THE JUGGLER OF NOTRE DAME

VOLUME 6

The Juggler of Notre Dame and the Medievalizing of Modernity

Vol. 6: War and Peace, Sex and Violence

Jan M. Ziolkowski

https://www.openbookpublishers.com

© 2018 Jan M. Ziolkowski

This work is licensed under a Creative Commons Attribution 4.0 International license (CC BY 4.0). This license allows you to share, copy, distribute and transmit the work; to adapt the work and to make commercial use of the work providing attribution is made to the author (but not in any way that suggests that he endorses you or your use of the work).

Attribution should include the following information: Jan M. Ziolkowski, *The Juggler of Notre Dame and the Medievalizing of Modernity. Vol. 6: War and Peace, Sex and Violence*. Cambridge, UK: Open Book Publishers, 2018, https://doi.org/10.11647/OBP.0149

Copyright and permissions for the reuse of many of the images included in this publication differ from the above. Copyright and permissions information for images is provided separately in the List of Illustrations. Every effort has been made to identify and contact copyright holders and any omission or error will be corrected if notification is made to the publisher.

In order to access detailed and updated information on the license, please visit https://www.openbookpublishers.com/product/822#copyright
Further details about CC BY licenses are available at http://creativecommons.org/licenses/by/4.0/

All external links were active at the time of publication unless otherwise stated and have been archived via the Internet Archive Wayback Machine at https://archive.org/web
Digital material and resources associated with this volume are available at https://www.openbookpublishers.com/product/822#resources

ISBN Paperback: 978-1-78374-539-5
ISBN Hardback: 978-1-78374-540-1
ISBN Digital (PDF): 978-1-78374-541-8
ISBN Digital ebook (epub): 978-1-78374-542-5
ISBN Digital ebook (mobi): 978-1-78374-543-2
DOI: 10.11647/OBP.0149

Cover image: Arman, *Jongleur de Notre Dame*, 1994, cast bronze statue with light fixtures, 231 x 90 x 82 cm, Arman Studio, New York. Photographer: Francois Fernandez, courtesy of Arman Studio, NY.
Cover design: Anna Gatti

All paper used by Open Book Publishers is SFI (Sustainable Forestry Initiative), PEFC (Programme for the Endorsement of Forest Certification Schemes) and Forest Stewardship Council(r)(FSC(r) certified.

Printed in the United Kingdom, United States, and Australia by Lightning Source
for Open Book Publishers (Cambridge, UK)

Contents

Note to the Reader	3
1. Juggler Allies	5
France	8
Great Britain	33
United States	34
2. The Juggler by Jingoism: Nazis and Their Neighbors	39
Virginal Visions	39
Belgium	45
The Netherlands	53
Germany	67
Curt Sigmar Gutkind	69
Hans Hömberg	73
After the War	76
Austria	77
3. Portrait of the Artist as a Young Juggler	89
Richard Sullivan, Notre Dame Professor	92
R. O. Blechman, Cartoon Juggler	103
Robert Lax, Poet among Acrobats	116
Tony Curtis, Prime-Time Juggler	120
W. H. Auden, *The Ballad of Barnaby*	123
Music from Massenet to Peter Maxwell Davies	135

4. Membranes of Things Past	147
Misremembering and Remembering	147
Getting a Rise from the Male Member	155
Jung's Jongleur	167
5. Positively Medieval: The Once and Future Juggler	173
The Juggler's Prospects	173
Gropius vs. the Gothic Ivory Tower	181
The Tumbler's Tumble	186
Michel Zink Reminds France	192
We All Need the Middle Ages	197
The Simplicity of Atonement	199
Acknowledgments	209
Notes	217
Notes to Chapter 1	217
Notes to Chapter 2	228
Notes to Chapter 3	248
Notes to Chapter 4	270
Notes to Chapter 5	276
Notes to Acknowledgments	284
Bibliography	285
Abbreviations	285
Archives	285
Referenced Works	285
List of Illustrations	305
Index	315

To Frits van Oostrom

"Who controls the past," ran the Party slogan, "controls the future: who controls the present controls the past."

—George Orwell, *1984*

Note to the Reader

This volume completes a series. Together, the six form *The Juggler of Notre Dame and the Medievalizing of Modernity.*[1] The book as a whole probes one medieval story, its reception in culture from the Franco-Prussian War until today, and the placement of that reception within medieval revivalism as a larger phenomenon. The study has been designed to proceed largely in chronological order, but the progression across the centuries and decades is relieved by thematic chapters that deal with topics not restricted to any single time period.

This sixth and final installment, labeled "War and Peace, Sex and Violence," follows the story of the story from the Second World War down to the present day. The narrative was put to an astonishing range of uses during the war years. In the fifties and sixties, it experienced what turned out to be a last hurrah in both high culture and mass culture. Afterward, it became the object of periodic playfulness and parody before slipping into at least temporary oblivion.

The chapters are followed by endnotes. Rather than being numbered, these notes are keyed to the words and phrases in the text that are presented in a different color. After the endnotes come the bibliography and illustration credits. In each volume-by-volume index, the names of most people have lifespans, regnal dates, or at least death dates.

One comment on the title of the story is in order. In proper French, Notre-Dame has a hyphen when the phrase refers to a building, institution, or place. Notre Dame, without the mark, refers to the woman, the mother of Jesus. In my own prose, the title is given in the form *Le jongleur de Notre Dame*, but the last two words will be found hyphenated in quotations and bibliographic citations if the original is so punctuated.

All translations are mine, unless otherwise specified.

---

1 The six-volume set is available on the publisher's website at https://www.openbookpublishers.com/section/101/1

1. Juggler Allies

> It would occur to only the most limited soul to investigate the Middle Ages in order to make them applicable to the present. At the same time, it confirms equal dullness if a person wished to reject the influence that the period must have on the understanding and proper treatment of the present.
>
> —Wilhelm Grimm

Our Lady's Tumbler and its prolific progeny have beguiled artists and authors of children's books again and again through the innocence of the protagonist, who is both firm and fragile, durable and defenseless. His unquenchable gusto for expressing devotion has voyaged in tandem with self-deprecation and self-doubt. Then again, compound words that get across the strength of his selfhood fail to do justice to his supreme selflessness. Even if the multitalented but unpresuming jongleur must enact his athletic art secluded under curfew in a private space rather than before a gawking public in open commerce, performing his routine means so much to him that he will pursue it through thick and thin. No matter what toll the practice exacts on his carnal constitution, he presses on with his worship through dance, and shows no fear in kicking up his Achilles' heels. In vexed times, these same qualities of emotional vulnerability, passionate creativity, and ceaseless persistence have rendered the entertainer irresistible to adults. As much as youngsters, these fans have craved the hope that can radiate from such a character—from such an underdog. Grown-ups in the belly of the beast have identified with the minstrel from the Middle Ages.

The most conspicuous pattern of all emerges during World War II, in tracts of land overtaken by the German army. The story elicited heightened engagement in those regions, subjected as they were to the humiliations and horrors of National Socialist racial laws and all the rest that Nazism entailed. Both the medieval tale and the many offshoots of Anatole France's and Jules Massenet's versions ignited special interest among Catholic writers, but the seductiveness of the narrative transcended denominations and religions. One noteworthy phenomenon was the attraction that *Our Lady's Tumbler* held for wretches who had been billeted in concentration camps or otherwise incarcerated. Jails and prisons of the mid-twentieth century shared a few arresting parallels with thirteenth-century monasteries. The later penal institutions were mostly single-sex places whose denizens were recluses in cells, and often such establishments imposed rigid rules and rituals upon their communities. Consequently, imprisoned individuals identified with the entertainer's esprit in outclassing those in the hierarchy above him and for establishing supernatural contact with the divine. Consciously or not, hounded minorities and Resistance fighters may have found the dancer's activities apposite to their own wartime circumstances. Like them, he refused to conform to what happened above ground so that he could go truly underground. In subterranean solitude he acted in accord with his conscience, only to be spied upon by alleged comrades. The action unfolds in a setting that centuries of Gothic fiction and art certified as sunless and sinister, shadowy and Stygian. The crypt may have made even the mildest monks seem a bit malevolent and monstrous.

In the sentence that caps *The Education of Henry Adams*, its strangely forward-looking author speculated plaintively about the contingency that after his demise he might reunite with his closest coevals and return to a better present in 1938. The wisdom of experience would allow no one grounded in twentieth-century history to wink at the poignancy of the year he plucked out of the air. Few commentators then or now would feel hopeful of finding at that point in the calendar, to quote the great man's *ipsissima verba*, "a world that sensitive and timid natures could regard without a shudder." In Asia, the Empire of Japan was already massacring and raping the Republic of China. In Europe, Hitler seized control of the German army, and in March directed it to invade and annex Austria. In October, its troops goose-stepped into Czechoslovakia. For the radicalization of the Nazis' anti-Jewish policies, 1938 has been termed "the fateful year." November brought Kristallnacht, the "night of broken glass" when paramilitary forces and civilian vigilantes carried out a pogrom against Jews throughout Germany. A year later, the blitzkrieg invasion of Poland marked the beginning of World War II in earnest.

Achtung! After the passage of eighty years, 1938 verges on slipping from within living memory: no survivor survives forever. In letters to dear friends and cherished acquaintances, Henry Adams plummeted recurrently into a loathing and loathsome anti-Semitism. Yet even his most noxious hate speech stood far apart from what two decades past his death in 1918 had been institutionalized within Germany for more than five years, and would soon infect not only the entire continent, but even the globe. Everything in the world changed, with no special allowance made for literature. Especially within Europe, writers resorted to *Our Lady's Tumbler* in divergent ways from those Adams had chosen in the early phase of the century, as he penned *Mont Saint Michel and Chartres*.

As the war wore on, the medieval story and its modern descendants became laced with ever more powerful valences. The medieval entertainer went on active duty in the early 1940s. In France and other nearby nations, the jongleur retained his abiding appeal to Catholics. In addition, he took on new associations thanks to his aria about freedom in Massenet's opera. In German-held France and its allies, the aura of liberty rendered him even more suitable and suggestive as a minor rallying point for underground movements against the Nazis. To those across the English Channel or whole oceans apart, the archetypal Frenchness ascribed to the protagonist made any artistic or artisanal adaptation of the tale automatically an expression of solidarity with the citizens and culture of the occupied nation. Enjoying the juggler was Francophilia, love of the French demonstrated allegiance to an ally.

A larger setting against which to view the wartime destiny of *Our Lady's Tumbler* is Gothic architecture and art, which continued to exercise a hold on the national identities of many European nations. We saw how, in World War I, destruction or damage that befell a medieval cathedral could be enlisted in propaganda battles between combatants. Reims constituted the foremost example. At a few crucial junctures in World War II, major structures from the Middle Ages were put deliberately in the cross hairs of trigger-happy efforts to obliterate cultural centers of opponents. Blasting places of worship to pieces offered a means to inflict payback, and in the process to demoralize nations that relied upon them for constructing and maintaining their very identities.

Fig. 1.1 Winston Churchill walks through the ruins of Coventry Cathedral. Photograph by William G. Horton, 1941. Washington, DC, Library of Congress, Prints and Photographs Division.

The air strike on Coventry on November 14, 1940 was the thin edge of the wedge. Afterward, a fitful plunge began into barbarity against the achievements of bygone centuries. High explosives and incendiaries rained down on the great church there. With one kaboom after another, they reduced the whole house of prayer to rubble, except for a small portion of its carapace. Although the ordnance also thudded into the armament factories nearby, the demolition of the fourteenth-century religious edifice was what seized the collective imagination. Without the vandalism of the Gothic structure, the city's devastation would never have become as searingly symbolic as it did (see Fig. 1.1).

The aggression against the borough in the West Midlands marked only the beginning of what became an architectonic tit-for-tat. Each side used its own most magnificent medieval buildings as bargaining chips in a game of mutual destruction, what devolved into punitive de-Gothicization. On March 28, 1942, the Royal Air Force of Great Britain pummeled Lübeck, whipping up a firestorm that disfigured the cathedral and other holy places in the historic medieval center of this Hanseatic port. In the ensuing vendetta, the German Luftwaffe reciprocated with a series of bombings against cultural sites in England. These retaliatory blitzes immediately earned the moniker of "the Baedeker raids," after the famous travel guides pioneered by the Leipzig-based publisher with this name. Though the medieval monuments of Norwich, Exeter, Canterbury, and York escaped, other iconic buildings fell. Even the mere endangerment of these churches brought the national style of architecture from the Middle Ages into the public eye. In effect, it made English Gothic a symbol that could rally patriotic pride and bolster fortitude. The assaults on the architectural style strengthened the grit of the British: the injured parties were determined not to be outplayed.

France

After the Germans leapt the Rhine and grabbed all the lands leading to the Atlantic, *Our Lady's Tumbler* enjoyed strong favor among conservatives in occupied France and under the Vichy regime. These collaborators followed their own path of least resistance, as they consented to a modus vivendi with the Nazis that many of their compatriots shunned. At the same moment, the medieval tale and its nineteenth- and twentieth-century derivatives became inspirations to the opposing side, in the persons of Resistance fighters. The occupiers waged psychological warfare; their adversaries partook in psychological resistance. Culture had its place in both strategy and tactics.

Many operas were performed in Paris while the Germans held sway there. Not too much should be made, then, of the enactment of *Le jongleur de Notre Dame* at the National Theater for Comic Opera in late December of 1940 and early January of 1941. Massenet's musical drama would have fitted the bill as light holiday fare, with no especially profound ulterior motives. A renowned tenor sang in the person of Jean, one of his signature roles (see Fig. 1.2). Whatever drove the choice of theme, it can still make the flesh crawl to see the printed program. A résumé in the occupiers' tongue complements the one in French. Full-page promotions, also in the speech of the invaders, promote the main newspaper in Frankfurt, as well as portable radios manufactured in Germany. Even the cast listing has at the bottom a bilingual text to bang the drum for the Berlitz language school (see Fig. 1.3). For a lesson in the difference seven years can make, compare the same side in the booklet for 1934: the advertisement for deluxe shoes, exclusively in French, speaks to a different ambience (see Fig. 1.4). At that point both apparitions of the Virgin and anxiety about the future ran rampant to the north in Belgium, but the war and occupation of France still lay a half decade down the road.

Fig. 1.2 Charles Friant as Jean in Massenet's *Le jongleur de Notre Dame*. Photograph by Studio Harcourt, 1941 or earlier. Published in a program for the Théâtre national de l'Opéra Comique (January 19, 1941), 2.

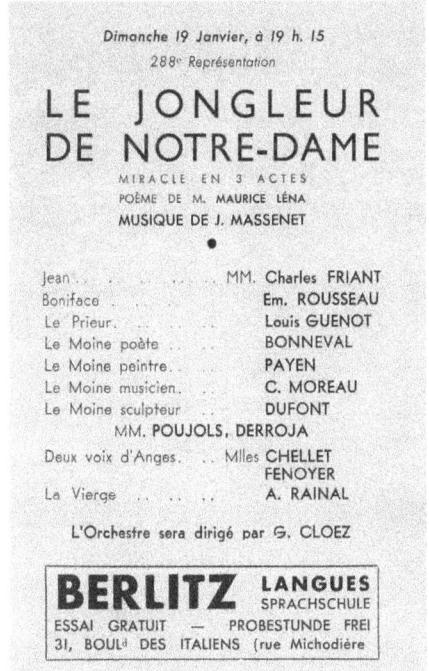

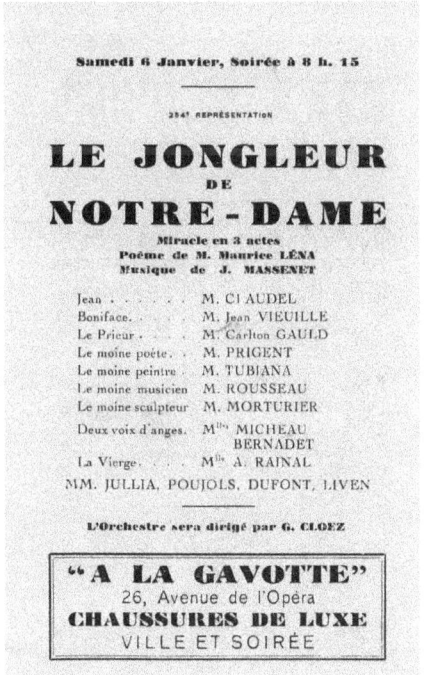

Fig. 1.3 Cast list for Massenet's *Le jongleur de Notre Dame*, with German language instruction advertised at bottom (in German). Published in a program for the Théâtre national de l'Opéra Comique (January 19, 1941), 11.

Fig. 1.4 Cast list for Massenet's, with deluxe shoes advertised at bottom (in French). Published in a program for the Théâtre national de l'Opéra Comique (January 6, 1934), 15.

In 1942, the authorities in occupied France threw themselves behind the revival of the opera, as part of the celebrations to commemorate the centennial of Massenet's birth: the jongleur met the threshold of acceptability to the Germans. Even so, the story was not the exclusive province of collaborators who played along with the foreign armed forces in their field-grey uniforms. It appealed identically to movements whose followers held dear political views that were radically unlike those of the Nazis. In both, many Catholics were implicated. Jews also took part in the co-opting of the story by the Underground. The development of the two extremes in the tale's reception in wartime France merits methodical examination and explanation.

More than any other author except Anatole France, Jérôme and Jean Tharaud (see Fig. 1.5) deserve remembrance for having kept *Our Lady's Tumbler* before the eyes of the French reading public during the 1930s and 1940s. These brothers were latter-day equivalents for their country to Jacob and Wilhelm Grimm, a formidable fraternal equipe who composed all their many books together over more than a half century. Without being physically as one, they were in their cultural production on the cusp of being conjoined twins. In due course their close to Siamese synergy would pose an occasional quandary. A Gallic wit opined that for being so closely allied with each other the two deserved to occupy only a single seat at the French Academy. Eventually they were both elected: Jérôme received the call in 1938, Jean in 1946.

Fig. 1.5 From right to left, Jérôme and Jean Tharaud, in their garden. Photograph Agence de presse Meurisse, 1932, https://commons.wikimedia.org/wiki/File:Frères_Tharaud_a_Meurisse_1932.jpg

Yet fame is fleeting. For all the formats and printings of their publications, the two siblings now wallow below the threshold in citation indexes. Indeed, anyone who studies them has to start by explaining why doing so pays any dividend. Countless copies of their volumes on the Virgin now molder in second-hand bookstalls, like an arsenal of obsolescent and unwanted munitions. The campaign for which the arms were stockpiled, in this case a cultural one, will not be waged again—but that does not justify forgetting that it once raged. The Tharauds' political proclivities did not match those of the brothers Grimm, and they just happened to be on the wrong side of almost every major ideological squabble. To have been aligned as they were with the mores of the petite-bourgeoisie and the clergy said nothing whatsoever in their disfavor, but we cannot discount that at one time or another they ranged themselves among the ranks of the opponents of Dreyfus, revanchists, pro-colonialists, anti-Semites, and rah-rah enthusiasts of Mussolini and Franco.

The two were attached to the elite institutions that had first projected *Our Lady's Tumbler* and *Le jongleur de Notre Dame* before the French public. Take for instance the bookstore of Honoré Champion, which in its glory days had been haunted by the likes of Gaston Paris and Anatole France. The proprietor himself had rubbed elbows with many local intellectuals and corresponded with foreigners, among them a whole gamut of literary scholars who concerned themselves with the Middle Ages. One of them was Wendelin Foerster, the Romance philologist in Austria who had edited the medieval French poem for the first time. As habitués of this shop, the brothers would naturally have encountered the story of the jongleur in a superabundance of forms.

As their input to the tradition over a half century, Jérôme and Jean Tharaud retooled miracles of the Virgin Mary for a mass audience. In 1904, a major show of so-called primitive French painters of the pre-Renaissance, from the fourteenth to the sixteenth century, went up in the Louvre and in the French National Library. In one spin-off from the enterprise, the two men furnished their versions of eight tales of the Virgin for an exhibition catalogue brought out in the same year. In 1931, they composed their own reworking of *Our Lady's Tumbler*. The venue was not a book of their own or even one devoted to Mary, but instead an anthology that collocated various short pieces by assorted French authors. Two of these, to wit Henry Bordeaux and Henri Pourrat, would later have occasion to produce their own adaptations of the tale. What can be concluded? The publication was reserved for well-connected, literate, conservative, Catholic authors. Afterward, the Tharaud brothers incorporated their version into their *Tales of the Virgin*, which evidently sold briskly, for the volume was reprinted at intervals between 1940 and 1960. To judge by the nearly annual rate of reprinting, the stories attained popularity in occupied and Vichy France. *Tales of the Virgin* was followed by *Tales of Our Lady*, although the latter did not contain *Our Lady's Tumbler*. In both cases Marian legends would have been enticing to Catholics during the godforsaken war years.

The most apparent change from the 1931 version to the one in the later volumes shows in the title, where the partly medieval "Le tombeor de Notre-Dame" becomes the fully modern-day "Le jongleur de Notre-Dame." The motivation away from the unfashionable spelling of the first noun would have been twofold. First, for reasons of rectitude the brothers would have had good cause to beat around the bush. As "lady's man" in modern French, *tombeur* awakens insalubrious connotations: the switch to *jongleur* made sense. Second, they may have avoided the more common title in 1931 because not even a decade had elapsed since Anatole France had been put on the

Index of Prohibited Books. The Nobel Prize winner had not been the first to use the title "Le jongleur de Notre-Dame," but even authors as well-taught and well-read as the Tharauds would not have known about the paraphrases by the consummately obscure Félix Brun that had inaugurated that wording, a half century earlier.

Before being absorbed into the book, the tale by the two Tharauds made its debut in a newspaper. In April of 1939, it took its place just below the fold on the front page of the periodical *Marianne* (see Fig. 1.6). To set the timing in context, the date fell not a month before France was invaded by the Germans. The patriotic infrastructure in which this illustrated weekly for politics and literature set the story could easily be overlooked. The opening paragraphs are bookended by political cartoons. On the left, one stigmatizes the recent invasion of Albania by Benito Mussolini of Italy. On the right, another satirical drawing renders pictorially the eventual costs to America that would come of not intervening against demagogues and dictators in Europe. The New World country is personified as Uncle Sam, who is being shown a tally of US dead and wounded in World War I, along with dollar amounts for defense spending. The message: staying sidelined in isolationism does not pay. Above the text looms a photograph of Hitler, along with a call for readers to propose captions for it.

As the context of the reprinting in the patriotically named *Marianne* would suggest, the brothers Tharaud were not collaborators who colluded with the enemy. Yet whatever their outlook on the German invaders, their views on Judaism were at best conflicted. An anti-Jewish incivility lurked not far beneath the veneer in some of their tales of the Virgin, which describe the Jews as "unbelievers who put to torture the Son of God." Such anti-Semitism alternated with Judeophilia on their part that at times extended even to admiration for Zionism.

To show the benevolence of Mary's intrusion in the rockiest moments of different lives, the brothers constructed other undoctored forms of pious stories. The times were unsettled, to deploy an adjective far too easygoing to describe what was taking shape in Europe of the 1930s. The sullen and scowling atmosphere may have tilted them and other devout Catholics toward the Mother of God even more than under ordinary circumstances. The conditions called for reassurance and a helping hand, and the Virgin specialized in dispensing both. In any case, the siblings were not alone, since in the early 1930s other scholars also had the notion of publishing anthologies of Marian miracles. The Tharauds were egged on by the French philologist Joseph Bédier to accumulate their collection of legends, and the printing history confirms that a market existed and awaited the fruits of their labors.

The selections include the narrative about *The Knight of the Barrel*, in addition to the miracle of the taper at Rocamadour. A third wonder is our story. The tale as told by Anatole France was known to the brothers. Whether they would or could have perused the medieval vernacular poem of *Our Lady's Tumbler* in full is an open question. Yet in the first sentence of their account, they claim to have tapped the material for their version from the *Acts of the Saints*, an immense hagiographic repertory in Latin that

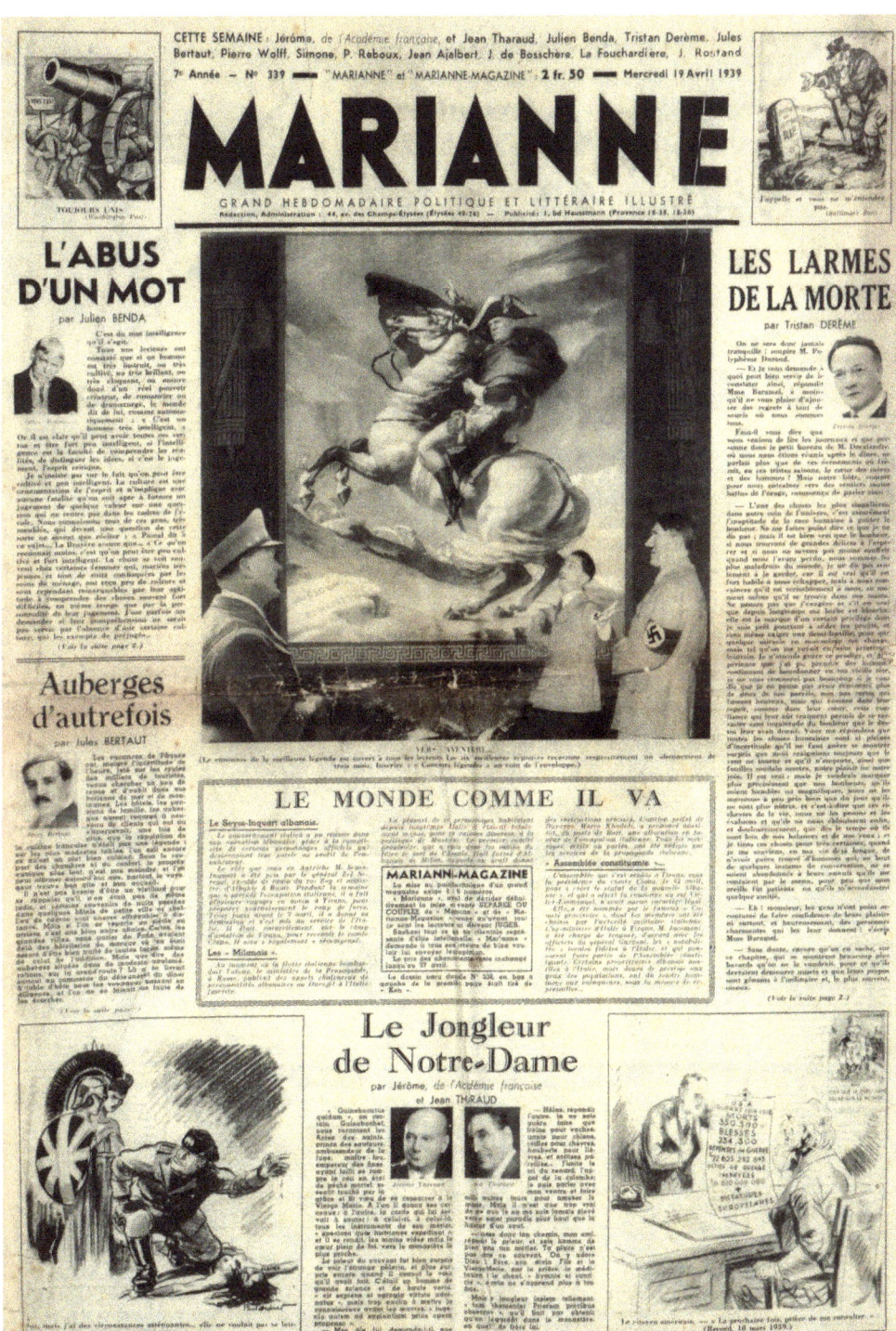

Fig. 1.6 Front page of *Marianne* 7, no. 339, April 19, 1939.

has been under way since 1643. Although the brothers opted for French prose, their pretense of having held fast to an original in the classical language may be considered pure poetic license, as no such story appears in the fifty-nine hefty folio volumes of the *Acts* that have been published to date.

In keeping with the pose they struck, the siblings seasoned their composition with lavish lashes of Latinity. If the assemblage were a drink to be swigged or sipped in a china demitasse, it would be an Irish coffee—light on the java, long on the whiskey. We could modify the recipe, to a similar decoction but with a little kick of Bénédictine. In any case, the brothers meant their tale for a bygone universe in which most French citizens remained practicing Catholics, many devoutly so. In France as everywhere else, Catholicism still depended on Latin liturgy, theology, and doctrine. In both state and religious schools, the most prestigious education rested on a bedrock of the learned language. Often the brothers reword in their French retelling phrases from the tongue of the Romans and Roman Catholics. Still, they felt free to incorporate remarkable quantities of the half-dead speech into their story, tattooing their refashioning of *Our Lady's Tumbler* with numerous, on the face of it authentic tags and quotations. Insouciant readers might infer that these embellishments had been transferred from a genuine source text, when instead the Latinity is often of the brothers' own devising.

The first two words of their version identify the protagonist in Latin as "a certain Guinehochet." This name is a dab of recondite wit drawn from the literature of the Middle Ages. It may well refer to a fabliau-like anecdote that John of Garland, a prolific Latin author of the thirteenth century, recounted as a side note in a treatise on poetry. In this episode, a peasant joins in a brief tête-à-tête with a demon who has taken up residence in a well:

> "What is your name?" The devil replied, in French, "My name is Guinehochet." And the peasant said, "How many sons do I have?" Guinehochet answered, "Two." The peasant guffawed, and said, "You're a liar; I have four sons." Guinehochet said, "No, you are the liar, you naughty peasant—two of your boys are the village priest's." "Which ones?" the peasant asked. And Guinehochet answered, "Go, peasant, feed both his and yours."

Lore about an evil spirit by this name could have been taken from other medieval texts as well, both Latin and French. But whatever their source of information, by the time the Tharaud brothers wrote, the appellation would have been insider knowledge, recognizable most readily by specialists. Henri Marmier, who wrote a novel-length version of the story about the tumbler, later made a similarly erudite reference to the same malignant being.

Two other adaptations of our tale were fashioned by authors with discordant political convictions from those of the Tharaud brothers. Both took the form of scripts for theatrical productions. Artists of all sorts have seized upon the jongleur as a model, for like other supposed "primitives" from before the Renaissance, he anticipated the detachment from the world around them that inventive minds sometimes cultivate. He toiled in inspired isolation, first as a common entertainer wandering through streetwise society and then as a misplaced lay brother in a monastery. To others, the jongleur has been appealing for the opposite reason that he is a cenobite, and thus a man bound to other men in an all-male social organization devoted to religion. This affiliation helps to explain the siren song that the account has crooned across the centuries to confraternities, both medieval and modern. Such groups, particularly theatrical ones, have recalibrated the narrative to render it suitable for performance.

One adaptation of the jongleur story for the stage was by Henri Brochet (see Fig. 1.7). This painter and playwright participated actively in Catholic theater of his day. With his close associate Henri Ghéon, he cofounded the troupe known as the Companions of Our Lady in 1924–1925. In this context, Brochet composed plays on Sister Beatrice and on Mary, Lady of Pontmain. Such activity demonstrates his deep immersion in Marian miracles from the Middle Ages to his own day. Further confirmation comes from the statuette of the Virgin and Child planted ostentatiously at one corner of the desk in the image of him. Forget about Jesus and Joseph: holy Mary!

Brochet's piece on the jongleur was produced in Auxerre in 1942. It was performed by the "Companions of Roger Good-Times," a company that the dramatist himself had established. This Roger Bontemps (see Fig. 1.8) is a storied personage, who pops up sporadically in French literature and culture. His dégagé and indolent lifestyle may not have been well suited to the grim constraints of scraping out an existence in occupied France or under the Vichy regime, but even in wartime people seek wish-fulfillment. They hunger after relaxation and the remedy of "good times" to come, especially from their fellow nationals.

Fig. 1.7 Henri Brochet, with Virgin and Child on desk in left foreground.
Photograph, date and photographer unknown.

Fig. 1.8 "Roger Bontemps." Illustration by Henri Gerbault, printed on lithograph promotional card, "Les chansons" (2nd series), by de Ricqlès & Cie, 1910.

Fig. 1.9 "Hippodrome au Pont de l'Alma: Cadet Roussel." Poster illustrated by Jules Chéret, printed by Chaix, 1882.

The play was entitled *Cadet Roussel, jongleur de Notre Dame*. The name of the title role belongs to a historical personage of the French Revolutionary era, known for his bicorn hat (see Fig. 1.9). Guillaume Joseph Roussel, a court bailiff who became legendary through a song, enjoyed special renown in Auxerre. The Auxerrois were reported to be enthusiastic about shows that drew upon the folklore and legends of their region. The relevance of such a patriotic theme to occupied France demands no gloss, and the positive response to this premiere justified the same company's production in 1943 of an old one-act farce "Cadet Roussel, Barber at the *Fontaine des innocents*."

The *jongleur de Notre-Dame* in the title of Brochet's script does not allude specifically to the medieval poem by the anonymous, the short story by Anatole France, or the three-act opera by Jules Massenet. Rather, it refers loosely to the narrative taken as a whole. In the penultimate scene of the play, Cadet Roussel engages in dialogue with a Madonna known as Our Lady of the Virtues. The statue is played by an actor, so that it can become animate as soon as the protagonist claps eyes upon it. The bailiff pirouettes before the living image to the accompaniment of offstage music. Otherwise, most of the scene takes the form of one-on-one between him and the Virgin on his ambitions as an artist and on his personal relations with his bride-to-be, Manon. At the end, Mary as marriage counselor reminds him of his duty to wed by drawing a parallel with her own acceptance of responsibility in the Annunciation. At that point she resumes being truly statuesque once again.

Fig. 1.10 Léon Chancerel. Photograph, 1942. Photographer unknown.

The other theatrical recasting of the tale, not simply an expropriation of its name because of its familiarity, was Brother Clown, or The jongleur of Notre Dame, Monologue. This script was the work of Léon Chancerel (see Fig. 1.10). The cover (see Fig. 1.11) and title page make false assumptions about both the ultimate provenance of the miracle story and its French author. They indicate that this actor, scriptwriter, and director produced his text on the model of a legend about the minstrel called Peter Sigelar. To be more precise, they signal that the dramatist followed a version in French verse from the thirteenth century by Gautier de Coinci. In the foreword, the twentieth-century author professes to have eschewed altogether the short story by Anatole France and the libretto to Massenet's opera by Maurice Léna. Instead, he claims out of purism or perfectionism to have adhered to Foerster's *editio princeps* of the medieval French, and the version by Maurice Vloberg. Mystifyingly, or at least paradoxically, Chancerel qualifies the adaptation as "free but very faithful." Like many readers for three quarters of a century before him, he regards the story of the jongleur as "naïve, pious, and tender."

The playwright frequented the same theatrical circles as Brochet from 1929 until 1932. The Dominican priest to whose memory the piece is dedicated wrote "spiritual letters" which when published in 1945 were preceded by a verse preface by the French poet and dramatist Paul Claudel. These circumstances substantiate the inference that Chancerel belonged to a Mariocentric coterie. One of his other close ties was with Gustave Cohen, a professor of literature at the Sorbonne who encouraged and oversaw reenactments of medieval plays. A medievalist, Cohen launched almost by happenstance a dramatic troupe dubbed the Theophilians. The name honored the Marian *Miracle of Theophilus* by Rutebeuf, a French poet who died around 1285. To

Fig. 1.11 Front cover of Léon Chancerel, *Frère Clown, ou Le jongleur de Notre-Dame* (Lyons, France: La Hutte, 1943).

Fig. 1.12 Front cover of Rutebeuf, *Le miracle de Théophile,* transposed by Gustave Cohen (Paris: Delagrave, 1934).

precipitate a revival of the play, the instructor approached the rostrum and told a lecture hall full of college students: "If you parceled out the roles and put it on the stage, you might be able to restore its marvelous stained-glass colors." This kind of synesthesia has been a recurrent feature of Gothic revivals. In any case, the resultant theatrical company staged its debut of Rutebeuf's *Miracle* in May 1933, with Chancerel as director. The professional scholar's "transposition" of the text was a low-profile hit (see Fig. 1.12). It came into print first in 1934, with a total of at least ten further editions over the remainder of the decade.

It pains the heart to parse the professor's dulcet words of hope about the young participants in his troupe in a retrospective published in 1937, since the German invasion and occupation would afflict France so soon afterward. The mobilization of students in amateur theatrical troupes in the 1930s, often driven explicitly by social and political goals, turned out to be almost a histrionic dress rehearsal for the Resistance. Chance would have it that medieval literature had a share in both movements. Cohen himself, being Jewish, was constrained to emigrate. Only during his exile in the United States did he convert to Catholicism.

The legend of Theophilus recounts a pact with the devil along vaguely Faustian lines. The lead character, purported to be a historical figure, is a priest. Although elected to the episcopacy, he brushes aside the preferment out of humility. Under the man who is named bishop in his stead, the padre loses his office. To recoup his position, he mortgages his soul to Satan in a charter. Through his later repentance, the father secures the intercession of the Virgin, who manifests herself to him in a vision and hands the signed legal document back to him so that he may retain his soul.

The story became traditional, retold time after time throughout Europe in both Latin and vernacular languages, and represented widely in art. In fact, it has fair claim to be accredited as the favorite Marian legend of the Middle Ages. That says a lot, since such a multitude of tales circulated about interventions of Mary. To look only at especially relevant medieval French versions, Gautier de Coinci produced the longest iteration of the account around 1200. Its marquee value shows from its placement in his *Miracles of Our Lady*, where it headlines the program. Later in the thirteenth century, Rutebeuf based his *Miracle of Theophilus* on Gautier's text. Despite the undeniable debt, the later poet makes a welter of sweeping changes. For example, he begins with the apostasy of the sinner from the Christian God after his loss of office, features a Jew named Salatin as the middleman to the devil, and has the on-again, off-again priest abide in his diabolical ways for a full seven years before inexplicably repenting. Eventually Mary recovers the charter in which her petitioner recanted Christianity and returns it to him (see Fig. 1.13).

Fig. 1.13 The staging of *Le miracle de Théophile*. Photograph, 1933. Photographer unknown. Published in Rutebeuf, *Le miracle de Théophile*, transposed by Gustave Cohen (Paris: Delagrave, 1934), 3.

In this photograph of the key early production, the whole stage is shown except for Paradise, which was stage left. Also to the same side stood the house of Our Lady, with God the Father and two of his angels at the entrance. As our gaze swings rightward, we see the Mother of God herself. Her clothing is modeled on that worn by a famed statue, known as the Golden Virgin, from Notre-Dame of Amiens (see Vol. 4, Figs.

3.26 and 3.27). Here Mary restores the written grant to Theophilus as he kneels before another Gothic edifice, the episcopal palace. Further in this direction stands his own home, with the bishop flanked by two clerics.

The last structure before the hell's mouth at stage right, where Satan awaits, is the domicile of Salatin. This name is plainly a slight variation on Saladin, the form current in the Western world for Ṣalāḥ ad-Dīn. By whatever name, he was the twelfth-century sultan of Egypt who famously resisted the crusaders. The sinisterly Semitic Jew of Rutebeuf's play is thus conflated with a legendarily dangerous Muslim warrior. Fittingly, then, Salatin's home features architectural elements reminiscent of medieval mosques.

The play remained in production throughout the 1930s, both before and after the German tanks rolled in. It does not require much imagination to see how the fancy of being spared by Mary from the eternal damnation of a pact with the devil could have held intensified appeal during the occupation. The association of the Theophilians with wartime patriotism in their nation is discernible even in the dedication of the final printed form of The *Mystery of the Passion of the Theophilians*: *Literary Adaptation* by Gustave Cohen (see Fig. 1.14). Although Chancerel was engaged with the group from the very start and would serve again later as its director, he came to be linked principally with the troupe of "Comedians on the Road." This company was instituted in 1929 as a French equivalent to the Boy Scouts, and helped to disseminate his ideas and techniques for reforming theater among working-class youths in France.

Fig. 1.14 Front cover of Gustave Cohen, *Mystère de la Passion des théophiliens* (Paris: Richard-Masse, 1950).

Sputteringly, Chancerel was drawn to God and religion. Although faith entered his life lastingly only after 1940, his epiphany presumably came in time to play a role in his choice of subject matter when he composed his version of *Our Lady's Tumbler*. The subscription to the foreword indicates that he wrote it in November of 1942. On the eleventh of that month, the lower portion of his country passed from being the nominally unoccupied seat of the French government, the so-called Free Zone with its capital in Vichy. Henceforth it was annexed as the southern district of occupied France. At this point the Germans began massive deportations of Jews to annihilate them in what we know now as the Holocaust or Shoah. Simultaneously, the occupiers intensified crackdowns, arrests, and executions to cow and quash the Underground.

When the enemy seized the territory, Chancerel found himself living on the edge. The dramatic group he oversaw unraveled. In the prefatory note to *Brother Clown*, he refers to entertainment programs that he hoped to organize for young people's associations called *Chantiers*. The French noun *chantier* means literally "worksite," but puns upon the verb *chanter* that denotes "to sing." At the same time, the name could allude to the playwright's own, the first syllable of which is homophonous with *chant* "song." The homophony resembles that in "Jean the Jongleur," which in French has analogous sounds in the initial syllables.

In setting the stage for the monologue of *Brother Clown*, the author asks the troop to intone in unison:

> Let's sing, to while away the time,
> Charming tales
> Of fair France,
> Let's sing, to while away the time,
> Charming tales
> Of its olden times.

In the light of his political partialities and activities, the final phrase implies not merely medieval but also more recent days, before the German occupation. On the following page the writer refers overtly to "this grievous year of 1943."

An intimate of Chancerel's, the French author Nina Gourfinkel, was an Odessa-born Jew. While active in the scrum against the German occupiers, she contrived for Abbé Alexandre Glasberg (see Fig. 1.15) the code name of *le jongleur de Notre Dame*. The good father was a Jew of Ukrainian extraction who turned to Catholicism and became a priest in France. During World War II, he contributed to the efforts of the Underground and helped to rescue numerous Jews, especially children, from Nazi death camps. He earned his sobriquet from his almost magical capability for discovering free play within the Church and other authorities for carrying out his projects, without occasioning political or diplomatic strains in the process. In Glasberg's innermost team, Gourfinkel was not alone in applying to him the *jongleur* epithet. A comrade of hers in the Resistance, Ninon Haït née Weyl, who went under the assumed name of Nicole Harcourt, allegedly also called him so. The scraps of evidence are disparate, but they more than suffice to demonstrate how much the jongleur of Notre Dame absorbed the minds of the occupied French. The blue-mantled Madonna stood ready to play her part in the cloak-and-dagger work of the Underground.

Fig. 1.15 Alexandre Glasberg at Chansaye. Photographer unknown, ca. 1941–1944. Image courtesy of the Mémorial de la Shoah. All rights reserved.

Shortly after passing away in 1912, Massenet was forgiven for having abandoned Paris and adopted Monaco as the regular venue for premieres of his new operas. In fact, he was soon extolled as an archetypally French artist. During the belle époque, the friction between Church and state had been resolved in the laicization of French society. Now, forty years later, the opera of the jongleur showed once again how it could exercise magnetic pull upon both of two starkly opposed political and social extremes. If one pole was advantageous to resistance, the other befitted collaboration.

During the Second World War, people had to decide where to situate the humble medieval minstrel, as they negotiated their own complex decisions about what it meant to be true to their nation in their own personal circumstances. Some were brave, others weak-kneed; for many, the reality was more complex than a stark either/or. In occupied Paris, Massenet's *Le jongleur de Notre Dame* enjoyed canonical status in the curriculum of musical education. In 1941 or earlier, it was enacted there in the national theater of the Opéra Comique. In Vichy, it played in the summer season. On July 12, 1942, the composer's musical drama was staged in open air on the square before the cathedral in Saint-Étienne, France (see Fig. 1.16). The year made sense for the performance, since it marked the centenary of Massenet's birth. At this point the Vichy government issued a commemorative stamp that bore his portrait (see Figs. 1.17 and 1.18).

The specific occasion of the show in Saint-Étienne bears note. July 12 falls only two days shy of Bastille Day. The date relates to both the storming of the Bastille in 1789 and the "Holiday of the Federation" in 1790, which celebrated the first anniversary of the

Fig. 1.16 Staging of Massenet's *Le jongleur de Notre Dame* outside the Cathédrale Saint-Charles Borromée, Saint-Étienne, France. Photograph, 1942. Photographer unknown. Saint-Étienne, Archives municipales, Bulletin municipal de 1942.

assault. It also commemorates the rampage that led eventually to the formation of the modern French nation. A staging of the opera on what has been known interchangeably as "the National Holiday" and "the fourteenth of July" would have been far too unsubtle, even rabble-rousing, a statement. Putting it on just two days earlier enabled those involved to play innocent if pressed about their motives, while at once the event would have still been a morale-booster.

And the year? Beyond being the hundredth anniversary of Massenet's birth, 1942 was—as we stare back with gimlet eyes from the all-knowing vantage of decades afterward—the nadir of the Second World War for those in Europe who regarded the Nazis as their nemesis. Although no terminus lay in sight, it represented the halfway point in the occupation of France. We shall revert to these 365 eventful days repeatedly in this chapter. Within the context of the occupation, Massenet was invoked, despite some implausibility, to uphold the morale of French families in the titanic tussle that enveloped them.

Fig. 1.17 Four-franc Vichy French postage stamp with portrait of Jules Massenet to commemorate the centenary of his birth (1942).

Fig. 1.18 First-day cover with portrait of Jules Massenet to commemorate the centenary of his birth (1942).

The opera's Catholic tone would have lent itself to the cultural politics of the regime. In addition, the Mother of God herself was regarded as the special, traditional buffer of France. Her guardianship constituted a valuable resource in an era of despair and need. A holy card printed in 1944 calls upon children to supplicate the Immaculate Virgin to safeguard France (see Fig. 1.19). It depicts a clutch of eight youngsters before Our Lady and Child, both clothed entirely in white. The infant Jesus grips a cross that hangs from a rosary. All the little ones who can be discerned with any clarity are likewise clinging to strings of prayer beads. The text within points out that Mary preferred to show herself to youths in France at La Salette, Lourdes, and Pontmain; and in Portugal at Fátima. Similarly, a postcard from the war years pictures a crowned Virgin with a Child on her left arm and a scepter-like lily in her right hand (see Fig. 1.20). She is flanked by the principal Gothic cathedrals of France, along with five large tapers that stand for key sites of Marian apparitions and that pay homage to Mary's special connection with beeswax and candles.

Fig. 1.19 Holy card of children in supplication before the Virgin (Paris: A. Leclerc, 1944).

Fig. 1.20 Postcard of the Virgin and Child, flanked by prominent French cathedrals and names of Marian miracle sites (1942).

Already in the aftermath of the Franco-Prussian War, the story of the jongleur had acquired patriotic associations. The entertainer's song of *Liberté*, "Freedom," would have obviously resonated for an audience of French citizens during an occupation by foreign invaders. These reverberations would have differed from the progressive connotations it carried for liberal and broad-minded Frenchmen during the nineteenth century. More expansively, this protagonist was a humble layman, who landed on his feet without help from those in his institution with more leverage and higher pay grades, if such terms can be applied when speaking of a monastery. Such a message held potential solace for a populace that for a long spell had no real option to embrace among the political movements that preceded or followed the German invasion. No workaround existed.

In 1940, Henri Perrin, at the sanctuary of Our Lady of La Salette in France, served as chaplain to prisoners of war. Sixteen years later, his memoir of Captain Jacques Darreberg was published. The clergyman had spoken to the hero-to-be about the miracles for which the shrine on the mountain was famed (see Fig. 1.21). Memory of the conversation stuck. While in the Resistance, the captain, called also "the herald of Our Lady," assumed the nom de guerre of *jongleur de Notre Dame*. As he embarked on a detail as a saboteur, he radioed in code: "The jongleur of Notre Dame goes off on pilgrimage. He calls his friends." An enciphered letter that came back after the mission was decrypted to read: "Our Lady of La Salette by her powerful mediation has allowed the clown to execute a perfect sabotage."

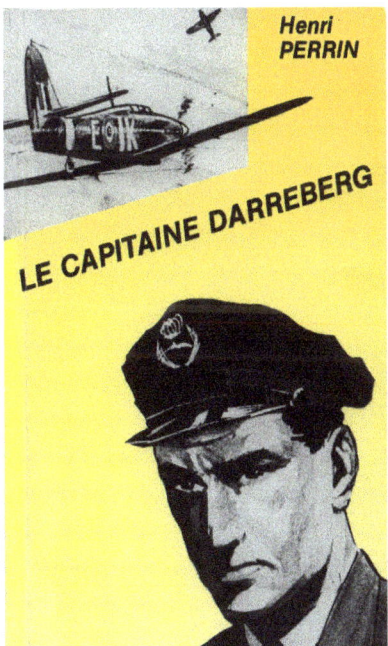

Fig. 1.21 Henri Perrin, *Le capitaine Darreberg*, 7th ed. (Corps: Association des pèlerins de La Salette, 1983), front cover. Courtesy of Association des pèlerins de La Salette.

An even later book on the occupation compares the Underground leader Gilbert Renault who also took the moniker of *jongleur de Notre Dame*, refers to the same man's devotion to the Virgin, and implies that he adopted the French phrase as one of many such coded designations. His other pseudonyms ranged from "Rémy," a common name for males in France, to "Fanfan la Tulipe," after a swashbuckling hero in literature, opera, and film. This Colonel Rémy's two-volume memoirs of his activities as a Maquisard describe his worship before a statue of the Virgin Mary and Child in Paris. The specific location was the basilica of Notre-Dame-des-Victoires. The inspiration came to him there to draw upon the formulation "Brotherhood of Our Lady" as a byname for one major network of the Resistance. The account of Rémy's activities flaunts a photograph of the statue of Notre-Dame-des-Victoires in the church of Notre Dame de France—which despite its impeccably French appellation is located on Leicester Place in London. The effigy there was a replica of the original in the Parisian house of worship. This other building and image also held importance for the secret agent, since he frequented them after he shifted operations to England in 1940. The biography, focused on the war years, also mentions other Marian incidentals, such as the application of the epithet *Stella Maris* or "Star of the Sea" as a cipher for a building. The Marianism stuck with the Underground fighter even after the war. Renault later devoted an entire book to the cult of Fátima.

A bas-relief medallion struck to commemorate Renault's role in the wartime struggle has on the front face his image, labeled simply "Rémy" (see Fig. 1.22). On the reverse is the head of the Virgin (see Fig. 1.23), bracketed on the left by the letters CND that abbreviate the French for "Brotherhood of Our Lady," and on the right by a cross composed of a vertical with two parallel bars. This symbol, known as the Cross of Lorraine, has long been associated with that region as well as with the whole of France. During World War II it stood for the Free French Forces and the liberation of the nation from the Nazi occupation.

Another tribute to the commonness of the phrase "jongleur of Notre Dame" as a code name or password in occupied France may be found in what a theater company was called in the commune of Dole, in the eastern part of the country. The group was organized in 1949 by a former guerrilla in the Underground. All told, the evidence

Fig. 1.22 Commemorative medallion (obverse) to honor Resistance, depicting Gilbert Renault (Colonel Rémy), ca. 1940–1944, by Jean-Paul Luthringer, struck in 1988 by Monnaie de Paris.

Fig. 1.23 Commemorative medallion (reverse), depicting the Virgin with the Cross of Lorraine and the abbreviation CND (Confrérie Notre-Dame), by Jean-Paul Luthringer, struck in 1988 by Monnaie de Paris.

Fig. 1.24 Front cover of Anatole France, *Le jongleur de Notre-Dame*, illus. Pierre Watrin (Paris: Éditions de l'Amitié-G. T. Rageot, 1944).

intimates that during the occupation, the phrase *jongleur de Notre Dame* became a minor rallying point for many citizens. They had been outmaneuvered even more rapidly and occupied longer by the Germans in the Second World War than in the Franco-Prussian War. The earlier debacle had formed the backdrop to the publication of the original poem of the miracle from the Middle Ages. Although not as directly, the black eye of 1870–1871 belongs to the context of Anatole France's story. In the first flush of the Liberation, the opera may have served in a minor fashion as a means of celebration; it was staged in Paris in the fall of 1944. "O liberté, m'amie" ("O beloved freedom") was aspirational during the Resistance. Once the Allies arrived, the aria became joyous and triumphant.

Also in 1944, the story of Anatole France's *Le jongleur de Notre Dame* was reprinted in a children's book, illustrated copiously in lighthearted, even garish colors by Pierre Watrin (see Fig. 1.24). At that juncture the illustrator was only in his mid-twenties. Artists not of independent means endure a perennial urgency about putting food on the table. Their bind would make a natural role model of the jongleur in the late nineteenth-century short story. He is presented as an impoverished performer who enters a monastery in large part to tide himself over during a financial hard patch. The usual need for an income would have been honed on the whetstone of social and economic conditions, by the deprivation of the war years and the aftereffects of the hard times immediately following. Additional motivations may have been less economic than political and ideological. For all the reasons that made the Underground hospitable to the entertainer, he would have been ideally suited as a peace offering for the articulation of joy over the Liberation. Further, he and his story were a logical choice to engender good cheer as the French sought to reestablish a semblance of normalcy after the humble pie that the occupation forced them to eat. Finally, the centenary of Anatole France's birth fell in April 1944. Watrin may have had a sentimental weakness for the once-idolized author. Otherwise, we would have to chalk up to mere coincidence that in 1946 he illustrated a limited print run of the Nobel Prize winner's 1914 *The Revolt of the Angels*. Seven years later his illustrations were reused in a bibliophilic English translation of the same novel. Whatever particulars went into his decision to illustrate France's *Le jongleur de Notre Dame*, the project took shape in a phase of febrile productivity for the young artist.

The same year of 1946 saw a further explosion of postbellum joy. The *Tales of the Virgin* by the Tharaud brothers, with its retelling of *Our Lady's Tumbler*, was reprinted in a luxury edition for connoisseurs, as lovely as it is rare (see Fig. 1.25). The cruciform colophon explains that the book was a labor of love by artists and artisans who worked for eighteen months, in 1945 and the first half of the following year, "to express in a tangible fashion the conscience that animates and guides them." The declaration spells out that the Italian-born but Paris-based painter Pio Santini invoked Mary for enlightenment in producing his art for the book. At a quick gander, the volume might look indistinguishable from earlier medievalesque printings of Anatole France's story, but that inference would be barking up the wrong tree. This printed work is old-fashioned, but it does not aspire to replicate a medieval manuscript in its typography. Even the dropped initial capital letters and the miniatures are not willfully anachronistic or archaizing. The pages exude self-possessed exaltation, if the last two words can be coupled without nosediving into bathos or worse.

In this Henri-heavy chapter, we come now to the last—with a final orthographic twist to furnish at least visual variety. Not everyone experienced an optimistic burst of high-octane energy in the years following the war. Some people had already run down what little they had stored in their flywheels. A last version of the narrative may well not have been conceived until afterward, but it speaks to another side of the nation than the Resistance. Henry Bordeaux (see Fig. 1.26) was a well-known author, elected to the French Academy in 1919. For a long stretch of his career, he had a reasonable claim to a fame that would long outlive him. As a novelist and essayist, he was prodigiously prolific, and the market ravened for what he could spit out. He was all the rage, and his books were bestsellers. Tied to the past of France, he was a conservative exponent of Catholicism, the provincial bourgeoisie, rural life and regionalism, and a conservative sense of national providence.

Before the flare-up of the Second World War, Bordeaux's conservatism led him to cheer the despots Mussolini of Italy and Francisco Franco of Spain. During much of the occupation he aligned himself also, as did many other traditionalist Catholics,

Fig. 1.25 The monks are appalled by the juggler's improvised ritual. Illustration by Pio Santini. Published in Jérôme et Jean Tharaud, *Les contes de la Vierge* (Paris: Société d'éditions littéraires françaises, 1946), between pp. 172 and 173.

Fig. 1.26 Henry Bordeaux. Photograph by Henri Manuel, date unknown. Reproduced on postcard stock (Paris, 1920).

with Marshal Philippe Pétain, who served as Chief of State of Vichy France from 1940 to 1944. An unswerving Pétainist, Bordeaux even glorified his old friend in a 1941 biography, closer to hagiography for its adulation of its subject. Once peace was reestablished, he backed his fellow author Charles Maurras, whom he had given a hero's welcome into the French Academy in 1939. Maurras turned to the Catholic faith near the end of his life, and was condemned for abetting the enemy as a Nazi stooge.

After World War II, Bordeaux too lived under a cloud. A staunch supporter of the Vichy government, he had been supine as it acquiesced in inhumane policies imposed by the Germans. His political preferences in wartime could have resulted in humiliation and far worse if other members of the Academy had not intervened to shield him, and with him the reputation of their institution. The immortality of the "immortals" would have suffered a lethal blow if any of their number had been punished for collaboration. This consideration held particularly true for those among them, such as Bordeaux, who could be counted as right-wing. Only one of them, François Mauriac, had entered the Resistance.

France went through wrenching debates between 1944 and 1954, as its citizens negotiated civil war and a purge of accused traitors. At the end came an amnesty—a collective pardon, both conscious and unconscious, that is an agreed or imposed attempt to forget what has preceded. What did Bordeaux need to put behind him? His stances were consistent with his values, many of them laudable, among them loyalty—but they give evidence of a doctrinaire bent in his personality.

At his stage in life, Bordeaux had ample justification for setting down the pen in his writing career, and so he did, soon, at least as a creative writer. He published his final work of fiction in 1951. In the English translation that appeared one year later, it bears the title *A Pathway to Heaven*. Closer to the original title would be *Our Lady's Thread*, preserving the pun in the French that plays upon gossamer. Among the rare examples of the juggler story expanded into a novel, it sutures together elements from both the thirteenth-century poem and *Le jongleur de Notre Dame*. The first chapter is even entitled "Our Lady's Tumbler." To go further, it opens with a recapitulation of the medieval tale. The conspectus indicates that the modern author knew the original in some shape or form, Anatole France's short story, and Jules Massenet's opera, and that he associated the composite of them with saint's lives in the *Golden Legend*.

Much of the novel gives an agreeable enough portrayal of the quotidian in a country parish. The primary personage is a minister of the Church called Father Calixte Merval. The focus rests on the relations between this priest and his recalcitrant flock. The central dilemma pits the protagonist's painterly avocation against his priestly vocation: this tension puts the pastor between the devil and the deep blue sea. Merval is an artist in the vein of the hero in *Our Lady's Tumbler*. A juggler or tumbler of light, he performs his art for Mary. A connoisseur of Madonnas, he concentrates his reverence on a thirteenth-century effigy of the Virgin in the little parochial church. So far, so good. The distastefulness bubbles to the surface at the end. Compelled to choose between his painting and his priesthood, Merval elects the ministry. After deciding to swear off pictorial craft for pastoral cares, the artist tears up his canvases and deposits them before the Madonna, along with his paint box and tools. Then he collapses face down, a deliberate imitation of the tumbler, before the statue. At that, Mary "dried the sweat of agony on his brow as she did the poor tumbler's in the *Golden Legend*. God be praised!"

The votive offering may well have an autobiographical subtext, since Bordeaux himself wrote no more novels after this one. We could say that the country priest was his alter (or altar) ego, and that like him, the author tore up his paper and cracked his pens in two. What is the ugliness? For the novelist to have forced his protagonist to opt for either his generative activity or his clerical calling distorts the contours of the medieval story. Worse, it deprives the tale of much of its salvific spirit. The padre (and Bordeaux, if we assume that the chief figure in the fiction represents the writer himself) puts before the Virgin as his benefaction not his art but his renunciation and destruction of it. He needs to redeem himself, but he does not petition for redemption by repenting. Instead, he cripples his means and products of self-expression, as if doing so constituted devotion — a votive and not vandalism.

The elision of repentance as the novel climaxes shows that he has failed to perceive the fundamental nature of his own defects and sins. In this case, the third-person pronoun means both Merval the priestly character and Bordeaux the real-life man of letters. The leading figure in the story behaves like a child who stays silent out of stubborn shame, rather than confessing evildoing and begging for a second chance. The book has been read as a spiritual triumph, but such an interpretation misses the point. On the contrary, it takes its author's conventional moralism in a direction that is not truly devout and certainly not redemptive, if absolution requires contrition. The novelist thought that he would sweep aside cobwebs, but instead unknowingly he became stuck fast in one of his own making. Gossamer is nowhere to be seen.

The close of the novel is tinged with an unwitting irony. Bordeaux's scene in which the priest and artist wrecks his equipment and his artwork nearly inverts a motif that lies at the heart of one wildly popular Marian exemplum from the Middle Ages, in which the Virgin saves a painter from a very close shave. In the life-and-death scene, the devil takes offense because the dauber in question has portrayed him as ugly. Out of Mephistophelian malice, the evil spirit causes a scaffold to come crashing down when the artist is toiling atop it. The painter tumbles in what would have been, without Mary's help, a fatal fall. The larger issue is that the wreckage of paintings and implements may be construed not as a sacrifice but as a snub to God. Such destruction is the exact countercurrent to one message that may be extracted from the medieval tale. The narrative tells of a miracle that brings succor and not punishment.

The story of the jongleur, despite its seeming simplicity, may be construed in multiplicitously, even infinitely. That openness to interpretation distinguishes the greatest art, including literature. In only two instances, both right after the war, has the tale been cheapened by being made a vehicle for violence against or involving art. In these two cases, the writers were not aligned with the Allies who won. Bordeaux abetted the Vichy regime, if not as an out-and-out collaborator. In his handling of the all-important offering before the Madonna, he bears a close resemblance to an Austrian Nazi whom we shall soon meet. Is this likeness sheer coincidence? Probably not. Bad choices in times of trouble have repercussions, even if the individuals who make them often slip away with official impunity. Neither the collaborationist nor the member of the National Socialist party seems to have been put on trial, but not being tried is a legal reality, and hardly the same as being exonerated morally. Among many outcomes of shameful decisions and malpractice are artistic ones: not only the artist's reputation may be hurt, but also the quality of the art that he produces afterward. Others will be more qualified to speculate about the psychic toll, but my own surmise would be that art and soul are inseparable. Committing infractions requires facing the music, even if its sounds reecho only within a person and not within a society that passes down a formal verdict.

Bordeaux in his prime might well have been set on a par with François Mauriac, a fellow Academician. But whereas the other writer went on to preach national reconciliation and secured the Nobel Prize in Literature in 1952, the inveterate Vichyist snapped the figurative brushes and slashed the metaphorical canvases of a career that had been fading for a decade. His oeuvre was diminished by the same foibles in his thinking that led him to collaborate with the enemy. In both his political and his literary decisions, he convinced himself that he acted out of principle, practicality, and patriotism. Yet he may have surmised that he was doomed after the war to be disgraced as a false prophet and to see his name blackened. He had staked out, all too openly, positions that were defeated along with the Nazis. How could an author who wrote novels of manners persist, when he had displayed such ill-mannered behavior? Rather than court the debasement of being dethroned by others, he unseated himself. He shuttered his fiction factory and devoted his energies instead to writing—or rewriting—history.

None of us now ought to be too quick to condemn anyone's chosen course of action amid such a calamity as the Second World War. The parlor game is all too facile, when armchair ethicists settle down snugly in plush upholstery more than three quarters of a century later and convince themselves that they would have been fearlessly resistant and not cowardly collaborationists, saviors of Jews and not anti-Semites, heroes and not heels. Hypothetical heroism after the fact counts among the worst forms of hypocrisy. It is a species of what is known as afterwit or *esprit de l'escalier*, those ripostes that occur long after the instant when they would have been clever. Yet relativism also affords an all-too-easy way out. No matter how compassionate about context we wish to be in excusing misbehavior, some circumstances are too grave and consequential for us not to take a stand. We must not hold in abeyance all decision-making about right or wrong. Reading literature, viewing art, and hearing music are multipurpose experiences. One point of such endeavors is to peer deep within the other people we examine, as well as within our own psyches. In the process, we learn from both past cultures and our present selves. All of this is to say that the humanities exist in part to deepen our sense of humanness. The human condition requires constant willingness to make value judgments, alongside equally constant striving for impartiality. Without education and effort, the human will not automatically become the humane.

Great Britain

Outside France, a mixture of nostalgia for a happier past and loyalty to an occupied ally may have spurred a pair of English professionals to join forces from 1939 through 1942. The one was a calligrapher and the other an artist, and their shared objective was to assemble an illustrated manuscript of *Our Lady's Tumbler* in the medieval French (see Fig. 1.27). The modern binding and medieval-style calligraphy were the work of Irene Wellington. The handmade book was illustrated by Sax R. Shaw. Then a young man, his craftsmanship belonged to a lineage that reached back to William Morris. The colophon indicates that the two artists completed their task in June of 1942 and made a gift of it to the painter Hubert Wellington. Wellington's first wife had passed away, and Irene took him as her second husband not long afterward.

Fig. 1.27 The juggler performs. Illustration by Sax R. Shaw, calligraphy by Irene Wellington. Manuscript of *Del tumbeor Nostre Dame*, lines 223–25 (Edinburgh, 1942), fol. 10r. Courtesy of Newberry Library, Chicago, Illinois.

From 1932 to 1943 the calligrapher made her home in Edinburgh, where she taught her skill part-time at the College of Art. In both her handwriting instruction and manuscript production, she carried on the revival of letter formation that had been initiated, under the sway of William Morris, by Edward Johnston. An Anglican who had a dalliance with Catholic medievalism, the last-mentioned belonged to the Arts and Crafts movement. He founded a new tradition of penmanship that was influenced by Morris's passion in the 1870s for medieval illumination and medievalesque calligraphy. Johnston never himself lettered any form of the juggler story, but he had demonstrated that a well-written codex could serve, like the dance routine of a tumbler, as a seemly articulation of devotion. For two decades, manuscripts from the Middle Ages and medieval-like texts provided Wellington with her major points of reference.

France may have been in distress under the crushing hegemony of the Nazis, but the lovingly lettered medieval French poem in this wartime manuscript reminded anyone who inspected it that a simple faith could prevail even in the face of monumental odds. The original-language text scrupulously followed the scholarly *editio princeps*, which dates from the years directly following the last German occupation of the country. Was this project mere escapism, jaw-jutting defiance, or both? How large did the ill-omened political backdrop loom over the new love that held sway or countersway in the scribe's personal life? How much was the tale a fond gesture by a woman who was not a Catholic to the denomination of her devout new husband-to-be? Did she espy more of him or herself in the humble tumbler?

In a note on the manuscript, the artisan of the quill discloses that at first she had been inclined to copy out Anatole France's version of the story. But before she set to work, a librarian convinced her that the thirteenth-century original "would give a more convincing reality to [her] calligraphy." Medieval is as medieval does, or maybe that thought should be rephrased as "medievalism is as medievalism does." In any event, the bibelotism of the fin de siècle carried on. In Britain, it remained alloyed with a conception of craftsmanship that had originated with William Morris. The "missal of my own" mania made its way even into the middle of the war.

United States

> War is the best subject of all. It groups the maximum of material and speeds up the action and brings out all sorts of stuff that normally you have to wait a lifetime to get.
>
> —Ernest Hemingway to F. Scott Fitzgerald

In the U.S.A. the experience of the Second World War differed starkly from what it was in France or Great Britain. Yet in the Land of Liberty too, the long-drawn-out conflict set in motion substantial social changes. Furthermore, the hostilities prompted personal reflections which authors sometimes elected to express using *Our Lady's*

Tumbler as the mechanism. The New World was regarded, as it had been after the First World War, as keeping alight the lamps of hope and learning. The Middle Ages were not the Dark Ages: today was. The Axis had draped the globe in an obscurity that the newest North American ally fought tooth and nail to dispel. In that effort, the States could use all the help they could get from the past as well as the present.

In 1942, an eleven-minute short *The Greatest Gift* was released. Based loosely on Anatole France, the hero of this handling of the medieval French tale is a juggler named Bartholomew. The out-of-luck performer is caught in a whiteout while crossing the Alps to Italy. When the blizzard closes the pass, he has nowhere to take refuge and is reduced by wintry cold to a virtual iceblock. Found in a close to cryogenic state by French monks, he is ushered into their monastery until the weather warms and they are no longer snowbound. While there, he becomes ashamed at his ineptitude and inability to repay the hospitality shown him. To make matters worse, his background as a vagabond makes the brethren suspicious. Throughout their hibernation, they devote the long dark nights to fashioning gifts to offer Our Lady upon the arrival of spring. As the season arrives, the misfit new arrival is eager to be on his way, but Brother Cyprian persuades him to tarry while the other members of the community make their donations to the Virgin. The discomfited juggler has nothing to present except his prowess in manipulating objects.

Before the Allies won definitive victory even just in the European theater, a married couple living in the New York City area published our story. The simple pamphlet that they commissioned contained the original language of Anatole France's *Le jongleur de Notre Dame*, along with an English translation of the classic French narrative. The title page is dated, in red ink, "Christmas, 1944." In a brief preface (see Fig. 1.28), the husband and wife made clear a few of the reasons why they chose to produce and distribute the booklet. Although their text is that of the short story, they see the tale through the lorgnette of the musical drama. Massenet gives them the setting of Cluny and its monastery. Thanks to the aria "O liberté, m'amie," his opera also promulgates the association of Barnaby with freedom.

If one lens of the opera glasses is appositely operatic, the other rests upon then-current events. The convent of Cluny sits near Vichy, where Pétain's pro-Axis government set up shop from 1940 to 1944. The possibility of war damage to the monastic complex is mentioned. The US public would have been well aware that the storied Italian abbey of Monte Cassino, where the Benedictine order was founded, had been heavily damaged in the first half of 1944. The male of the pair who commissioned this diminutive book would have had even more reason to harbor a special fondness for the medieval monastery: he had attended Princeton University as an undergraduate just after the reign of Ralph Adams Cram as house architect had ended. The Gothicist in chief may have taken his leave, but the collegiate buildings he had constructed defined the campus as never before or since: Princeton would be Cram-med with Gothic forevermore.

IN the little town of Cluny in Burgundy, a scant hundred miles from ill-famed Vichy, there still stands, we hope, a venerable Benedictine Abbey, built over a thousand years ago.

To this roughly cobbled market place, in a Yule season long past, there came the wandering juggler of our story.

Because both Christmas and "Barnabé" stand for freedom of spirit, and France has so recently regained hers; because our humble juggler was immortalized in song by Massenet and in words by Anatole France; but most of all because it's Christmas and we're friends, we want you to share with us this simple story.

J.W.S.-R.A.S.
December, 1944

Fig. 1.28   Preface to Anatole France, *Le jongleur de Notre-Dame*, trans. Frederic Chapman ([no place]: printed for the friends of Jarrett and Robert Schmid, Christmas 1944).

Still later in the War, Arnold Robert Verduin, at the time a college history professor who became for a patch an aspiring writer, placed as a freelancer a few fictions in a cross-section of periodicals. Most relevant for our purposes, in 1945 a single side in a journal for educators was taken up by his "Handsprings and Somersaults" (see Fig. 1.29). The piece is set in a sixth-grade class and centers upon an enactment of *Our Lady's Tumbler* as a skit by pupils in an elementary school. For all its elementariness, the account recounts a performance. For all its contemporaneity, it has the twist of telling a new exemplum ingrained in an old one.

Fig. 1.29   Cover illustration to the story "Handsprings and Somersaults" by Arnold Robert Verduin, published in 1945.

The zero hour of this one-page *Our Lady's Tumbler* strikes when a highly acrobatic girl who is meant to act the role of the tumbler trips and sprains her ankle. The day is saved by a recently relocated Japanese-American, who has been the object of heartless teasing because of her ancestry. The young lady steps, or leaps, in and plays the lead, to a crescendo of clapping. In a less-than-subtle hint of the climax to come, the author describes the teacher's perception of the child's frame of mind and chief objective as she approaches the living statue of the Virgin: "And then it seemed to Miss Benston that the little girl grasped the whole significance of her part. She would win the approval, not of the Virgin Mother, but of a Caucasian audience, the parents of the boys and girls who bedeviled her life." The final four sentences of the story make up a brief speech by the teacher which effectively constitutes the moral of the exemplum. They lead into what is meant as a supremely sentimental summation:

> "The tumbler's part was taken by Nana Tomita. When Sally Parcell sprained her ankle backstage, Nana volunteered to substitute. I am glad to introduce to you our new student, Nana Tomita. She has shown tonight the finest American spirit." Miss Benston's last sentence was swallowed up in a new thunder of applause.

During the war, more than 100,000 residents of Japanese background were interned in the United States. The sneak attack on Pearl Harbor by the military of Imperial Japan resulted in thousands of American deaths. The black-swan event induced what turned out subsequently to have been a groundless panic that the mainland would be invaded. To say that the internment was in some ways understandable is not to claim that it was excusable. On the contrary, it was a deeply regrettable reflex. A long-overdue apology was rendered to those victimized by the US government decades after the wrong was perpetrated.

One force driving the mandatory resettlement and incarceration was the dark cloud of suspicion seeded by the event in Hawaii. The bombing and strafing of the naval base in the Pacific archipelago caused people who looked nothing like the norm of white European descendants on the mainland to the east to be regarded (in most cases wrongly) as potentially traitorous newcomers and outsiders. The painful paradox is that such domesticated xenophobia takes hold cyclically in a nation that comprises mostly of citizens who come of immigrant stock. In the fullness of time, the new arrivals become hyphenated or even plain and simple Americans. In the shock of the moment, their countrymen felt distrust. Which side of the punctuation mark would take precedence? Would Japanese-Americans nurture greater loyalty as Japanese, because of birth or race, or as Americans, because of residence and citizenship? A very similar question about patriotism had led to hostility against German-Americans during and after World War I. Another part of the antagonism against Japanese-Americans arose from racism run amok. At the moment, the US had all in all less experience and acceptance of Asians than today. For all the benefit of hindsight, the reaction against Japanese-Americans cannot be papered over: it has long been recognized as inglorious. This very short story, despite being almost oversweet (but not overly optimistic?), speaks to a more capacious humanity, and one truer to what Americanism has meant at its best. It argues for shared humanity, rather than for tilting at windmills (or fellow citizens).

Verduin composed his words long after the wake-up call of "a date which will live in infamy," in the last year of a war that cost lives by the tens of millions. In a publication for and about teachers and pupils, he chose to bring home the broadest view of what the American dream and spirit could signify. Presciently, he implored the United States to be open to its immigrants, and particularly to hyphenated Americans from the Eastern Hemisphere. Before him, the twosome in the New York area articulated in their own distinctive way solidarity between the Western Hemisphere and France.

Neither of these two products, the printing by the Schmids or the short story by Verduin, has any glamour about it. Then again, much of a good life, great nation, and peaceable world is made by fitting together a jigsaw puzzle of many little pieces that are not overwhelmingly special but that make a constructive contribution to the goal of betterment. From the sidelines, we can easily fault what is affirmative for being simplistic, carp about love as mawkishness, and look for feet of clay perching upon every plinth that bears a heroic bronze. Yet bringing heroism down a peg or two and shattering myth will take us only so far. In the end, many forms of right and wrong have nothing at all in common. Not everything is gray. We can position ourselves to be touched by the better angels of our nature. We can stand to learn from this chapter in our story's biography, from these episodes in the long trajectory of the juggler across the second millennium, just as we can from the tale itself. *Homo narrans* is one wonder, *homo interpretans* its natural corollary. Let us, for the sake of our humanity, narrate and interpret well.

2. The Juggler by Jingoism: Nazis and Their Neighbors

> *The world becomes more amusing every year.* I am always in greater hopes of living to see it break its damn neck, which I calculate must happen by 1932.
>
> —Henry Adams

Virginal Visions

A not very incisive principle could be formulated: from the early Middle Ages on, in phases of high anxiety Christians have often sought to strengthen their engagement with the Virgin. When sailors batten down the hatches, the faithful fall on their knees before Madonnas. When the political ambience and military events swoop toward apocalypse, Marianism soars to new heights. One tangible token of these tendencies can be wrested from numismatics. Until the Vatican adopted the euro in 2002, it had its own system of coinage which was linked closely to the Italian lira. From 1929 through 1941, the reverse of the one-lira denomination depicted Mary. The design showed the Mother of God with her head encircled by a star-ringed nimbus and her calves framed by the horns of a crescent moon, with the globe beneath her feet as she tramples a serpent (see Fig. 2.1). In 1933, to mark the jubilee commemorating the death of Jesus, the area for signifying the date was enlarged. The years around this one proved to be uniquely important in far more than coins alone.

Fig. 2.1 Virgin Mary on crescent and globe, trampling serpent. One-lira Vatican commemorative coin (reverse), engraved by Aurelio Mistruzzi (1933).

The broad backdrop of Marian devotion and the uneasy atmosphere in the run-up to war all but guaranteed that apparitions would occur, and that they would attract ever more attention from the public. A first symptom of a craving for the immediacy of a sighting, and for the associated promise of mediation, took the form of Mariophanies in the spring of 1931. At Ezquioga, two children and others affirmed that they had caught sight of the Virgin (see Fig. 2.2). The faithful rallied behind the appearances of Mary by flocking on pilgrimage to this hamlet in the Spanish Pyrenees. Overzealous believers even wagered that the microscopic municipality in the mountains might manage to become a new Lourdes (see Fig. 2.3).

Fig. 2.2 "These four Ezquiogans saw the Virgin." Photograph by Charles Trampus, 1931. Published in *Le Miroir du monde* 2.78, August 29, 1931, 244.

Fig. 2.3 "Ezquioga sera-t-il un nouveau Lourdes?" *Le Miroir du monde* 2.78, August 29, 1931, 243.

These visions happened one month after the sacking of a hundred convents and places of worship in Spain. Anticlericalism surged once Cardinal Segura denounced the recently declared Spanish Second Republic. By decrying the regime, this Roman Catholic dignitary drew a line between the left-wing Republicans and the Church. He was sent packing into exile in France.

The flurry of virginal visions in the Pyrenees notwithstanding, the heaviest Marian activity came to pass in multiethnic Belgium. In the early 1930s, Belgian society wobbled and crumpled from the instabilities of its many internal rifts. As one of the most brutally contested killing fields in the First World War, the nation had been badly bludgeoned. During the combat, frictions between French-speaking Walloons and Dutch-speaking Flemings had pressed to the fore over language and culture as well as over might and money. In the interim, such spats had hardly been resolved and dissipated. If anything, they had intensified. The latent became blatant. Like the rest of Europe and the world, this factious land had endured the Great Depression. The economic hardship which dragged out year after year had furthered the political advance of socialists. In a 1931 encyclical, Pope Pius XI took a stand in condemning statist socialism. The stage was set for all sorts of dramatic brushfires: the country was on edge. A turn to the supernatural for reassurance made sense.

Circumstances were no more irenic in the hulking neighbor that loomed to the east of Belgium. Germany was mired in its own not-so-healthful muck of financial and political problems. In 1933, a mustachioed psychopath tightened his tentacles and centralized power in himself. On January 30 of that year, he was appointed chancellor. On August 19 of the next, he was confirmed as sole *Führer* or "leader" of the nation by a referendum. In the near term, Belgium, the Netherlands, and France would begin receiving displaced persons from the Nazis. Furthermore, Hitler's favor for *Lebensraum*, or "living space," to accommodate a loosely conceived pan-Germanic realm only fanned the flames of rivalries between French and Dutch speakers in Belgium. Under his rule, the German had a strong self-interest in fomenting Flemish nationalism and separatism. For all these reasons and more, many Belgians devoted themselves to the Mother of God, and contracted what verged on an epidemic of Marian visions.

The first of the actual or alleged Belgian epiphanies of Mary transpired in Beauraing, a small Francophone town in the borderland diocese of Namur, just a few miles from the frontier with France. Between late November, 1932, and early January, 1933, five children from two working-class families experienced apparitions of Our Lady. All the visions occurred close to a drab, scaled-down replica of the Lourdes grotto, with a modest-sized plaster statue of the Virgin (see Fig. 2.4). The simulacrum stood near a railroad embankment just beyond the garden of the convent school the youngsters attended. Another landmark in the sightings was a hawthorn tree.

At the outset, the young people spotted a luminous woman in snowy clothing. With her feet shod in puffy little cumulus clouds, she moved aloft above the railway bridge that stood at the top of a gradient not far from the children: she was truly walking on air (see Fig. 2.5). Subsequently they saw her, wearing a white gown and

Fig. 2.4 Postcard of the replica of the Lourdes grotto in Beauraing, Belgium (Brussels: Ernest Thill, 1930s).

Fig. 2.5 Postcard recreating the apparition in Beauraing, Belgium (Brussels: Marco Marcovici, 1930s).

emanating a blue light. More than thirty times, the five espied the Mother of God, communed with her, and received in return a beatific smile and a few instructive words. Mary's main memoranda to them were pithy and uncomplicated imperatives, such as "Pray always" and "Always be good." Initially no one put any stock in what the schoolchildren related, but eventually the report of the sightings drew the great unwashed of faithful (see Fig. 2.6). On August 5 of 1933 alone, 150,000 pilgrims or thereabouts descended upon the location. During the first ten months of the shrine's existence, the total number of visitors to it was tallied at 1,700,000. The wall-to-wall throngs included believers who themselves asserted that they had prospered from miracles, with visions and healings. One of them was the fifty-eight-year-old Tilman Côme (see Fig. 2.7).

2. The Juggler by Jingoism: Nazis and Their Neighbors   43

Fig. 2.6 Postcard of crowd at the hawthorn tree and bridge, locations of the apparition in Beauraing, Belgium (Brussels: Ernest Thill, 1930s).

Fig. 2.7 "The crowd hearing the revelations of Côme Tilman, Beauraing." A bit left of the middle, bareheaded and facing the camera, the farmworker who experienced a miracle. Photograph, 1930s. Photographer unknown.

A chain reaction took place, in which glimpses of Mary in one place led to subsequent recurrences in another. (Given the involvement of the Mother of God, the cumulative response could be better called a domina than a domino effect.) In the village of Banneux (see Fig. 2.8), between mid-January and early March of 1933, an eleven-year-old girl witnessed eight materializations of the Virgin. In this instance she showed herself clad all in white except for a blue sash, and radiant with light. In this guise she became recognized as the Virgin of the Poor, a title by which she identified herself in one of the showings. News of the visions drew immense concourses. At first, the seer was suspected of having been conditioned in her conception of Mary by having seen a statue of her at Lourdes. For obvious reasons, the young lady was thought to have been affected by the brouhaha at Beauraing. Additional visionaries, or alleged ones, caused some aftershocks, but the validity of their claims was challenged even at the time. As a result, these individuals are scarcely remembered today. A case in point leads us to events that played out in Onkerzele, another small settlement in Belgium. The episode began with Leonie Van den Dyck (see Fig. 2.9). Between August 9 and October 31 of 1933, she purported to catch sight of Our Lady of the Poor thirty-three times. The grim-faced housewife and mother came forth with many predictions. Eventually the Church rejected any supernatural legitimacy in the visions that she was supposed to have had.

Fig. 2.8 Postcard of the site of the apparition in Banneux, Belgium (Brussels: A. Dohmen, ca. 1934).

Fig. 2.9 Postcard of Leonie Van den Dyck, the visionary of Onkerzele, Belgium, outside her home, ca. 1933.

What conclusions may we draw? In 1933, Marian apparitions metastasized throughout Belgium, among both Flemish and Walloons. The epidemiology of their dispersal furnishes ample confirmation that in the stressful atmosphere, believers ached to apprehend the Virgin as a material presence. They hankered to witness the direct intervention of heaven on earth, through the person of the most approachable figure Catholicism could deliver. Although the rash of seeings would not recur, Mary would reappear in an even darker moment. Authors in the Low Countries found faith, solace, or even just parallels in the miracle of the medieval jongleur. Not by coincidence, like their countrymen who experienced Mariophanies, these writers are extraordinary in number and range.

Belgium

> God is in the detail.
>
> —Anonymous saying

> The devil is in the detail.
>
> —Anonymous saying

In Belgium and the Netherlands, the tale of *Our Lady's Tumbler* was put into Dutch at least three times during the occupation. The pen is said to be mightier than the sword. Whatever truth we assign to the truism, writing can offer a means of striking back against hostile forces. For all that, our story was not invariably a pièce de résistance in the Low Countries. The authors of these three versions inscribe a triangle, to which we may append the translator who was responsible for the only rendering into the language that had been made prior to the war. No one could have dreamed up a paradigm that would better communicate the starkly varying circumstances imposed and choices made under the Germans in these countries from 1940 to 1945.

The sundry translations and adaptations speak to the creativity that can be unleashed amid upheaval. All these Belgian and Dutch writers lived during the years leading up to the Second World War. The societies around them were beset by severe political and economic crises that called into question self-definition, church-state relations, and many other factors. Seen in the rearview mirror, the 1930s have been regarded as a heartwrenching crisis in Flemish and Dutch literature. Conditions in Belgium favored a turn to Mary and to the narrative of *Our Lady's Tumbler*. No wonder that people were receptive to manifestations of the Virgin, or that accounts of solace offered by her to individual penitents of humble backgrounds would strike a chord with artists and audiences alike.

In 1930, Franz Johannes Weinrich's German expressionist play of 1921 was brought out in Antwerp under the Dutch title meaning *Our Lady's Dancer: A Little Miracle Play* (see Fig. 2.10). The translator, Wies Moens, was a Fleming who wrote prolifically in his natal tongue. Already as a young boy, this future poet and journalist was exposed to two of the chief preoccupations that would intertwine erratically in his adulthood. One was Catholicism, thanks to which he evinced an unwavering belief in God and placed a special accent upon the Virgin. The other was Flemish nationalism. Both considerations held the foreground when he attended the College of the Holy Virgin (see Fig. 2.11) in a Belgian city in East Flanders and came into contact there with the Flemish Union. This institution, built in a gritty medievalizing architectural style, puts on show in an alcove over its principal portal a statue of its protectress, Mary.

Fig. 2.10 Front cover of Franz Johannes Weinrich, *De danser van Onze Lieve Vrouw: Een klein mirakelspel*, trans. Wies Moens, woodcut by Prosper De Troyer (Antwerp, Belgium: De Sikkel, 1930).

Fig. 2.11 Postcard of Het Heilige Maagdcollege, Dendermonde, Belgium (Brussels: Ernest Thill, 1930s).

Ghent remained the central locus of Moens's activities until the end of the Second World War. During the First World War, he studied Germanic philology in the university there. The city, one of the oldest in Belgium, was rent by social tensions. In it, the young writer had a hand in the Flemish nationalist movement. After the armistice, his activism landed him in detention twice, for much of 1918 to 1921. In the second stint, he spent twenty-two months in a prison cell, until spring of 1921. As a Dutch-speaking Fleming, he belonged to a population linguistically and culturally estranged from the French-speaking Walloons. His faction saw the so-called Flemish question as "a conflict of two civilizations, based on two different languages." In consequence, the group sought for the German occupiers to resolve the issue so that the Flemish could gain the upper hand by establishing a discrete Great Netherlands. This nation of Dutch speakers, known as Dietsland, would ingest not only the Netherlands and Flanders but also the Afrikaans-speaking portion of South Africa.

Politics is just part of the picture. Ghent, birthplace of the Belgian Nobelist Maurice Maeterlinck, saw vibrant intellectual and artistic experimentation. How much that extends to writing in Dutch remains indeterminate. During the two decades between World Wars, Moens (see Fig. 2.12) stands among his Flemish peers as an isolated and halfhearted advocate for modernism. More specifically, he could be considered a disciple of avant-gardism. In fact, he has a claim to literary-historical significance chiefly in this role. While imprisoned, he composed a booklet of expressionist poetry. The Fleming's absorption in this style of verse led him naturally to Weinrich's play, and he translated it faithfully into his native tongue not even ten years after its first edition. The German's drama innovates on earlier forms of *Our Lady's Tumbler* by having the dancer execute a progression of steps as he wrestles with his doubts over his calling to take monastic vows. The first is fleshly dance; the second, a mystical ascent to Mary; and the third, an outpouring of spiritual exultation that proves to be the monk-dancer's supreme effort before his death, after which he strings out perpetually his balletic career in the firmament as a star right next to Mary. In the later translation,

Fig. 2.12 Wies Moens. Photograph taken before 1926, photographer unknown.

the play pealed a note that resonated with the tastes of the times. The expressionism allows for actors and dancers to convey emotion through their acting, including their movements, far beyond the restraints of the uncomplicated words. The piece was soon appropriated for production by school and amateur groups in Belgium.

Prosper De Troyer (see Fig. 2.13), the Fleming who engraved the woodblock that embellishes the book jacket to Moens's translation of the play, is also a certified expressionist. The writer and he crossed paths in other collaborative projects during the early twenties. Like Moens, the artist for a spell synthesized expressionism with his Catholicism, and he has a reputation for religious themes. Graphic art in the new style constituted such a broad and well-balanced movement that generalization about it can be perilous. In many places, it was conditioned by the putative primitivism and primal vitality of African and Oceanic art, complemented by the work of Gauguin and Van Gogh, as well as by medieval woodcuts. Such medievalesque influence can be detected here in De Troyer's cover. The carving has an anguished blackness that is even harshened by the underlying grayness of the cardboard. The composition brings angular lines into stark juxtaposition, with the dancer's square mat set sideward to the oblong frame of the whole artwork. We make out only the back of the man doing his steps, with his tonsure and his medieval entertainer's garb. Up to the left, the apparition of the Virgin hovers. To the right, a monk in his habit carries between his hands what could be a stack of books or an accordion.

Fig. 2.13 Prosper De Troyer, self-portrait, 1929. From Frans Mertens, *Prosper De Troyer* (Antwerp, Belgium: Standaard, 1943), front cover.

Fig. 2.14 Henri Ghéon. Drawing by Jean Veber, 1898, https://commons.wikimedia.org/wiki/File:Henri_Ghéon_by_Jean_Veber.jpg

Moens viewed his generation as nurturing an entirely new and more positive outlook on medieval culture than had been endemic in the nineteenth century. He also pointed to the agency of expressionism. In conclusion, he singled out for special attention Henri Ghéon (see Fig. 2.14) and his *Play of Saint Bernard*. This French-language playwright was a lifelong devotee of the Virgin. He founded for young folks the "Companions of Our Lady," an amateur theater group for which he composed more than sixty plays. For content, he usually drew upon the Gospels and saints' lives, while for style he relied upon medieval mystery and miracle plays. His prolific corpus includes such titles, to give them in English, as *Mary, Mother of God* and *The Madonna in Art*. It also assimilates works on other holy men and women who were themselves pledged to the Virgin, such as *The Marvelous History of St. Bernard*, *The Secret of Saint John Bosco*, and *The Truth about Thérèse*.

Moens's attraction to medieval legends propelled him in 1923 to fashion the authorized Dutch rendering of a three-act German "legend play" on the pilgrimage to Compostela. The original-language edition from 1920 could not have placed less emphasis on the movement of pilgrims. Its cover art incorporated a 1520 woodcut that displayed a monk seated at a writing desk (see Fig. 2.15).

Fig. 2.15 Front cover of Dietzenschmidt [Anton Franz Schmid], *Die Sanct Jacobsfahrt: Eyn Legendenspiel in drey Aufzügen* (Berlin: Oesterheld, 1920). Woodcut by Johannes Othmar, 1920.

Additional impetus to translate *Our Lady's Dancer* could have come through G. K. Chesterton's *St. Francis*, which dealt in passing with the story of the tumbler, and which Moens put into his own first language in 1924. In the same year in which his translation of the German play appeared, the author published his Dutch version of an English volume on Saint Francis. At the same moment, he became a driving force behind the establishment of the Flemish Popular Theater by a cohort of Catholic theater producers and other movers and shakers. A further factor that may have lent gravitas to the notion of translating the German *Our Lady's Dancer* into his native tongue is the relationship between the tumbler and the Church. Until the end of the War, Moens propounded the view that the Flemish people could avert crisis by heeding the direction of its intellectual elite. Accordingly, the performer's ultimate obedience to the hierarchy embodied in the abbot may have resonated well with his thinking.

Our Lady's Tumbler has embedded within it a folkishness that could have coaxed attention from an essayist who belonged to a cadre known as *Volks-Dietsers*. "Folk-Dutchers" would be an indelicately literal way of putting this untranslatable word into English. Moens's own credibility as a folk-oriented writer is faultless. Indeed, his verse has been characterized as "folk-connected" (*volksverbonden*). A few years later he would even write a study entitled *Dutch Literature Viewed from a Folk Perspective*. The purportedly Picardian provenance of the medieval poem would have fortified the tale's relevance to the modern Flemish author. Even though the original was in a French dialect and not his mother tongue, the story still qualified as at least loosely regional. Finally, his reactions would have been colored by grappling closely with the narrative in a German-language form, in the play by Weinrich.

Moens's writerly activities are only one tranche of the context that screams out for scrutiny. The year after publishing his Dutch *Our Lady's Dancer*, he cofounded the National Socialist party of Belgium, the first full-fledged redirection of nationalism in Flanders toward fascism. With the involvement of the Nazis, the Flemish Question intersected eventually with the Jewish one. Although the author drifted from the Belgian movement not too long afterward, his efforts on behalf of extremists sympathetic to Nazism did not go unremarked and uncompensated later by the invaders—or unpunished when in turn the Germans were beaten down.

After the appropriation of Belgium by Germany, from 1941 to 1943 Moens directed the Flemish radio broadcasting operation instituted by Hitler's regime. During this same period, he published *The Flemish War Poem*, in an edition with the Dutch original and a German translation on facing pages. After the deathmatch between the Allies and the Axis drew to an end, he fell into a disfavor that went beyond being persona non grata: in 1947, he was condemned in absentia to execution for having consorted with the enemy. At that juncture, he took flight to the Netherlands. Instead of being extradited to Belgium, he found safe harbor there for three and a half decades as a teacher and administrator at a Carmelite college in Limburg. He died in 1982.

Whether the sentence was condign or not remains an open question. So too does the degree to which Moens deserves responsibility for the atrocities of Nazism in Belgium. Seventy-five years have flown by. Whatever verdict we reach on his connivance and culpability, the outcome he desired from his political activities was not the one exemplified in the German anthem "Germany above all." Rather, his ambition could be expressed in unwieldy English as "Dutchland above all." He espoused an ethnic nationalism that aspired to consolidate Flanders, the Netherlands, and other Dutch-speaking pockets, so that a greater Dutchland or Greater Netherlands might arise. This mirage of an emergent nation became befouled by collaboration with the Nazis. In both the First and Second World Wars, the Germans exploited the Flemish Movement to inflate their own supremacy. This writer's fate serves as another useful caution about the care to be shown in choosing causes and even more in picking allies. Regarding the enemies of enemies as friends requires being steeled to accept or at least tolerate their guiding principles—and standing ready to face the fallout for treason.

Was Moens's turn to the Middle Ages in the 1920s related somehow to his eventual descent into philo-Nazi Flemish nationalism and national socialism? The cover of his 1943 book *The Pointed Arch* offers a stylized view of lancets (see Fig. 2.16). The one in the foreground has a robustness that could be termed "muscular Gothic," on the model of "muscular Christianity." The dark-shadowed interiors of the invisible arches behind it obtrude joylessly, like the tips of bombs, torpedoes, or missiles. In one sense, the look marks an outgrowth of expressionism. Set in the context of the last few years of the war, it has a scowling air, with a potency reminiscent of the all too vigorous people and buildings familiar from the propagandizing of Nazism, Fascism, and Soviet Communism. Think socialist realism.

Fig. 2.16 Front cover of Wies Moens, *De spitsboog* (Bruges, Belgium: Wiek op, 1943).

The popularity, and even special status, of *Our Lady's Tumbler* in Belgium was not restricted to Flanders and especially nationalist fanatics there. For example, Arthur Masson (see Fig. 2.17) was a Walloon author recognized for a cycle of five novels in French known affectionately as the "Toinade," a neologism constructed to honor the likable personality of their protagonist, Toine Culot. In reminiscences, Masson recalled having been introduced to the story of the entertainer in the context of literature from more than a half millennium earlier, specifically fabliaux. He concluded the same piece by characterizing himself as "troubadour of the good days, bard of the humble beauties of my country, jongleur of the Walloon region."

Fig. 2.17 Arthur Masson in his student quarters in Louvain. Photograph, 1919. Photographer unknown.

Interestingly, the medieval French tale achieved its greatest success in Belgium, but not in the modern reflex of its original tongue. Instead, it spread riotously in Dutch—or Flemish, as the strain of that language spoken in the northern part of Belgium is often called. In November, 1933, a censor of the Roman Catholic Church in Bruges officially approved publication of *Wintze, or Our Lady's Tumbler: Legendary Account* (see Fig. 2.18). The name assigned to the leading character is unusual, with a suffix uncommon in Dutch personal names. In fanciful onomastics, the author puns on its elements with the phrase "Wintze wint Ze": Wintze wins you over—and not just by default.

The writer was E. H. Blondeel, a Fleming who resided in Mont-Saint-Guibert. This community, in Walloon Brabant, is located not far from both Beauraing and Banneux, and thus in the lands where Mariophanies were nearly as common as Madonnas for a few years in the early 1930s. This author published nothing else of substance. His tale makes no mention of the apparitions that occurred nearby as his book was being written and printed. Hence, we are not positioned to infer whether in composing his narrative he was inspired by them, or whether he was moved merely by the same anxious context. Two of our only major certainties are that he was a practicing Catholic and a teacher at a religious school. A third is that in 1929, the writer directed dramatic

Fig. 2.18 Front cover of E. H. Blondeel, *Wintze, of De Tuimelaar van O. L. Vrouw: Legendeverhaal* (Torhout, Belgium: Becelaere, 1933).

performances of Our Lady's Tumbler that the charitable St. Vincent Society in Ypres organized to raise funds for Flemings who went homeless. He is identified as having been a chaplain for Flemish workers in France. Apparently, Blondeel had already staged the play in various other towns in Flanders before then. The staging took place beneath the speechless smile of "the mother in white and blue, Our Dear Lady of Mercy."

The Netherlands

Also in 1933, August Defresne (see Fig. 2.19) published a remake of the story, under the Dutch title that corresponds to the English *The Pious Minstrel*. A playwright, director, leader of theatrical companies, and fiction writer, he showed an interest early in the literature of the Middle Ages. For example, he wrote a 1920 study on the psychology of the Dutch narrative cycle about Reynard the Fox. His engrossment in the human mind accorded loosely with his attraction to expressionism. In 1925, he published a study on the movement in modern German drama. Either in the original or in Moens's translation, this other Dutch man of letters would surely have encountered the play by Weinrich on *Our Lady's Tumbler*. Still, the standard biography of this dramatist's theatrical activities makes no mention of any other Dutch-language author who wrote a narrative or stage form of the story. From 1923 through 1956, Defresne was affiliated continuously with one or another theatrical company. The sole exception came during the wartime years. During that stretch, he refused to join a Chamber of Culture instituted by the Germans. Consequently, he had a gun held to his head (all but literally) to go into hiding.

Defresne's version of *Our Lady's Tumbler* is not a theatrical script. All the same, the photographic image that once graced the outer cover shows a woman in stylized monastic habit, almost like a glorified gown of the sort worn at American graduation ceremonies (see Fig. 2.20). Her eyes gaze upward, heavenward. Her hands are upraised and pressed against a bare gray background. Blackness billows from stage right, and shadows shoot out from her silhouette. The vignette bottles expressionism in its purest distillation, and it may even afford us insight into the lost German silent films of the story. In a decidedly different direction, the decision to cast the jongleur as a female here is due to the convention that welled up from the dissonant traditions connected with Mary Garden. On the back of the title page the author stipulated that no one but Charlotte Köhler might recite his version of the medieval account. This is the actor he married in 1920.

Fig. 2.19 August Defresne. Photograph by Hanna Elkan, 1940.

Fig. 2.20 Charlotte Köhler as jongleur, in monastic habit. Photograph by Godfried de Groot, ca. 1933. Published on the front cover of August Defresne, *De vrome speelman* (Amsterdam: "De Gulden Ster," 1933).

In his introduction, Defresne reviews the constitutive facts about *Our Lady's Tumbler* and its reception through Massenet. He observes "this medieval tale is as famed in French literature as Sister Beatrice is in Dutch." With great chronological precision, he situates the action in 1215. His reworking of the story departs from the original, especially because he "fantasizes" about what happened after the episode recounted in the miracle from the Middle Ages ended. In expanding the narrative, he sought inspiration in the mysticism of the thirteenth and fourteenth centuries.

In 1934, yet another version was reprinted in Dutch. Under the pseudonym of Anthonie Donker, N. A. Donkersloot, at that point in his early thirties, published a collection of poetry entitled *Broken Light*. The fourteen-line poem bears the title that calls to mind Anatole France and Jules Massenet from decades earlier, rather than visions of Mary in Belgium of his own day. In fact, Donker had published the poem already in 1928.

                Le Jongleur de Notre-Dame

> Before the Mother of God with the Child, in the grey niche,
> he entered, quick as a church thief,
> without saying a Hail Mary, without making the sign of the cross,
> but juggling with glittering balls,
> maneuvering in limber somersaults,
> and then clasped his legs, as quick as lightning,
> around his neck (the Chinese bridge),
> humbly performed his most difficult stunts,
> and finally went all out,
> and immobile, without trembling for a moment
> in his painful, taut wrists,
> stood minutes long on his hands,
> a prayer stretched motionlessly.

Mary watches it intently.

The first version of the tumbler's tale in Dutch during actual wartime preserved a story at variance with that of Moens, in several ways. It was a translation not of a twentieth-century German text but of the medieval French poem itself. Furthermore, the prose in the modern language issued from the pen of not a Fleming but a Dutch man of letters—and a Jew.

In his early twenties Victor Emanuel van Vriesland (see Fig. 2.21) had already come up against the contrast between the fun-loving tomfoolery of peacetime and the black-hearted soberness of wartime. As a student at the University of Dijon he had joined his classmates in donning a costume as a Pierrot, a sad clown (see Fig. 2.22). With the outbreak of the First World War, he soon had to curtail his studies to come back home. Owing to the hostilities, the frivolity of college life ended prematurely for him.

The Dutch Jew was well acquainted with the writings of Defresne. In fact, he even supplied the introduction to the latter's 1931 novella *The Restaurant*. During

Fig. 2.21 Victor Emanuel van Vriesland, age 70. Photograph by Jacob de Nijs, 1962, CC BY-SA 3.0. The Hague, Nationaal Archief, https://commons.wikimedia.org/wiki/File:Victor_van_Vriesland_(1962).jpg

Fig. 2.22 Victor Emanuel van Vriesland as a sad clown (top left), age 22. Photograph, 1914. Photographer unknown.

the occupation, Defresne lent a hand in in the Resistance. The story of the tumbler had drawn notice for mixed reasons in both Flemish Belgium and the Netherlands in the early 1930s. Partly it attracted note as a late avatar of expressionism in Germany. Equally, it responded to the Marianism connected with the apparitions of Beauraing and Banneux in Belgium. After the German invasion the tale gathered in renewed attention for different motives again, but from individuals who had been exposed to its earlier popularity.

Vriesland's version was printed in 1941. The illustration on the title page underlines the joyous self-expression of the dancer, to the exclusion even of the Virgin (see Fig. 2.23). Another vignette brings home the humility of the scantily clad tumbler, whom we see only from the rear as he enters the monastery (see Fig. 2.24). The scene focuses close-in on the worldly accoutrements he has relinquished. His horse is led away, alongside a monk who totes the sumptuous garments the minstrel has renounced. A third figure shows the performer, now a lay brother, again from behind. This time he looks identical in habit and tonsure to the choir brothers as they muster with their psalters, except that he is ducking down to skulk into the crypt (see Fig. 2.25).

The book wraps up with a note that offers scholarly orientation, since the author sticks closely to the medieval original. The world seemed tremendously parlous when Vriesland plied his pen across paper. In keeping with this fragility, the closing passage in the two pages emphasizes the tenuous transmission of the French text from the Middle Ages. Thanks to unwitting overstatement, we are apprised of a single, badly damaged manuscript. At least fourteen folios and most of its miniatures have gone missing during the past few centuries. After the war, the story writer stressed how artists had played a role in the Resistance. He could well have regarded

Fig. 2.23 Title page of Victor Emanuel van Vriesland, trans., *De potsenmaker van Onze Lieve Vrouwe*, illus. Bob Buys, De Uilenreeks, vol. 44 (Amsterdam: Bigot en Van Rossum, 1941).

Fig. 2.24 The juggler enters the monastery. Illustration by Bob Buys, 1941. Published in Victor Emanuel van Vriesland, trans., *De potsenmaker van Onze Lieve Vrouwe*, illus. Bob Buys, De Uilenreeks, vol. 44 (Amsterdam: Bigot en Van Rossum, 1941), 6.

Fig. 2.25 The juggler slips down into the crypt during prayer. Illustration by Bob Buys, 1941. Published in Victor Emanuel van Vriesland, trans., *De potsenmaker van Onze Lieve Vrouwe*, illus. Bob Buys, De Uilenreeks, vol. 44 (Amsterdam: Bigot en Van Rossum, 1941), 42.

both the jongleur and himself in this light at the instant when the poem first began to ensnare him.

The translator, illustrator, and printer are identified only in a colophon at the very end of the volume. This arrangement may give voice to an unpretentiousness that sits well with the thirteenth-century miracle, which is anonymous: whether by coincidence or design, the story is allowed to speak for itself. Alternatively, the minimizing of identities could have been self-protective discretion. Vriesland had ample incentive not to advertise his biodata. Although he had never made an issue of his background, he was indeed a Jew. Had the German authorities become aware of his ancestry, he would have faced all the travails that being Jewish entailed in the Netherlands under Nazi occupation. To make matters worse, he had been at one time a self-declared Zionist. Neither item in his dossier, Jewishness or Zionism, would have eluded detection by the Nazis. When the Jewry of the Netherlands began to be rounded up for deportation and mass execution, the man of letters had to go to ground. He spent the war years shuttling from one address to another with the help of bosom buddies and the Resistance. Although he evaded capture, his safety and survival were not at all assured. The goon squads of Germans and Dutch Nazis managed to track down between a third and half of the Jews in the country who went into hiding. Those they apprehended, they dispatched to camps and death. Socially isolated from hiding and psychologically pressured from worrying, Vriesland sunk into despondency.

The fugitive could have teased out parallels between the tumbler and himself. The medieval entertainer forsook his belongings and clothing, retired from the world to live a cloistered existence, and took on a powerful institution that seemed unsympathetic and uncaring to both him and his craft. The dancer of the Middle Ages, long before the concept of nonviolent resistance had been created, cordoned off a space and function of his own without confronting his institution directly. Similarly, the juggler of the Anatole France story goes unwittingly against the government of his organization. He resists by practicing his art. Even while wheeling physically or verbally, the two protagonists balk at being mere cogs in the social machinery they inhabit. A harried Jewish artist consigned to a living death in a country occupied by the Third Reich had good cause to identify with a protagonist who could express himself only surreptitiously.

Going farther out on a limb, we should consider the claustrophobia of a confined existence as compounded by the sequestered aloneness of the out-of-place lay brother. The gymnast spends most of his waking hours trying to breathe unbreathable air as he is cooped up in a stuffy space far from the light of day. Being in a crypt differed comparatively little from being walled off from society and secret police, as were most famously in Amsterdam Anne Frank and her Jewish family. Some hiding places of Jews who went underground to become involuntary shut-ins were in fact truly subterranean, oubliettes entered and exited through trapdoors. In addition, the Dutch word for going into hiding (*onderduiken*) means literally "to submerge"—to go under water. To speculate further, the term in the same language for the Shoah (*ondergang*), if broken down into its two constituents, corresponds to the English "going under."

The medieval poem portrays an artist cut off and excluded, from both the outside world he quits and the inside clique he joins. He is a loner in the pursuit of his art, and he dies partly through the practice of it. Yet the message and spirit of *Our Lady's Tumbler* are not defeatist. Without being triumphalist, the poem is nonetheless triumphant. Without knowingly trying, the gymnast or dancer vindicates himself against both the macrocosm of secularism and the microcosm of monasticism. He attains salvation through his commitment to his craft, even though he must rehearse it in windowless, lightless, and airless isolation. Vriesland may have been lured by the counterintuitively victorious spirit, which is uplifting in a very real sense. First the performer is assuaged when he is down, and then post mortem he is hoisted aloft to heaven by angels who levitate themselves and him at Mary's behest.

A final thought is that the Dutch Jew may have felt a rapport with the story out of appreciation for Christians who succored him in his time of need. More generally, Vriesland may have been fascinated by it as an expression of ecumenism. In this regard he can be compared with the German-language author Franz Werfel, who was Austrian-Bohemian by birth, but Jewish in ancestry. Werfel was exposed to Czech Catholicism through his governess and through the schools in which he was educated. After the 1938 annexation of Austria by the German Nazis, he fled his homeland. His flight took him to France. In the closing days of June, 1940, after the German invasion, Werfel and his wife found themselves among millions of evacuees in southern France. The couple was advised by one family to seek shelter in the major town of Lourdes, in the foothills of the French Pyrenees. The two received sanctuary in this so-called City of Miracles. After visiting the heralded holy place, the writer vowed to give an accounting of the spiritual serenity, and the kindness from the Catholic keepers of the shrine, that he experienced there.

Once Werfel gained asylum in America, he delivered on his pledge. In 1941 he published in German the historical novel *The Song of Bernadette*, which deals with the vision of the Virgin seen at Lourdes by the young woman from the Soubirous family. The "personal preface" to the book concludes with a paragraph in which the author explains movingly why despite religious difference he was impelled to set pen to paper by one goal:

> … that I would evermore and everywhere in all I wrote magnify the divine mystery and the holiness of man—careless of a period which has turned away with scorn and rage and indifference from these ultimate values of our mortal lot.

The émigré wrote about Saint Bernadette, not about the jongleur—but his ultimate faith in the sanctity of man resembles the spirit that has moved many, or even most, of those writers and artists who have engaged over the centuries with the story of the medieval devotee of Mary.

After World War II, Vriesland ascended to preeminence in the literary firmament of the Netherlands. Simultaneously, he maintained his commitment to the belletristic culture of France. He translated from French, especially poems and essays of Paul

Valéry, and left a bumper crop of verse in the same language. The Dutch writer is likely to have been drawn to the medieval French piece of poetry about the tumbler by way of Anatole France, with whose writings he was au courant. There even survives from his hand an autographed copy of a speech that Anatole France declaimed at the burial of the French naturalist writer Émile Zola at Montmartre in 1902, as well as abundant correspondence with the Anatole France Society.

However noteworthy his French retelling may be, Vriesland was even more prolific and varied in Dutch. Although he may have left his deepest mark by compiling a three-volume poetic anthology in his native language, he also wrote a novel, short stories, plays, poems, literary essays, and other journalism. Yet even amid this heterogeneous and eclectic outpouring, his prose of the tumbler's tale looks curiously out of place, making it all the more probable that his pick of material was dictated by the special strains of the German occupation.

Later came a bit of writing by another verse-maker, so freely rendered from the medieval narrative that its hero is accorded the name Reinoud, not until then assigned to him in any foregoing version. By Gabriël Wijnand Smit (see Fig. 2.26), the composition was printed by itself in an undated publication, perhaps also from 1941.

Fig. 2.26 Gabriël Smit, age 42. Photograph, 1952. Photographer unknown. Image courtesy of Katholiek Documentatie Centrum, Radboud Universiteit, Nijmegen, Netherlands. All rights reserved.

This poet, journalist, and essayist fraternized at first with a group of Protestant writers, but in 1933 he enrolled in the Roman Catholic community. His translation may have been welcomed with open arms, since it was reprinted four years later to cap a collection of seven miracles of the Virgin. In a closing note to the later volume, Smit points out that the first six of the legends had Dutch origins. In contrast, he describes the story of the tumbler as a repurposing of what he calls "a very Old French legend." In the same text he also underscores that in his rendering he has not sought to cling to the original verbatim, but rather to enable the quintessence of this priceless narrative to spring to life for a present-day reader. The later book was embellished by Cuno van den Steene (see Fig. 2.27), an artist and illustrator in the Netherlands. The volume was designed by a printer with whom Smit had coedited a magazine put out by the printing house in 1939 and 1940. The title of the periodical, *In the Light*, would presumably have referred both generally to the beacon of faith and more particularly to the light at the end of the tunnel of war.

Fig. 2.27 A monk discovers the juggler's performance. Illustration by Cuno van den Steene, 1945. Published in Gabriël Smit, *Zeven Marialegenden* (Utrecht, Netherlands: Spectrum, 1944), 80.

Smit's circumstances differed sharply from Vriesland's. Most notably, the Catholic writer found common ground now and again with claques under the sway of the Nazi occupation. In 1942, he was a featured speaker in cultural radio programs run by Netherlands Broadcasting, which was controlled heavily by the Germans and used by them in their efforts to Germanize and Nazify the occupied nation. Thereafter he participated actively in the Netherlands Chamber of Culture. As with Defresne, this agency required all writers, musicians, and other artists to be approved and to register, or else risk penalty. Smit has been vilified for the opportunism of taking both sides during the war. For all that, it is hard to size up how fully he, as opposed for example to Moens, embraced the policies of the occupiers. Was Smit a turncoat or not?

Throughout his writings, Smit gave utterance to a visceral yearning for the unmediated presence of God. Even before the war he addressed himself to religious topics (see Fig. 2.28). Nor did he scrap such subjects once peace had been rehabilitated and fences mended, as is confirmed by a compilation entitled Psalms. His faith may have given him strength, yet the hostilities weighed heavily on the poet all the same. His soul suffered from living under the Germans. His preoccupation may be gauged from a postbellum compendium of his, entitled *In Wartime*. During the occupation, he turned specifically to the Virgin for solace and support. His special reliance on her is borne out by the title of his 1939 verse miscellany, *Praise of Mary and Other Poems*.

Fig. 2.28 Caricatures of Gabriël Smit, with note indicating that originally he belonged to the Old Catholic Church. Drawings by M. J. H. M. Wertenbroek, 1936. Image courtesy of Katholiek Documentatie Centrum, Radboud Universiteit, Nijmegen, Netherlands. All rights reserved.

Frans van der Ven published his poetry under the pen name of Frank Valkenier. In 1944, he brought out under this pseudonym a private edition of *The Tumbler … A French Legend from the Twelfth Century*. The minuscule book was printed in Tilburg. It belongs to the high tide of clandestine literature that rolled over the Netherlands under the Nazis—far more for the size of the country than in any other occupied nation. This version puts the medieval French poem into Dutch rhyming verse. The cover (see Fig. 2.29) signals the poet's politics, since it bears the Cross of Lorraine. As in France, this mark symbolizes the Resistance.

The title page (see Fig. 2.30), deliberately creaky in its construction, rubricates the name of the work and the author's nom de plume. Beyond such basic facts, it provides much additional information in conventional black ink:

> *The Tumbler of Our Lady* is strictly speaking a French legend from the twelfth century. But because it is so old and still attractive to read, and your servant had very little to do, the one who sometimes also calls himself Frank Valkenier translated the tale one more time into Dutch rhymes when he was at the Major Seminary at Haaren and has had the revision (black with a little bit of red) printed now for you former seminarians with your trustiest friends, as a remembrance of the stay there, and it [the tale] then follows after this.

The outlook beyond this opening seems nothing if not sunny, until we become conscious of the fact that the place under discussion was officially Camp Haaren, a German-run prison and interrogation unit overseen by the dreaded Nazi paramilitary organization known as the SS. Peeking at the towering, Romanesque revival edifice in a photograph from the period (see Fig. 2.31), one can perceive easily why prisoners confined in the commandeered theological institution would have identified with a lay brother. Wish-fulfillment would have come into play in picturing how he slipped away from compulsory group activities to voice his heartfelt beliefs and desires. The fellow seminarians would be those who were detained along with him, most of them

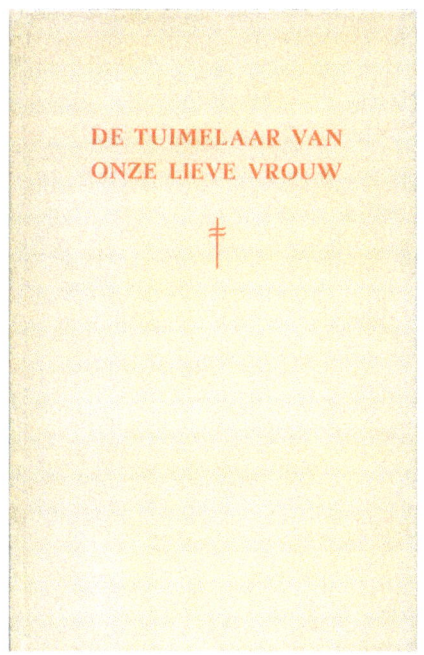

Fig. 2.29 Front cover of Frank Valkenier [Frans van der Ven], *De tuimelaar van Onze Lieve Vrouw* (Tilburg, Netherlands: Private printing, 1944).

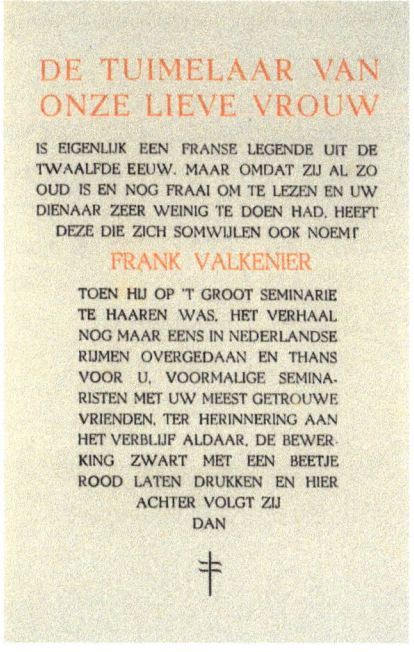

Fig. 2.30 Title page of Frank Valkenier [Frans van der Ven], *De tuimelaar van Onze Lieve Vrouw* (Tilburg, Netherlands: Private printing, 1944).

Fig. 2.31 Grootseminarie Haaren. Photograph, ca. 1942–1955. Photographer unknown. Image courtesy of Brabants Historisch Informatie Centrum. All rights reserved.

in the Resistance. Could the "black with a little bit of red" refer not only to the lightly rubricated printing but also to the results of beatings that left victims bloodied as well as black and blue—or does this amount to overinterpretation in the first degree?

Van der Ven's first poem was printed in 1936. In that same year, he released satiric verse against Anton Mussert, a founder of the National Socialist movement in the Netherlands. This boldfaced derision, ill-judged in retrospect, led to the poet's internment by the Nazi occupiers five years later, when the power of the ideologue he had mocked had attained its acme under the Germans. After another five years passed, Mussert himself faced the muzzles of a firing squad in the wake of the Allied victory. The satire is not par for the course in Van der Ven's oeuvre during this period. Some of his poetry, reflecting his Catholicism, is religious, while a share is devoted to his home district of North Brabant. In 1935, he cofounded Brabantia Nostra, Latin for "Our Brabant." He brought out his verse for the first time in this journal, came soon to be held in the highest estimation as a poet of the cultural and political reawakening in the territory, and eventually became the big fish in a small pond by being dubbed "the herald of Brabant."

The Brabantine periodical was produced by a corps of conservative young men between twenty-five and thirty years old. They were inspired by Toward a Catholic Order, a tract published in 1934 by the devoutly faithful Étienne Gilson, a French philosopher who throughout his distinguished career worked extensively on topics pertaining to medieval philosophy and religion. By and large the two causes of

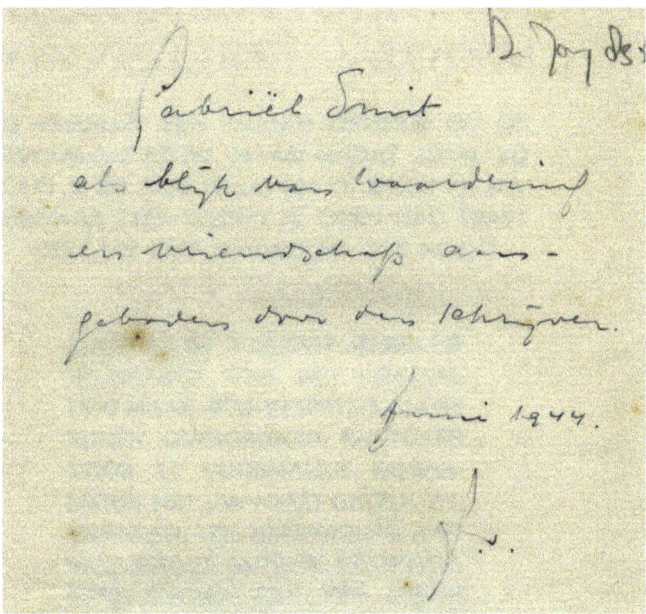

Fig. 2.32 Dedication of Frank Valkenier [Frans van der Ven], *De tuimelaar van Onze Lieve Vrouw* (Tilburg, Netherlands: Private printing, 1944).

religion and regionalism are interrelated: Catholicism and Brabantism commingle. Van der Ven wished to shelter the local color of his native region from the threat of industrialization encroaching from Holland. The cultural distinctiveness encompassed the zone's characteristic adherence to the Church—and its Gothic architecture. Thus the movement that pinnacled in the journal is related to the devotion evident in the Brabant student guild of Our Dear Lady. Both commitments, to traditional preindustrialism and to the Roman Catholic faith, would have fostered nostalgia for the Middle Ages as a golden age for the territory. This pattern has been familiar since romanticism.

Brabantia Nostra championed the idea that the province was "becoming once again visibly the core of the Netherlands." Such renewal carried within it an implicit reference to the sector's medieval heyday. The boosters of Brabantine pride undertook to dig out old traditions. If unable to rediscover them, they stood ready to invent them. The faction comprised elements congenial to the philosophy of the Greater Netherlands. It envisioned Belgium and what English-speakers call Holland as being two moieties of a nation that had been sundered only by an accident of history. In effect the pair was not separate countries, but merely slightly different latitudes of the same entity: North and South Netherlands.

Catholicism may have formed the great common bond between Van der Ven and Gabriël Smit. The first dedicated a copy of his tumbler translation to the second (see Fig. 2.32), with the inscription "As a token of appreciation offered by the writer in friendship." The momentous position that the Virgin has filled in Catholic religion helps to explain why both authors were captivated by the medieval miracle story that involved her. The journal *Brabantia Nostra* had a noteworthy religious component, and a singular devotion to Madonnas runs back many centuries in Brabant. Brabantia Mariana (see Fig. 2.33), or "Marian Brabant," a 1632 behemoth of around 1000 pages, is a repository of tales about miraculous images, many of which come to life, in shrines throughout the province. Mary has been dubbed "the Duchess of Brabant." The attachment to the Mother of God remained compelling on the verge of World War II, when a little Marian chapel was hammered together near Moerdijk Bridge. Because of subsequent road construction, the house of prayer was later demolished, but the image of "the Lady of Moerdijk" has been retained. The locality at issue straddles a political and cultural borderland, the boundary between the Netherlands and Belgium.

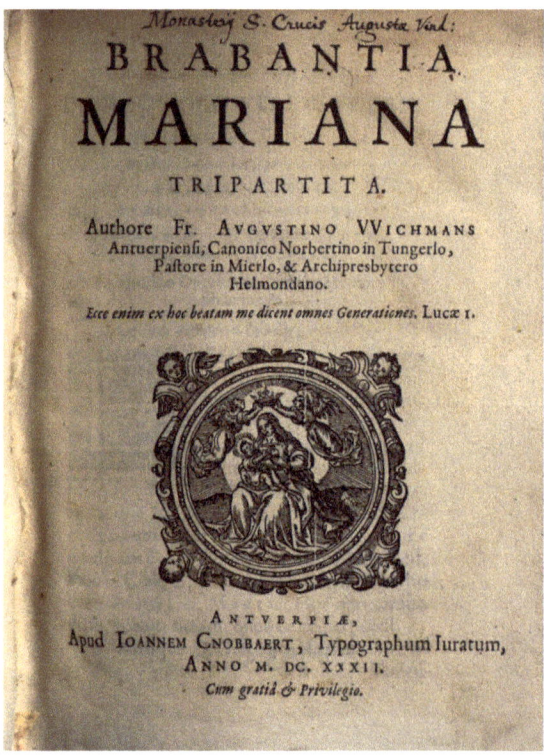

Fig. 2.33 Title page of Augustinus Wichmans, *Brabantia Mariana* (Antwerp, Belgium: Joannes Cnobbaert, 1632). Munich, Bayerische Staatsbibliothek.

Did mere happenstance ordain that three Dutch-language writers should follow—not that all of them were of necessity cognizant of doing so—a Belgian predecessor by translating *Our Lady's Tumbler* during the German occupation? Though in literary as in cultural history two points do not always determine a line, the coincidence of efforts by Vriesland, Smit, and Van der Ven carries all the greater force when one realizes that the story has been reworked in Dutch only rarely since then. Did the wartime literature exercise a later influence? The only clear evidence emerged a half century later, in a highly abridged and very free prose adaptation of Smit's poem. A mere three and a half pages, this rewriting is one of twenty medieval Marian legends retold by a [university teacher of medieval literature](). The narrative is hardly a household name among Dutch-speakers, but it has pulled through in some later variants. In 1958, Felix Rutten published [a prose version of the tale](). He wrote it in the dialect of Sittard, the town in the Limburg region of the Netherlands where he was born. This long-lived minor Dutch author turned to the tongue of his native town late in life, from his seventies on. The leading character in his telling is Brother Balderik.

The most significant subsequent treatment of the miracle in Dutch, more for its authorship than for its impact upon being published, may be [a short prose printed first in 1972](). Its composer was Gerard Reve. Along with Willem Frederik Hermans and Harry Mulisch, he has been regarded as one of the "big three" of Dutch literature after World War II. In Reve's reworking, the tale takes place in 799, the jongleur bears the name Henri de Maine, and the setting is Vosges. The performer, trekking by foot from Besançon to Poitiers, takes cover in a convent of nuns. He is allowed only to roll out his mat in the chapel. There he embarks upon an elaborate routine before an image of Mary. (Reve, who considered himself a convert to Catholicism, professed a particular devotion to the Mother of God.) As three nuns spy, the representation becomes animate, takes the showman into her arms, and mounts with him to heaven, as the organ thunders by itself and dozens of voices burst into song without any singers being visible. The narrative ends: "It was Christmas."

The clustering of various forms in Dutch before and during the German occupation leaves us to contemplate the curiously discrepant destinies of their four creators. Think of Moens, the Flemish expressionist, nationalist, and Nazi; Vriesland, the Dutchman who was a thoroughly assimilated Jew but at least for a spell a Zionist; Smit, the Dutch Catholic; and Van der Ven, the Dutch Brabantophile. The most salient overlaps among the foursome would appear to be their life spans; their love of Dutch and other literature, especially poetry; and their shared devotion to this one story. In its infinitely complex simplicity the miracle hypnotized all of them. But even with the basic goodness etched into its very essence, it could not save all its readers and writers from the darkness of the times, and in some cases of their own souls. Narrative can be redemptive, but literature or no literature, the best capacities of humanity have endured unending strife against the worst. Good does not always triumph over evil.

Germany

The performer's qualities of frailty, noncompliance with institutional norms, and perseverance in the face of chronic illness resonated with those writers in France, Belgium, and the Netherlands who suffered the occupation, but the same traits had failed to enthrall Germans in the late interwar and war years, from the 1930s through the mid-1940s. Although they made many turns to the Middle Ages out of [discomfort]()

with modernity, not all forms of antimodernism are equal. The Nazis spelled trouble for the early thirteenth-century tale and its later adaptations, and the climate that became conducive to Nazism proved to be uncivil to our little legend. During the cliffhanging of the Weimar Republic and the churlishness of the National Socialist period, the medieval entertainer all but retreated from Germany.

Why did the tumbler of the medieval French poem and the jongleur of Anatole France's story disappear from German culture for more than two decades? Among the multiple reasons for his temporary suppression, one is that French literature and art came to be branded as dissident and decadent. In his Frenchness, the character had little to recommend him. During this period, the government made *Völkischkeit* or (to approximate in English) pure Germanness at least a notional goal in language, literature, and all the rest of culture. Hitler, quarrelsome and inflammatory as usual, slurred the French as an enfeebled and effete people. Their vernacular had been a major concentration within higher education during the Weimar Republic, but the Führer decreed that the speech and culture of France should no longer hold such special prestige. This condemnation held especially true for authors who exacerbated their Frenchness by being Jews or having a same-sex sexual orientation. The public and publishers alike spurned imports from foreign arts and humanities that they regarded as debased and debauched, and spun around instead to supposedly genuine German fairy tales. Fiction felt to be more authentically Germanic in origin held larger appeal. In such an atmosphere, Wagner and his spawn were more spellbinding than Massenet; Old Norse sagas, than Old French narratives.

Other complicating circumstances existed, too. When groupthink and group action were the order of the day, the jongleur or juggler could be called a nonconformist. A peace-loving loner, he could have been parodied as a milquetoast. In the style of his shows, he resembled more the foreign and Jewish artists who were alleged to be degenerate than the autochthonous ideologues who elicited superlatives from the Nazis. In his intense and independent-minded religiosity, he stood miles apart from the state co-option of Christianity that Hitler prescribed. Lastly, the progressive political views that made Anatole France appetizing to Stalinists were anathema to the authoritarian Germany of the time. His famous dictum "it is a noble thing for a soldier to disobey a criminal order" comported poorly with National Socialism.

In the half century from 1873 to 1924, German-speaking Romance philologists displayed limitless zeal in cranking out editions, textual criticism, interpretations, and adaptations of *Our Lady's Tumbler*. During the second part of this period, the story's vogue peaked around 1920 among writers, theater producers, composers, and others, even possibly filmmakers. Likewise, the 1950s and later saw a steady succession of German-language revampings of the tale by nonscholars across various genres. Illustrators too chipped in their talents. In between, from the late 1920s through the mid 1940s, such scholarly and literary efforts to bridge the cultural divides between France and Germany were no longer appreciated. Whatever rapprochement took place among intellectuals soon after the First World War became a thing of the past.

Our lovely work, in all its manifestations, was effectively ostracized and suppressed, embargoed or eradicated. Attention to the French text from the Middle Ages slackened, new printings of Anatole France's story dropped off, Massenet's opera ceased to be staged, paintings and illustrations were not produced, and new versions cannot be documented.

In Germany, the last major fresh involvement of either a high-brow or a creative sort with the French tumbler for nearly thirty years was a philologically and poetically meticulous translation of the original octosyllables into four-footed iambic verse made in 1924 from the recent research edition of the medieval original. As we have already noted, the German form was printed as an appendix to a book by the art historian Wilhelm Fraenger. The man who put the poem into the modern language, Curt Sigmar Gutkind, made a conscious effort to outstrip his predecessors. In an afterword, he dismissed as failures the German versions of Wilhelm Hertz and Severin Rüttger, the first for being over-facile and the second for awkward and unidiomatic archaizing. If a comparison is to be drawn between this volume and any other scholarship written in the immediate aftermath of World War I, it would be with Romanesque representations, especially sculptural, of jongleurs as studied by Henri Focillon. This investigator was a French museum director, art historian, and professor, first in Lyons and later in Paris. The world had changed immeasurably in the quarter century since the 1898 *Religious Art in France, the Thirteenth Century* by his predecessor, Émile Mâle. The name of Focillon's study can be translated as "Romanesque Sculpture: Apostles and Jongleurs (Studies of Movement)." The pairing of high and low offices in the subtitle may bespeak a desire on its author's part to acknowledge or to intuit a social egalitarianism in the Middle Ages, not altogether unlike the leveling of class structure throughout Europe after the First World War. Previous research may have sought out and overemphasized the degrees of separation between the revered beings of sacrosanct evangelists and the immoral bodies of lowly minstrels. But Focillon's essay, like the world around it, departed from the traditionalism and unbudgeably anchored hierarchicality of the preceding generation.

Curt Sigmar Gutkind

Until now the demeanor of the jongleur had been nothing but bouncy, bubbly, and bright, but an evolution was under way. The fate that overtook Curt Sigmar Gutkind as a result of his Jewish derivation throws light on what befell the tumbler and juggler in the Germanosphere over the ensuing decades. Born in Mannheim in 1896, this German citizen returned wounded from the First World War. He rounded out his studies with a doctorate in philosophy from the University of Heidelberg in 1922. In the 1920s and 1930s, he displayed breathtaking sweep as he cranked out foreign-language anthologies and translations as well as scholarship of his own. His researches bore fruit, to say nothing of many essays, in books on wine and food history, the seventeenth-century French playwright Molière, and travel in Italy. The translating and anthologizing encompass a selection of Italian poetry and a sheaf of Italian short stories, alongside research on French philosophy and Italian novels.

Amid the outpouring of humanistic scholarship that flowed from his pen between 1927 and 1929, the name of one hardback looks peculiarly mismatched. The English would be *Mussolini and His Fascism*. The title page (see Fig. 2.34) conveys much quietly. For instance, it announces an introduction by no less than Benito Mussolini himself, who at the time had been absolute ruler already for four years. Below that text, a circle circumscribes a representation of the ancient Roman *fasces*. This bundle of wooden rods, bound around an axe, denoted the authority held by one class of Roman magistrates. In Mussolini's Italy, the symbol gave fascism its name, or at least the *auctoritas* of an association with the grandeur of Rome. Gutkind was not himself a full-fledged fascist, but he sympathized with the movement because of its stand on labor and union issues. Months before his book was published, he was handed the manuscript of Il Duce's introductory remarks at a personal audience with him. The German had no inkling of what lay in store for him and other Jews in the fatherland a half dozen years later, courtesy of the equivalents there of Mussolini's minions, namely Hitler's Nazis. After 1929, a long gap ensues in the publications of this otherwise steadily productive scholar.

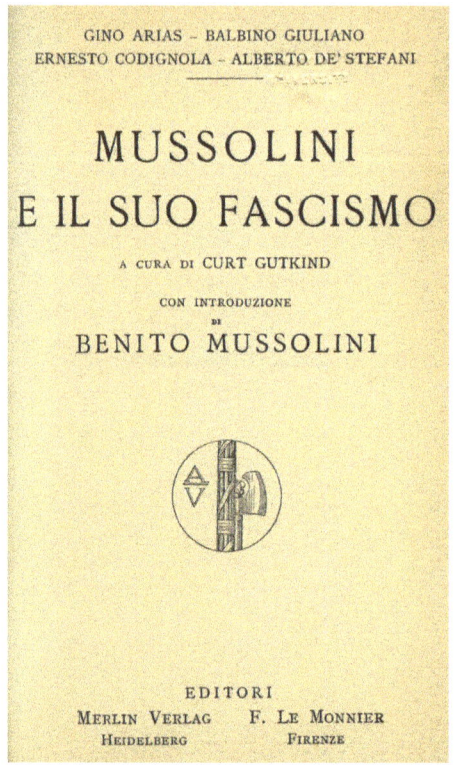

Fig. 2.34 Title page of Curt Sigmar Gutkind, *Mussolini e il suo fascismo* (Heidelberg, Germany: Merlinverlag, 1927), with introduction by Benito Mussolini.

Behind the banality of this hiatus in his curriculum vitae lies the grim reality of life for European Jewry under National Socialism. A Romance philologist who specialized in Italian, Gutkind first held a lecturership in Florence from 1923 to 1928. This initial position he owed to his dissertation director, Leonardo Olschki, an Italian Romance philologist also of German Jewish background. From 1929, his former student worked as a professor in his hometown of Mannheim, at a translation institute set up there in that year. He married the daughter of Theodor Kutzer, a Catholic who had been the elected head of Mannheim from 1914 to 1928. She went by the name Laura Maria Gutkind-Kutzer. Her husband directed the translation institute from 1930 to 1933, and in 1934 he was employed briefly on the staff of the business school in Mannheim.

Now neither Gutkind's status as a wounded veteran, marriage to the daughter of a notable mayor, nor proximity (even if only passing) to Mussolini could stave off what befell him thanks to the Nazis. After the racial laws cost him his position, in April, 1933 he joined the exodus of his coreligionists on the run from Germany. Within this larger displacement, he belonged to a skillful but ill-starred elite of Romance philologists bracketed as Jews. He made a quick exit to Italy, but despite having obtained Italian citizenship and developed amicable relations with the country's strongman, he could not secure a post there. The legend "Two Peoples and One Struggle" on a 1941 German postage stamp (see Fig. 2.35) proclaimed the alliance between the iron-fisted leaders of fascism and Nazism as well as between their nations. These relationships trumped any special consideration to which the German refugee may have hoped to be entitled by virtue (if that is the appropriate word) of his cordiality with the Italian autocrat.

Fig. 2.35 "Two Peoples and One Struggle." German postage stamp (12, with a supplement of 38). 1941.

In 1934, Gutkind went first to France, to unsalaried teaching at the Sorbonne in Paris, and then on a fool's errand to get into the clear south of the Alps. In 1935, he ended up in England, at Magdalen College in Oxford. In 1939, he obtained positions as an instructor at Bedford College and a reader in Italian at University College, both in the University of London. These arrangements turned out not to last long, because they (and his Jewish ethnicity) did not cushion him from suspicion owing to his national background and previous political affiliations. In Britain, the twofold setback of his

Germanness and erstwhile sympathy for fascism counted to his discredit more than the reasons for which he had failed to gain a haven anywhere on the Continent argued in his favor.

In 1940, hot on the heels of the German rout of France, the British authorities feared an invasion of Britain itself. Against that backcloth, they grew alarmed over the possible existence of a "fifth column" among Italians and Germans resident in the United Kingdom. Consequently, they resolved to defuse the danger of domestic treachery and trouble by deporting the individuals of concern to them. The forty-three-year-old Gutkind, registered as an Italian citizen, was arrested as a hostile alien, evacuated to Liverpool, and shipped to Saint John's, Newfoundland, to be interned in Canada.

The unfortunates in the same predicament as Gutkind boarded a steamship that until recently had been a luxury liner. Yet what lay ahead for the passengers and crew was anything but a vacation cruise. The *Arandora Star* (see Fig. 2.36) foundered off the coast of Ireland on July 2, 1940, after being torpedoed. The steamer came to grief when a German submarine, as it concluded a patrol, fired its one unspent missile. Later, the officers of the U-boat professed to have acted on the mistaken assumption that the weathered and faded old paint on the vessel was military colors. Concurrently (and contradictorily), they also maintained their belief that the weapon they shot was defective. In any case, several hundred people from the shipload of German and Italian detainees lost their lives amid the frigid waves of the squally Irish Sea, or in the bowels of the ship when it sank. A smattering of other Jews who had been rounded up with Gutkind, such as the Italian literary critic Uberto Limentani, survived the cataclysm, but the translator from Mannheim was among the unlucky majority who drowned in the Atlantic.

Fig. 2.36 Postcard of the *Arandora Star* (before 1940).

The First World War had badly battered the vitality and prospects of the European cultures that had first breathed life into the tale of the tumbler after his discovery or rediscovery in the aftermath of the Franco-Prussian War. In the late 1920s, 30s, and 40s, a miracle that had been a minor monument to the optimism and prosperity of the belle époque may have seemed frivolously irrelevant, when political anxieties were whetted to stiletto-sharpness, as many readers and artists struggled beneath the overfreight of political problems and worse. It could even have appeared contemptible, as nationalism took hold in more than one country and drove a boorish repugnance of foreigners or supposed outsiders. Yet whatever crises Europe had had to face before the Second World War paled into insignificance beside those it ran up against now, for the scale of suffering and death outpaced anything humanity had seen before.

Hans Hömberg

The biography of Gutkind tells one side of the story about the years of National Socialism in Germany. Another would be Hans Hömberg, who lived much of his adult life in Austria. Early in the Second World War, this German-born writer composed what may have been his most famous piece of theater, the 1940 *Cherries for Rome*. The play deals with Lucullus, a Roman general, politician, and plutocrat of unparalleled success. The text is touted sometimes for its pacifist traits.

In his drama, Hömberg may have made slantwise efforts to keep himself at arm's length from the National Socialists, but those attempts did not offset the closely contemporaneous book that he produced under the pseudonym J. R. George. The volume novelizes the notorious 1940 German motion picture *Jew Süss*. The cinematic costume drama, filmed at the bidding of no less a Nazi potentate than Joseph Goebbels, the Minister of Propaganda from 1933 to 1945, succeeded in packing movie houses and earning strong box office receipts. It presents a historical pageant that follows, with many distortions, the legendary career of Joseph Süss Oppenheimer, who had served as financial adviser and tax collector under Duke Karl Alexander of Württemberg from 1733 to 1737. While purveying intense anti-Semitism, it couched the propagandizing as entertainment. Goebbels commissioned the film after the conquest of Poland, with its large Jewish population. By demonizing the Jews as hook-nosed, conspiratorial predators, he intended it to build a supportive environment on the home front for the Final Solution.

The novel, close to two hundred pages, is not a whit better than the cinema in its demonization of Jews. Like the movie, it depicts the protagonist as he enlarges his pelf and power through dealings with the nobility, especially the duke. Here we can see Süss showing off the jewels and crown in his wall safe (see Fig. 2.37). Ignoring well-meant monitory words from his elderly rabbi (see Fig. 2.38), he keeps on increasing his riches by hiking taxes, tolls, and prices, and in helping his fellow Jews take over more and more of Württemberg. The project reflects the author's lifelong passion for moving pictures, which at this stage evidenced itself in the reviews he wrote as a cinema critic for the Nazi newspaper *Popular Observer: Militant Newspaper of the National Socialist Movement of Greater Germany.*

Fig. 2.37 Süß shows off his wealth. Photograph, 1940. Photographer unknown. Published in J. R. George [Hans Hömberg], *Jud Süß: Roman* (Berlin: Ufa-Buchverlag, 1941), facing p. 32.

Fig. 2.38 Süß's elderly rabbi. Photograph, 1940. Photographer unknown. Published in J. R. George [Hans Hömberg], *Jud Süß: Roman* (Berlin: Ufa-Buchverlag, 1941), facing p. 97.

After the hostilities, Hömberg worked energetically on the airwaves, as a writer of scripts and as a broadcaster. In 1961, he published (to put the name into English) *The Juggler of Our Lady*. The small book in fact subsumes three tales, of which the title story is only the first and not even the longest. In a compact afterword, the author set forth his conviction that the Middle Ages were more permissive than his own era in the treatment of certain themes touching upon religion and clerics. Furthermore, he observed that twentieth-century readers had trouble digesting miracles and deeds of saints as written in their original form, whereas they reacted with oohs and aahs of pleasure and wonderment when he read them aloud. This realization had prompted him to accept an invitation from a press and to go down "the shaft of the past." In additional remarks, Hömberg demonstrated his familiarity with the 1920 edition by Lommatzsch of the thirteenth-century original, the French poetastery by Borrelli, the French prose short story by Anatole France, the 1894 German retread by Robert Waldmüller of the medieval French, and the English radio (and recorded) version by John Booth Nesbitt. Hömberg's professional involvement in broadcasting would have heightened his interest in the American radio play.

In restructuring *Our Lady's Tumbler*, Hömberg fuses elements of the centuries-old legend with aspects of Anatole France's and other modern adaptations. He attaches to the leading character the name of Jean Vapeur, with the cognomen being the French for "steam" or "fume." This entertainer possesses the dancing skills familiar from *Our Lady's Tumbler*, alongside his juggling talents from the 1921 Nobelist. The story is set in France, to all appearances in Paris. Hömberg is noncommittal about the chronology, perhaps medieval but at the same time not closed to such modern-day features as the Café Apollinaire. The tale concludes with what is alleged to be a Latin inscription on a marble tablet in the crypt of the main church of Our Lady, where the protagonist is buried: "Here lies Mary's jongleur, a pure artisan, Jean Vapeur." Nothing cryptic here, save the location.

The narrative is enlivened by a couple of illustrations, one of which doubles as the cover art. The first (see Fig. 2.39) shows the jongleur, hat in hand, as he nerves himself to step through a portal with a pointed arch and set foot in the monastery. The second (see Fig. 2.40) depicts the Madonna poised on a sickle-shaped moon. She beams from ear to ear, as the child she cradles reaches out his arms toward the jongleur, costumed as a clown, who kneels before her and juggles nine balls. Both woodcuts are far more guiltless than the illustrator himself. The Austrian artist Ernst von Dombrowski had mixed himself up early in the National Socialist movement. During the war, he continued to fabricate inordinate quantities of Nazi propaganda, including anti-Semitic writings. His pieces harvested approving comment from Hitler himself, and were exhibited in collections of German art. After two years of postwar internment by the Americans, he resettled in Bavaria. He collaborated on projects with many ex-Nazis, belonged to extreme rightist organizations, and received a 1976 award from an association that was dissolved in 1998 because of its Nazi associations.

Fig. 2.39 The juggler arrives at the monastery. Illustration by Ernst von Dombrowski, 1961. Published in Hans Hömberg, *Der Gaukler unserer lieben Frau* (Vienna: Eduard Wancura, 1961), 13.

Fig. 2.40 The juggler performs before a smiling Madonna and Child. Illustration by Ernst von Dombrowski, 1961. Published in Hans Hömberg, *Der Gaukler unserer lieben Frau* (Vienna: Eduard Wancura, 1961), 25.

Hömberg's version of the story would appear to have attracted little notice even when first published. Along with the rest of his works, it languishes in oblivion today. Assiduous readers may seek it out, to determine for themselves whether the two collaborators' National Socialist background had any consequence on the choice or framing of the tale. Did the narrative offer a touch of redemption through worship and art to erstwhile Nazis who turned to it; were they unrepentant of their past and yet still capable of wallowing in religious emotionalism; did they do their best to shrug off their earlier misdeeds and go on with life; or did the coming together of their motivations and reactions to the account differ from any of these possible explications?

After the War

In the years of peacetime rebuilding, Germans, both erstwhile Nazis and not, turned to *Our Lady's Tumbler* and its later adaptations as much as did the writers and artists of any nation except the United States. The economic miracle of postwar Germany had the side effect of creating a yen for Marian miracles. To be entirely serious, the medieval setting may have had the appeal of seeming remoteness and innocence from recent events, while also being deliciously free of the Wagnerian stigma of Germanic myths and sagas from the Middle Ages. If any strain of medievalism fell as a casualty of the Second World War, it was of the Germanic and not the Picard sort. In fact, the French backdrop may have enabled Germans to pick up the strands of the détente with their neighbor that had been taken off the table during Hitler's rule. Moreover, the fact that the story stood then at a high point in US mass culture thanks to radio and television may have further burnished it.

To wax even more speculative, the German appropriators and adapters who had lived through the war may have liked to project something of themselves upon the jongleur. Among the regimented monks, the former lay entertainer found a way to retain his autonomy and to be true to himself while not capitulating to their conformism. He was, above all, squeaky clean and blameless. We know next to nothing of his past. Presented with a choice between simple and even simpleminded innocence or complicit guilt in a collective breach of ethics, who would not prefer the first?

Austria

> Christianity, and that is its greatest merit, has somewhat mitigated that brutal Germanic lust for battle, but could not destroy it; and if ever that restraining talisman, the cross, breaks, the savagery of the old fighters will rattle forth again, the absurd frenzy of the berserker, of which the Nordic poets sing and tell so much. That talisman is brittle, and the day will come when it breaks apart miserably. The old stone gods will then emerge from their forgotten ruins and rub the dust of millennia from their eyes. Thor, with the giant hammer, will spring up at last, and destroy the Gothic domes.
>
> —Heinrich Heine

Alongside classical revival architecture, Vienna possesses an *embarras de choix* of Gothic and neo-Gothic, running the gamut of original and renewal styles. At one end tower authentic structures built in the Middle Ages, such as Saint Stephen's Cathedral, erected in the fourteenth and fifteenth centuries. In the middle squat edifices with substantial later accretions and overlay that were refurbished centuries afterward to a more medieval-looking condition. To this group belong the "re-Gothicized" Church of the Augustinians and Church of the Minorites (see Fig. 2.41). From these buildings the renovating architect stripped away later Baroque accretions to the earliest designs. At the other extreme soar sheerly neo-Gothic buildings constructed during the revival in the second half of the nineteenth century.

Fig. 2.41 Postcard of the Minoritenkirche, Vienna (Vienna: Kunstanstalt Kilophot, early twentieth century).

Gothic revivalism manifested itself not only in houses of worship, but also in civic architecture such as parliaments and town halls, as well as post offices, universities and schools, and train stations. The Austrian capital has a handsome share of all these. Its places of prayer in the style include the Votive Church (see Fig. 2.42) and the Church of Mary of the Victory (see Fig. 2.43). Among municipal structures, the Town Hall deserves note (see Fig. 2.44). The architect of both the consecrated space and the city building had been a mason for the Cologne cathedral. Furthermore, the Votive Church could be interpreted as a downsized epigone of it. Thus, the Imperial City's architecture is studded with various strains of Gothic. The revival style predominated in the skyline as seen from key vantage points (see Fig. 2.45). The same prevalence may well hold true in literature.

Fig. 2.42 Postcard of the Votivkirche, Vienna (early twentieth century).

To all appearances, Austrian poetry and prose contain only one retelling of *Our Lady's Tumbler* in the lineage of the medieval French poem, as mediated through Anatole France and Jules Massenet. Before turning to that adaptation, we should pause for a beat to consider a 1931 play that, although set within a church, tells an utterly different story of two jongleurs, their stratagem to steal from a Madonna and Child, and their ultimate repentance. The playwright settled on the title *The Play of the Jongleur before Our Blessed Lady*, but he toyed as well with calling the piece *The Jongleur Legend*.

The writer was named Joseph August Lux. He was born in Vienna at the time of the Franco-Prussian War and died in a minor municipality not far from Salzburg in the

2. The Juggler by Jingoism: Nazis and Their Neighbors 79

Fig. 2.43 Postcard of the Kirche Maria vom Siege, Vienna (Vienna: K. Ledermann, early twentieth century).

Fig. 2.44 Postcard of the Rathaus, Vienna (Vienna: K. Ledermann, early twentieth century).

Fig. 2.45 Postcard of the Viennese Parliament, Rathaus, and Votivkirche (early twentieth century).

wake of the Second World War. Already in 1911, he evidenced a predilection for matters Marian with a book entitled *The Vision of the Blessed Lady*. After converting to Catholicism in 1921, he composed for the stage such scripts as the 1930 *The Play of Satan's World Judgment*, the 1930 *God's Minstrel*, and the 1930 *Play of a Holy Fool*. He was influenced by Ruskin and Morris. In addition, he was devoted to the genre of the mystery play. He founded a theatrical group called *Lux Spielleute Gottes*, which might be translated as "Lux's Jongleurs of God." During the Hitler years, his religion, Austrian nationalism (which has been termed Austrofascism), and politics brought him into immediate disfavor. His publications were publicly burned, and he was put under lock and key in Dachau, the first of the Nazi concentration camps that opened in Germany.

On a scale of negative or positive disposition toward the National Socialists, Lux stood at one end among sufferers. The only Austrian author to adapt the tale of the jongleur who may be pegged at the other extreme would be the hate-mongering Rudolf Elmayer von Vestenbrugg. During the Third Reich, he had been a lockstep and goose-stepping participant in Hitler's regime. In 1962, he scuttled out of the woodwork to publish a long, disconnected, and self-indulgent fiction in German entitled *From Death into Life: A Book of Love, Death, and the Hereafter*. The author recycled the main title from one he had used for earlier hymns, without any narrative, addressed to a male God. The later novel has as the central of its three sections one entitled "The Jongleur of Our Beloved Lady." The swastika would seem to sit uncomfortably in the presence of the tumbler and the Madonna, but the novelist was a former Nazi and an ex-Storm Trooper, no less. The question arises to what degree, if any, wartime anti-Semitism and Hitlerism infused this postwar piece of writing.

This hyperproductive author with a double-barreled moniker issued from a Roman Catholic family. Before becoming a writer, he made his way as a construction engineer. During the Nazi period, he lived in Germany, mainly in Munich, with a prolonged active-duty posting in what is now the Slovenian city of Maribor. In 1919, his brother Willy founded in Vienna a famous school of dance and etiquette that exists to this day. The fraternal connection with dance is intriguing, since the writer chose late in life to busy himself with a story that contains a big balletic building block. Another fun family fact worth registering, if only on the fly, is that the mother of both sons bore the name Maria.

Throughout his career, Elmayer von Vestenbrugg poured forth copiously under a host of different names both nonfiction and fiction. Two of the many identities under which this one man wrote were blacklisted during postwar denazification. In 1946, his books were included in the principal roll call of Nazi authors whose publications were to be weeded out of libraries. Why? Because during the 1930s and the Second World War, he had served as the equivalent of a lieutenant colonel in the Storm Troopers. In that paramilitary capacity, he compiled training manuals and propagandistic accounts of the martial exploits achieved by this private army.

During the hostilities, the onetime favorite lost standing among the Nazis as a scientific adviser—unless consigliere would be a more fitting word. Despite the drop in status, he never seems to have disowned any of his scientific or pseudoscientific views. Exactly what services he performed during his three years in Maribor are not known—but cannot inferences be hazarded? Initially, the brigade in Slovenia was charged with Germanizing the indigenous populace. As the conflict escalated, and the local movement intensified to cast off the yoke of the Nazi occupation, the onetime propagandist would not have been employed exclusively in educational or ideological issues. Too much dirty work needed doing.

Through the early years of combat, Elmayer contributed to the National Socialist cause as a hack who specialized in full-blown propaganda. To prove the case, nothing more needs to be said than to translate the title *Gravediggers of World Culture*: The Route of Jewish Subhumanity to World Dominion. Among other things, he lionized Georg Ritter von Schönerer, an Austrian who had advocated in favor of German nationalism. To the later Nazi in his role as publicist, this countryman and fellow anti-Semite had become a martyr by being clapped in jail for ransacking a Jewish-owned newspaper office (see Fig. 2.46). Hitler, to whom the author dedicated this book, held the earlier Jew-baiting vigilante in the same high regard. The future novelist encapsulated his precursor's outlook on religion, which was as inimical to the papacy as to the Jewry, in the unsubtle ditty: "Without Judah, without Rome / will be built Germany's dome!"

Fig. 2.46 Georg Ritter von Schönerer. Engraving. Published in F. F. Masaidek, *Georg Schönerer und die deutschnationale Bewegung* (Vienna: F. Schalk, 1898), frontispiece.

Fig. 2.47 Hanns Hörbiger. Drawing, 1930. Artist unknown. Published in Rudolf von Elmayer-Vestenbrugg, *Rätsel des Weltgeschehens*, Kampfschriften der Obersten SA-Führung, vol. 4 (Munich: Eher, 1937), frontispiece.

Before and during the war, some of Elmayer von Vestenbrugg's output pertained to cosmological pseudoscience grounded in the World Ice theory of his fellow Austrian and engineer, Hanns Hörbiger (see Fig. 2.47). This frosty drivel posited that glaciation thousands of years earlier had caused eugenic changes in Germanic peoples. We stand far from rocket science. These suppositions were alleged to find support in the mythological poems of the Old Norse Edda. In Hörbiger's system of deranged ideas, ice was the elemental substance of the cosmogony and in fact of all cosmic processes. On a grand level, the fake physics of this fringe thinking laid claim to explain how forces within the cosmos led to natural terrestrial occurrences. The occultism of this glacial reasoning became entwined tightly with National Socialism. The junk science had the backing of Heinrich Himmler, military commander of the SS.

The pseudoscientist took Hörbiger's World Ice theory, which was "close to the folk and important to them," and worked it into an official Storm Trooper training handbook he produced in 1937. In a tome he knitted together a year later, he hailed his predecessor as a Copernicus of his day. Going further, he argued that contemporary science refused to adopt the views of the earlier Austrian engineer only because of a cabal among Jewish scientists and their democratic henchmen. Laying out his train(wreck) of thought further, he made various contentions. One was that Nordic people had been toughened by having to survive Arctic cold. Another was that this "North Pole man" had also evolved to regard death in battle as self-sacrifice: each one was a subzero hero. Our author somehow contrived, however, not to embrace such self-offering for himself.

When the Second World War reached its conclusion, Elmayer von Vestenbrugg did not suddenly become lucid. On the contrary, he held on in espousing fake science about the workings of the cosmos. Furthermore, he did not put Nazism entirely behind him. He may have ceased to be an outright proponent, but he did not foreswear the entire ideology. Minds that had mustered behind the Führer as a white knight in the 1930s could not readily be unaddled (or un-Adolfed). But after the Allied victory, at least in public writings, the former promoter of National Socialism had no choice but to be circumspect. Owing to strict laws against Hitler and his causes, open profession of anti-Semitism and other related intolerance became socially and legally inadmissible. Yet writing literature afforded him the flexibility to pronounce obliquely—whether he even realized it or not—the same tenets to which he had subscribed before and during the war. In the later novel he gives no hint of having cast them off.

After the Nazis had been overcome and their army demobilized, Elmayer von Vestenbrugg settled in Graz, in Austria, but he published in Germany. Did he suffer even the slightest blot on his escutcheon for his long involvement in the Storm Troopers? Whether he underwent any systematized denazification and reeducation or not, he remained imbued in the ideology of the 1930s and the Second World War. His postbellum decision to pursue a doctorate in English studies may have reflected two inclinations. Since the Austrian city sat squarely in the British occupation zone after the war, it was pragmatic to study the language and literature of the victors. He knew how to bend with a prevailing wind—or he may have been a chameleon with a survival instinct. Yet in retraining himself, he appears to have nohow repudiated his previous intellectual and cultural biases. For instance, his 1958 dissertation centered on the poem *Beowulf*. Significantly in this context, the epic is not merely Old English in language, but Old Germanic in cultural trimmings and trappings. It contains ghouls, dragons, and devilry, and it ends in the death and mortuary rites of its hero. It orbits in the same solar system as the Old Norse Edda which had so entranced Hörbiger.

Against this political and intellectual backdrop, no one should be thrown off balance to find that Elmayer von Vestenbrugg's novel is unapologetic. Even if not explicitly and consciously, it still suppurates with the ugliness and nastiness of Nazism. Some stains do not fade with time, especially in souls that cannot come clean. The book puts on display, knowingly or not, the long-lasting slime of the inhumanity into which its unredeemed author descended before and during the Second World War. Once a Nazi, always a Nazi.

The fiction is dedicated to the owner of the publication house that printed it. The front of the dust jacket has emblazoned upon it a symbol (see Fig. 2.48) that looks like an X with a slightly longer bar added directly down its middle, from top to bottom. The same motif is stamped in gold on the maroon cloth of the front cover. In addition, it reappears on the first printed page, the half-title page. In other words, no one handling the book could help but spot the pattern. The runic sign under consideration is known as *hagal*, representing the Old Norse word that means "hail" in English. This would be hail of the subzero brand, larger pellets even than in sleet of the same stuff that the World Ice theory presupposes. The rune is the seventh, and fundamental, in the eighteen that make up the Armanen Futhark. This letter in the twentieth-century runic alphabet is called the mother-rune, because its shape correlates to the structure of a supposed hexagonal crystal that was the starting point of an occult system. This kind of Futhark and the mystical beliefs orbiting it were created by Guido von List (see Fig. 2.49). This Viennese author and occultist became obsessed with reviving Germanic paganism after a eye- and mind-opening experience in an 1862 visit to the underground cemetery beneath the great church in Vienna.

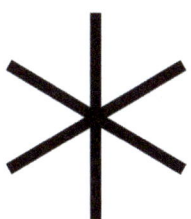

Fig. 2.48 The *hagal* rune. Vector art by Melissa Tandysh, 2016. Image courtesy of Melissa Tandysh. All rights reserved.

Fig. 2.49 Guido von List. Photograph by Conrad H. Schiffer, 1909. Berlin, Deutsches Bundesarchiv, CC BY-SA 3.0.

Elmayer von Vestenbrugg's novel contained, among many digressions, a subsection entitled "The Resurrection of the Dead in the Catacombs at Saint Stephen's." Earlier, he had written another book of fiction in which he accorded one chapter to each century in the life of the cathedral, from the twelfth through the twentieth. Crypts and Gothic ecclesiastical architecture occupied special locations in his fictive landscape.

The *hagal* rune combined the *algis* letter, interpreted as signifying life, with the same mark flipped upside down, to symbolize death. The melding of the two is understood to mean "all-enveloping" or "everything-in-one." *Hagal* was already associated with the swastika in the theosophy of Fidus. This symbolist artist and social reformer joined the Nazi Party in 1932. In his system, it embodied the unity of God and man. Under the National Socialists, the old Germanic alphabets figured prominently in both the pseudoscholarship and the symbology of the infamous SS, whose principal device consisted of two of another sign drawn side by side to resemble lightning bolts. The figure was called the *sig* rune, in the Armanen system. Originally it had been equated with a Germanic word for the sun, but this change by Guido von List equated it with the concept of victory. The *hagal* rune was also important. In learned literature, it can be found flanking the swastika on the 1936 title page of a folkloristic journal (see Fig. 2.50). The Norse letterform also served Hitler's underlings as an emblem. For instance, it appeared close to the Hakenkreuz on the SS Honor Ring (see Fig. 2.51), known unofficially as the death's-head ring. This item of jewelry was conferred personally by Himmler as a token of honor and belonging. In the citation issued to recipients of the ring, he declared "The swastika and the Hagal-rune should keep before our eyes our unshakable faith in the ultimate victory of our worldview."

Fig. 2.50 *Hagal* runes flanking a swastika, on the title page of *Die Kunde* 4 (April 1936).

Fig. 2.51 SS Totenkopf ring, with *hagal* rune visible. Image courtesy of
Craig Gottlieb, 2015. All rights reserved.

As part of the postwar denazification, the German criminal code outlawed many symbols that had become tainted through use by the Nazi groups that had created or co-opted them. One token that slipped through the prohibitions was the *hagal* rune. Although Elmayer von Vestenbrugg was in the SA and not the SS, he could not have failed to be alive to the meaning the Nazis attached to the sign. The final paragraph in his novel that contains the story of the jongleur relates:

> Now it will also be evident, why the age-old Hagal rune has been imprinted upon the cover board of the book: it comprehends at once the life rune with outstretched arms and the death rune with lowered arms, as death and life unite as one in it, and thus lead into God the Father.

This elucidation posits that this spread-eagled letter combines two conventional ones. Nothing whatsoever is said of Hitler, who was long dead by suicide in a bunker in Berlin, and the passage could be construed as having only a broad cosmological meaning without even any artesian reference to Nazism. All the same, it defies imagination that a man with Elmayer's résumé could have confected these sentences without recalling beliefs associated with them that he had expounded for nearly a decade and a half, not even a decade and a half earlier.

Beyond the *hagal* rune that Elmayer von Vestenbrugg incised into his novel from beginning to end, can any indication be located that in shaping his narrative of *Our Lady's Tumbler* he was affected by lingering National Socialist beliefs? Simply put, yes. Of all the many modifications and even transmogrifications the story has undergone since the earliest extant form was composed eight centuries ago, his stands out for taking the tale in uniquely abhorrent directions. First and foremost, the ex-Nazi set his long fiction during the hostilities from 1618 to 1648 that are known collectively as the Thirty Years' War. The choice of a wartime setting is itself significant. Among other things, this long-drawn-out strife was the most baneful through which Austria and its neighbors had trudged before the Second World War. Furthermore, the conflict had as one of its major motivations a clash between religions, in this case Protestantism and Catholicism. The bedlam extended to mass trials for witchcraft, which in many instances led to burnings at the stake.

The section in the story that deals with *Our Lady's Tumbler* opens with a scene in which a woman from the "traveling folk" approaches a local baron, a gentle and judicious soul who agrees to help her. The German term for her "people" designates the undernourished and unschooled vagabonds who were a phenomenon of life in the late Middle Ages and in the early modern period. This class had questionable social status, and a common complaint against it was thievery. In Elmayer von Vestenbrugg's world of the twentieth century, the closest equivalent to this group would have been the gypsies. The mass murder of the Romany, as they are more formally known, could hardly have escaped his notice during his years as a Storm Trooper. Members of this minority were subjected to the same systematic persecution and extermination—in a word, genocide—as were the Jews.

The female turns out to be the common-law wife of a character called Hanns. More important than the given name of this musician and dancer is his byname: he is nicknamed Our Lady's Tumbler. He earned the sobriquet from fiddling and dancing before a Madonna and Child that he found in a church ruined by marauders during the warfare. Whatever we call him, this man needs medical attention urgently: that is why his spouse has sought out the baron.

Now she tells how he ended up in this condition. A mob of "drunk and disorderly" caught sight of the performer as he did his routine. They accused the itinerants of having stolen the statue. In the ensuing altercation, the ringleader lashed out wildly with his sword. When he severed the infant Jesus from the Mary, Hanns became furious. He had previously given no evidence of having a hair-trigger temper, but the manhandling and desecration of his beloved carving were too much for him to stomach. In the subsequent melee, his antagonist continued to ply his blade. In self-defense, the unarmed Our Lady's Tumbler weaponized the Mother of God: he wielded like a club the chunk that had been split from the sculptural grouping. In the end, both he and the drunkard were wounded.

The motif in which the carved Child is cloven from the Madonna by a man's blade has a medieval precedent, not that Elmayer von Vestenbrugg had reason to know or invoke it. In the late twelfth century, at the town of Déols in northern France, truculent soldiers confronted local men and women who could not enter through the north portal of the abbey church. In the ensuing scuffle, the military men mocked the townspeople. One of them threw a rock that broke off an arm from the infant Jesus. In a heartbeat, blood spilled from the projectile that fell to the soil, and the man-at-arms who committed the outrage collapsed lifeless to the ground. Early the next day, a local eminence made off furtively with the fractured limb by swaddling it in a veil. At nightfall, a second miracle involving the sculpture was perceived: the image first made a feint as if she wished to depart, and then rent the veil covering her breast, so that her chest was laid bare.

But it is high time to return to the novel and to relieve the suspense about the fate of Hanns. Eventually he is hauled to the baronial manor, where he rattles off his life story to the nobleman. Before the war, his father was prosperous. He even owned a financially rewarding tin foundry. Yet during a set-to, he was taken hostage and disappeared. The overseer of the facility was his former second in command. After this scoundrel tried without success to persuade Hanns's mother to marry him, the man denounced her as a witch, and she was put to torture. During this ordeal, she betrayed one of her daughters, an eleven-year-old. Her son went into exile.

Once the main narrative resumes, we discover that the aggressor who tussled with Hanns is himself flirting with death: a splinter from the shattered Madonna has caused blood-poisoning. Both this brawler and the fiddler end up passing away. The first perishes from septicemia in a way that bears out his intrinsically putrid nature, while the second dies with his characteristic good-heartedness. Eventually the aristocrat turns out to be none other than Saint George himself.

The incoherence of the twentieth-century novel is perceptible from even a cursory summary of one subsection. The narrative seesaws between violence and schmaltz, between the profundity of myth and the vapidity of melodrama. Most Christian denominations allow for the possibility of redemption until the very moment of death. In most of its countless forms, *Our Lady's Tumbler* too expresses optimism about the prospects for salvation for those who are sincerely penitent. By fulfilling their chosen crafts to the best of their abilities, they may bounce back from their earlier shortcomings. Yet even a generous-hearted intermediary such as the Virgin can butt against uncrossable lines beyond which her mediation has no effect. How can a man who has drenched his inmost being in foul and pernicious thoughts find the clarity to purge himself of them and save himself? Not everyone who wants a lifeline will get it. A zealot who for years dispenses hate and death cannot readily scour the traces of such conduct from mind and soul. Such an individual will not easily become a clean-spirited, child-like adherent of loving worship. In fact, he may not even manage to recount the story of such a simple person without warping both the tale and the character, deforming a source of wonder into one of revulsion.

The juggler does not lend himself well to use by the jackbooted, either while they are still in active service or decades afterward. This fiction by Elmayer von Vestenbrugg offers no salvation and no penitence. In fact, he does not even take the time or have the imagination to tell us about the redemptive performance by the minstrel. Other forms of *Our Lady's Tumbler* stage the action against a backdrop of war. The difference is that they present the entertainer as anything but warlike. Instead, the leading figure in the narrative holds out the promise of another path to take. Only this author makes the lead character into a belligerent. Only he spends more time on fighting than on dancing. Finally, only he has, to all appearances unwittingly, the temerity to have a Madonna serve as a bloodstained murder weapon. At the end of the tale as he recounts it, the jongleur has met his maker, with no miracle and no deliverance. The nature of the life to follow death in the book's title remains a fog. The only surety is that we have been shown much dying, violence, and torture. Those scenes run counter to all earlier manifestations of the legend, in which the death of the tumbler either brings deliverance and transcendence or is averted. What accounts for the idiosyncrasies of this version? During a decade or so of Nazism, Elmayer had cloaked himself in pitch-blackness. Afterward he could not shed his own personal dark Gothic to drape himself in the light one.

3. Portrait of the Artist as a Young Juggler

> The cathedrals belong to France, and Manhattan is American. What a good opportunity to consider this fresh, twenty-year-old city against the background of one's awareness of the skyscrapers of God. This new place in the world, New York, examined by a heart full of the sap of the Middle Ages. Middle Ages? That is where we are today: the world to be put in order, to be put in order on piles of debris, as was done once before on the debris of antiquity, when the cathedrals were white.
>
> —Le Corbusier

During the Second World War and the two decades following it, *Our Lady's Tumbler* became ever more solidly entrenched as a Christmas entertainment, thanks to broadcasts of plays and readings on both radio and television. Unlike France, Belgium, and the Netherlands, the United States underwent no German annexation, nor indeed any other military incursion that affected its reception of the juggler story. The sole exception would be when the Japanese pounced upon Pearl Harbor. Eventually, the attacks of September 11, 2001 may well leave their mark somehow on the tale, if enough works of literature and art are made through retelling it in our not-so-brave not-so-new century—but that has not happened yet. For the time being, the story continues to radiate a cheery and cozy optimism that made it a December darling for a quarter century.

Many versions created through the 1960s are straightforwardly sentimental and sanctimonious, for family audiences especially in the then-thriving middle class. They may seem deliberately stodgy and sugary, intended to divert and reassure a home front during a decades-long war that ran first hot against the Axis and then cold against the Soviets. The narrative lends itself to such platitude and piety—which is not to say that it is doomed inescapably to manifest those qualities and nothing else. At the opposite end of the artistic spectrum from the more jejune of the commercialized versions, the miracle has demonstrated again and again a potential to transfix great talents. In equal measure, its emphasis on aboveboard simplicity and its capability for displays of virtuosity have sparked the interest of gifted writers and composers.

Prose writers, poets, and illustrators in America have not waged their skirmish with clenched fists or clutched weapons, to maintain their morale in the face of invasion and occupation by a foe. On the contrary, they have fought the good fight on a different battleground, to attain recognition in a society that often prioritizes individual industry, personal productivity, and financial viability over adventurous artistry. They have now and again made the agony and the ecstasy of the jongleur the opener for conveying their own floundering as creators. They have aligned the story with the present day much less through blunt allusions to current events than through drawing subtle parallels between the plight of the earlier artist and their own.

The disaffected minstrel of our story lives in a comprehensively "other" period and place. The narrative of his vicissitudes is set in the long-ago medieval days. The chronological remoteness of that earlier era differentiates it from our own times. The tale takes place in Europe, until recently a far-off place that lies an ocean away from the New World. Analogies to the here and now can be elicited from accounts of what the jongleur or juggler experiences, but they oblige the audience to become involved in the thoughtfulness of at least basic "compare and contrast."

The performer depicted in the tale from the Middle Ages has had the facility to represent everything his modern counterpart has been fearful to have lost. The medieval character renounced materialism and achieved immediate contact with the divine through his senses. The entertainer felt himself an outsider, both in broader society and in the closed confines of the cloister, and his alienation has attracted the notice of creative agents who themselves feel marginalized and estranged, although often within an anomie that is more modern or postmodern than medieval. As a lay brother who seems siloed among the choir monks, he passes his life in a situation that could have great relevance to writers, musicians, and others. He is naïve, guileless, unshackled by materialism, and happy-go-lucky about having an audience or receiving a handout. He angles for no acknowledgment, certainly not from human beings. As a free spirit existing in a state that is supposed to be artless and unsullied, he is an authentic primitive.

In an odd way, modern artists and poets have turned full circle. Instinctively, they have normalized the story to its medieval roots. The poem and exemplum from the Middle Ages enacted on a narrative level the precept of right or proper reason. In the Christian sense of this concept, an action is good if it conforms to rational dictates. God, in this case through his deputy Mary, is nothing if not reasonable. By capturing the Virgin as she lavishes her favor upon the juggler and intervenes to save his soul, the authors of the treatments that will be examined in this chapter imply that the person who wishes to display artistry can be redeemed by making a sincere effort. Both art for God's sake, which was the common medieval situation, and art for art's sake, the cliché today, can lead to deliverance. Does this mean then that the protagonists of both are rationalists, even though at first sight they may appear to be anything but that?

In a 1948 study by Wallace Fowlie, *Our Lady's Tumbler* and *Le jongleur de Notre Dame* do not greet the eye in the table of contents. Yet the juggler or jongleur in fact occupies a nodal place in the book (see Fig. 3.1). In codifying types of poets, the professor of literature presents as one subset the *voyou*, a subcategory that comprehends both the fifteenth-century François Villon and the nineteenth-century Arthur Rimbaud and Guillaume Apollinaire. The critic sees such hell-raising derelicts as shunted aside in a bourgeois world; this peripheralization sharpens their edginess. In any event, such outsiders have a close sibling: "This brother is called at times clown or acrobat or fool. Once he was called a juggler. He has even been called by the polite name of Harlequin. And from time to time fate lends him the pretentious name of poet."

Fig. 3.1 Wallace Fowlie, age 60. Photograph, 1968. Photographer unknown. Durham, NC, Duke University Archives Photograph Collection. Image courtesy of Duke University Libraries. All rights reserved.

Fowlie posits that the clown bears all the stronger resemblance to the verse-maker for being speechless. He goes further to put this sort of entertainer in the catbird seat as a companion to the *voyou* and as a characteristically medieval character, in the sense of being "both solemn and naïve." In this way the literary historian, while easing the juggler or jongleur even further into the modernity of the second half of the twentieth century, retains the nineteenth-century conviction that the Middle Ages are wide-eyed and insouciant. He sees the naïve and clownish *voyou* of *Our Lady's Tumbler* as the "founder of a long race of weak men who live outside of their real life and whose sole vigour is their poetry."

The pages to follow will touch upon four examples, none of them Fowlie's. One dates from the 1940s, another from the 1950s, and the final two from the 1960s. Only the first is overtly religious, but all of them have touchingly spiritual dimensions. Each gives prominence to the parallel between the medieval tumbler and the modern literary artist. The final two offer evidence of both the interplay between Christmas-related commercialism and artistry and their creators' conflicting efforts to get at the essence of the medieval story, which in today's terms may be framed as through and through non- or even anticonsumerist.

Richard Sullivan, Notre Dame Professor

> They need to apply that lovely old fable of *Our Lady's Tumbler*, and to remember that the artist normally honors God, not by preaching or teaching, but by practicing his art!

For reasons that barely call for glossing, the jongleur carries special connotations at the University of Notre Dame. The name of the entire Catholic institution is dedicated to the Blessed Virgin Mary, as designated by her most common French appellation. As we have seen, a college literary magazine that has been active in start-and-stop fashion there since December of 1919 has borne the title *The Juggler of Notre Dame*, or the later truncation *The Juggler*. Beyond the vagaries of nomenclature, the university fosters devotion to the Mother of God. The cult of the Virgin stood out centrally in French Catholicism after the Revolution in France. That being the case, Marianism held a general importance in the cultural formations of the transplanted Francophone founders of Notre Dame. The French priest Edward Sorin and his fellow Brothers of Saint Joseph, who later came to be known as the Holy Cross Brothers, made their way to Indiana as missionaries and arrived at the site of the future educational establishment on November 26, 1842. Sorin's own commitment to the Virgin was lifelong, being evident from the first sermon he wrote in 1837 through later years. He kept her, or at least an image of her, near to him at all times (see Fig. 3.2). He believed that the Mother of God had extended her exceptional protection to the mission of the Holy Cross Brothers in America. He took pride in having started the weekly journal *The Ave Maria* (the "Hail, Mary") in 1865 (see Fig. 3.3). For all these reasons, no one should wonder that from the outset he and the Brothers called the institution they had created "The University of Our Lady of the Lake."

The location near South Bend in Indiana where the alma mater was founded prides itself on two lakes; one named in honor of Mary, the other of Joseph. The campuses of Notre Dame and its sister college, St. Mary's, were remarkably invested with reminders of places where, sometimes through a Madonna but at other times through independent apparitions, the Virgin had exercised a powerful sway over the hearts and imaginations of humble folk in locales in faraway Europe. The Joseph-and-Mary topography contained simulacra of key Marian pilgrimage sites in the old country.

Fig. 3.2 Edward Sorin, with Madonna. Photograph, before 1890. Photographer unknown. Image courtesy of the University of Notre Dame Archives. All rights reserved.

Fig. 3.3 *The Ave Maria* 10.9, August 30, 1919. Image courtesy of Ave Maria Press. All rights reserved.

In April of 1843, Sorin masterminded a plan for honoring the Virgin in May, the month of Mary. He consecrated a provisional altar to her, which he raised on an islet blessed as "the Isle of Mary of the Lake." In November of the same year, he informed a correspondent that the Mother of God had signified her precious patronage to his community by saving first a nun and then one of the brothers from untreatable illness. She had interceded after he and the others vowed to build a chapel to the holy Virgin on the island named after her. The university's devotion to Our Lady only grew when on December 8, 1854, Pope Pius IX endorsed the dogma of the Immaculate Conception, the doctrine that Mary had been preserved from the smirch of original sin.

Already in 1859, a copy of the Chapel of Loreto had been constructed at Saint Mary's College (see Fig. 3.4). Its altar stands before a sculpture of the Madonna and Child (see Fig. 3.5). The ensemble constitutes a facsimile of the Holy House in the town in Italy. Legend held this to be the girlhood home of Mary, where the angel Gabriel announced to her the coming birth of Jesus and her role in it. In the legendary account, heavenly couriers ferried the structure from Nazareth to different stops across the Mediterranean before relocating it in a shepherd's field in the village near Ancona after which it is now known.

In 1861, the first replica of a Marian shrine was raised up under the aegis of Notre Dame itself, when the Portiuncula Chapel of Our Lady of the Angels replaced the island shrine dedicated to Mary that had been erected there in 1844 (see Fig. 3.6). It imitated

Fig. 3.4 Replica of the Chapel of Loreto, Saint Mary's, Notre Dame, IN. Photograph, before the Church of Loretto (sic) was built in front of it in 1886. Photographer unknown. Image courtesy of Sisters of the Holy Cross Archives and Records, Notre Dame, Indiana. All rights reserved.

Fig. 3.5 Altar (with Madonna in center and *cap i pota*-style replica at left) in the replica of the Chapel of Loreto. Photograph, before 1886. Photographer unknown. Image courtesy of Sisters of the Holy Cross Archives and Records, Notre Dame, Indiana. All rights reserved.

Fig. 3.6 Our Lady of the Angels, Notre Dame, IN, replica of the Porziuncola, Santa Maria degli Angeli, near Assisi, Italy. Photographer unknown. Image courtesy of the University of Notre Dame Archives. All rights reserved.

Fig. 3.7 The Porziuncola, in the Basilica of Santa Maria degli Angeli, Assisi. Photograph by Ludmiła Pilecka, 2007, CC BY 3.0, https://commons.wikimedia.org/wiki/File:Santa_Maria_degli_Angeli_(Porcjunkula).JPG

a church in the plain below Assisi where Saint Francis received his vocation, founded and headquartered his first order, and died (see Fig. 3.7). The equivalent was built at Notre Dame when the Holy Cross Brothers obtained the canonical establishment there of the Portiuncula indulgence. The likeness, until dismantled in 1898, attracted pilgrims on August 2, the Feast Day of Our Lady of the Valley of Josaphat or Angels.

These duplicates afford evidence of conscious striving *ab ovo* (if that turn of phrase is not inapt for a virgin) to invest the site of Notre Dame with a Marian geography and history. At first these endeavors could seem both out of place and out of time. In days gone by, nothing could have looked much farther from the Marian sites of medieval Christianity than the consummately exotic New World state of Indiana. Think about the very name of the territory, which means land "of Indians." South Bend, the city adjacent to the university, stood thousands of miles from Lourdes, Loreto, Assisi, and other such stopping places for pilgrims. Yet this very remoteness constituted a formidable reason for bringing likenesses of distant holy places to Notre Dame itself, where they could serve as focal points for Marian devotion.

In Italy, a faithful Christian who vowed to go on a religious excursion could fulfill the pledge by making an expedition to a nearby shrine to Mary, often a place where Our Lady had been sighted, heard, or somehow touched or felt. For example, the Italian regions of Piedmont and Lombardy contained no fewer than nine "sacred mountains," where chapels and other architectural features were created during the early modern period as an embodiment of the Counterreformation. Two of these hilltops were dedicated to the Blessed Virgin, with sanctuaries that contained the obligatory Madonnas (see Fig. 3.8). But such ready proximity of long-established pilgrimage sites was not the case in North America.

Fig. 3.8 Postcard of the Santuario di Oropa, Biella, Italy (Turin: S.A.C.R.O., 1943).

The commitment to the Virgin by the papal endorsement of the Immaculate Conception was paralleled on a popular level in France. We have only to remember the public reaction to the eighteen apparitions of Mary that Bernadette Soubirous experienced in 1858. Those sightings were declared authentic in 1862, and they elevated Lourdes as first a national and then one of the world's foremost international destinations for pious journeys. Sorin made more than two dozen crossings of the Atlantic and traveled several times to the Pyrenean village. Yet only late in his life did he scheme to lead an inaugural peregrination from America to Rome, with a first stop in Lourdes. Until then, the most practical means for conducting such an expedition was to make the campus itself a theme park for Marianism, through its simulation of sanctified topography across the Atlantic.

The centrality of Mary in the revival of pilgrimage in the nineteenth century and after ought not to be underrecognized, and it relates cogently to the reintroduction of Marian images. Early on, copies began to be made of the Grotto and statue of Our Lady of Lourdes. For instance, in 1875, construction of a reproduction was begun at what became by and by the National Shrine Grotto of Lourdes, and in 1891 a facsimile of the statue was installed at what is now Mount St. Mary's University in Emmitsburg, Maryland (see Fig. 3.9). At the University of Notre Dame, the devotion to Our Lady of Lourdes was concretized in miniature only five years later, in 1896, in the famous Grotto on the campus (see Figs. 3.10 and 3.11), replicating in downscaled form the site of the miracles in France. The sanctuary, one-seventh the size of the original, is situated in the shadow of the Golden Dome, another earlier monument to the Virgin on the campus in Indiana.

Fig. 3.9 Postcard of the National Shrine Grotto of Lourdes, Mount St. Mary's University, Emmitsburg, MD (Gettysburg, PA: L. E. Smith Wholesale Distributors, date unknown).

3. *Portrait of the Artist as a Young Juggler* 97

Fig. 3.10 The Grotto, University of Notre Dame, IN. Photograph, ca. 1896. Photographer unknown. Image courtesy of the University of Notre Dame Archives. All rights reserved.

Fig. 3.11 Postcard of the Grotto, University of Notre Dame, IN (South Bend, IN: City News Agency, early twentieth century).

The Main Building and the Madonna that tops it are emblematic of the whole university. They stand at the heart of the campus, not far from the lancets of the church (see Fig. 3.12). The gilded image was affixed atop the rounded vault in 1888, the same year in which it and the dome were outfitted with electric lighting (see Fig. 3.13). At that point Mary's head was circled by a halo of twelve incandescent lights, while below her feet another bank of bulbs was positioned in the shape of a crescent moon. The effigy was modeled after a sculpture that Pope Pius IX erected in Rome to commemorate the doctrine of the Immaculate Conception (see Fig. 3.14).

Fig. 3.12 Postcard of the Basilica of the Sacred Heart and Main Building of the University of Notre Dame, IN (early twentieth century).

Fig. 3.13 Workers maintaining the electric lights on the Main Building dome, University of Notre Dame, IN. Photograph, ca. 1922. Photographer unknown. Image courtesy of the University of Notre Dame Archives. All rights reserved.

Fig. 3.14 La Colonna dell'Immacolata, Rome. Photograph by Monopoli91, 2014, CC BY-SA 4.0, https://commons.wikimedia.org/wiki/File:Immacolatacolonnaroma.JPG

One half century later, as an undergraduate at Notre Dame from 1926 to 1930, Richard Sullivan would have experienced an institution that bore the pervasive impress of Gothic. The university's buildings even included a dining hall (see Fig. 3.15) designed by the premier architect of the style, Ralph Adams Cram, with the help of others, including the architecture professor Vincent F. Fagan. While still an undergraduate, Fagan had been instrumental in the inception of *The Juggler* as illustrator of the cover for the inaugural issue. As for Sullivan (see Fig. 3.16), after a few years outside as a freelance writer, the fond alumnus wended his way back to his former college to teach English from 1936. In due course, he proved himself as a fiction writer, with dozens of short stories and a few novels to his name. He remains unforgotten at his university, although he never fulfilled his early ambitions for literary fame on a national level.

Sullivan composed a retrospective that he dedicated to *Nostra Domina*, the Latin for "Our Lady" and the equivalent of the French *Notre Dame*. In it he meditated upon the fulcral place within the campus and its life of the gilded representation of the Virgin on the Dome. The Madonna was even portrayed on the face of his best-known book when it came out in paperback (see Fig. 3.17). The professor and writer expresses a perspective on the masculinity of the University of Notre Dame that held particularly true until 1972 (less than a decade before he died), when the institution took up coeducation. Before the arrival of women, it could be argued that a special romance, or at least a special bond, tied the image of Mary to the men who taught and learned at the university. A postcard that displays the Basilica of the Sacred Heart with the Main Building beside it by moonlight brings home this nexus (see Fig. 3.18). The moon may be above the golden Madonna rather than at her feet, but the linkage is present all the same. We have here a distinctively Notre Dame form of moonstruck.

Fig. 3.15 Postcard of the South Dining Hall, University of Notre Dame, IN (Notre Dame, IN: Notre Dame Bookstore, date unknown).

Fig. 3.16 Richard Sullivan. Image courtesy of the University of Notre Dame Archives. All rights reserved.

Fig. 3.17 Front cover of Richard Sullivan, *Notre Dame: Reminiscences of an Era* (Notre Dame, IN: University of Notre Dame Press, 1951).

Fig. 3.18 Postcard of Sacred Heart Church and the Main Building by moonlight, University of Notre Dame, IN (Fort Wayne, IN: Fort Wayne Printing Co., early twentieth century).

The institution's endemic Marianism helps to explain why an alumnus and professor with a passion for writing should have gravitated toward the tale of *Our Lady's Tumbler*. The same observation could be made later of the Catholic poet Samuel John Hazo. After graduating from Notre Dame, he spent his professorial career at Duquesne University, in Pennsylvania. In 1975, he collected under the title *Inscripts* extended interior monologues that he called "scripts." One, entitled "Windscript: The Oslo Solo," takes as its starting and starring metaphor the figure of the tumbler. The speaker aspires to imitate the performer as he worships God by enacting his craft. Like the protagonist in the tale from the Middle Ages, the persona of the poem is at once a mischief-maker and a melancholic: "I am God's clown. From glee to grief I go."

Sullivan and Hazo resembled each other in being Catholic writers on campuses of the same denomination. They also took similar approaches to the story of the juggler or jongleur. The Notre Dame academic and author, when drawn to the medieval narrative, took the less obvious course of not focusing on the protagonist who had been made familiar by Anatole France and Jules Massenet. Instead, he directed his energies toward the leading light of the verse miracle from the early thirteenth century. In 1940 he published *Our Lady's Tumbler*, a play in one act that he identified as deriving from a French legend of the Middle Ages. The script is minimalist, only eleven pages. From a quick peek, the production notes give rise to the impression that their four sides are incommensurate with the length of the piece itself. Then one realizes that the playwright envisages as his target audience inexperienced neophytes who need to be walked through such basics as stage positions. The unprepossessing venue he has in mind emerges from a desultory remark about "the grey drapes with which many community theatres are equipped."

At the same time, Sullivan has grappled searchingly with the medieval text, but we can presume that he did so in a translation and not in the French. He divulges his alertness to the original in both a cursory note and the drama itself. The introductory author's note locates the dramatic action in Clairvaux, clearly pointing to the tale as recounted in the poem from the Middle Ages. He explains that this foundation was Cistercian. Despite making the brethren white monks, he calls for the actors of his theater piece to be dressed in the brown of Franciscans. In the body of the play, the unnamed brother, who had been a tumbler before entering the abbey, uses technical terms of dance and acrobatics, such as the French Vault and the Leap of Champagne. This terminology was an impactful feature of the original poem. It also proves how familiar the author was with jongleurs, not just of a literary inclination but also of a physical sort.

The twentieth-century stage production may be most intriguing not for its fidelity to its wellspring of inspiration but for its departures from it. In the thirteenth-century poetry, the performer expresses exasperation at his inability to earn his keep among the brethren, because he lacks the skills to produce anything. Sullivan's version puts front and center the worthlessness of this Brother Wat. Despite suffering from an irremediable cough which soon turns out to be symptomatic of a fatal affliction, the former professional seems pestered less by his compromised health than by the prick of his troubled conscience. The convert's first speech is a prayerful soliloquy, in which he admits: "I do not earn my bread in this holy monastery." As in many versions going back to the earlier of the two medieval ones, he has jitters that by not paying his own way in the cloister, he has become a parasite, as he never was in the world. But he has in mind a salve for his guilt about freeloading. In his next breath, he claims to have offered his tumbling to Mary. As the dramatist reconceives the story, the statue of the Virgin does not spring miraculously to life until after the tumbler's death. The theatrical event draws to a close with an exchange between the young monk, who has been implacably condemnatory of Brother Wat for his parasitism, and the abbot, who moments before had given the entertainer his walking papers: he would have to absent himself from the convent.

Sullivan's text gives scant sign of aiming at any contemporary social or political relevance. All the same, in it the writer almost puts his finger on social tensions that artists in America at the time must have felt ever more penetratingly. Some of those who had recourse to the tale of the juggler in the 1950s and 1960s made it even more a parable, yet ever less in an overtly Christian sense, of their own anxieties and aspirations as creative forces. The play would never have been common knowledge to untold numbers of spectators. For all that, it had its transitory moment in the experimentation that took place in the early years of television. A 1953 production of *Our Lady's Tumbler* was broadcast in a series that showed the activities of Catholic schools in the diocese of Cleveland. No information is forthcoming that the script was ever staged again, but other recastings of the story have continued to catch the fancy of producers and the public in different locales for similar school productions.

A woman known as Hannah Blue Heron professed in an autobiography that in the early 1950s she composed a modern musical version of *The Little Juggler of Our Lady* for performance at Christmas. Back then she was Sister Teresa. Her Catholic religious order, the Sisters of the Good Shepherd, has specialized in ministering to women and girls who need buttressing as they recover from domestic violence, adolescent troubles, addiction, abortion, and other major bumps in the road of life. At the time the religious of her nunnery chanted or sang daily, among other portions of the liturgy, the Little Office of the Blessed Virgin. The memoirist indicated that she chose to make the narrative into a theatrical piece partly because the school where she taught English to wayward high school girls lacked a budget to pay royalties. In her version, the drama ends when the juggler is found dead, with a gorgeous red rose laid across his heart, by monks who have gone to bring back the abbot to see the blasphemy of the man juggling before the Madonna. Blue Heron made no secret that she identified with the character of the medieval performer in her musical, "with this simple character, who had known both success and failure, and for whom love was the primary motivating force." No exact diagnosis is feasible of the narrative she had read, heard, or seen. In referring to "the Old French medieval play," she is right about the time and region of origin but just plain wrong about the genre.

The likelihood runs strong that the onetime Sister Teresa had been influenced by the tradition, going back to Mary Garden, of having a female enact the role of the jongleur in the dress of the opposite sex. The specific detail of finding a girl who could dance but who for want of juggling skill must pantomime that activity calls to mind American campus productions and television presentations of the early 1950s. Still, Sister Teresa's selection of the name Cantalbert for the juggler points to a thoroughgoingly distinct version, as we will soon see. After leaving the nuns, Blue Heron eventually realized, or at long last admitted to herself, that her romantic attractions were same-sex. Her acceptance of her sexuality may have played a considerable role in her choice of topic for the musical, her identification with its hero, and the overall nature of her adaptation. This is to say nothing of her decision to entitle one of her novels *The Virgin*. For a story that in many tellings has no space for a woman beyond the Mother of God, *Our Lady's Tumbler* and *Le jongleur de Notre Dame* have attracted no meager attention from female writers who have either been alleged or avowed to have same-sex attraction. The standouts would be Mary Garden, who was first to bend the gender of the lead role in the opera, and Katharine Lee Bates. Beyond the distinctive history of *en travesti* performances, both the medieval poem and its modern adaptations had embedded in them a hero who was an outsider, in a minority of one within a larger fellowship of men who were all something else from him. The situation may have resonated not only with lesbians but also with many gay authors and artists.

To return to the markedly different world of the early 1950s, the time was especially ripe for the tale of *Our Lady's Tumbler* to flourish. Pope Pius XII declared in an encyclical that the first Marian year in the history of the Roman Catholic Church should run from December of 1953 through December of 1954. He directed that these twelve months be filled with cultural, theological, and devotional initiatives to honor Mary, and that special observance be shown to the Virgin in Marian churches and shrines, especially the Grotto of Lourdes. Elsewhere, houses of worship were bidden to have "at least an altar, in which the sacred image of the Blessed Virgin Mary is enshrined." A few years later, Bernadette Soubirous's visions at Lourdes had their centenary in 1958. For these reasons and more, the 1950s have been called "very much the decade of Mary, as far as her prominence in popular periodicals is concerned."

Outside local and specifically Catholic milieus, times had changed enough by 1953 that the juggler's story would demand severe reshaping to achieve more than a regional vogue, and also to be transported further beyond its Christian roots than it had ever before gone, in the United States and even internationally. Just such a new version was on its way.

R. O. Blechman, Cartoon Juggler

> If you cannot improve on a story, then there is no sense in retelling it.

In 1952, an American student by the name of R. O. Blechman received his bachelor's degree from Oberlin College in Ohio and resolved to become an artist, although he had yet to place any work with a publisher. An editor-in-chief at a trade press, after leafing through the portfolio of the young man's art, urged the fresh graduate for commercial reasons to attempt a theme that lent itself to the Christmas retail market. Accordingly, Blechman set out to design a publication on a Noel theme. The book that resulted, *The Juggler of Our Lady*, was published in 1953. On both the dust jacket and the title page it bore the subordinate title *A Medieval Legend*. On the page where a dedication or an epigraph might be expected, it has emblazoned the words "A sort-of Christmas story." Forty-five years later, a reprint merited a preface by the much-ballyhooed Maurice Sendak, the late American author and illustrator of children's literature. In at least two forms of the wrapper for the reedition the original subtitle was omitted. Instead it was replaced by the phrase "A Reissue of the Classic Christmas Story." Therein lies a story. ...

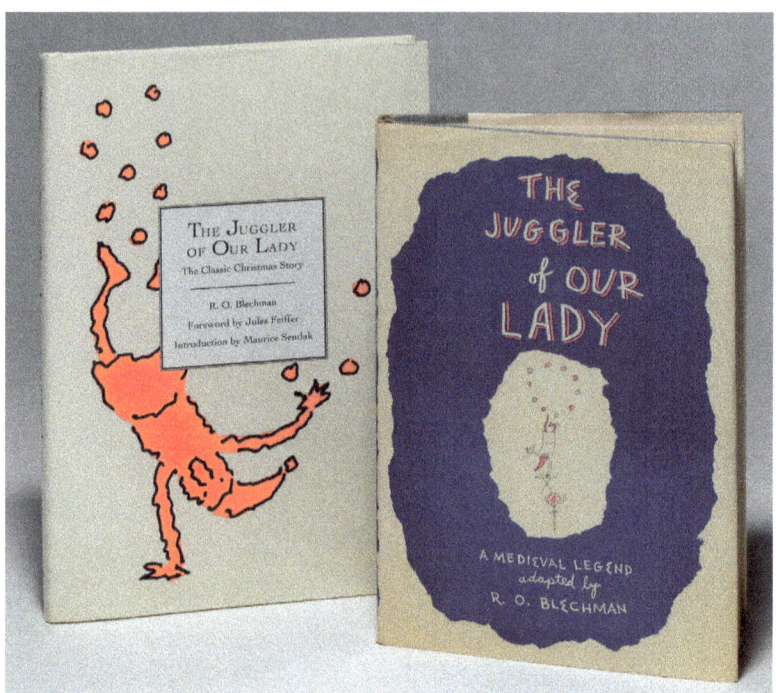

Fig. 3.19 To left, R. O. Blechman, *The Juggler of Our Lady: The Classic Christmas Story*, 3rd ed. (Mineola, NY: Dover Publications, 2015); to right, R. O. Blechman, *The Juggler of Our Lady: A Medieval Legend*, 1st ed. (New York: Henry Holt and Company, 1953). Photograph by Joe Mills, 2018.

The prospect of having to cater to the yuletide season at first alarmed Blechman. He was Jewish, knew little about the holiday, and had no real interest in it. But time and again, the miracle's deep-rooted associations with Christianity and even with Catholicism have not interfered with its use by Jews. A few examples will suffice as evidence. The actor Tony Curtis played the lead in a 1960 made-for-television movie that transposed the narrative to the small screen. The American football coach Allie Sherman related the narrative in 1963, as a call to arms for the professionals of the New York Giants team before they played a game a couple of days after the assassination of President John F. Kennedy. The writer Louis Untermeyer retold the narrative in a 1968 volume of "legends that live forever." Although Blechman had no way of knowing that coreligionists before him had been instigated to draw upon the story, he made the decision on his own not merely to recount it but even to anchor it as firmly as it had ever been in the days between Advent and Christmas.

In quest of ideas, the aspiring young artist flailed about for dear life. In need of a brain to pick, he telephoned a buddy, who encouraged him to adapt "The Juggler of Our Lady." At the time, this word of wisdom was reasonable, since both Blechman and his prospective audience of publishers and readers would have been familiar with the tale. In fact, the author reminisced, in his autobiography *Behind the Lines*, that he was already acquainted with the legend and that the next day he reread it. How did he happen to be acquainted with the account and choose it to be his pilot project? He does not specify which version he looked over again. In the United States the most readily available form of the medieval *Our Lady's Tumbler* would have been a used copy of a reprint by Thomas Mosher of the Wicksteed translation. There is no point in speculating about the Anatole France: at this juncture, the short story and its imitations were everywhere to be read.

Many people who read the story would also have heard or seen it. In this case, Blechman could have studied the text of the miracle from the Middle Ages in English at his alma mater, or been told about it by a friend who had done so, in a course offered by Frederick Artz, a medievalist on the faculty who had dealt with the narrative in his widely used textbook. By the same token, the young man could have attended a dramatic performance or heard about one from a classmate. Artz had mounted productions of pageant and staged them plein-air at Oberlin in the late 1920s and 1930s. His shows had swept up more students and spectators than any campus production before or since.

In the early 1950s, a person need not have encountered the juggler through any single, local conduit. The tale was ubiquitous. An endnote in a gift book, printed in America for Noel of 1951, adumbrates the history of "Our Lady's Juggler" by tracing a slightly inaccurate itinerary. It sets out from twelfth-century France, leads through mid-nineteenth-century Germany, Anatole France, and Jules Massenet, and arrives in the year of its publication. By then, the author reports, the narrative had become a minor classic in yuletide publications on both shores of the Atlantic, belonged to the stock holiday repertoire on radio, had been recorded on an album, and seemed to be instituting itself likewise on television.

The following year saw published in England a theatrical work that purports to be "based on an ancient legend and on the story of the same name by Anatole France." The adjective about the age of the tale can be applied only inexactly, since the miracle originated in the Middle Ages and not in antiquity. More problematic, the observation that the medieval poem and the late nineteenth-century short fiction have the same title is mistaken. Be that as it may, Rex Knight's *Our Lady's Jester: A One-Act Play*, takes in a whimsical direction the inclination to have the jongleur's suffering overshadow the Virgin's response to it. In this piece, Brother Barnaby is an ex-jester who struts his stuff before a statue of the Madonna. The monk's vaudeville act involves both rudimentary acrobatics, such as capers, cartwheels, and somersaults, and "a jester's stick, surmounted with a carven head of Punch." He calls the thin piece of wood Master Punchinello, or Nello for short. The term of endearment is taken from a short and stocky buffoon in the Italian puppet shows that arose from seventeenth-century commedia dell'arte. The culminating miracle in Knight's drama occurs when this character is transmuted to gold, which the old entertainer takes as "the beatitude of his playmate." The piece ends with Mary nowhere in sight, but instead all eyes trained upon Barnaby, who "stands, 'Nello clasped to his bosom, with rapt, unseeing eyes, listening perhaps to the applause of celestial voices. The evening sunlight, through the stained-glass windows, throws a glory round his head." *Our Lady's Jester* is written in an uncolloquial archaizing style we have met often. Not many audiences, even if we traveled back more than a half century to conduct our test, would respond well to hearing such a script delivered.

As the 1951 Christmas book and the 1952 English play go to show, the tale was in the air. Consequently, we should not feel obliged to identify any one text as Blechman's source. By the early 1950s, the account had perfused all levels and extents of American culture, through all the channels that we have now seen and that various adapters of *Our Lady's Tumbler* had themselves enumerated. A college-educated student would have somehow naturally become versed in the juggler and his story. The narrative was in the early stages of being first trivialized and then forgotten. Its success may have been mistimed: it peaked too strongly and too early. But at that point no one could foretell the obsolescence that lay not far ahead.

Beyond imparting intelligence about his sources, the graphic artist goes on to tell how he related to the narrative because of his personal circumstances: "The juggler desperately performing before an indifferent world might have served as the parable of my own life." Then he relates how he quickly brainstormed before tossing off his story. Overnight, he dreamed up his version, based on this masterstroke. Although for him the paramount theme was the correlation between the artist and the world, he could not circumvent altogether the religious element—but he could transmute and ecumenize it. No wonder he utilized the word parable. Bidden to produce a book with a holiday theme, he called the bluff.

By choosing a legend set within a medieval monastery, he even raised the stakes by intensifying the religiosity that Christmas alone would have involved. Getting the monasticism right required acquainting himself in a flash with what was relevant in the cultural and institutional history of the Middle Ages. To this end, he took The Age of Faith by the bestselling historian Will Durant as his reference work in ascertaining how to portray medieval faith in general and medieval monks in particular. This book, a encyclopedic study of culture that had come out only recently, was the fourth volume in a series called "The Story of Civilization." The eleven tomes in the series furnish an integral transhistorical overview of two and a half millennia of Western culture that the author and his wife, Ariel Durant, wrote over four decades, from 1935 to 1975. The view of the Middle Ages as an Age or Ages of Faith, or as one of Belief, is old but not antiquated or superseded, and not entirely wrongheaded. The outlook has proven winsome to those in quest of a golden past as an antidote to the shortcomings and especially the spiritual bankruptcy of their own times. As we have seen, people in the West who have deemed their own days soulless have often replenished their spirits by resorting to the earlier epoch.

The publication of *The Juggler of Our Lady* marked the first major milestone in Blechman's walk of life. The sparseness of lines and frugal application of color in its images were attention-getting. The accompanying text was penned in a spidery hand that was simultaneously neat and tremulous, regular and squiggly, linear and wavy. The combination was at once understatedly minimalist and over-the-top innovative, faux-naïf and expressive. The young artist alluded to both the character of his leading man and the nature of his own artistry when he articulated the wish that his modernism not be eclipsed by the medievalism. A Franciscan who reviewed the volume soon after its publication zeroed in on the author's originality in modernizing a story from the Middle Ages.

For two decades the book's éclat put a low-grade hex on Blechman, who in his modesty shared with the diffident protagonist a sense of undeservingness. He stuck with the theme, on the hunt for a sequel or prequel that refused to gestate, and worried that he might be nothing more than a one-hit wonder. But the biography of the artist achieves a happy denouement, like that of the monkish hero of his first great success, with creativity continuing now deep into his octogenarian years (see Fig. 3.20). Building on *The Juggler of Our Lady*, Blechman retained the special affinity for Christmas themes that he gained from his first breakthrough. He also persisted in seeking out foreign folktales.

Fig. 3.20 R. O. Blechman at work. Photograph, November 2013. Photographer unknown. Image courtesy of R. O. Blechman. All rights reserved.

Although the story of the artist's own destiny has had many chapters since his youthful triumph, it remained bound up with that of the juggler for a little longer in the 1950s. Within a few years, his brainchild passed from paper onto celluloid: in 1957, a nine-minute animated short entitled *The Juggler of Our Lady* was released. The month of distribution was December, most definitely no mere coincidence: the animation was meant as holiday fare.

The cartoon, anything but cartoonish in quality, came about through an improbable partnership. The Terrytoon Cartoons/CBS Productions studio, in operation for four decades from 1928 to 1968, became best known for anthropomorphic animals: a rodent superhero known as Mighty Mouse, a canine deputy sheriff called Deputy Dawg, and a pair of magpies named Heckle and Jeckle, who spoke with English and Brooklyn accents, respectively. All these birds and beasts were standouts of animated children's entertainment and comic books, unimaginative and uninspiring, that attained their high-water mark in the 1950s and early 1960s. As far as production values are concerned, the most famous saying ascribed to Paul Terry, after whom the facility was named, runs "Disney is the Tiffany's in this business, and I am the Woolworth's." By this, the businessman did not allude to the glorious Gothic skyscraper that the dimestore magnate had built as a cathedral of commerce in Manhattan. Rather, he meant that his footholds in the market for animations resembled nickel-and-dime or five-and-ten mass retail outlets—corresponding to what inflation has made today's dollar stores. The metaphor is through-and-through commercial: Terry not only says plainly that his cartoonmaking is a business, but he puts himself at the bottom of its food chain. We are not talking here about high and low art, but high-value at low volume and low-value at high. In the end, the moving-image mammals were all cash cows to Terry, to be milked as often as their udders could bear so that he could market every conceivable dairy product.

Blechman's animation was created in a momentary interlude when the studio was endeavoring to move upmarket. In effect, new management sought to make a leap toward producing the cartoon equivalent of the top-dollar wares on sale in the high-class jewelry shop that Terry had identified. The animated short had voiceover by Boris Karloff (see Fig. 3.21), whose renown until this juncture in his career had rested upon his stardom in horror films. He was best known as Frankenstein's monster (see Fig. 3.22). The actor later maintained a stake (not of the vampire-killing sort) in entertainment for the December holiday: he narrated the on-screen animation of the Christmas book by Dr. Seuss, How the Grinch Stole Christmas.

Fig. 3.21 Boris Karloff, age 45. Photograph by MGM Studios, 1932, https://commons.wikimedia.org/wiki/File:Borris_Karloff_still.jpg

Fig. 3.22 Boris Karloff as Frankenstein's monster in The Bride of Frankenstein (1935), CC BY-SA 4.0, https://commons.wikimedia.org/wiki/File:Boris_Karloff_as_Frankenstein's_monster.jpg

The Terrytoon short is just as much a gem as Blechman's book. Both have sparkling facets of social criticism that passed unremarked in contemporary reviews but that make them both qualify as graphic commentary. The two tell of a medieval juggler who wishes to revamp the world through his craft. Named Cantalbert, this well-meaning but hapless fellow cannot make a living, cannot reform a class structure divided between serfs and freemen, and believes he has no way to shine. Despite his right-minded aspirations, he cannot compete with the witch-hunting and warring that draw away his wished-for audience. Spectators greet his displays of juggling with shrugs of indifference and wander away.

What is Cantalbert to do, if he cannot alter humanity? First, he dons a garment of haircloth so as to become an ascetic—but now his only viewers are other flea-bitten and louse-ridden recluses, equally itchy in their own hairshirts. Finally, chagrined by the failings of society and by his lucklessness in mustering a following, he joins an abbey in the hope of leading a humble existence. There he witnesses how all the other brethren ennoble Mary with their elan in cooking meals, illuminating manuscripts, writing poetry, sculpting statues, and composing music. Subsequently he tries to pitch in in each of these endeavors, but he turns out to be to the same degree incompetent and ineffectual in all of them. After a bit, his colleagues hold a festival for the Virgin on Christmas, and each brother tenders the gift he has completed, but the juggler can think of nothing to grant. Feeling even more keenly than before his scarcity of talent, the performer steals into the chapel and renders to the Mother of God the only skill he has. He does his utmost for her through the night. When his fellow cenobites plod into the space in the morning, they watch the exhausted entertainer, bone-weary and weakened, swoon just before Mary enacts a miracle. The statue of the Virgin becomes animate and gracefully accepts his juggling by conferring upon him a single red rose. After she has rewarded him, the whole community at last recognizes his facility: the secular schlimazel has been unveiled as a monastic mensch. In a mass "monks see, monks do," they all take up juggling in emulation of him. The closing message to the brothers—and to the rest of us, when greeted by innovative art—is not a reproachful "You should be ashamed of yourselves" but a peppy "You too can do it." Wonders are at our fingertips, and artists can be as life-giving as the highest and holiest religious figures.

In the eloquent language of Christian signs and symbols, the Mother of God was associated most closely with the lily. Its whiteness stood for her purity and virginity. Although less commonly, she was connected also with the rose. This other flower has tended to represent martyrdom, for the self-explanatory reason that blood is red. The theology of the Immaculate Conception was fine-tuned only after the medieval poem of *Our Lady's Tumbler* had been written. It held the Virgin to be exempt from the stain of original sin, helping to testify to the notion of her as a "rose without thorns." This Marian flower leads ineluctably to the rosary. The term derives from the Latin for "garland of roses." The noun is applied both to a rank order of prayers, with emphasis on the "Hail, Mary," and to a necklace-like string of beads used to count them.

Although the verbal formulas and the physical objects fulfill multiple purposes, the two have been tied especially to devotion to Mary in popular contexts from as early as the thirteenth century, building upon meditative practices of Cistercian monks going back to the twelfth.

What would Blechman have known and made of all the iconography and theology? He was an early-career graphic artist of Jewish background, and not a budding theologian steeped in the doctrinal nuances of Catholicism. If symbolism and dogma were not on his mind, he may have been spellbound by red because of its vividness. For the most part, he cleaved to chromatic minimalism in both the book and the later animation of it. The strictness prevails until the disembodied hand of the Virgin is shown bestowing a rose upon the juggler as he lies prostrate near the end of the story. The fleck of spot color, intensified by yellow (used here and only here across the whole book) for the epiphany, is all the more effective in contrast to the black and white elsewhere.

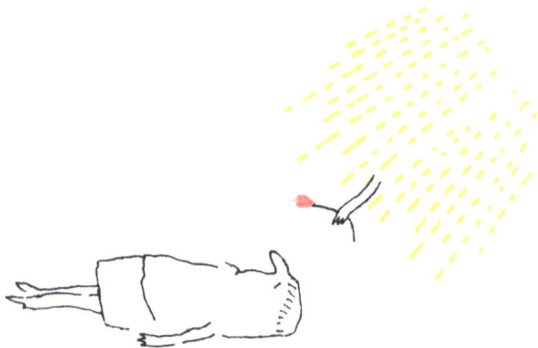

Fig. 3.23 The Virgin's hand extends a rose to the juggler. Illustration by R. O. Blechman, 1953. Published in R. O. Blechman, *The Juggler of Our Lady: The Classic Christmas Story*, 3rd ed. (Mineola, NY: Dover Publications, 2015), 110 (unnumbered). Image courtesy of R. O. Blechman. All rights reserved.

For the underlying meaning of *The Juggler of Our Lady* as Blechman tells the tale, we need to look not at Christian symbolism but instead at the 1950s. He said: "I hope people won't be fooled by the mediaeval setting. Cantalbert is strictly a modern man." The last assertion holds equally true for the author and designer himself. From today's vantage, his version of the story not only presents the portrait of an artist as a young man but it is also defined by the mood of the Cold War. The hostility and anxiety, even neurosis, of the period manifest themselves all the more in the animation. For more than four decades, from 1947 to 1991, the United States and its allies were pitted in political and military tension against the Soviet Union and its client states. The frictions were in formation when *The Juggler of Our Lady* was conceived. Two circumstances in current events of the day are particularly evident. One was the recent crisis of the Korean War; the other was the witch-hunt for communists that a Republican Senator from Wisconsin, Joseph R. McCarthy, conducted over roughly the same stretch.

Less starkly and more gently, Blechman's story elaborates an implicit inquiry into the remedial functions that art can fulfill when its beholders behave in accord with mob mentality or psychology. In his narrative, paranoia goads war-mongering crowds to rush headlong into dissension and persecution. Left implicit but indubitable is his opposition both to the constant military action during the protracted political hostility between the Soviet bloc and the Western powers and to the related red-baiting in McCarthyite America, with its stalking of so-called commies and pinkos who were felt to be supportive of the enemy. These angles are brought home with even greater emphasis in the animated short than in print: the film version makes a more overt case for anti-militarism and pacifism. Both the book and the cartoon answer the unspoken question about the functions of art by positing that no matter how unfavorable the climate, a performance that springs from the heart will in due course win favor, both divine and human.

In form as well as in content, the brief film marks as profound a change within the incipient tradition of juggler films as the book that harbingered it did in literature. To compare it on a split screen in our mind's eye with the juggler segments of the Waring hour taped at Christmastime in the early 1950s requires the perspective of Janus, the two-headed Roman deity who lent his name to the first month of the year ([Janu-ary](#)!). With the visage that faces backward, we can look in best retro fashion, through the entertainment arranged by Fred Waring on his television variety show in the early 1950s (see Fig. 3.24), to the earliest years of the twentieth century. We can also discern the intensifying commercialization of Christmas, since the program is coupled with

Fig. 3.24 Filming *The Fred Waring Show*. Photograph, ca. 1949–1954. Photographer unknown.

other such products as sound recordings. Nadine Gae, the woman who mimes and dances the role of the juggler, was far from a diva. She arrived at television from a career as a dancer, including stints on Broadway. Yet by the very trait of being female, she owed an ultimate debt to Mary Garden. The Chicago-based soprano, virtuosic as a media presence no less than as a singer, set the stage for all subsequent recreations of the jongleur's story by women in musical drama, ballet, and other media. The head of the divine Janus that stares forward sees nothing of the gilded opera houses of Monaco and France. Instead, it gazes at the modernism centered on New York City in the 1950s, when abstract expressionism ruled uncontested.

From the earliest attestations in the thirteenth century, we can make out how the miracle of the juggler has been restyled. At intervals, it has elicited treatments in successful texts that for a while have fixed in their audiences' consciousness new motifs that had not been part of previous instantiations. At other times, the narrative has been received by authors who have either chanced upon it in only a synoptic form or felt themselves deputized to reimagine liberally whatever fuller handling of it they have encountered. Thus, we have beside the medieval French poem the précis in the later Latin exemplum, and alongside the Anatole France version the sundry radio broadcasts and other remoldings of the tale. Those who have transformed the story in texts seem often to have dived into floods of waning memories. In the wash of these recollections, they have adjusted and even overcorrected details, consciously or not. The tale is so short and simple that the temptation must be uncontrollable simply to plop down and write out a fresh adaptation. Why go through the folderol of fixating on whatever older iterations one has at hand? Why bother with such niceties? The narrative has belonged to the common domain from the very beginning. Copyright has not been a constraint, since no one artist has ever had a monopoly over it.

Both Blechman's book and the animation take the story in a new direction. On the one hand, they keep the spirit true to the Middle Ages, or at least medieval-like. On the other, they depart from the tendency of many earlier and subsequent illustrators to replicate qualities of age-old manuscript illumination. Even in the printed version, the author illustrates the tale more extensively than did any of his predecessors, particularly to judge by the head count of illustrations in proportion to the number of words in his narrative. In effect, Blechman creates a proto-graphic novel. His volume differs in length from the ones that decades later have become an accepted genre. He even forms the lettering of the text in his distinctive hand, with its elegantly controlled wavering. In the same squiggly script, he records on the jacket of the first edition that *"The Juggler of Our Lady* is a retelling of the famous legend in picture-and-caption form." Despite the enchanting simplicity of both text and images, the relationship between the two is sophisticated. The book marks a great initial stride in Blechman's development as a graphic storyteller. The famous children's book author and illustrator Maurice Sendak observed that his friend and fellow artist's chief sources of inspiration were newspaper funnies, animated cartoons, and silent-movie comedies. Once again, Charlie Chaplin makes his presence felt in the environs of the object manipulator.

Blechman achieves graphic sparkle by adhering throughout to a disciplined minimalist style which, although very much his own, is simultaneously recognizable in a flash as belonging to the second half of the twentieth century rather than to the first. His look, even today, remains redolent of what was the then-new abstract expressionism, or American abstraction, of which New York of the early Cold War era was the hub. *The Juggler of Our Lady* anticipates the ecumenism that would become enshrined in the nondenominational Rothko Chapel in Houston, Texas. In a distinctively different artistic milieu, Blechman's understatedness shows a kinship to that of the limited animation associated with the United Productions of America studio. This type of production has come to be associated with vacuous commercial cartoons of low quality from the 1960s and 1970s. Yet it began life a little earlier as a deliberate artistic experiment. In the case of *The Juggler of Our Lady*, the form accords well with the gentle and simple irony with which the artist conveys his themes. It also suits the economy of line and color that typifies all his work across the decades.

Blechman's handwriting bears comparison, or contrast, with the meticulously personalized, pseudo-Carolingian minuscule that Wilhelm Preetorius employed in his interpretation of the medieval story from 1964.

Fig. 3.25 The tumbler dancing. Illustration by Wilhelm Preetorius, in Wilhelm Preetorius, *Der Tänzer unserer lieben Frau* (Zurich: Die Waage, 1964), 29.

Fig. 3.26 The tumbler dancing. Illustration by Wilhelm Preetorius, in Wilhelm Preetorius, *Der Tänzer unserer lieben Frau* (Zurich: Die Waage, 1964), 31.

The juxtaposition reveals two diametrically opposed styles of sparing, mid-century modern minimalism. The German artist produced artwork to accompany various short narratives, many translated from non-German source languages, that could entice audiences of both cultivated adults and juveniles. In keeping with a family culture of heavy engagement in theater, the Swiss book illustrator was also an actor and marionettist. In 1984, he established in the German town of Esslingen am Neckar a "literary marionette theater" modeled on a medieval house chapel. In this venue he performed puppet plays based on literary inspirations. Preetorius's book presents the story of *The Dancer of Our Lady* anonymously on the title page. He relegates acknowledgment of his own role to the edition notice, where he subsumes the narrative as legend or pious tale. Not unreasonably, he was misled by a swatch in the text itself into identifying its source as being one reflex of the thirteenth-century French *Life of the Fathers*. In his modernization he adapts the medieval poem freely. While leaving the basic actions unaltered, he introduces many modifications to make the psychology of the tumbler more digestible. For the art, he applied a centuries-old craft of paper cutting. Loosely comparable to silhouette, this technique is known in German as *Scherenschnitte*, "scissor cuts." It was by way of being a family tradition: the illustration work of Wilhelm's uncle Emil Preetorius stood out ineradicably in this artistic form.

Blechman's style in both the book and the subsequent animation can be read as a small-scale summa, in which a man who came of age after the Second World War looks back on the genres with which he had grown up and come of age. In response, he synthesizes them so as to meet the artistic expectations of a new era. The illustrations contain their fair share of Gothic architectural features, but the pointed arches are not part of a sustained effort to translocate us as viewers into a fanciful medieval past. Instead, we are moderns, as are our artists, who inhabit temporarily a Middle Ages that all of us concede never was. The aesthetics prompted pundits of the day to be complimentary, although the strong stylistic novelty put them in some perplexity. At least one reviewer of the animation had doubts about how many viewers would take kindly to the experience of watching it.

Gene Deitch, who produced the animated *Juggler of Our Lady*, gave an account of the process, stressing the strain of subsuming a story about art for art's sake within the catalogue of a commercial cartoon studio. In fact, he suggested that his commitment to making this short hastened his ouster from the firm not much later. A little history is in order. Paul Terry departed from Terrytoons after selling it to the CBS television network in 1955. In the aftermath Deitch, aged all of thirty-one, was ushered in as creative director in the following year. He was drawn to the undertaking because he saw an opportunity to achieve an unprecedented wedding of form and content. The latest technology allowed for shooting wide-screen movies. The precocious new appointee grasped that the spectacular width allowed by the innovative format would facilitate sensational contrasts in Blechman's illustrations, "playing off those tiny timorous figures against the vast expanse of that very wide screen." The effect is striking, since the size of the backdrop accentuates the wriggliness and sinuousness of the artist's style. Deitch has made no attempt to hide his assurance that this short was his "highest achievement at Terrytoons."

For the project to yield results, Deitch had to serve two masters, with antithetical aims and values. One was the head of the studio, who had to be persuaded that the cartoon would bring sufficient prestige to the company to warrant the payroll for staff time and the outlay of other resources it would entail. The other was Blechman himself, who the director reports "was well aware of the Terrytoons product, and was terrified we would convert his little juggler into Mighty Mouse." After close to a year, Deitch prevailed upon the young man to accord the rights for his masterpiece to be animated. In the animation, Al Kouzel clung rigorously to the artist's visual minimalism. Both the music, limited to a woodwind quartet, and the narration enhanced the same spare aesthetic.

The matter of genre intensified the challenges inherent in the manner. The simplicity of Blechman's story makes it resemble a children's book, while its Christmas setting could trick the unwary into mistaking it for a religious one. When the hardback first hit the market, it was listed in the *New York Times* with a brief mention under the heading "Religion." Both the confusion with children's literature and that with religion had ample justification. By being childlike and simple, the tale resembled youthful reading. By being a miracle, it had a footing among religious studies. The distinction between childlike and childish can easily be overlooked, just as simplicity in an adult can be misconstrued as being sophomoric. Today the book has leapt out of juvenile literature into graphic novels, a literary form that did not even exist as such when Blechman's stroke of genius was first published. Coincidentally, it is now flagged on its cover as "The Classic Christmas Story." As far as creed is concerned, we may find ourselves bemused and even taken aback by the answers if we ask whether the thirteenth-century poem promotes organized religion or individual devotion. By the same token, Anatole France's version is deliberately enigmatic, even ironic, in its presentation of the juggler's faith and indeed of medieval Christianity. These conundrums, handled adroitly, may deepen the narrative, as the undercurrents of such imponderable questions keep its simplicity from becoming simplistic. They prevent its childlike truths from degenerating into unadulterated childishness.

From *The Juggler of Our Lady* on, Blechman's special magic has been to evoke profound issues, often through juxtaposition of different registers or eras, but at once to elicit chuckles. Forty years after conceiving the book, the cartoonist created the cover art for a now defunct magazine entitled tout court *Story* (see Fig. 3.27). To the left slumps Hamlet, cupping Yorick's skull in the graveyard scene with the "To be, or not to be" soliloquy that everyone comes across in mass culture. To the right a jester sits perkily, with his belled cap and shoes, tossing a sphere in his hand. The viewer need not recall the specific that Yorick had been, before his death twenty-three years earlier, just such a court entertainer. The mere contrast between darkly pensive and brightly smiling figures gets at something elemental about the human condition. Rather than being ordered to suggest a sequence of life and death, as Yorick to the left and Hamlet to the right might have done, the two are flipflopped. Overarching

Fig. 3.27 R. O. Blechman, cover art. To left, Hamlet with Yorick's skull; to right, Yorick the court jester with juggling ball. *Story*, Spring 1992. Image courtesy of R. O. Blechman. All rights reserved.

both are the heavens, with the mysteries of the cosmos (see Saturn and its rings?) floating above the suicidally brooding Hamlet and the bubbly balls above the jester. In Blechman's universe, juggling's levity wins the day.

Robert Lax, Poet among Acrobats

> The juggler is therefore the being who leaves himself—like the poet in the deepest sense of his vocation. The clown and the poet are two men, very slightly limited by their bodies, who aspire to be invaded by God.
>
> —Wallace Fowlie

The future American poet Robert Lax met the mystic (and monastic) theologian-to-be Thomas Merton when the two were undergraduates at Columbia University. Among other shared pursuits, both young men served as editors of *The Jester* (see Fig. 3.28), a collegiate humor magazine that was founded on April Fool's Day of 1901. Their college acquaintance mellowed into lifelong friendship, and it resulted in a goodly number of letters sent and received.

Merton was rebuffed when he attempted to enter the Franciscans. At the end of 1941, he joined instead the Abbey of Our Lady of Gethsemani. The brothers there are Trappists, a reformed order that descended from the Cistercians, the monastic society with which the thirteenth-century French of *Our Lady's Tumbler* associated the miracle that some six hundred fifty years later morphed into *Le jongleur de Notre Dame*. At the monastery in Kentucky, Merton wrote voluminously. The output of this American Catholic author encompasses books of autobiography, biography, biblical exegesis, contemplation, and meditation.

In 1943, Lax laid aside Judaism and embraced Catholicism. In October of 1949, the twenty-seven-year-old addressed a letter to his former fellow student—now a white monk—that referred to the legend of the juggler. In the same year, the not-so-new believer mingled with a troupe, the Cristiani Family Circus. That summer he traveled as a kind of roustabout or carny with this ménage of peripatetic performers. He developed with one member of this squadron what would blossom into a long-time attachment. Mogador Cristiani was an acrobat and equestrian, as accomplished a death defying daredevil as he was a debonair devil.

While keeping company with the Cristiani clan, the poet acted episodically as a clown. Still more germane to our purposes, he play-acted at being a wandering minstrel of the Middle Ages. The artistic upshots of his spell with the peripatetic company did not stop there. His exposure to the family, their way of life, and the high-achieving feats demanded by their line of work caused him to take a soulful turn and coincided with his composing a profusion of impassioned prose and verse. His passion would seem to have been driven in equal measures by the big top and by the winsome Mogador.

The signal outcome of the experience was *Circus of the Sun*, a cycle of poems that Lax published as a complete volume only a decade later, in 1959. Literarily, he cast

Fig. 3.28 From left, Thomas Merton, Robert Lax, and Ralph de Toledano, editors of the *Jester*. Photograph, ca. 1937. Photographer unknown. New York, Columbia University Archives. Image courtesy of the Columbia University Archives. All rights reserved.

himself as the ringmaster of a three-ring circus. The lyrics are arranged according to stages of the day, deliberately like the canonical hours. Against this backdrop of spirituality, medievalizing, and wayfaring, the poet was drawn unsurprisingly to the tale of the medieval acrobat. The parallels between his reactions to the circus routine and the story of the jongleur would have been intensified by the circumstances in which he devised his book, in the spring of 1950. A Franciscan of Saint Bonaventure advised him to hunker down to write daily at the same hour in the same place. As his location for crouching to dedicate time and effort to composition, the writer chose the lower level of the library. Expressed differently, this drill means that he drafted his poem by himself in the basement of a building where he was fenced in by friars. How would an author not deem the minstrel on-topic in such circumstances?

In the 1949 missive to Merton, Lax rhapsodized dreamily about filming the performer who infatuated him: "[I] want to make a movie ballet of Juggler of Notre Dame. Mogador Cristiani turning the right kind of sommersalts. I wish we could make it in the Church, for the Church." No must-watch cinematic magnum opus ever emerged, but the story clung to the poet in his life as well as his literature. From 1962, for the final three and a half decades of his existence, the man of letters resided on the Greek island of Patmos, in what was regarded in some quarters as a self-imposed hermeticism. Without going so far as to become a Cistercian like his classmate and close crony Merton, he managed all the same to traipse down a pathway that made him similar to the juggler. The difference was that, as with all writers of the tale since the original poet, Lax's craft was verbal rather than acrobatic. In a lyric called "Acrobat's Song," he likened the faith of believers in Mary to the exaltation, literal and figurative, of aerialists while aloft. Many of his pieces about the circus can be interpreted as having the jongleur in their background. In one, the medieval lay brother pokes his way into the foreground.

Although Lax never brought to fruition his castle in the air of making a motion picture, by the 1940s cinema had become an obvious conduit for the story of *Our Lady's Tumbler*. Television soon followed. Later still came videos designed for home viewing. Most representations of the story on celluloid, whether for the big or small screen, whether for public or private viewing, fall into an underwhelming zone between intimate and amateurish. Thus, Benedict Groeschel, a Catholic priest who died in 2014, recounted three inspirational saintly legends of the early church in a 2008 videotape for children, which was informal to the point of appearing homemade. One of the triad was about the juggling monk who witnessed a statue of the Virgin move, a miracle he identified as being seven hundred years old. For the mentions of juggling and six balls the good father, who belonged to the Community of the Franciscan Friars of the Renewal, owed an ultimate debt to Anatole France, and beyond him to Raymond de Borrelli. The animation of Tomie dePaola's *The Clown of God* was more commercial, but not much more polished and professional. Neither would qualify as slick or Hollywoodish. Then again, why should they? The tale can be construed as a paean to the would-be artist, but it affords more certitude about his faith than about his flair.

A made-for-television film from 1982 entitled *The Juggler of Notre Dame* has reaped the most enthusiastic praise of all big-screen versions. The production aired first in late November as a TV special, a timing chosen in all likelihood because it fell in the temporal outskirts of Christmastide. Although the broadcast brought in some laudatory notices, positive assessments were hardly universal. Even to knead the story into a movie of fifty minutes requires substantial leavening of the plot. The fictitious character of the juggler, predictably named Barnaby, has suffered one major deprivation before the narrative even commences. Flashbacks fill the viewer in that while previously in the circus, the heartsick man suffered the trauma of witnessing his newly wed wife slip as she performed on the tightrope and hurtle to her untimely death. As the psychodrama begins, he is busker, tormented and alone, but he soon shares his life with a fellow street person. This fresh comrade, called Sparrow, assists him and picks up the rudiments of juggling from him. In return, the entertainer opens his heart a crack to living again. Not long afterward, he is racked by loss once again, when his buddy is slain by other drifters while being robbed. At this juncture, the entertainer forsakes not only his métier but also all hope. Yet in his meandering he is taken in as a model by a sculptor who himself has endured tragedy and sorrow, when his family perishes in a house fire.

As the story unfolds, it turns out that this Jonas has carved a Madonna. The sculpture turns out to be the very likeness of the juggler's late wife. Barnaby resolves to abscond from the community, driven away by the artist's distrustful and harsh-hearted sister, who faults him for having no gift to offer the statue for the Mass on Christmas Eve. Before parting, the former performer comes back to the chapel of the church, which was ruined by an earthquake but has been restored and reconditioned. Offerings are arrayed before the effigy, as is a life-sized crèche. The dead Sparrow materializes and cajoles his living friend to do homage through his craft before the image of Mary, which after some time he does. The final miracle in this version of the tale, as in many others, takes the form of a floral motif, as the Virgin presents the circus artist with a rose.

The television special partially addressed two deficiencies of the narrative for modern times. In the first place, it introduced female characters, in the persons of the juggler's deceased wife and his host's inhospitable sister. For all that, the movie would scarcely pass the Bechdel test. This measure evaluates whether a motion picture or other work of fiction features at least two females who converse with each other about a topic other than a man. For the story to go down well now with general audiences in Western or Westernized countries as anything other than a short skit, it may need to be reconceived to allow more scope for women, girls, or both. In a second enhancement of the medieval miracle, the collaborators from the Paulines and Walt Disney studios may have been right to add splashes of color with both the romance with the dearly departed wife and the bromance with the deceased best friend. General viewers may not be gratified by would-be entertainment that depicts no love save that for God.

Tony Curtis, Prime-Time Juggler

One "what if" is to wonder whether the trials and tribulations of the juggler would be better known if the telegenic Tony Curtis had followed through on his woolgathering: he thought of adding footage to the color made-for-television film of 1960 entitled *The Young Juggler* (see Fig. 3.29 and 3.30) so that this miniaturized historical drama could be released as a feature-length production. The idea of creating such a movie made sense at the time, since the career of this fine-looking golden boy of Hollywood was at its zenith: he was then a top-class celebrity, still married to the prominent actress Janet Leigh. To single out only two motion pictures, both *Some Like It Hot* with Marilyn Monroe and *Spartacus* with Kirk Douglas and Laurence Olivier that co-starred Curtis were blockbusters at the box office, in 1959 and 1960, respectively. The story of the juggler was also at its height in television, for the year 1959 alone saw versions aired in France and the United States. But any dreams that a reworking with such a high-profile actor could succeed beyond the small screen in movie theaters came out of a pipe. After airing once, the telefilm went nowhere further than the vaults where it has degraded ever since. It was a sneak preview for nothing.

Fig. 3.29 Tony Curtis as the juggler in *The Young Juggler*, dir. Ted Post (1960). Photograph, 1960. Photographer unknown.

The Young Juggler, known now only to the most passionate of film buffs, gave Curtis room to show off circus skills, which he had deployed already in the 1956 *Trapeze*. This coincidence belongs in a larger context. The big top is the only major institution in which the juggler, the clown, and all their kin live on. These professions are the modern iterations of premodern vocations, calcified within a guild that stands apart from larger society. The juggler is one type of jongleur, the clown perpetuates the jester, and the present-day mime narrows the unbounded range of the medieval mime player to a single specialization. The nexus between jongleur and circus in real life is brought home most vividly by a 1967 French press photo that captures a posse of prelates, some seated, others standing, in a circus round (see Fig. 3.31). Like masters of

Fig. 3.30 Tony Curtis contemplates the Madonna in *The Young Juggler*, dir. Ted Post (1960). Photograph, 1960. Photographer unknown.

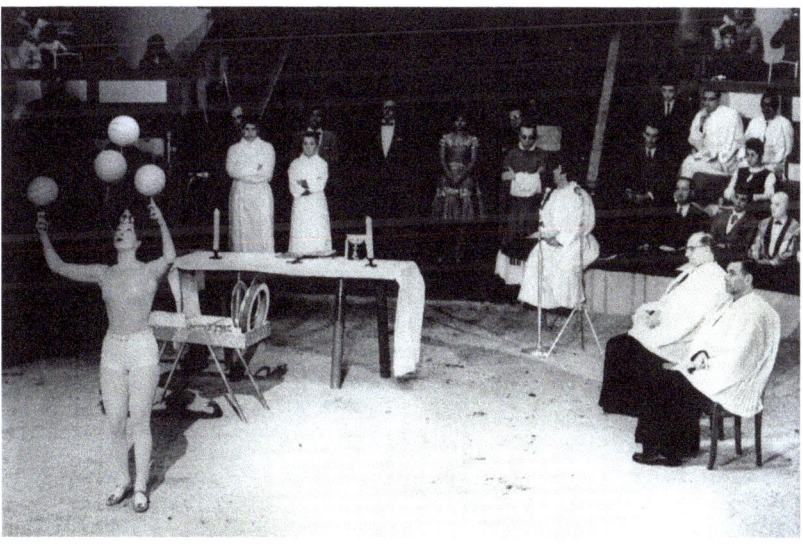

Fig. 3.31 French prelates in a circus round watch a juggling performance. Photograph, 1967. Photographer unknown.

ceremony costumed in cassocks, they watch as a female juggler knocks out a routine involving the manipulation (with mouth, head, and hands) of four twirling balls. The ceremony was a Mass to mark the end of "circus week," a tradition that has been alleged to extend back a half millennium or more. The liturgy was officiated by a chaplain tasked with ministering to fairground and traveling people.

The inherent limitations of Curtis's movie would have precluded it from achieving much greater success, even if it had been put into a shape that had allowed it to be screened in theaters. Although elaborate sets at Universal Studios gave the semblance of a lush ambience, *The Young Juggler* was in fact filmed on a tight budget. Additionally, it was broadcast not during the Christmas season but instead during Lent. The actor, who had the birth name Bernard Herschel Schwartz, retained his whole life long a working-class Bronx accent, which garnered him the sometimes affectionately teasing nickname "Boinie." The manner of speaking functioned to better effect in comedies than in an early modern period piece. The star himself may well have recognized some of the substantial blemishes in the version that was recorded: he never pursued the project further.

The film claimed to be set not in the Middle Ages, as conventionally delimited, but in sixteenth-century France, between the medieval and the early modern. Likewise, it purported to be based upon a legend of the same period. The movie opens during the Feast of Fools. This celebration, popular from the fifth century through the sixteenth, allowed the prevailing social hierarchy among both clergy and laity to be overturned. For a brief spell, the world was altered dramatically. The carnival-like misrule of the festival received vivid expression in Hugo's *The Hunchback of Notre Dame*, published in 1831. There the tale begins on this very feast, which is said to occur on January 6, 1482, to mark the holiday of Epiphany, when the three Magi visited the Christ child.

In the story as the screenplay developed it, the athletic Tony Curtis acts the part of a young entertainer who is poor and proud, unable to beg or to believe in God, but fully proficient in juggling both real plates and ladies' hearts: "If I can't believe in the power of a woman, what can I believe in?" The womanizing of this dark-haired blue-eyed charmer incites doting from the fair sex but dislike from wronged husbands. From the late nineteenth century on, researchers and artists went to great lengths to cleanse the protagonist of the medieval poem from any inadvertent associations with later Lotharios or Casanovas. Although in the dark about the unseemly ambivalence that the word carried in French, this screenplay makes the timid *tombeur* of the original into a total tomcat. It embroiders further upon this titillating tangent by implying repeatedly that the outraged spouses of the adulteresses seek to avenge their abasement by castrating the oversexed performer.

Together with his best friend, the character played by Curtis ends up being accosted by a gang of vigilantes enraged at having been cuckolded. He saves his own skin by playing Judas: he pushes his companion into the hands of the thuggish mob. The betrayed buddy is first beaten and then hanged in a Christ-like fashion by his bloodied arms from a large beam, mocked by being necklaced with a juggling ring. After a scene with a vague visual resemblance to the Descent from the Cross and Pietà, the juggler ends up being found and stabbed. Although the brethren of Our Lady nurse him back to more or less fine fettle, the itinerant can no longer ply his trade: one arm has been left partly paralyzed. To complete his convalescence, the monks ministering to him give him counsel to pray before a statue of the Virgin. Professing himself ever a believer in the might of the fair sex, he does so. When the Madonna miraculously warms to life and restores full mobility to him, he gains faith and tenders thanks by giving his only gift. Reducing any narrative to such bare bones (and that proverbiality is right for a lightly clad acrobat) does not smooth the way for equitable judgment, without fearfulness or favor, but the well-worn elements that have just been described held out little promise of great success.

In the Anglophone world, the narrative has been told and retold, written and rewritten, shown and reshown so often that much of the flavor has been washed out of it. By the principle of "familiarity breeds contempt," it has run the jeopardy being rendered into watery pap. Alternatively, the juggler's decline may reflect not the ubiquity of the tale but instead the debased quality of many recent tellings. The information aggregated in the present book makes no pretense of being exhaustive, but it may be enough to disabuse future adapters of the illusion that they are pioneers. It compensates by opening paths for attentive readers and writers to go not for the jugular but for the juggler—to locate many different versions to which to react and respond.

W. H. Auden, *The Ballad of Barnaby*

> We who must die demand a miracle.
> —W. H. Auden, *For the Time Being*

Fig. 3.32 W. H. Auden, age 60. Photograph by Jill Krementz, 1967.

The fifth of my six examples, and among the most bewitching efforts ever made to recast the legend, was by a poet, born an Englishman but later an American citizen (see Fig. 3.32). In the initial stages of his métier in metrics, W. H. Auden was not gripped by Latin and French texts from the twelfth and later centuries of medieval Gothic architecture.

Instead, his heart went out to Germanic literature of the early Middle Ages. His given name of Wystan memorialized his parents' interest in medieval England as it was constituted before the Norman conquest in 1066. He was so called after a saint who suffered martyrdom in 849, in the thick of the Anglo-Saxon period, and who hailed from Repton, the village in Derbyshire where his father attended school. The elder Auden maintained that his side of the family traced its lineage back to a settler by this name who figured among the earliest Norse in Iceland. The poet's cultural formation, from childhood through the last gasp of his life, included a heavy accent on myths from the Germanic past, both directly in the original and indirectly in translation. His mother taught him the words of Richard Wagner's opera *Tristan and Isolde*, duets from which she and he belted out arias together. He was exposed to the English of Icelandic sagas by William Morris and the Icelandic scholar Eiríkr Magnusson, studied Anglo-Saxon at Oxford and became friendly there with the philologist and fiction writer J. R. R. Tolkien, admired Old English poems such as *Deor*, and teamed up with a scholar and lover of English literature in bringing out three volumes of translations from Old Norse poetry.

In college Auden also sampled from Middle English poetry and prose. His tastes ranged too widely to forestall him from responding to good reading from beyond the chronological pale that separated the early Middle Ages from the twelfth century and later. If an exquisite and intriguing text from the high or late medieval period caught his attention and suited his poetic purposes, he did not hesitate to immerse himself in it. Particularly after his emigration to the United States in 1939, he developed a curiosity about pre-modern Christendom that is evident in his adaptations of medieval writings. He engaged closely with Julian of Norwich, an English anchoress and mystic who died in the early fifteenth century. The modern poet also poured himself into the vernacular of the *Second Shepherds' Play*, which merges the sublimity of high religion with the farcicality of low culture. It takes scant imagination to see why a person mesmerized by such a mystery play on the Nativity would have found *Our Lady's Tumbler* both genial and congenial. Auden's "Ode to the Medieval Poets," dated June 1971, addresses first by name a foursome of Middle English and Scots poets—"Chaucer, Langland, Douglas, Dunbar"—but then acknowledges the innumerable cohort to which the French poet from the Middle Ages belonged—"with all your / brother Anons." Despite the valiant efforts of medieval scribes and modern scholars to attach identifiable names, the pipeline of literature from these distant centuries carries an unstanchable flow of texts that remain nameless or incognito.

So much for generalities based on biography. In this case Auden had a specific instigation. He drafted *The Ballad of Barnaby* as the libretto for a musical that was composed and performed in 1969 by the pupils of a girls' school in Connecticut. A longtime friend of his who taught and directed the music program at the institution created the score, in conjunction with the students in his class. The narrative text of the poem was released officially months later along with the musical notation as sheet music. The poet had collaborated in a similar venture years before, when he wrote the narration to the medieval Latin liturgical drama, the *Play of Daniel*. In 1958, this thirteenth-century mystery play had been recorded as an opera in the environs, at once monastic and pseudo-monastic, of The Cloisters, the medieval European branch of the Metropolitan Museum of Art in New York City. Auden retained the connection with youth when in 1972 he first published the ballad in *Epistle to a Godson* and *Other Poems*. He gave the piece of poetry, the longest in this collection, center stage arithmetically, as number seventeen of thirty-three items. He also brought home its centrality by a symmetry: to produce a mini-chiasmus, he bracketed it between "Shorts I" and "Shorts II."

Before appearing in the volume of verse, *The Ballad of Barnaby* came into print in the fortnightly cultural magazine *New York Review of Books*, a forum intended very much for adults. The front cover from December 18, 1969, labeled as a Christmas issue, offered the poem in two columns. The text was flanked by six decorations by Edward Gorey in the left and right margins. This artist (and writer) was an apt choice as illustrator. He lavished meticulous care upon the craft of illustrating and cultivated a style that was vaguely Gothic—but viewers must decide for themselves in which specific senses the descriptor would apply here. Whatever we call Gorey's manner, his diverse output included coverings for the English translation of *The Romance of Tristan and Iseult* as retold by Joseph Bédier, and *The Perfect Joy of St. Francis*: A Biographical Novel by Felix Timmermanns, to say nothing of the typography for Henry Adams's *Mont Saint Michel and Chartres*. Beyond generalities of style and content, Gorey admired Auden's verse greatly. As an undergraduate, he memorized the poet's whole canon.

The Ballad of Barnaby lives up to the conventional definition of the literary form that its title trumpets. That is, it offers a simple narrative of a dramatic episode to be chanted or recited to a rounded tune. Furthermore, Auden's poem makes use of the repetition common in run-of-the-mill balladry. For example, it repeats verbatim a list of four specific vaults that the tumbler accomplishes. It also adheres to convention in relying heavily on dialogue. Beyond such formal matters, the poet's decision to cast his version of the tale as balladic is doubly apropos, since folk songs of this sort are often long-established by custom. The genre squared too with the context of the entertainer's activities as a popular performer. A ballad automatically conjured up the oral-traditional literature of bygone centuries. What is more, the literary-historical associations dovetailed with the lack of Latin and illiteracy of the protagonist. Finally, misleadingly or not, the generic term has embedded in it a root that implies, as does the word *ballet*, an intrinsic relationship with dance.

The disarmingly, and deceptively, straightforward nature of the verse has been styled "faux-naïf." That last modifier, splicing two foreign elements, emphasizes falsity that undermines seeming innocence. Such a characterization is not the fairest designation for the genial ingenuousness of Auden's poem. Simple is not the same as easy, still less the same as facile. In life as in mathematics, simplicity may be at

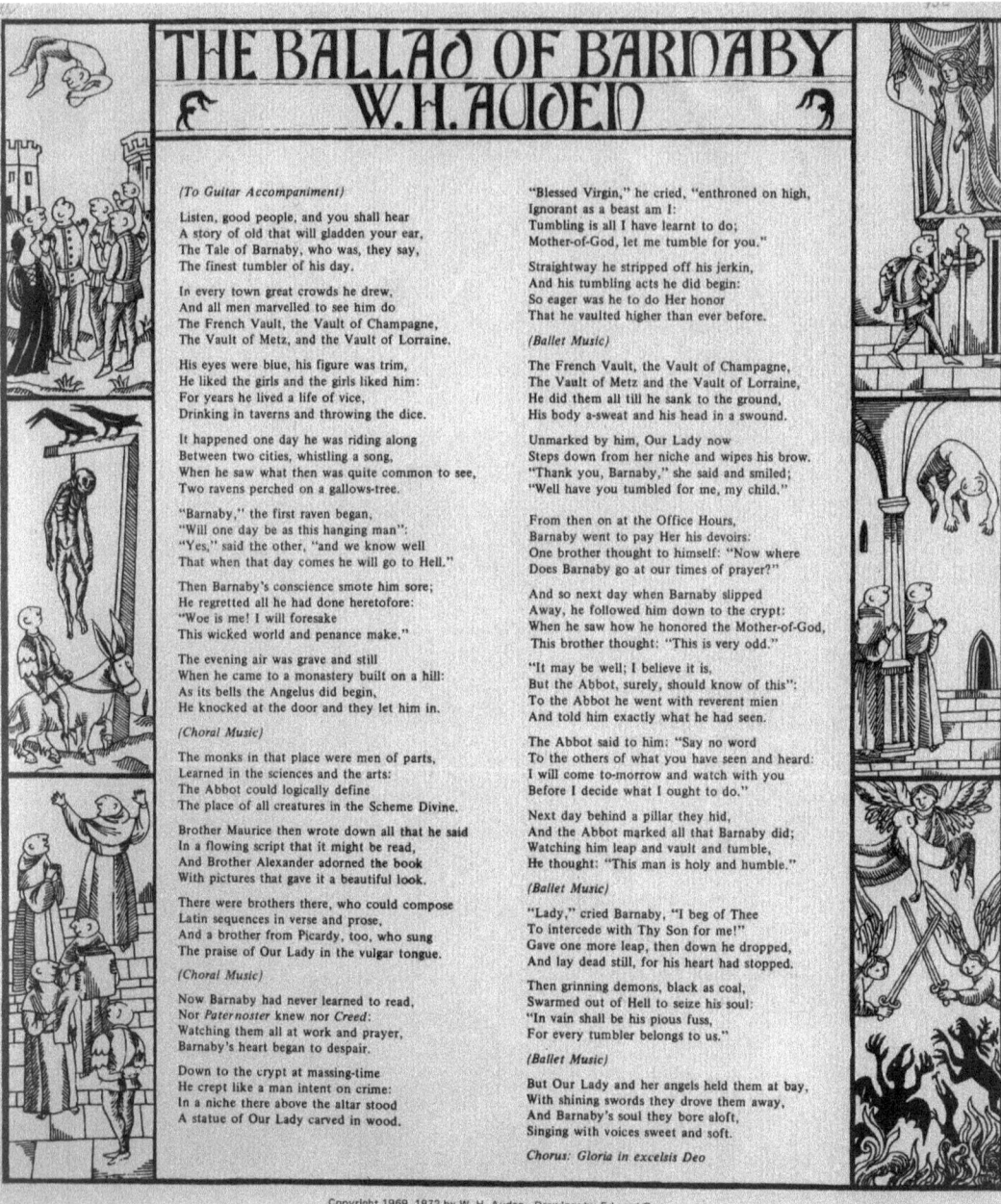

Fig. 3.33 W. H. Auden, *The Ballad of Barnaby*, illus. Edward Gorey. Pre-existing poem and artwork, distributed to complement the Memorial Service in St. John the Divine, New York City, Wednesday, October 3, 1973. All rights reserved.

once suave and impregnable. The spirit of the ballad, whatever we vote to call it, is crystalized in the four lines that set forth the passing of the personable dancer:

> "Lady," cried Barnaby, "I beg of Thee
> To intercede with Thy Son for me!"
> Gave one more leap, then down he dropped,
> And lay dead still, for his heart had stopped.

Two further stanzas follow. One recounts how gleeful demons swarm out to take hold of Barnaby's soul, since all tumblers are demoniacs—all jongleurs belong to the devil and his henchmen. The other tells how the Virgin and her angels drive away the hellions and bear the entertainer heavenward. The melodious event that Auden envisaged closes with the chorus intoning the Latin of the so-called angelic hymn or great doxology, "Glory to God in the highest." Through the musicality, he brings us all, auditors or readers alike, to the communal high note of *Gloria* as chorused in Latin. This commonality has arrived only lethargically. At the beginning, the entertainer is accepted more with forbearance than with open arms. Whereas the other monks are literate, high-culture, polyglot artists, he is illiterate and "ignorant as a beast," with no skill to his name but his tumbling.

Less than four years after composing *The Ballad of Barnaby*, Auden succumbed to cardiac arrest after a poetry reading he gave in Vienna on September 29, 1973. That he gave his tumbler the same cause of death could have been sheer coincidence, not a sign that the poet had a prophetic premonition of his own heart failure. Did he have other reasons to identify with the young athlete—or did he associate him with past lovers? Whatever the reasons, this poem was supposedly a personal favorite of the author's. For that reason, a few days after he gave up the ghost alone in a hotel room in Austria, copies of the ballad were handed out as leaflets to the mourners at a two-hour memorial service in New York City (see Fig. 3.33).

The ballad has not been universally loved or respected. One critic faulted the choice of this piece to cap an anthology of narrative poetry. He conceded that its placement as the last item "allows the book to end as sweetly and softly as the voices of the angels who bear Barnaby to Heaven." All the same, he gave voice to doubt at a selection he damned with faint praise as "inoffensive, almost apologetic." Another scholar was equally stinting when he described it as standing on a plateau rather than a mountaintop. Such unadmiring potshots reflect a frequent divide among Audenists. Some favor his early compositions, whereas others prefer the later ones he crafted in what might be called his American phase. A fair number regard Auden's evolution as a poet after his naturalization as a US citizen as a decline and fall. In this interpretation, he cascaded from the full-bodied subtlety and sophistication of his career in Britain and glided into a watered-down facility that elided difficulties. His new style sidled away from challenges—esthetic and artistic as well as psychological and emotional. Criticism in this vein reads the song of Barnaby as nothing more than fluff.

The negativity fails to register that outward shows of simplicity are often attained only through Herculean toil and Orphic virtuosity, and that the gentleness of the poem makes Auden's joy manifest in offering up the best of his art, in an act as hallowed as that of the tumbler himself. In recent years, "The Ballad of Barnaby" has been given renewed musical outlet in the version by Alla Borzova. The composition by this Belarus-born resident in the United States premiered in 2002. It infiltrates such medievalizing features as Gregorian chant-like monody. As the musician explains on the second page of the score, the "ballad" quotes three medieval melodies. One, a tune the tumbler whistles while astride his horse, is extrapolated from the thirteenth-century *Play of Robin and Marian*, by the thirteenth-century Adam de la Halle. The second brings together extracts from the *Lay of Our Lady* by the trouvère Ernoul le Vieux de Gastinois, likewise of the thirteenth century. Finally, Borzova incorporates the medieval Latin hymn *Day of Wrath* as a sequence intoned by a male chorus. The composer was won over to the poem by its message of unflinching, lifelong commitment to art by an artist.

The simplicity of Auden's text may give the impression of extempore creation, but nothing could be further from the truth. Like many other classic men of letters, this one had a proficiency for ferreting out his sources and zeroing in on their key features. In *The Ballad of Barnaby* he distilled and blended the essences of both the medieval poetry that constitutes the earliest extant form of our story and Anatole France's late nineteenth-century French literary revision. This is exactly as it should be. Great fashioners of poetry and prose should have the freedom to wrestle with the narrative to isolate for themselves what they regard as its determinants. They should not be constrained by the thirteenth-century poem, the late nineteenth-century short story, the early twentieth-century libretto, or any other version.

In an interview, Auden once made clear that he would have seen no contradiction between what we have called medieval studies and medievalism. To the wry amusement of the few who earn their keep as professional medievalists, he admitted that on occasion in real life he posed as a historian of the Middle Ages, a pretense that enabled him to sidestep the gauche and importunate questions that he faced sometimes when he admitted to being a verse-maker. He clarified that because of his family upbringing, he had never viewed what he called art and science as being at loggerheads.

When had Auden first happened upon the medieval French original, in translation or adaptation? He may have come across the medieval miracle first through the prism of Henry Adams. The poet's "New Year Letter" of 1940 places on display an intimate familiarity with Adams's "Virgin and the Dynamo." His mastery of Adamsiana presumes knowledge of the chapter in *The Education of Henry Adams* entitled "The Dynamo and the Virgin." It may suggest an acquaintance too with *Mont Saint Michel and Chartres* and its excerpts from *Our Lady's Tumbler*. The historian's book remained essential reading among intellectuals. To the author of the 1940 ballad, North America as a continent and the United States as a culture have the appeal of allowing personal development by lacking or not imposing, at least relatively, a deep past—of having "worshipped no / Virgin before the Dynamo."

Later in the decade, Auden expatiated on his engagement with the scion of the political dynasty in a disquisition called "The Virgin & the Dynamo." In this essay, the poet took the reader's mindfulness of *The Education of Henry Adams* so much as a given that he adverted nowhere to its title. In fact, he identified the autobiographer's own name, on the third page of his meditation, only to take issue with him. In the discussion, the later writer examines human existence, without descending to smooth-talking dichotomies, within a context of polar questions about the dynamic between the social and poetic order as well as between religious belief and hard science.

The twentieth-century poet's musings on "The Virgin & the Dynamo" twist their way to a passage of more than a paragraph that relates strongly to his short stanzas about the tumbler. Four sentences bear quoting in full:

> The subject matter of a poem is comprised of a crowd of recollected occasions of feeling, among which the most important are recollections of encounters with sacred beings or events. This crowd the poet attempts to transform into a community by embodying it in a verbal society. Such a society, like any society in nature, has its own laws; its laws of prosody and syntax are analogous to the laws of physics and chemistry. Every poem must presuppose—sometimes mistakenly—that the history of the language is at an end.

The Ballad of Barnaby gives an account of just such an interaction with a revered entity, since the Madonna strides forth from her nook and as the Virgin blesses the title character. A later amplification also holds significance:

> Every beautiful poem presents an analogy to the forgiveness of sins; an analogy, not an imitation, because it is not evil intentions which are repented of and pardoned but contradictory feelings which the poet surrenders to the poem in which they are reconciled.

Against this backdrop, it becomes harder to niggle at what could be called the optimistic simplicity of the pseudo-traditional song. At its crowning point, the ballad demonstrates a benediction. Such blessing lies within reach of the presently or even momentarily irreproachable, no matter how un-innocent their pasts.

The modern ballad-writer had only indirect access to the medieval French of *Our Lady's Tumbler*. He would not have read the poem in the original, but by the avenue of the Wicksteed translation. He may have also come across allusions to the tale by other versifiers, although by the 1960s most of the verse translations or explicit references to the narrative in poetry could be seen only through a glass darkly. Obviously, Patrick Kavanagh would have been known to Auden, but the Irishman's *Our Lady's Tumbler* is among his most opaque compositions. In any case, Auden's influence on the Irish poet is more easily charted than vice versa.

Like past authors, counting Anatole France, Auden seems to have been roused by features intrinsic to the story from the Middle Ages that reechoed across the centuries even when it was abridged and made into prose. The pivotal event in the thirteenth-century poem is in fact the bolt from the blue of an unannounced meeting with a sacred emissary. Encircling the austerity of the tumbler and the Virgin are concentric rings, first of the onlooking abbot and monks, and then of the entire community beyond them. From France's short story the Anglo-American drew the name of the tumbler, which he interjected already in the first stanza of *The Ballad of Barnaby*. From the medieval text he lifted the terms for two of the liturgical texts, the Paternoster and the creed, that the performer could not recite in Latin. From the same source, he derived the designations for the moves that are specified in the second stanza—the French Vault, the Vault of Champagne, the Vault of Metz, and the Vault of Lorraine.

The third stanza, in which the youth's looks and morals are delineated, is all Auden's own. The tumbler, blue-eyed and trim, with sensual and even sexual appeal, susceptibility to quaffing and gambling, and showiness about his tumbling talent, caught the poet's eye and heart. The athlete's willowy allure is reported to be unambiguously heterosexual: "He liked the girls and the girls liked him." For this reason, it would be overinterpreting to lay too much emphasis upon the balladeer's same-sex attractions. Although we may picture the juggler's wasp-waisted and lissome body as sculpted by exercise, the poem is (to put it mildly) mostly not about sex. Mary is barely described, since the focus rests to the end on Barnaby's spiritual condition, yet nonetheless her vivacious physicality comes through. The "Blessed Virgin" and "Mother-of-God" all in one, she is never whittled down to being merely a static wooden "statue of Our Lady."

The ballad is not only deeply religious but also deeply Christian. Through the tumbler, Auden gave vent to the passion of artists, for whom their art and their life, or their art and their salvation, are one and the same. "The finest tumbler of his day" has a talent to which he remains true to the last gasp. His soul is then spared. Salvation comes despite the earlier-mentioned concession that "for years he lived a life of vice." He is redeemed despite the gloom-and-doom statement of two large crows on a gallows-tree which caw that Barnaby "will one day be as this hanging man." That is to say, he will be damned to hell. For all his sins, the gymnast proves in time to be as redemptive in his humility as he has been ignorant. Even more, he achieves holiness through the appeal of his artistry. Thus, there is neither hollowness nor gallows humor in the profession "this man is holy and humble."

The bird talk near the end brings to mind the most famous poem by François Villon, in which putrid corpses on a gibbet deliver an apostrophe (see Fig. 3.34). The late-medieval poet's stock has risen by leaps and bounds since the Gothic revivals of the nineteenth century, with a decisive groundswell in the 1860s and 1870s. A dependable thumbnail sketch of his character and conduct is hard to give; for that matter, it does not come easy to put a finger on his occupation or the demimonde in which he lived. Ultimately, the title of an 1877 essay by Robert Louis Stevenson sums up the situation best: "François Villon: Student, Poet, and Housebreaker." Although the Frenchman's activities as a wayward student and felonious lawbreaker have shouldered aside close popular attention to his lyric poetry, Auden gave equal weight to all three aspects of the genius's biography.

3. Portrait of the Artist as a Young Juggler 131

Fig. 3.34 Hanged Criminals. Woodcut illustration to François Villon, *Le Grant Testament et le Petit, Son Codicille, Le Jargon et ses Balades*, 1st ed. (Paris: Pierre Levet, 1489), https://commons.wikimedia.org/wiki/File:PendusVillon.jpg

Villon's ballad, supposedly composed while its late medieval maker languished on death row, refers to the fate of the hanged. According to the judicial practices way back when, those who have been so executed are afterward to be exposed to the elements and torn apart (by fowl play). In the exclamation, the bodies cry out to later living human beings for their sympathy and prayers. Auden makes the final motif very much his own. The chance conversation with the two ravens about a body suspended from the scaffold with a noose around its neck results in a revelation. True gallows birds, they taunt the carcass with gibes about the prospect, or threat, of hell. This prospect induces his resolution to repent, leave the world, and take the cloth. To the end, the tumbler retains his unassuming bearing. Without his saying it expressly, we understand when he sees the corpses that he knows "there but for the grace of God go I." The only qualification may be the theologically problematic substitution of the Virgin for God.

In 1968, Auden perused *Rabelais and His World* by Mikhail Bakhtin. The book had been drafted decades earlier, but owing to the political and cultural vagaries of the Soviet era it saw publication in English translation only in the year in which the poet read it. Auden seems to have been struck forcefully by the notion of the carnivalesque laid out in it, which refers to types of literature that leverage whimsy and grotesquerie to upend the dominant hierarchy. The Anglo-American poet shows similarly subversive flashes of waggishness when he refers to the canonical hours of worship as "the office-hours." The Russian emphasized the origins of the carnivalesque in carnival and festivals similar to it, with the medieval Feast of Fools holding high importance. The popular ramifications of this literary mode accorded nicely with Auden's choice of an old-fashioned form for *The Ballad of Barnaby*, since broadside poems of this sort were originally aimed at a readership of commoners. The poet fused Bakhtin's concept with his own unique interpretation of the monastic ideal of *ora et labora* ("pray and work!") to forge a view of poetic creation. About 1970, Auden wrote an essay, entitled "Work, Carnival and Prayer," that he had not polished at the time of his death. He concludes the piece by advocating our human need to pursue a triad of "prayer, work, laughter." This was the last pronouncement on faith he issued before dying.

In the prose critique, Auden observed at one point that "the primary task of the schoolteacher is to teach children, in a secular context, the technique of prayer." In *The Ballad of Barnaby* he furnishes instruction, as a pedagogue to the girls of the Wykeham Rise School but as a poet to us all, in understanding all-encompassingly the forms praying can take. To him, this activity amounts to an homage of praise and a petition for salvation. He presents this message so as to match a seeming simplicity of style and language with the commensurately simple piety of the tumbler he depicts. He puts forward for deliberation that a show given sincerely, no matter how humble the art or unschooled and sinful the artist, can attain deliverance for its giver. This credo is to be cherished by all of us who work with words, which of all things in the world are simultaneously the cheapest and most precious, most readily available and yet elusive, most ephemeral and yet perennial.

Both *Our Lady's Tumber* and *Le jongleur de Notre Dame* tell of a man whose skills run to the corporeal and not to the cerebral, a physical performer who has no panache for foreign tongues or even sign language. At first blush, it may strike some as incompatible that later poets should have co-opted such a story as a parable for what they have to furnish the world and their readers through their art. Yet this anomaly may have been embedded in the tale from its inception. The vernacular poem asserts that a person untrained in the words and movements of formal worship has the capacity nonetheless to transcend his humanity by making an offering to God of the skill he has.

Propelled to anatomize Anatole France's short story on more than one occasion, the American literary critic John Ciardi (see Fig. 3.35) once recapitulated it for instructors of fine arts, especially of English literature, and elaborated its meaning for them. He envisaged the entertainer as being much like a teacher and verse-maker. In the opinion of this twentieth-century man of letters, a master of literature is automatically a self-appointed bard. As the poet and professor spins out his analogy, the monks who catch the medieval minstrel in flagrante delicto and who clamor to hurl him out of their community correspond in present-day terms to the school committee; the prior, to the superintendent of educational system. In the peroration to the address that this essay records, the author sets forth in detail how the juggler's act relates to a poet's shaping of a poem. Ciardi wrote an introduction to poetry and to the criticism of it that became standard fare in the 1960s. In it, he distills France's prose (but not prosaic) tale to bring home the kind of wordplay that sets a lyric apart from other brands of artistic expression. An antinomy of the jongleur is that the length and elaborateness of the language in which he has been purveyed has been as elastic and bendy as he is sometimes reported to be himself. His story has been pared down to nothing, only thereafter to regenerate itself in manifestations that are ever different, and yet sufficiently the same to be instantaneously recognizable.

Fig. 3.35 John Ciardi. Photograph from late 1950s, photographer unknown. Image courtesy of Rutgers University Libraries. All rights reserved.

If *The Ballad of Barnaby* suffers from two imperfections, they are mutually opposed. One is that the lightness of its exterior puts it at hazard of being faulted as frivolous and overused. The other is that its excellence may have imposed upon later writers an anxiety of influence: the phrase describes the insecurity of successive authors when confronting great literary antecedents. Various other verse-makers since Auden have judged his piece in a far more favorable light than nitpickers have done. Some of them have even been suborned by the loveliness of the story into devising songs of their own about the jongleur or juggler. Many enterprising mortals, including those who write verse, have lives with energetic ups and downs. Without reference to the medieval story, Robert Lowell wrote metaphorically in a letter to his fellow American poet, John Berryman: "You and I have had so many of the same tumbles and leaps. We must have a green old age. We both have drunk the downward drag as deeply as is perhaps bearable. I feel we have better work and better lives ahead."

The 1970s generated at least a couple of specimens by American poets. The little-known Massachusetts-based Nina Nyhart exercised her skills as a verse-maker in fashioning a beautifully compact version in nine sestets. (Could she have been galvanized to put the lyric into this number of stanzas by her first name, with its resemblance to the noun nine?) The groupings of lines have contours in which the shortest come at the beginning and end, the longest in the middle. This shape echoes the poem's emphasis on the arch or bridge, such as that formed by the body of a gymnast. After falling flat in a performance, the acrobat (of unspecified gender) receives direction from a bridge "my fellow arch" that he should enter the monastery of Clairvaux. There, after despairing of having a calling, the tumbler does a routine "under Our Lady's arch." In concluding, the composition concentrates exclusively upon the performer, who bounds about ever faster until his or her head bursts:

> with fervor
> and I tumbled down. I swear I felt
> her hand, yet waked to a still crypt. To this day
> I covet no other's rite or talent, knowing how I may,
> by the simple spending of myself,
> deserve her.

Entitled "Our Lady's Tumbler," Nyhart's piece makes full sense only if the reader is previously acquainted with the events in the original medieval narrative. Through the words "trick," "vault," and "somersault," the text gives a hint that the author may have consulted all three of the main translations from the late nineteenth or early twentieth century, by Wicksteed, Butler, and Kemp-Welch.

Fig. 3.36 Turner Cassity. Photograph, date and photographer unknown. Atlanta, GA, Emory University, Robert W. Woodruff Library. Image courtesy of Emory University Archives. All rights reserved.

A second effort from the 1970s to lyricize the tale from the Middle Ages would be a short poem by Turner Cassity that was first published in 1976 (see Fig. 3.36). The American poet's "Our Lady's Juggler" may respond to Auden's:

> The miracle is mine, My Lady
> Do not think your lifted hand,
> Your so late simper count. The steady,
> Prompted poise of no hoops in the hand
>
> And some hoops in the air surpasses.
> This I make for you of rest,
> Eye, wrist—a going magic—grace's
> Access neither harms nor much assists.
>
> Grace is to have no need of grace,
> And I who send out no prospectus,
> Leave no memory, give phase
> To fall, in giving mass my little ictus.

Be that as it may, the lyric grabs a reader's interest by valorizing the persona of the versifier over the Virgin and for casting him as the juggler (or the manipulator of objects as the writer of poetry). To turn to another example which is not a complete poem, Peter Porter did not retell the story of the juggler, but he did allude to it in the sentence "We watch / Le Jongleur de Notre Dame perform before / His plastic Virgin." Although this Australian did not refer to Barnaby or juggling, the connection to the ballad is palpable: the composition is entitled "Scrawled on Auden's Napkin."

Another word of encouragement is owed to aspiring poets who are wondering what remains to be done. The troubadours had Ezra Pound. Such canonical medieval authors as Chrétien de Troyes and Dante (to single out only a couple of other instances) have coaxed numberless lyricists into versifying medieval poetry and occasionally even into turning it into its genuine modern equivalent. In contrast, *Our Lady's Tumbler* has wasted away in sometimes grimy, dog-eared books. In the versions preserved in them, the nettlesome diction that was already unnaturally archaic when they were printed in these plain-looking volumes a hundred years ago may outweigh the compensation of quaintness. The person who could follow the text of the original without slavishness but with loyalty, and who could enable its spirit and sounds to speak to us across the centuries and over the gulf between the French of the Middle Ages and the English of here and now, would do it and its eventual readers a service as great as the jongleur fulfilled for the Virgin. Mary might not ventilate him in this life as a reward, but the verse-maker who accomplished the feat of truly translating *Our Lady's Tumbler* for our times would be sure to win many fans of another sort.

Music from Massenet to Peter Maxwell Davies

Jules Massenet's feat with *Le jongleur de Notre Dame* both blessed and cursed the story's subsequent fate in music. Had Richard Strauss written the opera Cosima Wagner urged upon him, or had Giacomo Puccini beaten the French composer to the punch, the destiny of the tale in the twentieth century might have looked different—and dimmer. Massenet's day in the sun would have paled without the contributions of the awe-inspiringly hard-driving and ingeniously manipulative Mary Garden. In his handling of the theme, he was driven to no inconsequential degree by his desire to demonstrate that he could score a favorable outcome without resorting to women; he thirsted for this one triumph with no pandering to leading ladies, female opera-goers, and romantic love. But despite all his efforts, the sultry soprano tugged his creation back toward fair sex by interposing herself as the lead. Her initial ploy and subsequent gamesmanship ensured that the narrative would be propagated in the United States, certainly far more widely than if its continuance after the Frenchman had rested solely on the many little boutique volumes with English translations of the medieval *Our Lady's Tumbler* that we have seen, most of them published in northern New England around the turn of the century.

The last assertion holds true even if, for the sake of argument (and in the face of all the countervailing evidence), we hypothesize that without the Scottish-American prima donna, dramatizations of Anatole France's story would nonetheless have been enacted on the radio and television. Her operatic road trips throughout the nation belong in the context of the legendary head-to-head rivalry between Oscar Hammerstein and the Metropolitan Opera Company of New York. They set the stage, really and truly, for the dissemination of the jongleur's juggling song-and-dance across vaudeville stages, college campuses, community and company auditoriums, and everywhere else where minor professionals and rank amateurs had a sporting chance to strut their stuff.

The 1920s saw the fame of the jongleur reach a summit, or the beginning of a drawn-out high plateau, in the United States. Let us take two different examples from 1925. To appreciate the reach that Garden's star turns achieved, we first need do no more than glance at an activity book for children. Entitled *Young Folks' Picture History of Music*, the item contains images to be cut out with scissors and glued into their proper places. A section "How Music Grew Up" concentrates on the nonecclesiastical musicians of the first thousand years of the common era. Massenet's opera is singled out, and the picture to illustrate it shows—could there be any doubt?—the diva as the jongleur. In Europe, the French composer's achievement almost put an end to experimentation with the theme by other musicians, as not many felt the slightest exigency to replicate, quite possibly not as artfully, what their predecessor had done already. But this is not to say that *Le jongleur de Notre Dame* was without influence, even though its ripples seem to have arisen more from its storyline than its music. In Germany, the First World War and expressionism brought enough of a rupture to permit experiments in adapting the tried-and-true tale. In 1921, at the very dawn of his career, Alfred Huth (see Fig. 3.37) composed his Opus 4: *The Dancer of Our Dear Lady*: *Legendary Play in Two Acts, for Soloists, Choir, and Orchestra*. By the end of 1932, this minor composer had enrolled in the National Socialist German Workers' Party, and he remained an active member to the end of World War II. After the deep freeze of the hostilities came a long thaw that has not ended. The Nazi diktat against French and other corrupt cultures no longer applied; in fact, the postwar framework for Western Europe encouraged Franco-German amity. Its effects, amalgamated with the emphasis on the Virgin within Catholicism at the time, meant that by the early 1950s German musicians and playwrights became amenable once again to re-energizing the underutilized story of the jongleur. In two cases, it bears note that titles highlighting *The Dancer of Our Blessed Lady* explicitly and unprotestingly acknowledge the French pedigree of the miracle.

Those who had been active and outspoken as National Socialists in Germany could not effortlessly wash away the taint of the belief

Fig. 3.37 Alfred Huth. Photograph by Ernst Huth, date unknown, CC BY-SA 3.0, https://commons.wikimedia.org/wiki/File:Alfred_Huth.jpg

system in which they had been implicated for years. A case in point would be *The Dancer of Our Blessed Lady*, the libretto for a ballet in two acts by Konrad Karkosch and Ludwig Holzleitner. The first of the pair wrote his early criticism on literature, and his later mainly on film. He participated actively in the Nazification of culture, among other things as the proponent of "a biologically based *Bildung*—a true *Volk* education."

Karkosch's self-published script for stage, film, and television has a few features that reflect the baggage of the 1930s and the war years. For example, it makes the principal character, named Louis de Clairvaux, the leader of a dance troupe, whose crew has given him unequivocal obedience: he is in effect a Führer. The entertainers are presented as prompting a squall of protest from the monks. In effect, the two groups are pitted against each other in ideological conflict. After a long scene devoted to a balletic play about the treacherousness of luck, Louis undergoes a conversion experience and joins the brethren. Within the abbey, he feels the inadequacy that was recounted in *Our Lady's Tumbler*, Anatole France, and Jules Massenet, but the three brothers who make the newcomer feel inadequate are not the artists and artisans familiar from earlier versions of the story. The second one beats his breast and wrings his hands in anguish, and the third is a flagellant who whips and welts his back with a flail. The traditional and normal focus on different types of artistic expression has metamorphosed here into something less salubrious and more violent. Remember the unspeakable turn that the tale took when retold by the Austrian author Rudolf Elmayer von Vestenbrugg. If those developments were psychopathic, this episode seems instead sociopathic.

The narrative did not necessarily suffer sinister twisting from all those who rode out the storm and lived to appropriate it after the Second World War. The account of an artist who goes into internal exile within a monastery may have appealed to many who had been through the Nazi era, giving them a way to feel as if they had resisted and struck out on their own through acts of devotion apprehensible to no one except God. Such speculation would have to be put to the test artist by artist, with uncompromising attention to their biographies—if their life stories could even be reconstructed today with sufficient granularity to justify the effort.

In France, a young Catholic artist who found a role model in the jongleur was Francis Poulenc (see Fig. 3.38). Various elements point to the early familiarity of this composer with the story. In 1918, he began drafting a piece entitled *Le Jongleur* for a music hall session that the writer Jean Cocteau planned for the end of the year. In 1919, the musician partially orchestrated the two-piano score he had composed, but he did not finalize the work. Eventually a composition by this name was staged in 1921, with both juggling and intricate acrobatic dancing, by the avant-gardist known as Caryathis (see Fig. 3.39). The show included a dance suite by Erik Satie that the same entertainer and choreographer also performed, in a costume designed by Jean Cocteau (see Fig. 3.40).Since none of the music survives, it remains a long haul to know whether any of the versions related closely to *Our Lady's Tumbler*.

Fig. 3.38 Francis Poulenc. Photograph by Joseph Rosmand, before 1922. *Miniature Essays: Francis Poulenc* (London: J. & W Chester, 1922), 2.

In 1936, Poulenc was agitated by the gruesome death by decapitation of a close friend and fellow musician in a car wreck. Returning to the Church to which he had mostly paid no mind in the intervening years, he made a penitential pilgrimage to the Black Virgin at Rocamadour. There he had a mystical experience that inspired him to compose three Litanies to the Black Virgin of that village. After 1936, he began to compose some strictly liturgical music. In 1952 the composer undertook Dialogues of the Carmelites, but the enterprise gave him migraine-level vexation. The opera was first staged only in 1956. During the interim, he wrote to the American John Howard Griffin, and declared his despair of completing it. He asked the Texan journalist to have the Discalced Carmelite Fathers at Mount Carmel Seminary in Dallas pray for his recovery. Poulenc's comparisons between himself and the jongleur of Notre Dame verge on being a leitmotif in his writings.

Fig. 3.39 Poster based on a watercolor by Léon Bakst, for a 1921 dance recital by Caryathis.

Fig. 3.40 Caryathis, in a costume designed by Jean Cocteau, in a dance show that included a performance of *Le Jongleur*. Photograph, 1921. Photographer unknown.

In the United States, the story had become indelible in popular and mass culture through the decades of vaudeville, radio, and live enactments by students in foreign-language teaching and other scholastic contexts, by staff members in corporate productions, and by families in domestic settings. Many such presentations have prompted the musically inclined to create their own treatments, some of which have been preserved. In the case of schools and church groups, composers and librettists have sometimes teamed up to publish versions for use by classes or congregations. Even the scripts of family stagings have been brought into print now and again. Only seldom have musicians endeavored to take the tale back up the ladder into high culture.

It speaks to the salient profile and all-inclusive reach of the narrative in the mid-1950s that just as Fred Waring incorporated his backward-looking adaptations of the episode into his variety show on television, Ulysses Kay (see Fig. 3.41) should have gravitated to *The Juggler of Our Lady* as the subject for a one-act opera that he composed in 1956. An African-American, he had a given name that in part would seem likely to pay tribute to Ulysses S. Grant, commanding general of the Union Army during the Civil War and prime mover in the Congressional Reconstruction. Then again, the appellation could allude directly to the hero of the *Odyssey*: most descendants of those who had formerly been enslaved could identify with the wily wanderer and shrewd survivor of Greek myth.

Fig. 3.41 Ulysses Kay, left foreground, at the reception after the premiere of his opera *The Juggler of Our Lady* at Xavier University, February 23, 1962. Xavier University of Louisiana Archives and Special Collections. Copyright by Xavier University of Louisiana. All rights reserved.

On the face of it, the story to which Kay gravitated for this opera was one far removed from, and unsoiled by, the slave era or its aftermath. He favored a neoclassical style. *The Juggler of Our Lady*, partly by dint of being detached from America and its history, offered its composer and librettist a free hand in dealing with the nature of veneration and art. The libretto was the creation of Alexander King. This Vienna-born US author and media personality claimed to have taken a French morality play as the basis for the dramatic action.

In the musical drama the lead is called Colin. His poverty is contrasted with the condition of two monks (see Fig. 3.42). Other characters include two street singers, one of them a boy soprano. The events unfold in 1554, in the French city of Tours. The juggler takes a suggestion from his musician to spend the night in an inn, but the host tells Colin that not a bed is free. Down the road, the minstrel finds a cloister that allows him to lodge overnight. There he endures various vicissitudes before doing fancy footwork before the statue of the Virgin, including magic tricks and playing music (see Fig. 3.43). At the end of his act, the image comes to life, and Mary flashes Colin a smile of approval and gives him a blessing (see Fig. 3.44).

Fig. 3.42 The juggler Colin and his musician are received by the monks. Ulysses Kay's opera *The Juggler of Our Lady* (1956), premiere at Xavier University, February 23, 1962. Xavier University of Louisiana Archives and Special Collections. Copyright by Xavier University of Louisiana. All rights reserved.

Figs. 3.43 and 3.44 The drama unfolds within the monastery. Colin performs before the Madonna. Ulysses Kay's opera *The Juggler of Our Lady* (1956), premiere at Xavier University, February 23, 1962. Xavier University of Louisiana Archives and Special Collections. Copyright by Xavier University of Louisiana. All rights reserved.

The opera lay neglected for six years before premiering in New Orleans. In a letter, Kay once offered pithily: "opera is not the medium for our time." His thinking seems to have been spot on, as far as any broad reception for this composition of his is concerned. Still, the local response in Louisiana to the performance of his musical drama before a full house of 450, and to his own involvement as composer and guiding spirit, could not have been more enthusiastic and approving. *The Juggler of Our Lady* was deemed "a melodic triumph" in a front-page story in the local student paper, and a "melodic affair" in a local city daily. The heavy emphasis on the tunefulness and sonority of the work may have been a deliberate corrective to the widespread prejudice among racists that African-Americans had rhythm but not melody.

Word trickled outside the South in the African-American press. One decade after the belated 1962 opening, the musical drama was revived in 1972 in Jackson, Mississippi, to modest national fanfare. King's libretto need not have been tailored to the experiences and sensibilities of non-white audiences. The composer makes no show of being intent on striking a blow against the segregation, disenfranchisement, and racism of the Jim Crow laws. Yet the motif of the lodging place that refuses to accommodate a would-be patron would have resonated with blacks who had to contend with housing segregated by law when traveling in the United States before the ratification of the Civil Rights Act of 1964—and by lingering custom even long afterward.

A few years after Ulysses Kay, Juan Orrego-Salas composed a ballet based on *Our Lady's Tumbler*. It might be tempting to connect the initiative of this Chilean composer with the children's story published in his homeland by the Spanish author José María Souvirón in 1942. Yet the certainty is that the narrative from the Middle Ages came to the musician's attention when a host presented him with a copy in English during a sojourn in the United States in the early 1950s. Behind that gift stood the non-metaphoric lone-wolf killing of a child that had taken place a quarter century earlier. The murder was stranger than either the medieval fiction or the slightly later kidnapping and infanticide of Charles Augustus Lindbergh Jr. in 1932. Enough suspensefulness: hear the ghastly facts about what happened in both 1953 and 1927.

While spending a few days at the home of an executive of the Bethlehem Steel Corporation, Orrego-Salas found one night that a translation of *Our Lady's Tumbler* had been placed on the pillow in his bedroom. After reading the tale right away, the musician was inspired by it to envisage a ballet. The next morning, his hosts responded to his enthusiasm by commissioning him to create his work in honor of the wife's younger son by her first husband.

The boy had died as a little one about twenty-five years previously in a grisly mischance. As a hobby, his wealthy father had traded in exotic birds and boarded a menagerie of wild animals. In 1926, a leopard slipped free from its cage. Fortunately, the feline fugitive was recaptured before causing harm. The next year, a wolf that escaped from its pen turned out to be anything but a paper tiger. In a grim rampage, the escapee leapt upon the two-year-old as he played on the back lawn with the son of his parents' live-in domestic. Both the maid's three-year-old boy and his year-younger playmate bolted, but only the first of them reached the safety of the house. There the housekeeper's son shrieked to his mother that a big dog was biting his friend. The childcare provider raced out to find the carnivore slinging the child in the air repeatedly and mauling him. She kicked to shoo away the creature, gathered up the youngster, and gunned down the predator with a rifle. But the deed was done. Like a fairy tale gone terribly wrong, no woodcutter arrived to effect a miraculous rescue. In this reality, the bloodthirsty beast won. More than twenty bite marks were counted on the lacerated corpse of the toddler Tommy. In one sense, that's the end of the story.

The traumatized mother of the fatality never put the catastrophe entirely behind her. Her first marriage dissolved: it would have been hard for her not to feel that her husband had fed their boy to the wolves. She took the American corporate boss as her second spouse. Still disconsolate, she pitched herself into stitching needlepoint tapestries. As a textile artist and quilter, she formed ties with a muralist from Chile, who sewed embroideries that used colcha crewel work. Through this surrealist named Carmen Orrego-Salas, the American developed a connection with the musician.

And the little book with the translation of the medieval miracle that landed on the pillow of the Chilean composer—why would the US artist have known it and cared about it? However facile the psychologizing may seem, it can be readily imagined how the bereaved parent of a son who had been killed while still a tot would find *Our Lady's Tumbler* therapeutic. The narrative has an almost medicinal potential: its balm appealed to authors who were Jews in hiding from the Nazis or other individuals in the resistance in World War II. Likewise, the tale was invoked later by the poet Adair, who made a practice of book therapy.

With the passage of decades, the mother of the boy who had been killed could have discerned in the tumbler the adult into whom her son would have grown. The story of an angelic dancer could have helped to banish the mental picture of a beastly wolf juggling a boyish preschooler. Moreover, when projecting what her lost child would have become in boisterous manhood, she could have arrested his development to retain intact all the positives of puerility. In effect, she could have juvenilized her Tommy to freeze-frame him before he could experience alcohol, sexual awakening, and other distinguishing traits and sometimes failings of grown-ups. She could have visualized him as undergoing a vague maturation that left him still sinless and physically active, simple and asexual. In *Our Lady's Tumbler* and *Le jongleur de Notre Dame* the jongleur and the Madonna commune in silence, in some ways like children playing: in no version do the two actors speak with each other. Whatever may have motivated his benefactor, Juan Orrego-Salas threw himself into composing the orchestral score in fits and starts, taking four years to clinch it. In performance in both Chile and the United States (see Fig. 3.45 and 3.46), the resultant music bears as its title the Spanish term for tumbler or acrobat.

Fig. 3.45 The image of the Virgin with the jongleur after his collapse. Ballet Nacional Chileno, November 17, 1961, Viña del Mar, and Teatro Victoria, Santiago, April 19, 1962. Image courtesy of Juan Orrego.

Fig. 3.46 The jongleur, holding his *vielle*, with one of the young women serving the Virgin. Ballet Nacional Chileno, November 17, 1961, Viña del Mar, and Teatro Victoria, Santiago, April 19, 1962. Image courtesy of Juan Orrego.

After Massenet, a distant second as the most important musical work of art to deal with the story of the jongleur would be a 1978 theater piece in one act. With both music and libretto by Peter Maxwell Davies (see Fig. 3.47), the composition is entitled *Le Jongleur de Notre Dame*. Staging the masque requires the services of an actual mime player with the ability to juggle, as well as a chamber ensemble of flutist, clarinetist, and percussionist who play three of the brethren, a baritone who sings the abbot, and a children's band that makes music at the beginning and end.

Fig. 3.47 Sir Peter Maxwell Davies. Photograph by the University of Salford Press Office, 2012, CC BY 2.0, https://commons.wikimedia.org/wiki/File:Peter_Maxwell_Davies.jpg

In this piece of music theater, the English composer and librettist departs from his usual practice by relating a miracle rather than sketching a character. His version of the legend, in which the juggler is truly a starving artist, focuses on the difficulties that an entertainer faces in fitting into his environment. On a higher level, it conveys what is essentially a memo that those endowed with musical talents should use and share them. As in other pieces in his oeuvre, Davies showed himself in this chamber opera to be attracted to older literature and dramatic forms, engrossed by Catholicism and ritual but revolted by the affectations of the religious, and eclectic in seeking out fountainheads of inspiration in earlier music, such as plainsong. *Le Jongleur de Notre Dame* was not Davies's first foray into material relating to the Virgin.

The masque "is based on the well-known story of the starving juggler whose performing made the Virgin Mary smile." In it, the musician presents the lead, named Mark, as a clownish mime player and juggler who enters a cloister as a neophyte. In this riff on the medieval tale, the jongleur first is humiliated for the lability of his earlier life by being assigned as janitor, washer, and cook for the brethren, and then is enjoined to leave the abbey. On the Virgin's birthday the other three monks, portrayed as smugly self-righteous and self-satisfied, make their offerings. Mark is told that because of his past sins he cannot do the same, but nonetheless he renders a performance as an entertainer. In response to the sincerity of his artistry, the statue plays a violin solo, through which the Virgin smiles and (after a fashion) speaks. The abbot recognizes that Mary has appreciated what Brother Mark has given in humility and devotion. Beyond that appreciation, she has a special destiny in mind for her conscript. She does not want the juggler to hide his light under a bushel—or his talent in a monastery. She bids him to abandon the closed community and carry his talent into the wide world. Afterward, the leader of the cloister sends off Mark so that he may refine and share his artistic talents.

Fidelity to the internal workings of the medieval account would argue for connecting it with Our Lady. This affiliation is part of what motivated Davies to base his fifty-minute "masque" or sacred comedy on chant for the Nativity of the Virgin. This festivity is customarily celebrated in the Catholic and Anglican churches on September 8. To make the tale into a birthday party and present for Mary would make sense, since the climactic event within the narrative as it has often been recounted is the presentation of gifts to an effigy of her. He also made the Mother of God a more active agent than is usually the case, by directing that she be a violinist.

Despite the composer's efforts to accentuate the tale's Marian qualities, the magnetism of Christmas could not be withstood. Davies's masque was written and scored for "The Fires of London," the special ensemble with which he teamed up at the time. The sacred comedy premiered on June 18, 1978. The first sentence of an early review described it as "a charming music theater piece which would be especially effective during the Christmas season." Yuletide is overpoweringly suited, it would seem, for short, traditional narratives. All the same, the holiday market is now also congested. In large part, it has been co-opted by old favorites. *Our Lady's Tumbler* and *Le Jongleur de Notre-Dame* got their foot in the door many times, but the slippery snow of a white Christmas makes traction insecure. Yes, another chancel drama for children's choir has come to light in the past twenty years. Yes, a Beirut-born and European-based composer has in this decade set three poems based on the story to music for soprano and organ, with a prelude of alternating clarinet and organ. Yes, the tale has been made into a one-hour musical. Yet the narrative has not received treatment in a genre with a broader reach—with the mass appeal that the story once commanded, in the golden age of short story, opera, and radio. These days it hides in plain sight, having had much past success, remaining extant in a few beautiful renditions, but not being widely known. What lies ahead? What will the juggler make his next act?

4. Membranes of Things Past

> *What's past is prologue.*
> —William Shakespeare

Misremembering and Remembering

> I told the joke about the woman who asked her lover "Why is your organ so small?" He replied, "I didn't know I was playing in a cathedral."
>
> —Prince, "Vicki Waiting"

If Blechman's animated short could be televised in the holiday season alongside one of the juggler segments from the Waring show, the collocation would deliver the invigoration of roving into the past through a time machine. While accessible to the youngest children, the juxtaposition would be provocative to adults receptive to cultural history, since it would throw open windows that faced in opposite directions from the start of the 1950s. The bandleader's program looked across an all-embracing vista of America back toward the diva Mary Garden earlier in the century: it transported the spectator to the first quarter of the twentieth century. In contrast, the cartoon surveyed a panorama forward toward a future that included hazily even what has become the present day: it anticipated the last quarter of the century, if not even beyond. But let us face the facts. Setting side by side a seventy-year-old snippet from an old television show and a sixty-year-old animation, no matter how absorbing and excellent they may be, respectively, would deliver more in deep critical appreciation than in fast commercial gain. Both a clip from the variety hour and the short animation have the wrong duration for today's market, which favors the extended viewing of feature-length movies. This is to say nothing of attention spans: who could seduce viewers nowadays into watching a long snippet of very old-time television? Eyes are glued too much on this day and age. Scant breathing room is left for the bygone.

Trying to hinge together a diptych of two old versions on the big or small screen would make a start, but better would be to stimulate live performances and delivery. Before radio, cinema, and television took hold of mass culture, the tale insinuated itself most durably into hearts and memories through the magic of musical drama, shows recreating opera in more intimate settings, and bedtime reading. Both children and adults could be engaged through song, dance, juggling, mime; medievalizing costumes, sets, and artwork; or any or all of these in combination. The challenge would be to achieve the coziness of modest-sized groups without battering the narrative into mediocrity. One conduit for innovation could be to act out the story as a vignette within a longer form, whether novelistic or cinematic. The decision by a single filmmaker to retell or reenact the exemplum somehow as a scene in a hit movie could bring *Our Lady's Tumbler* or *The Jongleur of Notre Dame* back into common parlance. In turn, that might be enough to generate imitations in other genres, or at least casual ponderings on old literary and operatic acquaintances that have been forgotten. All of these hopes may be unrealistic: the presence of Christianity within the narrative as it has traditionally been told may raise an insuperable barrier to its absorption into broader circles of the humanities and arts. In this case the legend may persist only where it has become deep-seated, first and foremost in children's books.

A recurrent phenomenon in this study has been clusters of groundbreaking adaptations and of knowledgeable interest that have come on the heels of performances, or even just of publications. An epidemiologist with a taste for investigating how literary-historical contagions ramify could secure fascinating results by logging into a spreadsheet the assorted dates and places where texts have been written, music composed, and ballets and operas staged. Obvious patterns would materialize. For instance, the sustained familiarity with the story among students and staff of the University of Notre Dame should catch no one unawares, since the juggler is by way of being an unofficial college mascot there. Less expected are the many other clumps of curiosity about the miracle.

For the tale to have become less well known than it was back in the day could be a resoundingly good thing. Now the narrative can be the secret discovery of every group or individual that usurps it through recitation, retelling, or performance of some kind. The story occupies an odd position. It became excessively familiar off and on for a century, but its pervasive familiarness led less to contempt than to oblivion. Since then, long neglect has made it seem a private discovery, a personal eureka for a multitude of individual authors and artists. Older ones remember having read it or seen it performed in school, heard it on the radio, or watched it somewhere else decades ago. Younger ones chance upon it much more randomly.

In the end, what matters is that people should have the chance to encounter and relish the tale and its events and characters, especially the protagonist. The specific vehicle in which the doings of the tumbler or juggler are purveyed matters less than the overall quality and spirit. A first-rate reenactment sets the bar high. It makes the fictional events memorable and allows audience members the latitude to interpret them independently—and to accommodate them to their own values and applications. The experience would be enhanced if readers, listeners, or viewers could be exposed to two or more versions of the narrative, preferably in separate media, to ease comparison of the various messages that have been encoded and decoded in the jongleur.

The broadest and richest approaches to literary pièces de résistance—as to life—require interpretive pluralism, which is not identical with cultural relativism. We need to view each text from multiple perspectives, just as if we circumambulated a cathedral to peer at it and appreciate it from different vantage points. In Hugo's sprawling novel about Notre Dame of Paris, we are encouraged to think about how the great church appears to a gypsy girl, a hunchback, churchmen, students, and others, as they meet the building from outside, inside, above, and below. Our tale is shorter and simpler, but it too takes us down and up, from the world outside into the one within, from the laical to the monastic. Another set of outlooks is diachronic. To cast our net wide, further viewpoints would include those of the researchers and artists who composed, recorded, received, and transmitted to us the medieval poem and its sundry subsequent rehandlings. In *Our Lady's Tumbler*, any effort to gain entry to these chronological contexts constrains us to engage with bygone days which (truism alert!), thanks to the inevitabilities of passing time, are ever more distant from us.

On the off chance that anyone has failed to notice a blatant conflict of interest, here comes my full disclosure. As a professional medievalist, I cannot pretend to have a disinterested outlook. A playwright responsible for a not very successful revamping of our story inaugurated his rollout of it with the observation: "It is possible to love the Middle Ages, or to detest it; but not to ignore it." The medieval miracle warrants much more examination and appreciation than it has earned, except from a handful of specialists. In 1921, Maurice Vloberg served up a long and mannered retelling. In his concluding apparatus he sung the praises of the "delightful short story from the beginning of the thirteenth century." By his reckoning, its desirability overtopped that of any modernization, and he challenged his audience to compare the original for themselves with the other versions then to be had. The Old French might still win a taste test hands down, even against a liqueur glass poured to the brim with a stiff snort of Bénédictine. Despite the many redeeming qualities of later permutations, the earliest is the best. To sever contact with it would be tragic.

Passing nods to the juggler are legion. Not ten years ago, the author of a book on the style of "the Monumental City" in Maryland made the oddly counterintuitive move of likening an immobile edifice to the protagonist of our tale. Calling an unpresumptuous apartment house "a gem of nonimportance," he ventured the view that "this building stands as Le Jongleur de Notre Dame of Baltimore architecture. It's not important, but it does what it does perfectly, and more people should notice." Less foreseeably, the juggler of Our Lady bid fair for a while to become boilerplate in *Festschriften*. Meaning in German literally "celebration writings," these omnium gatherums of learned articles have traditionally afforded a means for students and colleagues in academic settings to commemorate the advancing years and careers of esteemed professors. At the same time the editors and contributors demonstrate their solidarity and heighten their own visibility through affiliation with those same worthies. Even scholars as far removed from tumbling, juggling, the Middle Ages, and literature as physicists have liked to acknowledge the jongleur when proffering lectures or essays to honor senior members of their guild.

For want of detail, it is usually impossible to pin down whether such citations of the story result from viewing a film, perusing a literary variant, or being acquainted with allusions made to it in earlier scientific writings. These glancing references mean that the gist of the tale remains well enough known not to seem hopelessly recherché, while they also portend that the narrative still retains enough prestige to make mention of it a feather in the cap—if such a head-covering makes a suitable image for cultural literacy. The invocation of the juggler in appraisals of collective volumes is attested already at the latest by 1960. In that year, a reviewer of a book on evolution praised the essay-writers for having offered, "like the juggler of Notre Dame," their best expositions of general topics on which they had written more specialized or longer studies.

If a fiction may be viewed as a living creature, such usages make this one an oyster spooned alive and raw from a shell for consumption. Alternatively, it could be likened to molten metal that loses its quickness upon being struck for a low-denomination coin. Another example is the way the author of a tome on jurisprudence discusses in wearisome detail the comparability of the juggler and a judge. To the writer quoting, the authority put on parade, and their presumptive readers, the medieval exemplum is as well known as a parable. Still, whereas an allegory formulated by Christ has had the power of a faith behind it, the account at this point was put on the line by becoming too well known. Outside religion and high culture, familiarity, sooner or later, breeds contempt. The same point could be made when a thumbnail précis of the late nineteenth-century French short story makes clear how poor command of orthography can dent popular trust in the competence of professionals such as medical doctors.

> If a physician would spell as follows, he would certainly have great difficulty in gaining people's confidence in his knowledge of medicine: "Barnaby [in Anatole France's 'Our Lady's Juggler'] found faveror in her [the Virgin Mary's] I by puting his hole hart and sole in his jugling."

Already by the same date, exhaustion or even exasperation with the miracle had become evident in some quarters. In the United States, at the very start of the 1960s, the jongleur's jig was up. A kind of "fable fatigue" or "tale tiredness" manifested itself long ago among foreign-language instructors in the United States. At the time French, which since then has been unhorsed by the surging advance of Spanish, reigned preeminent in many regions of the country among modern languages studied in high school and college. The curriculum rested heavily on poring over literature, especially prose fiction. In anthologies relied upon by teachers, *Le jongleur de Notre Dame* was all-too-regular fare. Enough decades have elapsed for the familiarity-bred contempt to dry up and blow away. A tale that seemed shopworn more than a half century ago may have been rejuvenated in the meantime. Still, huge challenges exist now in the American market for schoolbooks. One is that the status of French among foreign languages has declined precipitously. Another is that the short story (and even fiction as a whole) has been displaced by other types of fare—and language learning is ever less text-based anyway. A third is that in many public schools almost nothing remotely religious can be introduced into a classroom without fanning controversy over the division between church and state.

Upon close inspection, data-driven research may turn out to be data drivel. Tritely, statistics can be manipulated to prove anything. That said (more than thirty-five million times), interesting explorations can be transacted within the vast Google Ngram database of digitized books written in English for the phrases "Jongleur de Notre Dame" (see Vol. 1, Fig. 4.1), *Our Lady's Tumbler* (see Vol. 1, Fig. 4.2), and "Juggler of Notre Dame" (see Fig. 4.1 below). The graphs that result from such inquiries force the conclusion that these designations have declined steeply from their apogees. The first two titles or characters crested in use around 1920. At that time, Mary Garden had singlehandedly heaved Massenet's opera to its all-time high of popularity. Moreover, countless editions and translations of the medieval original in translation and of Anatole France's story in both his language and English circulated, being used in schools as well as in pleasure reading. After the French phrase was nativized, "Juggler of Notre Dame" rose to a peak just as the Second World War was getting under way. These inferences from the outcomes of word searches are undergirded by evidence that can be amassed by rummaging in archives of historical newspapers.

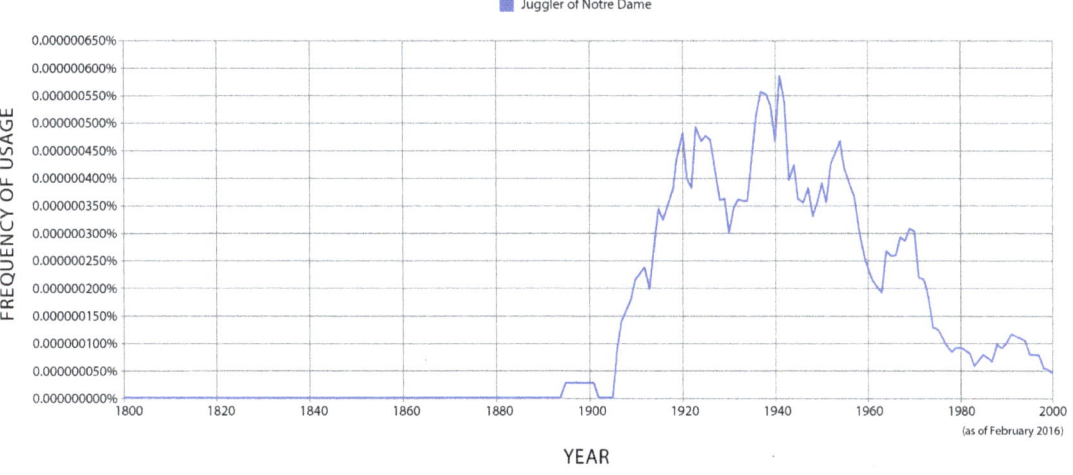

Fig. 4.1 Google Ngram data for the phrase "Juggler of Notre Dame." Vector art by Melissa Tandysh, 2016. Image courtesy of Melissa Tandysh. All rights reserved.

Do the diagrams establish that the narrative has become familiar to fewer people? Not unavoidably. Before leaping to any hasty conclusions, we ought to recollect that the jongleur, tumbler, and juggler have metamorphosed by turns into the acrobat, clown, and jester, while Our Lady or Notre Dame has given way to God or an angel. In at least one instance the name of the main actor has even been modified, by conflation with Notre Dame of Paris, to become "Le jongleur de Paris." The same designation, as for example in the title of a 1969 oil-on-canvas painting by the artist Marc Chagall, may serve to denote a [Parisian circus-type entertainer](), rather than the hero of our story. As the protagonist's profession has changed, and as the nature of the higher power who materializes on his behalf has varied, so too the proper nouns deployed to identify the leading character have proliferated. In 1920, one could have ascertained whether another person had encountered the narrative simply by asking about jongleur or tumbler, Barnaby or Jean, and Notre Dame or Our Lady. All these features, and even the involvement of a statue, have grown into more of a mare's nest. Consequently, straightforward consultation of data sets by two or three phrases will not unmask the realities of popular exposure to the tale as well as it would have done a half century ago. Don't expect an all-purpose algorithm for the purposes of this cultural-historical search-and-destroy anytime soon.

The account of the jongleur is hardly impervious to being misremembered and re-membered as well as misrepresented and re-presented. It even thrives under such treatment and mistreatment. The gist of the narrative in all its major guises is so pithy and punchy that it must seem needless to check it before referencing it. And why scruple about verifying anyway, since no single definitive version exists? In the past, people formed their impressions and memories of the tale from many different media and forms. Few individuals would impose upon themselves the punctilio or pedantry of tracking down a text to see if they had the fine points right when adducing, especially just offhand, Cinderella, Little Red Riding Hood, or other fairy tale greats. Why should they do so when instancing the juggler, who could be cousin if not brother to such literary-cultural personages? In fact, the medieval performer gives even more pause to those who might long for definitude. Is the miracle to be designated as *Our Lady's Tumbler*, *Le jongleur de Notre Dame*, or one of the dozens of other titles? Is the protagonist a tumbler, juggler, joker, jongleur, dancer, buffoon, gymnast, or fool; an adult or child, well-to-do or destitute? Is he anonymous, or called Barnaby, Cantalbert, Jacob, Jean, Jean Vapeur, Pierre, Pietro, or by another name? Do the events take place in Clairvaux, Cluny, Compiègne, Piegne, Touraine, Tourlaine, Sorrento, or somewhere else real or fanciful?

The tale's instability in such rudimentary characteristics has helped to maintain its essence and status in the common domain. In turn, the story's belonging to everyone but no one has freed the hands of artists who have wished to remake it as their own. The downside? The malleability sometimes leaves the down-and-out juggler prey to deformation. He can be handled or mishandled, sometimes deliberately, even by those with a genteel sensibility. When credited only incidentally, he can turn out to be the equivalent of literary-historical roadkill—a wretched creature that has been struck and left to expire on the shoulder of the cultural throughway.

Here we may ponder another example, this one from the Slavic world. Czesław Miłosz (see Fig. 4.2) characterizes his fellow Pole Konstanty Ildefons Gałczyński (see Fig. 4.3) not only as a buffoon but also as having "assigned to himself the role of the medieval *jongleur de Notre Dame*, of a weak man, a drunkard, a vagabond thrown into a world alien to the true desires of his heart, but trying to survive and to bring people something of beauty." Precise as the Polish winner of the Nobel Prize in literature tends to be in his choice of epithets, this analogy gives an inadvertently blurred impression. Not all these traits would very aptly fit either the medieval tumbler or the jongleur of either Anatole France's or Jules Massenet's versions. The three protagonists were vagabonds, but none of them truly an incorrigible inebriate, and the jury would be out on the fairness of calling any of them a spineless weakling. For all that, the likeness is not an out-and-out mistake. The most scathing adjectives are meant to qualify Gałczyński more than the tumbler or the jongleur. Renowned for alcoholic overindulgence and especially for vodka-saturated binges, he was the impotent vagrant whom the 1980 laureate sought to describe.

Fig. 4.2 Photograph of Czesław Miłosz, 1976, by G. Paul Bishop. Image courtesy of G. Paul Bishop. All rights reserved.

Fig. 4.3 Konstanty Ildefons Gałczyński. Photograph by Henryk Hermanowicz, 1947, https://commons.wikimedia.org/wiki/File:KonstantyIldefonsGalczynski1947.jpg

To look toward a different point of the compass and another hemisphere, an argument has been advanced that the Brazilian writer Paulo Coelho, in his bestselling 1988 *The Alchemist*, relied heavily on the narrative treasury in the anthology of children's stories by the Mexican Arreola. Whatever the merits of the case, the original Portuguese edition and translations into many other languages (but not the English) contain a preface that ends with a very distinctive redoing of what is ultimately a heavily modified form of the Anatole France version. In the novel, the eponymous alchemist speaks about three

Fig. 4.4 Advertisement for J. B. Gothic bras. Showcard, 1940s.

Fig. 4.5 "Notre-Dame, Quai de Montebello, Paris." Photograph by Bettina Rheims, 2009. Published in the series "Rose, c'est Paris." © Bettina Rheims. All rights reserved.

types of practitioners who exemplify his profession. To illustrate the third, he tells the young protagonist Santiago a tale in his laboratory. Once, he says, Our Blessed Lady, with the infant Jesus in arms, resolved to return to earth and to visit a cloister. The brethren lined up so that they could step forward one by one before the Holy Virgin to show her honor. One recited beautiful poems, another displayed his miniatures of the Bible, and the third reeled off a list of all the saints. Thus all of them, one monk after another, proved their reverence for the Mother and Child. Backmost in the line stood the lowliest among the brothers, who had never had their noses in learned books. His parents had been simple circus folk who had imparted to him no skill beyond a negligible amount of juggling. When his turn rolled round, the other community members wanted to cut the homage short, because the former juggler had nothing suitable to offer and might become a blot on the monastery's reputation. But he felt an irrepressible insistence to give something to Jesus and the Holy Virgin. Abashed, with the reproachful looks of the contemplatives weighing heavily on his back, he held a pair of oranges and began to juggle with them, since that was the only thing he could do. In response to his antics, the infant Jesus gurgled, giggled, and clapped his little hands on the bosom of Our Blessed Lady. The Virgin extended her arms to the juggler and allowed him to hold the baby.

Getting a Rise from the Male Member

> A peculiarity of the piece is that it contains only male parts.

Gothic architecture can be sexual and even sexy. Most familiarly, in novels of the genre the dark byways of abbeys and churches can morph into erogenous zones. Sometimes they furnish settings for venery that range from the titillating to the tormented. Even apart from any literary traditions of sexualizing buildings, the femininity of Notre Dame—Our Lady, the Virgin—has entailed opportunities first to personify the constructions and then to eroticize them. The cathedral can be conceived as a living body of flesh and blood, and not just any physique, but specifically a sexualized womanly one. In the late-nineteenth-century Parisian beauty contest between Notre Dame and the Eiffel Tower, the great place of prayer was dolled up as a belle.

In the mid-twentieth century, the whole point of Gothic could be condensed in an advertising showcard to the sultry geometry of female breasts as shaped by a brassiere (see Fig. 4.4). If men could have their heads lidded by the angular rigidity of hats with "Gothic crowns," women could have their figures cupped and girdled in similar architecture. The American artist Anne Stokes, who has illustrated books and record jackets, created in 2007 an image "Gothic Siren" that portrays a tattooed Goth-style vamp(ire) against the backdrop of a many-spired tower in the expected architectural vernacular, adorned prominently with skulls and crossbones.

The most artful equation of a shapely woman and a Gothic cathedral comes in a snapshot. An illustrious French photographer has nimbly brought out correspondences and complementarities between the soft slopes and sinuous swells of a voluptuous feminine figure, as seen from the rear, and the lancets, rose windows, and flying buttresses of Notre Dame in Paris (see Fig. 4.5). Called Bettina Rheims, the professional who conceived this ravishing image has good reason even solely from her family name to be attuned to houses of worship from the late Middle Ages; the great church of the French city in question has made repeated appearances in this book. Beyond such onomastic coincidence, Rheims manages in this photograph to point to the resemblance between the rounding of a buttock and the circularity of a rose window. The draping of the lines on the model's dress, and the triangular neckline dipping down to the middle of her back, enhance the similarities between the inanimate medieval edifice and the animate human being. Both are well-proportioned.

However propitious Gothic generally and Notre Dame particularly may have become to sexualization, the suggestiveness in treatments of the juggler relates more often to the male than to the female body. *Our Lady's Tumbler* in its earliest incarnation involves an athletic man, au naturel apart from his most intimate apparel. Although the medieval poem leaves no doubt that the acrobat is scantily clad rather than nude, at least one modern reader completed the striptease in his mind. The gymnast, often pictured as a virtually and virtuously naked young man, exerts himself to the utmost for a woman and falls prone from debilitation in the finale of each encounter. Described thus, the story could spark connotations that are anything but pious. In this context, the French idiom of *la petite mort* for a sexual climax is not of no consequence: the phrase for this sometimes athletic but always unascetic type of catharsis means literally "the little death."

Our Lady's Tumbler has much to say about love, but the tale may be far from romanticism or eroticism and even further from libido. The thirteenth-century poem is no limerick. In a highly reductive interpretation, the meaning of Anatole France's narrative is too wholesome to require any mincing of words: "The essence of religion is the love of God and of our fellow men." The ease of arriving at such a reading explains why the narrative would be absorbed into anthologies entitled *Treasures of the Kingdom: Stories of Faith, Hope, and Love* or groupings headed "Love Never Ceases": the issue is not stamina in intercourse. In Mary Garden's usurpation of Massenet's male lead, and in countless recreations of her cross-dressing by other women who have acted, sung, danced, or juggled the part, the leading role has been made pre- or parasexual. He is not record-low- but no-testosterone. The character has not been neutered, but in effect any overt sexuality has been sublimated for the sake of the kingdom of heaven. Androgyny has worked well for the hero of *Our Lady's Tumbler* and its descendants. Then again, we may be justified in wondering whether the passion is so unearthly, or whether the tale exudes no earthly and earthy passion. Look at the cover of another collection into which the story has been incorporated, this one entitled *A Century of Love Stories* (see Fig. 4.6). Does the monastic setting restrict the relationships in our story to ones among men? Is any romantic attraction between males and females dormant in the medieval original—as in the tales we have seen of youths who plight their troth before (and with) statues that turn animate?

Fig. 4.6 Front cover of Gilbert Frankau, ed., *A Century of Love Stories* (London: Hutchinson & Co., 1935?).

The narrative's intrinsic piety would seem to present an insuperable obstacle to a sex-driven explanation. Why should anyone seek to advance such a reading of the poem, anyway? In the end, the relative importance of a libidinal charge in the medieval text matters less than whether the writers, artists, composers, and filmmakers who have reworked the tale have sensed in it or sought to impose upon it any sexuality. Those intent upon finding hot-and-heavy sex will discern double entendres wherever they train their gaze, but what one woman or man views as a provocative innuendo may spark no response at all in another. An old chestnut, ascribed with no real basis to Freud, holds that "sometimes a cigar is just a cigar." By the same token, sometimes a half-naked jongleur is just that and nothing more. The mind of the entertainer in the medieval poem, insofar as we are granted any entrée into his interiority, is planted in the crypt and not in the gutter.

The entertainer is French. Strange presumptions about his nation—even though if truth be told, it was not yet one in the Middle Ages—have long been rife, nowhere more than in the English-speaking world. Consequently, some broad stereotypes about Gallic gayness and garrulity have come into play in exegesis of our story. In such pigeonholing, a common factor of Frenchness, at least in the eyes of foreigners typecasting it, across the ages has been sensuality. If we cruise for sexual elements within the tradition of *Our Lady's Tumbler* and *Le jongleur de Notre Dame*, we might evaluate differently some of the works we have surveyed.

We saw how in 1898 the boutique-like Boston firm bankrolled by Fred Holland Day published Isabel Butler's translation of the medieval poem. Yet although we met a few of the cronies with whom Day banded together to launch the visionist movement, we did not delve into the sexuality with which he has become aligned. In 1894, Copeland & Day brought out Oscar Wilde's *Salomé*, and for two years afterward the ten American issues of *The Yellow Book*. The company's list of titles in print alone cements its ties to the aestheticism and decadence of the Irish author, who in 1895 was convicted of sodomy. In fact, the inaugural volume, printed by the publishing house in 1894, was even entitled *The Decadent: Being the Gospel of Inaction*. Although written by Ralph Adams Cram, it was left anonymous by its author for fear of adverse consequences: slings and arrows, sticks and stones. Association with the bohemian counterculture of the visionists that it depicted fancifully might not have resonated well in Boston, which was then still a conservative city.

Fig. 4.7 "Vita Mystica [Monk in Cell]." Photograph by F. Holland Day, 1900. Image courtesy of The Royal Photographic Society, Bath. All rights reserved.

Day was close-mouthed and buttoned-up about his sexuality as about much else in his private life. All the same, he became deservedly known for his inclinations toward a personalized and (homo)sexualized brand of philhellenism. In the ambit of late nineteenth-century Boston, his predilections approached closely to outright "Greek love." To make known same-sex proclivities was already skating on thin ice. For evidence, we need rummage no further than his many photographs of young men posed nude or half-clothed. Such images have been diagnosed as symptomizing proto- or crypto-gay sexuality and culture. The male-male eroticism sometimes simmered in conjunction with a turn to the Middle Ages. The relationship between the two phenomena was undebatable, for instance, in one of Day's role models as a cultural figure, John Addington Symonds, the English poet whose translation of medieval Latin student songs made famous the phrase "wine, women, and song." Do such scattered facts render plausible the inference that Copeland & Day selected *Our Lady's Tumbler* for publication because they perceived affinities between the story and their decadent aesthetic values, or between the protagonist and their gay subculture? Members of their coterie may have felt a yank toward the Middle Ages for many reasons, sexuality being only one of them. Day's 1900 photograph Monk in Cell has nothing overtly erotic about it (see Fig. 4.7). The cast of Massenet's musical drama in its original form was, at least from what could be seen on stage by spectators before the conclusion, all male. But did *Le jongleur de Notre Dame* harbor elements we might suspect of being intentionally or unintentionally gay? For that matter, did the opera acquire any hitherto-absent sultriness—heterosexual, gay, lesbian, or all three (and more?)—when Mary Garden pulled on pants and took over the lead *en travesti*? To hopscotch forward several decades, Auden's "Ballad of Barnaby" gave its tumbler, we may recall, blue eyes, a svelte figure, and an aura of conceited and even cocksure heterosexuality, and these qualities may well relate to Auden's own gayness and affinities; but it would require considerable, even exorbitant, ingenuity to argue that the poem is mostly or even largely concerned with sex.

Less arguable cases in point of how banally susceptible to sexualization the story can become may be gleaned from literary and movie criticism of the 1970s and 1990s. First, a 1973 interview of the American pornographic filmmaker and distributor, Radley Metzger, devolves at one moment into a raunchily outré interchange between him and the influential American cinema critic Richard Corliss:

> CORLISS: What might be called the obligatory shot in a Metzger picture is a closeup of the heroine simulating orgasm as the man performs cunnilingus. In hardcore it's usually the reverse.

> METZGER: The only example of that in one of our pictures was *The Dirty Girls*, where the prostitute is in a commercial situation. But there the motive wasn't commercial. The woman was expressing her gratitude to the man—a little like the Anatole France story, "The Juggler of Our Lady." Where the juggler in front of the icon can only juggle, the only thing *she* can do is give him the best lay he's ever had. Mind you, I'm not saying I'm not a male chauvinist pig. I'm not saying I am, either.

Come again? *Our Lady's Tumbler* may give evidence of being a short religious tale at its most basic, with the jongleur representing humanity; the brethren, formal religion; and the image of the Virgin, God. The protagonist's stance vis-à-vis the Madonna has been described as gratitude by interpreters as far apart in attitudes as Charlie Chaplin and William F. Buckley Jr. Here the same religiosity of a male devotee of Mary is desacralized within the mind of a pornographer inured to thinking in the physics and physicality of smut. In this context, the narrative and the manner of conveying appreciation are boiled down to man, sexual exchange, and woman. From devout monks we have moved to consenting adults.

Freud, the founder of psychoanalysis, coined the notion of what is called the Madonna-whore complex. The theory runs that men are inclined to demarcate between some women whom they respect but do not desire and others whom they desire but disrespect. Such binary processing divides females into two groups, virginal mothers and continent homemakers in contradistinction to sexual sluts and promiscuous slatterns. Whether knowingly or not, Metzger's off-color color film rings a strange change upon the antithesis of Madonna and whore in the foundational Freudian formulation. Two acts in seclusion are compared, a fille de joie's thankful fellating of a man and the jongleur's pious juggling before the Madonna. Such reduction of *Our Lady's Tumbler* could be a deathblow, if that choice of words may be forgiven, to the story.

The motion picture under discussion is not Hollywood, in either place of production or style. The skin flick could be better called sexploitation: taking commercial advantage of sexually explicit material. Nonetheless, the interview demonstrates, whether consciously or not, a degree of cunning subtlety. Through the deft crudity of its allusion to the French short story, it props the sleek and slick pseudo-Europeanism of [Metzger's films](#) such as *The Dirty Girls*, released in 1965. Many of his motion pictures, filmed in Europe, were based heavily on French and Italian literature. Early ones were directed by him under the telling pseudonym of Henry Paris—fortuitously, Henry Adams bumps into Gaston Paris in the strangest context! Small wonder that the director's corpus has been called "[erotic kitsch](#)" and "[glamorous European-accented romances](#)." The article based on the conversation between the cinema critic and the filmmaker was subtitled "Aristocrat of the Erotic."

At the same time, it would be misreckoning to attach too much importance to the sheen of urbanity in Metzger's remark. By no stretch of the imagination are we dealing here with an auteur. He does not so much wink as leer at the audience. In the end (and take that phrase as you wish), what gets worked out in his films are not mental powers but body parts. We find ourselves in the very zone of deliberate shock and schlock that the Mexican edition of *Playboy* for December of 2008 inhabited (see Fig. 4.8). For this solecism against mores, the central office in the United States [apologized](#), while in the same breath gainsaying any intended blasphemy. The front photograph of the offending publication showed, expectably, a topless and ostensibly nude young female: what cover of this monthly has failed to flaunt such a vista? The provocation was that the model in question, not likely to be either immaculate or virginal, was draped from head to foot in unblemished white cloth. The seemingly nubile knockout was an Argentine named, conveniently, María Florencia Onori. Furthermore, she stood in an obviously Marian pose, with her hands placed to herald the absence of the infant Jesus a Madonna would usually hold. Whereas Christianity originates in a baby conceived without sexual congress, the porn magazine is all about coitus without procreation, getting without barnyard begetting, and fertility without fertilization. In sum, the religion and the review set their sights upon altogether different dream girls.

Fig. 4.8 A man looks at the front cover of the Mexican edition of *Playboy* (December 2008), featuring a suggestive Virgin Mary. Photograph, 2008. Photographer unknown. Image courtesy of Getty Images. All rights reserved.

Heightening the air of pseudoreligiosity, the flesh-and-blood mannequin was positioned with a colored window just behind her left shoulder. The lancet signified church and religion. The substance may also have recalled medieval iconography. In common symbolism, the conception of Jesus by parthenogenesis resembled the penetration of lumens through unruptured panes. Stained glass allows translucence: rather than being reflected, light pierces—but it does so without causing fragmentation.

Just below the level of a partially unconcealed breast ran Spanish words translatable as both "[we adore you, Mary](#)" and "we love you, Maria." A quick theological aside: in Catholicism, Mary may receive veneration or devotion but not adoration or worship. Inside the periodical, a spread of eight photos employed to provocative effect such accompaniments from the cult of the Virgin as white veils, blue mantles, flowers, and crowns. Everything about the cover conveyed a calculated effort to affront by presenting this supposititious Mary all but full frontal.

The decision to publish in December was an added calendrical irritant. The month is chockablock with Marianism everywhere where Catholicism is found but nowhere more than in Mexico. For all the foregoing reasons, the issue triggered immediate and intense protest. What to do? The front shot and centerfold feature pages were too extensively offensive for expurgation. Instead, the whole run was pulled from newsstands. Even after its removal from the kiosks, the hue and cry among devout Catholics continued, leading to such grumbling headlines as "Playboy's Not So Virgin Mary."

The jongleur has a reputation for being pure, simple, and childlike. The last quality, owing to the very definition of child, would extend to being asexual or presexual. Like the proverbial red flag before a bull, these very associations have incited some later authors to mutiny by mentioning the star of the miracle in overstatedly sexual contexts. Fifteen years before Metzger drew his parallel between oral sex performed by a female sex worker on a male client and the devout juggling done by the jongleur for the Virgin, René Étiemble lambasted André Malraux's *Encyclopedia* for its superficial and self-absorbed mix of sham exoticism, pseudoheroism, and sexual excitement. In doing so, the French comparatist likened the encyclopedist to the protagonist of *Our Lady's Tumbler*:

> Until this juggling of proper nouns, I admit to imagining a pathetic version of the *Jongleur de Notre-Dame*—the second transformation of a man who, disappointed by the gods of many revolutions, has come out of it by making himself the pious juggler of simultaneously Notre Dame and the Buddha of Nara [in Japan], the Lady of Elche [an ancient stone bust in this city in Spain] and the Devout Christ of Perpignan [a carved crucifix in this southern French city]: tossing into the air heaps of names, he succeeds marvelously in catching them without too much breakage, although he has made them collide in the air for a coitus interruptus that makes a pretence of overcoming fate.

The old entanglement of the Middle Ages with orientalism, eroticism, and primitivism has died an awfully slow-paced death.

A third, later example of an analogy that sexualizes Our Lady's Tumbler (or that pinpoints a sexuality latent in it?) would be in a book published in 1991 about Djuna Barnes, a poet, novelist, and journalist of early American modernism. In one essay, a literary critic stakes the claim that in the acclaimed 1936 avant-garde novel *Nightwood*

> Barnes privileges the penis. But she celebrates the nonphallic penis, the limp member of the transvestite Dr. [Matthew-Mighty-Grain-of-Salt-Dante-] O'Connor—who masturbates in church like the Jongleur of Notre Dame doing tricks for the Virgin Mary. …

Doughboys in World War I dubbed "Our Lady of the Limp" the shell-shocked effigy that sagged at less than half-staff atop Notre-Dame de Brebières. They had no premonition what kind of legs (if that is even the right limb) their five-word witticism would have three quarters of a century later, when a lesbian socialist feminist intellectual would liken the juggler's devotion before the Madonna to misfired onanism. Service to the Virgin becomes sexual self-service. In neither this academic prose nor the preceding paradigm does the original work, the film, or the novel allude explicitly or even implicitly to the story of the juggler. Both similes are formulated by exegetes altogether independently of the content of the creations they make a pretense of elucidating. They impose the performer upon the movie and the book, just as they foist carnality upon the juggler.

A 1994 artwork entitled *Jongleur de Notre Dame*, by a French-born American who went by the name of Arman, also sexualizes the entertainer (see Fig. 4.9). The designer dubbed this kind of fabrication transculpture, on the model of the term *transsexual*. In such sculpting, the artist crosses compositional and generic boundaries, just as individuals who undertake sex reassignment surgery do in sex and gender. In these works, he joined classical statuary with found objects, everyday items that are not recognized for their artistic potential because they customarily fulfill a nonartistic function. In this sculptural composition, the sculptor sliced a replica of an antique bronze statue, with gold and gray patina (now weathered to a bright green), to form out of its *membra disiecta* the juggler. In so doing, Arman perhaps held unwittingly true to the frequent medieval practice of spoliation: he took conventions from antiquity and reshaped them to achieve a revolutionary reuse.

The eight orbs juggled by the male figure double as lighting fixtures welded to his body. In the medieval tale and its modern adaptations, a carving comes to life. In this sculpture, Arman takes a different approach so as to freeze motion in unmoving mineral matter. He transmutes into light the kinetic energy of the juggler and his balls. But even more is going on. The lamp is simultaneously a lampoon; the bulbs, burlesques. Viewers cannot help but observe the bottommost globe, which is mounted right where the glans of his engorged male member would be expected. The shank projecting from his pelvis that the glass fitting rounds off is larger than those for all the other spheres, apart from the main one that transects the juggler's whole torso. The projection makes the construction resemble the type of ancient Roman statue known as a herm, a squared stone pillar topped with a head and often adorned also with an erection midway down the block. In this case, the rod for the wiring to illuminate one electric light was one of the creator's tools. The stiff shaft protrudes ithyphallically from the title character's groin, more out of deliberate whimsy than structural necessity. This clever placement obviates the need to cover the man's genitalia, but it is anything but a stock sculptural fig leaf. The device also casts the spotlight (very really) upon the well-endowed organ it removes. The protrusion, with its well-hung and nonlimp lampshade, evokes the tumid bulge of a phallus. The entertainer, as the sculptor represents him, was first effectively castrated and then, before the eunuchism became irreversible, shorn of his scrotal

Fig. 4.9 Arman, *Jongleur de Notre Dame*, 1994. Cast bronze statue with brass and glass light fixtures, 231 × 90 × 82 cm. New York, Arman Studio. Photograph by Francois Fernandez. Image courtesy of Arman Studio, New York. All rights reserved.

sack but outfitted with a prosthetic penis of the most awe-inspiring dimensions: no call for any Freudian envy here. As we see him, he holds himself erect, frozen forever in a paroxysm of untreatable priapism. Despite needing to be turned on by a switch, he is in other ways perpetually aroused.

The desire to upset prudes by playing upon prurience may be categorized among the phenomena captured by the French phrase *épater la bourgeoisie*. In plainer English, the objective of such objectification is to scandalize the bourgeoisie or middle class. A demonstration of fin-de-siècle decadence, this impulse can lead to many ends. The same ambition to prize shock value from a story and character perceived to be staid and traditional can go in various directions. Sex is not the only one; other bodily functions and products can become equally involved.

Fig. 4.10 Chris Ofili, *The Holy Virgin Mary*, 1996. Mixed media. Image courtesy of Chris Ofili. All rights reserved.

The painter Chris Ofili, British-born of Nigerian parents, kindled a public outcry for a few years in the late 1990s with a piece of art entitled *The Holy Virgin Mary* (see Fig. 4.10). The assemblage, created in 1996, includes a lacquered sphere of elephant dung on the canvas, while the whole rests on two more balls of the same scat. Furthermore, the depiction of the Virgin is swarmed by collaged images of naked female derrières and crotches clipped from pornographic magazines, resembling the angels that often encircle the mother of Jesus in more conventional artworks. Like Gustav Klimt's *Woman in Gold*, this painting nods toward Byzantine and medieval representations of Mary. The composition is also a Black Madonna, in this case an African Virgin that neighbors on the parodic in its physiognomy and endomorphic body type. Like many medieval Madonnas and Byzantine Panagias, this Mother of God faces out and stares directly at the viewer.

Ofili has explained the depiction as transposing paradoxical elements in Christianity into the terms of modern mass culture. He was exposed to conventional features of Marianism as a youth, raised in the Catholic Church. If we follow this line of argument, the sexuality is not imposed by the artist today. Rather, it highlights what is present but unrealized already in medieval icons and paintings. A glancing connection with our story comes into sight in a scholarly article that describes the inclusion of a pachyderm's droppings in the canvas as "an ironic symbol of Ofili's African heritage (as if he had been staging himself as a kind of postcolonial hip-hop 'Jongleur de Notre Dame')." The writer reaches for a correlative that will distill the painter's relationship to the Virgin Mary he has depicted. Through the seeming incongruity, the researcher also aims to match at least a little the potential of the construction itself to provoke disgust.

Is our tale's condition to be deemed to be terminal when its narrative and message can be rendered as superficially simple as the jongleur became after the mid-twentieth century? The sexualizing of the narrative, both heterogeneous and erogenous, looks like the flares from a dying star, except that the cosmology of human art and creation defies the usual fiats of astrophysics. What does it augur, that the key pair of figures in the story can be reduced to shorthand symbols of sexual and even pornographic act? For the asexual account of the jongleur of Notre Dame to have been sexualized with the world's largest penile implant and even to have been caricatured may betoken vivacity. At the same time, it may form an inevitable counterweight to the po-faced solemnity with which the miracle has been treated by some of the preachier authors who have invoked it. In literature familiarity leads to special manifestations of contempt. An axiom of literary theory could be concocted: once a tale has become trite, it will be coopted in one direction for children's literature and in the opposite for parodic reformulation in adult media. The fate of a classic is to be treated as plastic, to be spun out and shortened, stretched and stunted, solemnified and satirized, but never set aside and disregarded. The juggler, holding his arms akimbo and tapping his toes, awaits his Chris Ofili.

Jung's Jongleur

> Q: Who's the toughest guy in the circus?
> A: The juggler, of course: he's got the most balls.

The founding father of psychoanalysis could have made much from the opportunities supplied by the "transculpture." For obvious reasons of chronological impossibility, Sigmund Freud never had the chance to put on a well-upholstered sofa for talk therapy any of the sculptures, films, photos, or texts we have been dissecting. Indeed, he gave no sign of having known the tale in any of its forms, or at least did not take the trouble to mention it if he did. But even without recourse to the grand master himself, Freudian readings could be constructed. In fact, a 1915 tractate by John Cowper Powys (see Fig. 4.11) draws to a close with a highly pertinent peroration on the essence of poetry. In it, the jongleur stands for any and every human being who yearns for a lover forsaken. The final pair of sentences in his essay presents the inmost desire of the heart as a shrine, in front of which the poetic soul dances stark naked:

> Not one human heart but has its hidden shrine before which the professional ministrants are fain to hold their peace. But even there, under the veiled Figure itself, some poor poetic 'Jongleur de Notre Dame' is permitted to drop his monk's robe, and dance the dance that makes time and space nothing!

Fig. 4.11 John Cowper Powys. Photograph, ca. 1930. Photographer unknown, https://commons.wikimedia.org/wiki/File:John_cowper_powys.jpg

The scene summoned up calls to mind King David's wild dance, as D. H. Lawrence transmogrified it. In Powys's interpretation, the official practitioners of religion, learning, or anything else can furnish no help in such instances. Individuals must depend upon their poetic spirits if they wish to cope through art with frustrations too secret to acknowledge outright.

To move from the covert to the overt, a thinker who showed an easy acquaintance with the story was Carl Gustav Jung (see Fig. 4.12). His abstract idea of the soul emphasizes what he termed the process of individuation: the integration of opposites within the individual, among which the conscious and the unconscious are an important match. The great thinker advocated for the existence of a collective unconscious that all human beings share. In Jungian psychology, archaic images that he called archetypes derive from this common pool.

Fig. 4.12 Front row, left to right: Sigmund Freud, G. Stanley Hall, and Carl Gustav Jung; back row, left to right: Abraham A. Brill, Ernest Jones, and Sándor Ferenczi. Photograph, September 1909, at Clark University, Worcester, MA. Photographer unknown, https://commons.wikimedia.org/wiki/File:Hall_Freud_Jung_in_front_of_Clark_1909.jpg

Jung's theories arose from his correspondingly excursive interests in religion, literature, and art, among other things. From them, he would have had ample motive for being riveted by the tale of *Our Lady's Tumbler*. His conception of the unconscious mind rested heavily upon a syzygy—a pairing of two connected but opposite qualities. He differentiated between a feminine inner personality within the male, called *anima*, and a masculine inner personality within the female, called *animus*. The psychologist regarded the first in this coupling as having four separate levels. The progression began with the biblical Eve, woman in a purely biological sense, as a mother to be fertilized. The next stage led to Helen of Troy, a muse associated with artistry. In turn, she yielded to the Virgin, who spiritualizes eros. Lastly, Sophia embodied an undiluted, transreligious all-knowingness. In this framework, Jung named Mary after the one in Christian theology. He paid phenomenal attention to the Virgin, going so far as the label the Church's official edict, at the end of 1950, of her bodily and spiritual assumption into heaven "the most important religious event since the Reformation."

In the 1950s, the narrative of *Our Lady's Tumbler* attracted no small share of attention in German-speaking Switzerland. This Alpine mini-boom stands out as imbalanced in contrast to what Germany produced during the same decade. Four instances will suffice. First, we have seen already that for Christmas of 1955 the Swiss graphic designer Fritz Bühler dealt out copies of his hand-painted little juggler book as gifts among confidants and colleagues in Basel. A second example is Josef Elias (see Fig. 4.13), who in 1958 printed his detailed script, with sketches and photographs (see Fig. 4.14), for a school production of *The Dancer of Our Dear Lady: A Play for the Stage, Based on an Old Legend*. Third comes Rudolf Moser, a Swiss music professor and composer who at some point before his death composed a work on the same theme. Finally, in 1964, Wilhelm Preetorius published in Zurich his calligraphed version with his own illustrations. The fact that he took the same title for his effort as Elias did is suggestive— but what were Preetorius's specific inspirations? To pan back further, another issue thrusts itself forward. Did these four individuals chance to learn of the story and to be enthralled by it independently? Was there a shared conduit, a buzz caused by school reading, radio listening, or opera going? Or was the cultural macroclimate for other reasons especially hospitable to miracle tales of the Virgin Mary?

Fig. 4.13 Front cover of Josef Elias, *Der Tänzer unserer lieben Frau: Ein altes Legendenspiel für die Bühne* (Belp, Switzerland: Volksverlag Elgg, 1958).

Fig. 4.14 The jongleur, in full motley with dunce cap, before the Madonna. Josef Elias, *Der Tänzer unserer lieben Frau: Ein altes Legendenspiel für die Bühne* (Belp, Switzerland: Volksverlag Elgg, 1958), 23.

The question about the reticulation and distribution of influence becomes even more tantalizing when as noted and transformative a person as C. G. Jung enters the scene. His reference to the *Le jongleur de Notre Dame* surfaces in a letter to a female therapist in London. The document is a masterful performance of effective concision. The renowned psychologist has been sent unsolicited paintings by the English analyst. In replying to her, he responds to the interrogative she directed at him: "For whom did I paint these pictures?" His goal is to shift the interpretive task back on her, and to return her personal portfolio to her.

As we have seen, Anatole France and Jules Massenet treated the medieval exemplum with an ironic compassion that would have left an opening for both believers and unbelievers among their readers or listeners to construe the account to their satisfaction. Although the Madonna plays an essential though silent role, the author and composer of the fin-de-siècle versions presented the events in such a way that they could later be desacralized or at least secularized. In the process, the focus came to rest ever more firmly and fixedly on the jongleur or tumbler, particularly as an image of the individual artist.

Jung may have encountered such an interpretation of the story in a literary rewriting of it. Then again, he may have arrived at his analysis all on his own. He was a lifelong, professional explicator of people and peoples as well as of works by both individuals and collectivities. As such, he would have been well positioned to peruse an already existent decoding of the miracle, or to proffer one himself. The twists and turns that he contributed make the tale's dynamics relevant to his disciplinary theories. In his reading, the action of the narrative is functionally solipsistic. Both the jongleur and the Virgin to whom he devotes his energies are beings who create art for their own selves. While laying hold of the entertainer as an exemplum, the Swiss scholar displays his own deftness in both rhetoric and etiquette as he graciously declines to retain artwork he does not want either to keep or to analyze. Mailing back the packet of images, he states that they must remain with the person who produced them, since "they represent the drawing together of the two worlds of spirit and body or ego and self." Touché.

More than a half century later, the letter provides a verbal portrait of a busy and brainy man who brings into service a clever allusion and employs it as a means of acknowledging receipt, extending spiritual guidance, and concurrently parrying or at least holding back. Through the simple story and its central figure, all these ends are made gentler and more resonant than a bald "return to sender" with an accompanying manicule would have been. He takes for granted that the protagonist will be immediately understandable to a professional and peer in Britain, just as within his milieu in Switzerland. At that moment, the juggler still had not budged from the cultural lexicon with which well-educated Westerners were assumed to be conversant. But culture undergoes constant renegotiation, and a few decades after Jung, *Our Lady's Tumbler* ceased to be an essential term in the horse-trading. The jongleur, while not a deal-breaker, was no longer a deal-maker.

5. Positively Medieval: The Once and Future Juggler

> It is a sad old age that loses all its memories. If it were true, as some have said, that St. Thomas was a child and Descartes a man, we, for our part, must be very near decrepitude. Let us rather hope that truth in its eternal youth shall keep our minds always young and fresh, full of hope for the future and of force to enter there.
>
> —Etienne Gilson

The Juggler's Prospects

> It's tough to make predictions, especially about the future.
>
> —Yogi Berra

This biography of a once-touted story has turned out to be, no typo and pardon the groaner, a jugglernaut. Yet despite the length and girth of this study, much more remains for future sleuths and bloodhounds-to-be to scrutinize. Loose threads could be sewn up—or, to put it more cheerfully, allow for pioneering new beginnings. More whys and wherefores could be analyzed and slotted into the great crossword and across-tale puzzle. Thanks to the ongoing digitization of archives and ever more detailed metadata for items being sold on the web, additional particulars come online daily. With further investigations by others, the chronicle that outlines the reception of the medieval tale might be dragged out unendingly.

What lies in store for *Our Lady's Tumbler* in years ahead? The relative unfamiliarity of this exemplum from the Middle Ages today makes its earlier successes in the late nineteenth and twentieth centuries even more impressive and surprising. Authors die in time, but literature is not subject to the bylaws of mortality and impermanence. Rather than being unique artifacts that can be destroyed at one fell swoop, tales retain a life force. They have a potential longevity beyond that of any human teller or writer. None other than F. Scott Fitzgerald averred that there are no second acts in American lives—but this ground rule may not pertain to narratives. Old ones die hard. To kill off a story requires total annihilation. For one to be declared dead by the coroners of literary history, all documentation relating to it must be extirpated. To go further, all memories of it must be expunged from the minds of living readers, listeners, and viewers—and making people unread, unhear, and unsee a tale is not easy. When it comes to fiction, character assassination does not happen at the snap of a finger.

When a tale possesses the richness of implications that this one has, the universe of wormholes into its meanings knows no limits. This account may be small change, a low-denomination coin in the transfer of cultural capital from one time and place to another around the globe. Yet in its best iterations, this miracle achieves exactly what the most sublime of human creations are supposed to do: it quickens emotions and prompts thoughts of the transcendent. Behind it, the humanities sweep in, to inspire and inform readings of those immediate reactions. The coexistence of many possible interpretations is a fact of life and language. Likewise, this heterogeneity constitutes a reality and part of the charm of literature and art. The infinitude of texts in verse and prose, unmoving and moving images, read aloud or acted out, explains why we might speak of our species as *homo interpretans*.

With its truly storied past and its propensity for provoking many significations, will the account in *Our Lady's Tumbler* and *The Juggler of Notre Dame* live on in broader culture? Will either or both versions be encountered in general reading, popular entertainment, school assignments, church sermons, or all the above? Notwithstanding a feebly elegiac note in the epigraph that put this conclusion in motion, I remain sanguine that the narrative will not merely scrape by but even thrive. Good guys come last, but the romance of stories often turns out otherwise. The medieval poem and its multifarious heirs may have appeared moribund, but they have always been, in their humble ways, revivified. As the world turns, the worm will turn.

The important thing is for enough of the past to be kept living. To take up, reject, adapt, or do all three at once, the here and now must comprehend a minimum of what has prefaced it. Bygone languages, lore, and art together form the taproot that nourishes the present. Bad luck will befall us if we chop or uproot it without getting to the bottom of what we do. For their mutual well-being, the past and present must converse constantly, and their dialogue contributes immeasurably to the differences between bestsellers—whether stacked in brick-and-mortar bookstores, stocked in libraries, or retailed digitally—and classics. The back-and-forth enables literary traditions to burgeon, in which authors and texts infuse each other.

More expansively than the tale, the Middle Ages themselves do more than merely subsist. Indirectly, they often stay very much alive in residues from the Arthurian legend. More directly, they survive in such twentieth-century authors, now canonical and even hoary, as C. S. Lewis, J. R. R. Tolkien, and Umberto Eco; and in fantasy role-playing games such as *Dungeons & Dragons*, action-adventure video games such as *Assassin's Creed*, and series for cable and television such as *Game of Thrones*. Such entertainments have accustomed us to hybrids of the medieval and postmodern:

without blenching, we accept unthinkingly and unblinkingly the hyperbolically in-your-face anachronism of the self-contradictory phrase "medieval video game."

In many settings, the architecture of the imagined Middle Ages surrounds us. The Gothic revival that was in the good old days so central in European, American, and British Commonwealth countries tailed off to an end a century ago. Yet before passing from sight, it insinuated itself into many cityscapes. Consequently, to this day neo-Gothic belongs to the palette of architecture and decorative arts to which everyone is exposed sooner or later on both sides of the Atlantic. The style rings the horizons of the flaneur who prowls urban streets, promenades by old buildings, patronizes art museums, or even just samples literature widely. In Europe, the original or revival cathedral, closely followed by the town hall of the same type, signals that a city is a city and in fact that it is European. In the United States, the same building style is especially salient in universities and churches. We have seen that the manner is by no means limited to these two kinds of construction, but dailies will plant pointed arches in the background of an illustration to inform their readers that the topic of an article is college or religion.

For all the times we lay eyes upon Gothic, do most of us ever stop to sniff out what stands before our noses? How often do we smell the roses—or in this case, the windows shaped like the flowers? Even less do we ponder the pros and cons, aesthetic or symbolic, of either the authentic medieval form or its multitudinous modern revivals. In a 1957 essay, Roland Barthes drew a parallel between the automobiles of his day and the Gothic cathedrals of the Middle Ages. Ten years later, he juxtaposed the modern and the medieval even more famously in "The Death of the Author." In French, the title of the disquisition just mentioned plays upon that of a fifteenth-century English text. *Le Morte d'Arthur*, written by Sir Thomas Malory, means "The Death of Arthur." Imagine that: the literary theorist and professional problematizer rolled in medieval literature to be his heavy artillery—catapults and trebuchets—as an opening gambit to terminate authors and replace them with texts, while doing away with literature and bringing in discourse.

Let us dawdle to soak up the intellectual intoxication of the City of Light in the mid-twentieth century. In the meanwhile, we can about-face from textuality to technology. In comparing motor vehicles with ecclesiastic architecture, Barthes referred to the Citroën DS. This model was manufactured from 1955 to 1975. Reversing our expectations, the French theoretician construes the medieval cathedral as a consumer object and the late twentieth-century car as effectively a magical carpet. His hypothesis that the auto is enchantment rests (and capitalizes) on its witty name. In French, the letters DS are enunciated the same as the word for "goddess" (*déesse*): the two are homophones. The essayist explains the pun in the second paragraph, and he brings it home again in the final sentence of the short essay.

In 1988, a tongue-in-cheek spoof of an automotive advertisement in a major German newspaper quoted the first statement in Barthes's observation as its caption (see Fig. 5.1). Below stood a cutaway drawing of a Citroën DS, with lines to identify features and potentials. "Eternal light" radiates from the headlights. (The make of car is wrong, but we have here a clear case of *Fiat lux*.) The dashboard enjoins the reader to "put up a Saint Christopher medal here." The back seat offers ample "seating for a middle-sized church choir." The fuel tank, by metonymy for gas consumption, is "modest as a churchmouse." "Incense-like exhaust" spews from the tail pipe. The ad finds affinities between automobiles and great churches that medievalize technology, but for parody rather than, as had been the case only a little more than a half century earlier, comfort.

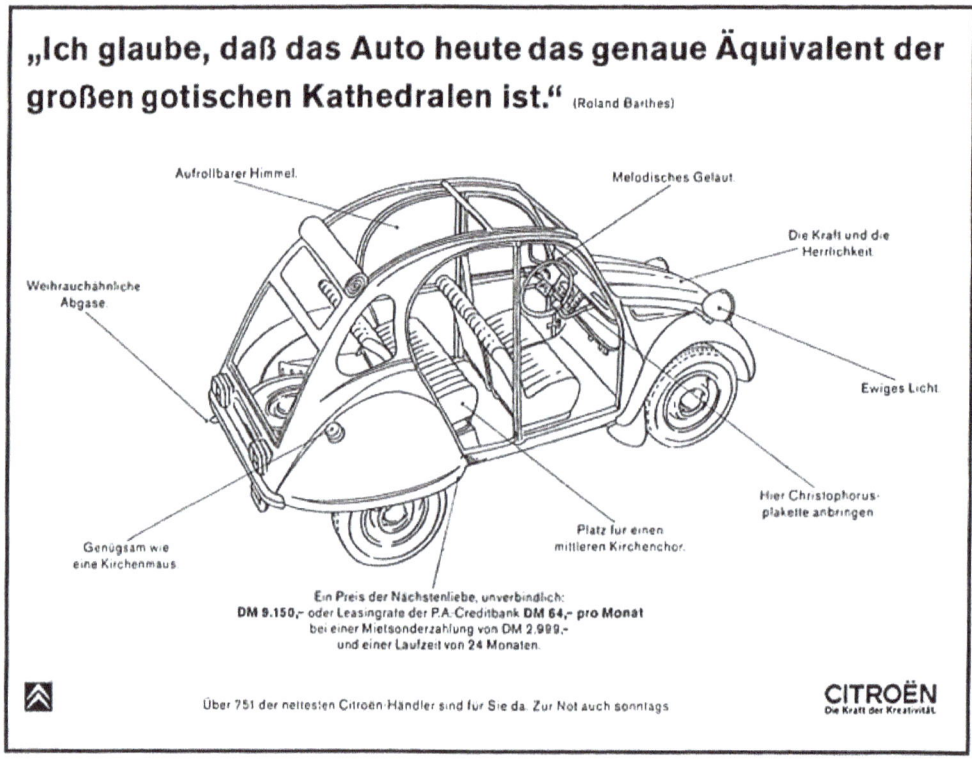

Fig. 5.1 Advertisement from 1988 for the Citroën DS, featuring a quotation from Roland Barthes that compares automobiles and cathedrals.

Closely related commonplaces from eight hundred years earlier have been solidified in two phrases, "transfer of empire" and "transfer of learning." In a widespread view, medieval people inherited from antiquity both a scepter of dominion (political and military) and a lamp of culture (philosophical and artistic) that had resided first among Greeks of Athens and later among Romans of the Eternal City. In the early decades of the twentieth century, Americans achieved a commensurate transference or appropriation of their own, by arrogating the European Middle Ages to themselves.

Individuals of incomparable wealth in the United States siphoned the material culture of ye olde days from Europe by buying up and bringing home art objects and architectural elements. These one-in-a-million millionaires also raised a trail-blazing Middle Ages of their own making in three dimensions, by taking in an altogether fresh direction the sham ruins that had been constituents of medievalism in the romantic era. In consecutive Gothic revivals, they built imagined medieval structures throughout not only Europe but even more the New World and beyond. These buildings were anything but ruins. Rather than shyly sham, they presented themselves as self-confidently medievalesque. Yet they stopped short of claiming to be authentically medieval. The architecture came arm in arm or arch in arch with literature, as the readers and writers of this much later period translated the earlier epoch to suit their own cultural environments. This is the nature of historicism.

To take the example that has propelled this multivolume book, they made modern versions of medieval literary texts. The process was moving, both literally and figuratively. Among many other consequences, the transference across time and space redounded to the legacy of closeness between Europe and the United States that had persevered for a few hundred years. Does it make sense for America to disinherit itself and recoil now from appreciation of either of these pasts, the Middle Ages or the nineteenth and twentieth century? Does opening up to new stimuli presuppose swiveling away from previous ones? Are the arts and history a pie that never grows larger?

Medievalism has been construed as a colossal, cathedral- or college-sized failure. It has been critiqued as a gremlin that instigated a breakdown or stasis in culture, a phantasm that turned out to be ill-founded, or at best that evaporated into nothingness. The Gothic revival itself has been presented in this same light, as a backward-looking flight from modernity into a fanciful past that was not suited to meet the ultimatums of the present—and even less those of the future. But is that reverse teleology not a caricature and mischaracterization? In 1831, John Stuart Mill described, not specifically Gothic revivalists, but more generally "those men who carry their eyes in the back of their heads and can see no other portion of the destined track of humanity but that which it has already traveled." Was the revival retro in so hideously Dantesque a physiognomic fashion? Did it in fact fall apocalyptically flat? Is the only brand of traditionalism stodgily and even asphyxiatingly self-justifying? Is a penchant for studying and savoring aspects of the bygone inherently reactionary? If you have done no more than skim even one of these six volumes this far, you can guess my retorts. Label me a pugilistic Pugin, call me a Cram redux (or prolix). Flip open my billfold and find a thin oblong wafer of granite: the contents of the wallet prove me to be a card-carrying Gothophile, out to redevelop a story and revive a revival—but that does not mean being out to make Gothic great again, or to make a vain and ugly effort to reinstate culture, society, and demographics as they were constituted a century or a millennium ago.

Reaching a negative verdict on the architecture at least is not entirely fair. Few structures are erected today in strict classical style, as was frequent in the nineteenth century, but the absence of Corinthian columns from present-day buildings is not taken as a rejection or failure of classicism. Old Gothic edifices remain around us on all sides. In many American cities, apartment buildings in the manner survive aplenty uptown. Skyscrapers with all the appurtenances of the style can still be spotted in major municipalities, even if overtopped by sleeker, more modernist successors. The architectural topography of the United States is stippled with collegiate Gothic, both towers and otherwise. We fare all the better for the variety. Why should contemporary cultural diversity be good, but not its chronological equivalent—past cultures?

How many who grind away inside colleges in Britain with Gothic architecture, or in North America with collegiate towers of similar sort, treasure their years of undergraduate education as being distinct, and in positive ways, from the rest of their lives? If students in growing older nurture such fondness, it happens in part because the spaces they inhabited while in residence are marked apart as being quaintly separate. Is that detachment a prime cause for regret? Should it be? It would be foolhardy to root like a cheerleader at a pep rally for a return to any recreation of the Middle Ages, any more than to plead for the no-win effort of dialing back the clock to any slice of the medieval period itself. That endeavor would be especially hard once we arrived at the portion of the era when such timepieces did not exist. Yet I hope to have advocated at least implicitly for the pleasure and even the utility of looking back across the centuries to the best of what was expressed in far earlier literature and art. Many watches should not be rewound, but human machines need to unwind or wind down, and one way of decelerating is to travel back hundreds of years.

Sure, rumination on days of yore may be melancholic or even burdensome. By the same token, it may also be a source of buoyancy. Those bygone times may be both explicated and enjoyed. Gestures may be made to precedents, and honors may be accorded to them, without being unfaithful to the present. The title of Tom Wolfe's novel, mined and refined posthumously from an unpublished manuscript for publication in 1940, proclaims *You Can't Go Home Again*. While many memories are not as enriching as the experiences when lived, it holds equally true that others oxidate to become even better: changing coloration need not be chastised as discoloration. Likewise, there is indeed no going back—but we can fumble forward to a new back. In fact, I see no meaningful progress for human culture that does not come with cognizance of the past. Relegating to the dustbin of history everything that transpired before us is not an option. Old-fashioned need not be outmoded and should not be considered a pejorative, but an alternative. It is something that we can hold, after we have understood it. That is often more than we can say about the new-fangled. (How many of us have even the most indistinct inkling of what "fangled" means?) Like many other reactions and pleasures, nostalgia may be used occasionally or abused habitually. In some religions, it may be classed as a virtue or a vice.

Gothic revivals fell out of vogue in the Me generation, but now we are deep into the meme generation of millennials. Time and tide wait for no man (or woman, or any other human gender category now existent). The pendulum of tastes swings without respite, both inside and outside the timeless but time-filled cases of grandfather clocks. Could a refreshed and revitalized revival go viral? It would not need to be as a style that could or should predominate as it did for much of the nineteenth century. Yet at least it could have a resurgence as one among various choices on the stylistic palette at the disposition of artists to recombine and for others simply to revel in. The medieval, Gothic, and the juggler will all return, though we cannot reckon on the specifics. They are all deathless. Nothing will fail to live except the conceit that any of them will die: perish the thought!

Could or should we re-Gothicize, by reclaiming the style from the mascaraed Goths in fishnet stockings? Can Gothic go from shibboleth to a buzzword once again? Can medieval be something good, rather than the almost exclusive negative that it seems to have become? Or are architecture and literature in this vein doomed to decompose in forgottenness? Are they extraneous to global audiences that know and show no need for the fine points of European history or the parsing of past Western literature? My comeback would be that we are all entitled to self-select, and that one choice is to relish the old differently from the new. The expressions "old favorites" and "golden oldies" hold continued traction for good reason. We have the prerogative of constructing our memory palaces in whatever modality we choose, and a cathedral may serve very well, thank you. Quarried stone may be 24-karat gold.

For obvious reasons, culture must be culture-bound—but being bound need not be the same as enchainment or enslavement. Historicist revivals, such as Gothic ones, by their very nature relate to renewal and recreation. They are spells of cultural energy that eventuate in reprises of literature and architecture, of stories and buildings, among many other things. The duplicates succeed all the better when they do not exactly replicate their models. The recreated forms belong to the constant pulsation between the poles of tradition and innovation, or conservatism and progressivism, that is essential to the common weal of societies, cultures, and civilizations. In the beginning, Gothic carried bad associations, but those were converted at least some of the time into positives. People hungered for order and innocence. Far worse appetites have existed. If at a given point individuals stopped wanting or putting credence in such principles and qualities, the blame is not to be pinned on the Middle Ages. Medievalism did not miscarry. To risk being anachronistic (and when is any movement by this name ever not so, at least to a degree?), it was too big to go wrong and fail. But nonetheless it has been tagged a failure.

Like a pointillist painting on a continent-wide canvas, the United States remains dotted here and there with pretty neo-Gothic buildings. A surprising number of places even preserve bits and pieces of authentic architectural elements in the original manner. In the Northeast and mid-Atlantic, we can point to the collegiate Gothic of universities such as Yale, Princeton, and Duke, and Gothic revival churches such as Saint John the Divine and Washington National Cathedral. However easy it may be to grumble about such phenomena, the design style of that phase, flanked by Edenic landscapes laid out by designers such as Beatrix Farrand, is unchangeably associated with campuses throughout the United States. It ties them to the colleges of Oxford and Cambridge. Much of the fabric has become threadbare and frayed in both architecture and landscape architecture, although not so much as in broader culture. As institutions of higher learning have sought to shoehorn buildings where they were not meant to be wedged, they have flouted the presiding notions that formerly governed the delicate interdependencies among buildings, lawns, gardens, groves, orchards, paths, roads, and other spaces. Others can make up their minds whether universities have also renounced the spirit and separateness that the architecture of the buildings and land were intended, or at least pretended, to achieve. For the time being, the not-undisputed dream of the ivory tower has fallen flat, if it was not conceded to be an illusion from the get-go. Right now, the image has become to many a pejorative—an object of aspersion for its pie-in-the-sky elitism. Yet not everything in the conception of universities in the early twentieth century deserves to be jettisoned irrevocably. In fact, the elusive reverie of an aerie atop a turret has often gone hand in hand with the American dream, if such a wraith can be imagined as having a body and walking. For this reason, if not for many others, the precipitous decline in stature of the ivory tower should prompt reflection (see Fig. 5.2). The steeplechase has undergone a miserable cutback: we suffer collectively from turret syndrome.

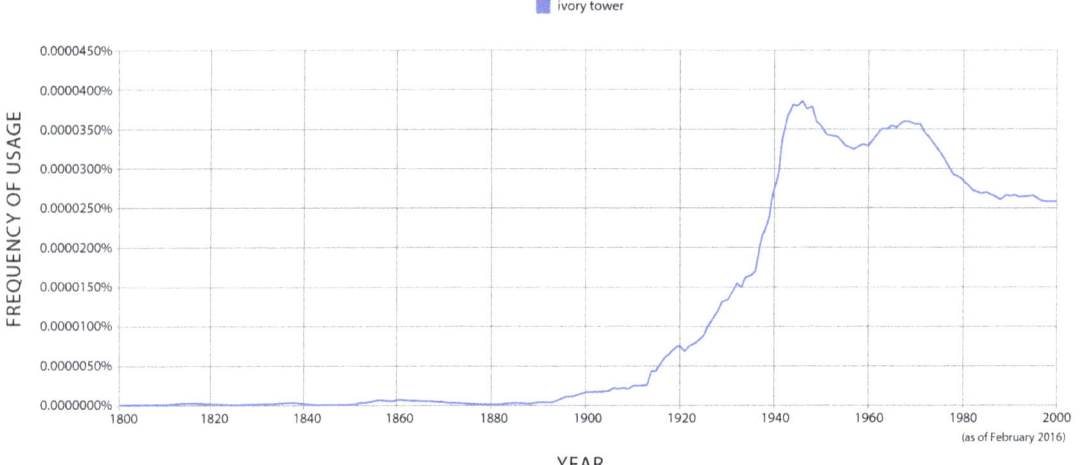

Fig. 5.2 Google Ngram data for "ivory tower." Vector art by Melissa Tandysh, 2016. Image courtesy of Melissa Tandysh. All rights reserved.

The ivory tower in its Gothic iteration is schizophrenic. It is shut off, if nothing else because it often forms part of a quadrangle, like a cloister. At the same moment, it lies open and exposed. It draws the viewer into a movement that is inherently elevating and can be transcendently illuminating. Because of its style, the tower instantiates contact with a heritage of intellectual camaraderie and exploration that stretches deep back into an earlier millennium. It offers centuries of soulfulness as an antiserum to the dispiriting toxins of the present.

And the juggler? Sure, he has suffered habitat loss. The environmental damage has come not in a shortfall of Gothic buildings but in a spiritual change in surrounding society. Like an ivory tower, our entertainer has his feet planted firmly on the ground but his head in the clouds. His spiritualism could play today, unless his religiosity disqualifies him from the running. In days of victim-chic, the tumbler of the original story shows potential. He arises from an underclass of physical laborers—peons. If he belongs to a caste, it comprises untouchables. In his sexuality, he defies quick classification. We have no information by which to subsume him as heterosexual, gay, bisexual, transgender, questioning, or asexual. Yet to judge by his later fate, especially once the opera by Massenet took off, he could be and has been filed under most of those headings—so long as that spirit of his does not go missing in the process, since it defines him. At least sometimes, the unexamined pieties of the past have been repudiated and replaced by the identity politics of today. In due course, our own perspectives and preoccupations may be recognized also to have been flawed and fragmentary: in the fullness of time, we too will prove to be dated. The juggler's way urges us to boost within ourselves humility and humor. Such habits will make us as acutely aware of our own failings as we are censorious of our predecessors' or contemporaries'. Others may decide for themselves if knowledge is power; whatever conclusion they draw, self-knowledge is good.

Gropius vs. the Gothic Ivory Tower

> Neither medievalism nor colonialism can express the life of the twentieth-century man.
>
> —Walter Gropius

Modernist vivisections of the ivory tower bear scrutiny. One of the most incessant assailants was Walter Gropius. Especially in his guise as director of the School of Architecture at Harvard University, this mouthpiece of the "New Bauhaus school" when transported to the United States sought the opportunity to shape "young people before they have surrendered to the conformity of the industrial community or withdrawn into ivory towers." He constructed a bridge between the delicatessen European avant-garde and homegrown American architecture. In an address in Chicago, he expressed his wish for the artist, including the architect, to be reintroduced into the collectivity: "From his ivory tower he will move closer to the latest laboratory and to the factory; he will become a legitimate brother of the scientist, the engineer, and the business man." Gropius saw the university as facing three choices: to partake in the real world by applying art to achieve socially progressive goals, to yield to the compliance required by industry, or to retreat into the ivory tower world. Without hesitating, he opted for the first. Even in the late 1960s the same professor stood ready to declare: "The ivory tower man is out. The artist needs to swing."

The German-born architect had not always made a straw man of the ivory tower man. In the beginning, he did not buck at the ideal of reviving or transforming Gothic. On the contrary, in a 1919 speech he espoused his commitment to making his contemporary reality the "best time of Gothic." In that very year the painter Lyonel Feininger carved a woodcut of a great church to adorn the manifesto for Bauhaus—and to solemnize Gropius's conception of the "future cathedral" as an avatar of modernity (see Fig. 5.3). Later, the architect reacted differently to the structure and spirit of the style as it was appropriated for collegiate settings in North America. He became anti-historicist and even anti-history.

Among acolytes, the German architect went by the affectionate nickname "Grope." When modernist constructions fell under siege by traditionalist Harvard graduates, these faithful followers picked up his language and metaphor to defend the embattled new buildings against those who villainized them. Parroting their past master, they too made the ivory tower a whipping boy. One wrote:

> Must we take the word of our older alumni that an ivory tower is the only true architecture? An ivory tower, to be sure, is a beautiful thing—ivory costs even more than marble. And a tower certainly is functional—it protects us from the sight of all the grubby creatures below. But Harvard, as she has on recent occasions reminded the world, prides herself, not on her ivory tower, but rather on her "free marketplace of ideas."

Sad to say, such reduction of thoughts to commodities paved the way toward the corporatized university of today, in which the onetime ivory tower sometimes melts away to the most ill-defined of memories. Is it so very inexedient for a society to have some members who, helped by the thrust of steeples, have their heads in the clouds? Doesn't the world need dreamers alongside pragmatists, pure scientists along engineers? It takes all kinds to make a world.

Universities are entrepôts for the refinement, assembly, quality-testing, storage, and transshipment of knowledge, culture, and values from one generation and one society to another. The Olympian detachment and independence required for many stages of the process have fallen out of vogue. Instead, institutions of higher learning now aim to incubate among undergraduates the kind of innovation that happens in the corporate workshops of software designers. At the same time, universities seek to commoditize learning and to profit from retailing the results. Finally, they have taken upon themselves responsibility for solving the teething problems of the world. Giving back in outreach and exhibitions is one thing, but how good a job are academic institutions doing as self-appointed saviors in areas where government and philanthropy have been the traditional actors? Is the world in better shape? Are

Fig. 5.3 Lyonel Feininger, *Die Kathedrale*, cover design for the Bauhaus manifesto, 1919. Woodcut, 30.5 × 19 cm.

they more appreciated for their efforts? Can they pick up the slack without losing their essence?

In the meantime, corporations have requisitioned for their own purposes the term *campus*, which until comparatively recently belonged without question to educational institutions. The noun first cropped up at Princeton, when it was still the College of New Jersey, in the eighteenth century. Others must determine whether it was meant to denote cultivated plots in an agrarian sense, the countryside, military training grounds, or a combination of the three. In soldierly use, think *Campus Martius* and remember that the campus of the private university has a cannon holstered muzzle-downward in it—a mode of open carry that makes no one feel endangered.

If phrases were stocks that could be traded on Wall Street, the up-and-coming blue chip to buy these days would be "corporate campus" (see Fig. 5.4). By comparison, the future growth of "college campus" (see Fig. 5.5) and "university campus" (see Fig. 5.6) does not promise to be robust. Put in the sell order—but, come to think of it, the vending has been under way for a long time already. Indeed, the fact that academic campuses must be explicitly marked as such is by itself a sign that the corporate ones have tugged *campus* away from the exclusive purview of institutions of higher learning.

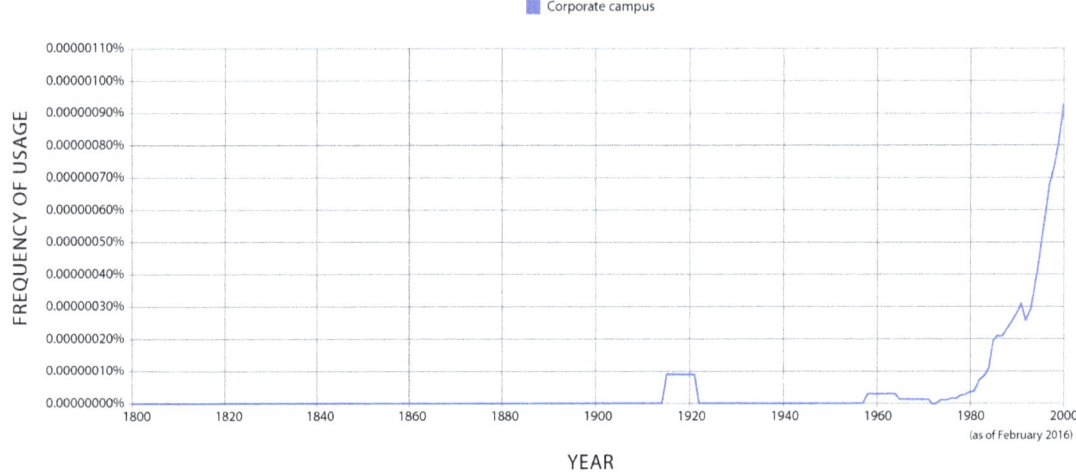

Fig. 5.4 Google Ngram data for "corporate campus." Vector art by Melissa Tandysh, 2016. Image courtesy of Melissa Tandysh. All rights reserved.

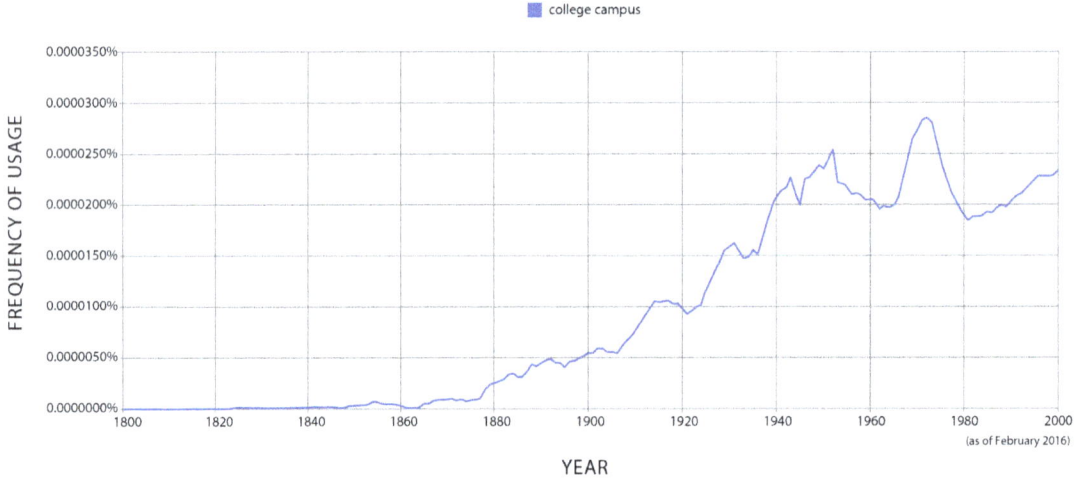

Fig. 5.5 Google Ngram data for "college campus." Vector art by Melissa Tandysh, 2016. Image courtesy of Melissa Tandysh. All rights reserved.

The fiery oratory of Gropius's groupies did a disservice. They knew full well that no tower was ever built one hundred percent of ivory, but they pounced upon the image with all the might they could muster. What has abided in some design schools is the legacy of their master's argumentative ahistoricism, which led him initially to oppose even highly successful courses on the history of architecture. He made a concerted effort to delegitimize historicism. Why not live and let live?

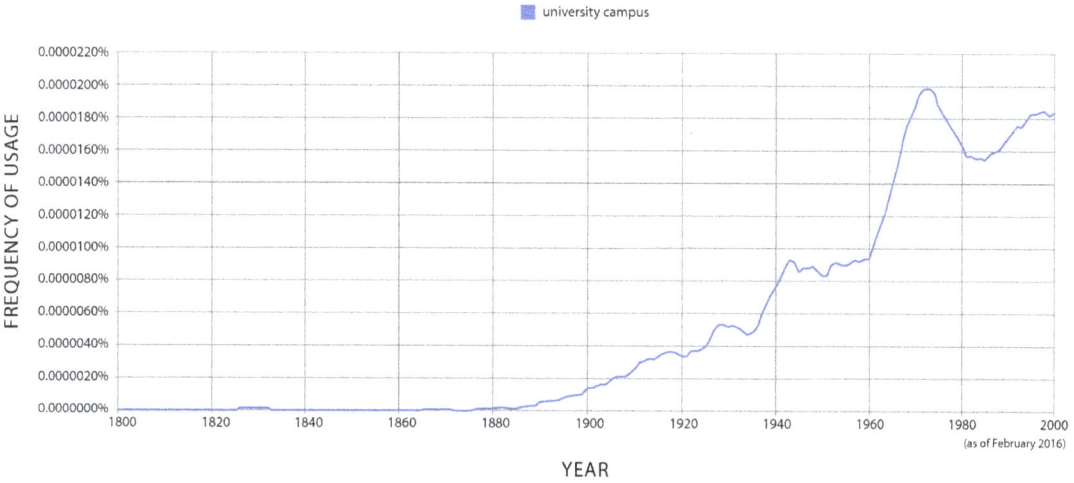

Fig. 5.6 Google Ngram data for "university campus." Vector art by Melissa Tandysh, 2016. Image courtesy of Melissa Tandysh. All rights reserved.

To transition from theory to practice, the edifices Gropius himself dreamed up (since even modern men who swing have their daydreams) have not all stood up well to time. The inhabitants and users of what he and his adherents erected could best compute the success of the so-called Gropius complex, on behalf of which its chief proponent polemicized explicitly against collegiate Gothic. The erstwhile Harkness Commons and the Graduate Center at Harvard have their deserved nostalgists, as most any style could and should (even brutalism has its aficionados), but where are the postcards? If the buildings suffered destruction, would they be rebuilt painstakingly at immense expense out of nostalgia decades later, as the Gothic revival tower of Memorial Hall was reconstructed in 1999 after having burnt down in 1956? A search in collectibles that focuses on Harkness Commons nets thin results in comparison with the other construction. To all appearances, not too many people have wanted to revive or share the sight of the first, whereas multitudes have been sweet on the second.

In the United States, the Gothic revival does not really merit the prefix re-. Precious few monuments in the original style existed, and those that did were such belated manifestations of the architecture as to stretch the limits of the word "original." The advent was effectively an arrival. The manner, particularly in the collegiate vein, was an innovation that brought with it resonances of many virtues, such as faith, peace, strength, order, placidity, learning, creativity, devotion, munificence, and more. Paradoxically, in America universities as institutions have become wedded to conglomerates and government far more closely than they were when the pelf of robber barons poured into their cashboxes, and when a head of higher learning was not disqualified de facto from becoming commander in chief of the nation.

Just as individual artists do, so periods create their own antecedents, changing both themselves and those very models in the process. In the mid-twentieth century, the whole medieval era could have seemed paradigmatic. Take by way of illustration an issue of *Life* magazine from 1947, where a photographic essay on "The Middle Ages" presented as one of eight headings "The Cult of Mary," adding "the virgin mother was a symbol of love, and heroine of legends like 'The Juggler.'" In the immediate aftermath of the Second World War, whether rightly or wrongly, these long-ago centuries were regarded yearnfully. Through sheer strength of conviction, the period held out a stability to be regained by a world that had fallen apart. Remember Le Corbusier's reflection in *When the Cathedrals Were White*: "Middle Ages? That is where we are today: the world to be put in order, to be put in order on piles of debris, as was done once before on the debris of antiquity, when the cathedrals were white." The interpretative corollary to this perspective remained current into the 1960s, when an anthologist presenting Anatole France's adaptation saw the earliest attestation of the jongleur story as a testimony to "the intense and simple faith of the Middle Ages."

The medieval tale of the juggler or its close modern French relatives commanded canonical status for at least a half century, particularly in France, England, and the United States. In one revelatory development in America, the miracle was included in a 1956 volume that eventually evolved into the long-lived and big-selling *Norton Anthology of World Masterpieces*. Yet the selection was not to retain its privileged niche forever. By the turn of the century, it had been expelled from the compendium. Could the sunniness and simplicity of the story have made it a foreign body that had to be dislodged?

The heavy commercialization of *Our Lady's Tumbler* and its descendants in the mid-twentieth century seems to have rendered the narrative too well known. In fact, its ubiquitousness in the 1950s may have contributed to its first causing disaffection, or at best a reaction of "ho-hum" or "same old, same old." Later it became virtually quarantined in children's publications and religious literature. Nowadays, unlike fifty years or more ago, few adults appear to have encountered either the account from the thirteenth century or any of its reformulations since the late nineteenth century. Those who do know the story have become familiar with it through books for young readers, the titles of which often camouflage the juggler or jongleur and even more frequently the Virgin Mary.

The Tumbler's Tumble

Individuals matter. In the trajectory of the tumbler, a few specific ones stand out for their contributions. The unknown medieval poet should be lauded as the first. Next we have Gaston Paris, charismatic communicator. Third in line would be Anatole France, urbane ironist. After him, Jules Massenet, glossy music maker, made an intense but short-lived mark. Mary Garden deserves as much credit as any modern for product development and marketing. Yet for even great women and men to work their magic, the surrounding context has to be sympathetic and receptive. Blechman's and Auden's minor masterworks have been sand castles in the face of a storm surge that has eroded the former salience of the Middle Ages and such tales as this one. Why the washout?

Not all Nobel prize winners withstand the onrush of time. That said, Anatole France lost ground or altitude with dizzying rapidity. His name recognition has dropped precipitously and perpendicularly (see Fig. 5.7). Among the musically inclined, Jules Massenet's reputation has suffered a devaluation as vertiginous as Anatole France's (see Fig. 5.8). Outside the inner circle of opera aficionados, the three-act "miracle" from 1902 rates as little more than a men-only oddity. *Le jongleur de Notre Dame* retained just enough cultural traction late into the twentieth century that in 1981 the avant-gardist Laurie Anderson would not only dedicate her song "O Superman" to Massenet, but even slip into it lyrics that parody an aria from the opera. When the musical drama of the early twentieth-century composer has been revived, it has been greeted with good-humored favor by connoisseurs, but for all that, each revival has the look of an atypical and temporary occurrence.

In American culture, Henry Adams remains a name to conjure with, but far more as a figure of biographical interest, and to a slighter extent as a US historian, than as a medievalist. Tellingly, the chapter of his *Mont Saint Michel and Chartres* that leads the reader learnedly from Gautier de Coinci, and what Gaston Paris made of him, all the way to *Our Lady's Tumbler* was spotlighted as a case study in Paul Haines's *Problems in Prose*. From 1938 through 1963, this volume delivered yeoman's service to students taking college courses in English composition. By its final printing, the tale had suffered a pratfall in its ranking and lost its charm. In a fit of housecleaning, the editor went so far as to excise this extract with no comment beyond the perfunctory "several of the less rewarding essays have been dropped." Speak no ill of the dead.

For fifty years or so in the mid-twentieth century, both Adams's *Education* and his *Mont Saint Michel and Chartres* were treated, perhaps bizarrely, as literature. Now their time in the public eye clicked past its expiration date. At the same instant, *Our Lady's Tumbler* fell from grace. The thumbnail exemplum boasts a theme that could enthuse equally the religious and the hedonistic: joy. Yet this version has never made much headway in achieving recognition. In contrast, the French poem from a few decades earlier in the thirteenth century has a pronounced penitential element—not a strong selling point in a world unsold on penance. Whatever the reasons, the tale's glory years had deteriorated into an early development of grunge by the 1960s. Yet from its fame of over a century, echoes from the medieval story and its adaptation by Anatole France reverberate that are still perceivable even today. The narrative entitled "Anonymous, 'The Tumbler of Our Lady'" is incorporated in a 2008 compendium on *The Joy of Reading*.

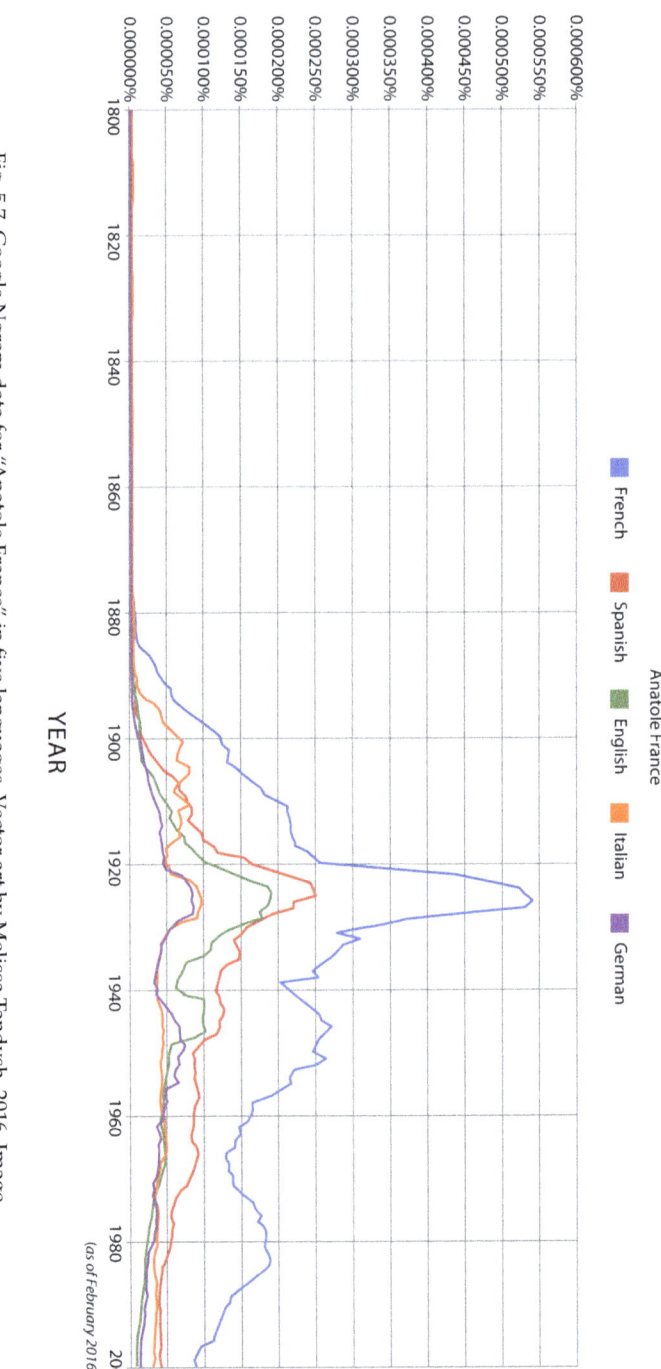

Fig. 5.7 Google Ngram data for "Anatole France" in five languages. Vector art by Melissa Tandysh, 2016. Image courtesy of Melissa Tandysh. All rights reserved.

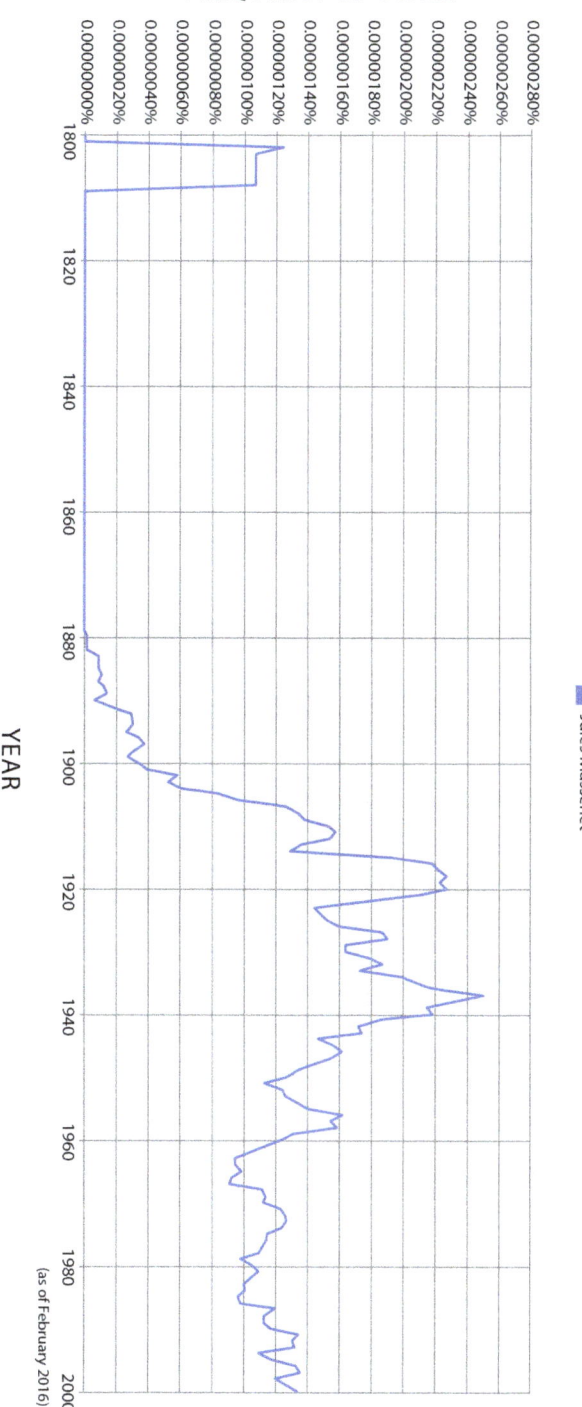

Fig. 5.8 Google Ngram data for "Jules Massenet" in English. Vector art by Melissa Tandysh, 2016. Image courtesy of Melissa Tandysh. All rights reserved.

The only genre to which narratives of short length lend themselves easily is the children's book. A familiar pattern takes shape: literature for young audiences, along with religious instruction, is the venue where the medieval miracle is likeliest to thrive right now. The tale has sometimes been shaped for youths with the lesson that even if a person's size and skills are average at best, what counts is to put forth one's best effort in the proper spirit. The story of the tumbler has been expounded as emphasizing above all the signal that under the right circumstances, individuals with uneventful lives and without incredible talents can outdo those who possess "special professional or social status." God, or at least not mere mortals and human beings, decrees which devotees have a right to recognition. The account gives people courage, even or particularly those who perceive themselves as having middling ability or less. Take Julie Harris (see Fig. 5.9). The American stage personality first acted the juggler when she was fourteen, in her school's Christmas play in the late 1930s. Eventually highly successful on screen, she loved the fiction and found that it perked her up first when she most doubted her own abilities.

Fig. 5.9 Julie Harris. Photograph by ABC Television, 1973, https://commons.wikimedia.org/wiki/File:Julie_Harris_1973.JPG

What was the original floor show like, as described in *Our Lady's Tumbler*? To be forthright, we do not know ourselves how properly or poorly the jongleur executed it. The compassion of the Virgin may have been prompted by his stamina and sincerity rather than by his virtuosity. Furthermore, her gesture of ventilation may well have been meant as much to telegraph a communiqué to his fault-finding fellow Cistercians as to provide calmative care to the jongleur himself. Now and again artists who have conceded that their talents have severe limits and their performances serious flaws have taken solace in the story and have pledged themselves to it. The tale has given hope to the mediocre.

Then again, the responsibility for the neglect of *Our Lady's Tumbler* and *The Juggler of Notre-Dame* may lie with its potential audience. Already in 1951, a

Hungarian-American comparatist subsumed the narrative among other gems of poetry and prose that belonged to what he called "world literature." At the time, that final term pertained first and foremost to texts that were regarded then as chefs-d'oeuvre of the European canon. Dashes of Russian and American could be injected for extra tang. So the mid-twentieth-century professor ranked *Our Lady's Tumbler* alongside Dante's *Divine Comedy*, Cervantes's *Don Quixote*, Shakespeare's *Hamlet*, François Rabelais's *Gargantua and Pantagruel*, Swift's *Gulliver's Travels*, Molière's *Tartuffe*, Goethe's *Faust*, Dostoevsky's *Crime and Punishment*, and Melville's *Moby Dick*. If these masterpieces were deemed worthy of being appreciated all over the earth, anyplace outside the Western world qualified as extraterrestrial. Despite the high standing this champion of global literature accorded to the story of the tumbler, he saw arts and letters in his day as having been at least partially commercialized, and some of its potential readers as succumbing to "the reluctance or incapacity of searching for a deeper meaning in the printed word." He is lucky not to be measuring the quality of reading today. Furthermore, he presented the jongleur in our miracle as distinct from the other heroes in his must-read list. Despite weighing in unwafflingly about Dante, Don Quixote, and Hamlet, he discoursed with more distance about "a medieval *conte dévot* such as *The Tumbler of Our Lady*." In the process, he made the tale seem special, while concomitantly generic.

The English translations in the second half of the twentieth century contributed nothing to making the medieval story accessible to a broader readership. On the contrary, they helped to corroborate the impression that it was rarefied—that its rightful place was to be stowed in the icy-cold vaults of scholarship rather than nestled in the fond hands of general readers. In none of these forms could the versions be expected to reach a wide audience. The greatest hope for the narrative's propagation across social classes and throughout the world lies in the spate of retellings that has gushed forth in poetry, prose, drama, musicals, music, opera, and other genres. Thanks to the infiniteness of human imagination, not even the shortest among all the rewritings I have encountered has not added an unheard of wrinkle or two to the corrugations already there, often without any apparent intent to innovate.

The authors of children's picture books and religious manuals have demonstrated an affection for reworking the tale. Such adaptations have carried the narrative, like a Gospel on a humble scale, to all four points of the compass and all five continents. In Russia, the juggler's story was recounted in a short verse narrative by the poet Galina Gordeeva in 2006. The title can be translated as "The Juggler of the Mother of God," the words by which both the short story and the opera have been known in the Russian language. No doubt other twentieth-century versions also exist in the Slavic world. The medieval poem from the thirteenth century may have had resonance among Slavs because of interest in "fools of God." During the Soviet era, the tumbler's lay status and the "moral of the story" that showed him prevailing over the church hierarchy could have been appealing. Additionally, Anatole France was a revered author, whose writings carried special weight because he had been a bulwark for the

Bolshevik cause in the early years of the Soviet Union. Among communist literati, he may have been the foremost French author. His *Little Box of Mother-of-Pearl* was put into Russian repeatedly, with spikes in the first decade of the 1920s, and in the 1950s: "Rarely is a work of prose translated into a foreign language so many times and under such different circumstances." Of the fictions contained in this jewel box of narratives, the tale of the juggler was one of the two most well-liked: it was rendered at least sixteen times into Russian.

The movement of the story may not have been universal, but it was transglobal. Owing to the prestige of French in Japanese culture in the early 1900s, Anatole France became well known there already during his heyday, and all his novels were put into the language at that time. But his version of the jongleur attracted no special notice. Through children's and religious literature, the miracle has permeated East and Southeast Asia. In the Philippines Catholicism dotes on the Virgin Mary, and local dance traditions may involve saints. Korea too has a sizable Christian population, around half of which is Catholic. The children's books that have lugged the lead character to such eastern countries have been mostly illustrated ones in translation that originated in European countries or the United States.

In the Southern Hemisphere the account has so far put down nothing but a footprint upon beach sand. In Chile, a transient Spanish exile pieced together the text for a children's book, while a native of his land who has remained Chilean for the balance of her life embellished it. Two decades later, a composer born in the same South American country flew home for performances of a ballet that he composed in the United States. In Brazilian fiction, an author recapitulated the account en passant in a fiction. In cultures interlaced with the original Gothic and its revivals in Britain through the Empire, many more examples are likely to be discoverable. In South Africa, a ballet was danced long before the dissolution of apartheid. Australia, home to much Gothic, has literary and musical treatments of the tale in various genres.

Michel Zink Reminds France

> The age of chivalry is gone. That of sophisters, economists, and calculators has succeeded; and the glory of Europe is extinguished forever.
>
> —Edmund Burke, *Reflections on the Revolution in France* (1790)

Edmund Burke, stalwart proponent of the beautiful and the sublime and latter-day exponent of knightly nobility and the Middle Ages, commented thus as he reflected upon the sequelae of the French Revolution. Has history repeated itself? By extension, should we arrange the exequies for the juggler and pronounce a funeral oration over this charismatic character, who took France by storm not even a hundred years after

Fig. 5.10 Michel Zink, secrétaire perpétuel de l'Académie des inscriptions et belles-lettres, an *immortel* of the Académie française. Photographer: Brigitte Eymann. Copyright Académie des Inscriptions et Belles-Lettres, Paris. All rights reserved.

the Irish statesman scratched his quill across paper, but who may now be cascading (or tumbling) from his one-time popularity? An optimistic diagnosis would be that the miracle, in spite of and because of its brevity, has an elasticity that may stop it from ever completely expiring, however moribund the humdrumness of most versions retailed in the mid-twentieth-century cultural market may have left it. Chivalric days may be long gone, but the lay brother has not breathed his last.

The elementarity of the story is one of its captivating qualities. The narrative can be readapted effortlessly from the tiniest concentration of words that a person has read. It resembles a bouillon cube that can be reconstituted into broth. Such regeneration was the plan for the exemplum in the Middle Ages: that was the whole idea behind the genre. The same sort of reconstruction recurred centuries later, when Anatole France composed his short story after happening upon a fleeting recapitulation by Gaston Paris. Exceedingly few elements are required to regrow, in ever-shifting ways, the quintessential contours of the tale—and mutations, deliberate or accidental, are not inevitably for the worse. The haziest remembrance of hearing or seeing a performance in the past may lead to a new and even better presentation.

For much of its history in the twentieth and now twenty-first centuries, the story has evinced a knack for being constantly recreated by scholars and artists. Many recreators have set great store by the unmerited fantasy that they have been doing something epoch-making by reshaping the tale, and they have found creative satisfaction in their creation (which has been unwitting recreation). In effect, the narrative has derived authority from its seeming venerability. Along the way, it has afforded the illusion of being a once-in-a-lifetime discovery to many who have bumped into it and chosen to retell or illustrate it.

Early in the twenty-first century, the legend may enjoy its healthiest reception in two places. One is France. Contrary to the proverbial wisdom that a prophet is not appreciated in his own country, the jongleur has held his own in his native land. If so, his obstinate continuance there owes to Michel Zink. As both a highly respected scholar of medieval French literature and a well-known writer of modern French fiction, this dual-threat man of letters (see Fig. 5.10) has perpetuated the best of what Romance philology incarnated in the late nineteenth and early twentieth centuries. Gaston Paris would be very contented. As it happens, the nineteenth- and twentieth-century Frenchmen share major credentials. Like his predecessor of more than a century ago, Zink holds the seat for the literatures of medieval France at the Collège de France; co-owns responsibility for the journal of Romance philology, *Romania*; and has demonstrated a can-do keenness to traverse not only the lofty byways of erudition but so too the more busily traveled highways of pop culture.

The littérateur has touched upon the French original from the Middle Ages in several of his own monographs. Outside his scholarship, in 1999 (see Fig. 5.11), he gave broad currency to thirty-five medieval pious tales that contend with preoccupations of Christian faith, by overhauling them in soignée but accessible French prose. As the eighth among these hagiographic narratives and miracles of the Virgin, he presented "Le jongleur de Notre Dame." He commenced the four printed sides of text with the well-worn fairy-tale exordium: "Once upon a time." The phrase features as the stock opening for all the fictions in the collection. The children's story author Violet Moore Higgins employed this same rhetorical technique in the corresponding English in her 1917 book.

The present-day French belletrist stringently simplifies the story. In his portrayal, the jongleur takes the shortcut of dancing just one time, not repeatedly. He does his act for the infant Jesus, not for the Virgin. The narrative reaches its meridian when the statue of Mary leans down and uses her veil, with motherly love, to wipe the sweat-sodden brow of the dancer when he has sat down out of exhaustion. The narrative thrift finds its stylistic match. The author himself describes the style as being simple, in imitation of medieval tales themselves, to give "an impression of unaffected limpidity and of unreserved adherence to the tale and its lesson." Of course, the person who wrote the story has at least some license to give it window dressing, here through a

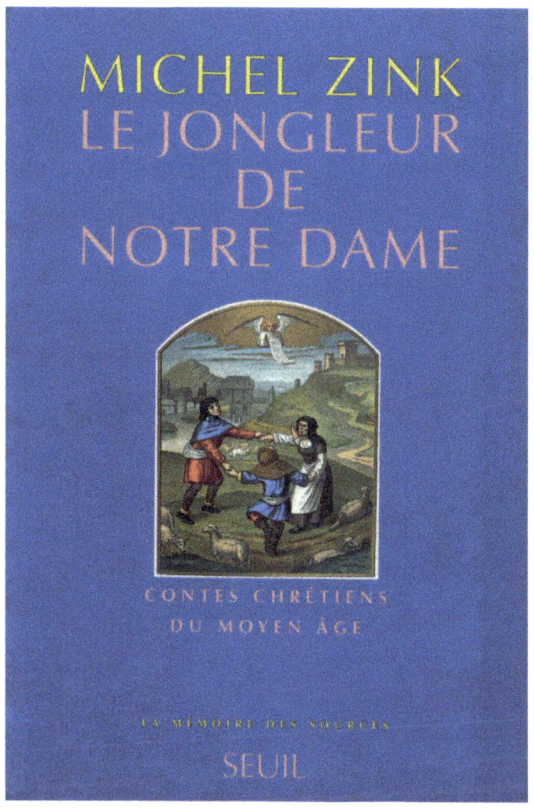

Fig. 5.11 Front cover of Michel Zink, *Le jongleur de Notre Dame: Contes chrétiens du Moyen Âge* (Paris: Seuil, 1999). Image courtesy of Seuil. All rights reserved.

tumbler-like humility. He also declares: "*The Jongleur of Notre Dame* is not the best of my tales. It is strongly didactic." Others might beg to differ.

The professional philologist and the public popularizer meet when Zink intercalates into his retelling, in modern French translation, a long quotation from Saint Bernard. The invocation of the *doctor mellifluus* has its scholarly backdrop in Zink's broad view of the relationship between poetry and conversion in the Middle Ages. One chapter of his book-length study on the topic, in 2003, dealt with the conception of the "jongleur of God," which he traced from the biblical David down to Saint Bernard. He explored the seemingly irreconcilable range of reputations attached to the figure of the jongleur during the medieval period. In discussing *Our Lady's Tumbler*, he coordinates it with the tale "Fool" in the *Life of the Fathers*. In both narratives, the onlookers fail to recognize or appreciate the wisdom of a seemingly silly person, and instead are misled by his ostensible folly into disapproving his performance.

In recapitulating the account of the jongleur, Zink owed an unmistakable debt to Anatole France, to whom he has resorted on many other occasions, without making a secret of his dependence. Beyond the Nobel laureate, the reteller placed himself squarely in a French academic tradition—a sidebranch of philology—that Joseph Bédier (see Fig. 5.12) had plotted out and laid down in modernizations of Old French romances published in the late nineteenth and early twentieth centuries. At Bédier's behest the Tharauds had gathered Marian miracles—narratives in which the Virgin interposes herself in human affairs. The connection between the philologist and the brothers went beyond the mere casual, since Jérôme Tharaud when elected to the French Academy in 1938 assumed the chair that had belonged to Bédier. His brother Jean also became an Academician, as a member of the academy is called, in 1946.

Fig. 5.12 Joseph Bédier. Photographer unknown, 1920s, https://commons.wikimedia.org/wiki/File:Joseph_Bedier.jpg

Zink's endeavor to perpetuate *Le jongleur de Notre Dame* before a larger audience by highlighting it as the title story met with mixed success. In 2002, fourteen of the thirty-five tales in his 1999 collection were reprinted under the reduced and de-Christianized name Tales of the Middle Ages. This time the narratives were brought out, with illustrations, in a series destined for readers (or listeners?) six years and older, whereas earlier as far as one can judge they had been pitched at adults. Unaccountably, the miracle of the jongleur was omitted. Outside France, the transmission of this volume may owe something to caprice. The book has been translated into Spanish, Czech, and Italian, though not yet into English or German.

2002 was a banner year for *Le jongleur de Notre Dame* in French. Fifty years after its first appearance, R. O. Blechman's *Juggler of Our Lady* was released in France for a young readership under the imprint Gallimard Jeunesse. Was it, like Zink's tale, being implicitly made infantile or at least juvenilized? Contradictorily, this edition of the critics' favorite from 1952 purveys by way of appendix a "bio-graphic" dossier to convey the spectrum of its author's work—a gallery that would be appreciated much more by adults than juveniles.

We All Need the Middle Ages

> I would not like to live in a world without cathedrals. I need the luster of their windows, their cool stillness, their imperious silence. I need the deluge of the organ and the sacred devotion of praying people. I need the holiness of words, the grandeur of great poetry.
>
> —Pascal Mercier, *Night Train to Lisbon*

> Whether we like it or not, there is no "pure" medieval; there is only medievalism.

If commercialism must be dueled in the market, the juggler may be overdue a new advertising campaign to publicize his aptitudes and appeals. Massenet may have done the right thing by puffing the liqueur Bénédictine. By taking on that promotion, he helped to keep before the public not only himself but also his Jean. Furthermore, the jongleur himself bears no small resemblance to such an after-dinner restorative, since he proffers a pleasure that everyone should experience at least once but not necessarily indulge incessantly.

A taxing trick for authors, and not just of literature but of scholarship too, will be to keep the story in the foreground of the here and now while also not violating the medievalness that belongs to its inmost fiber. It may afford a degree of consolation and even a fount of inspiration to recognize the long view. The present sort of study helps to make evident that mediating between the medieval past and the modern present has for many scores of years been complex and difficult but rewarding. This tunneling should also remind us that the texts of yore require a brain trust, such as philologists, literary historians, critics, and historians, who can discover, reconstitute, and interpret them. Those gurus, mostly in the groves of academe, rely for their education and employment upon the support of the societies and cultures that encircle them. In return, they have an obligation to repay the favor by bringing forth whatever in history and story can enlighten, entertain, and electrify all the audiences they can reach. To be relevant, nonfiction and fiction do not have to be determinative. They contribute more than enough by merely increasing the stock of wisdom and beauty upon which we may draw. We require all the reenchantment we can get.

From the millennium or so that constitutes the Middle Ages derives a large part, even the lion's share, of what civilization remains even today in Europe and North America. Consequently, we will fail to fathom ourselves as we are if we shy away from looking back at our earlier selves. Not to take part in cultural retrospection (and it need not all be rosy) is nearsightedness that coincides with narrow-mindedness. For a culture not to know the past out of which it has grown is chrono-narcissism. Like all manifestations of exaggerated self-love, it lays down a minefield that is dangerous not only for the narcissist but also for the innocent bystanders.

When change occurs at a rapid clip, the past can serve not only as a distraction or a safe haven, but also as an orientation point. More than just the Middle Ages, we should take stock of later images of the period, which we often encounter even before we brush against its own realities. To have the measure of that long-ago era, we have to tackle not only those centuries themselves, but also the recent ones that have most informed our own presuppositions about it. We must come to terms with the revivals and reenactments we tag as medievalisms, as well as with the medieval itself.

This book has not taken us on a clandestine or quixotic quest to reimpose a pastel-painted past. First, such a retrograde endeavor would be unprofitable: there is no going back. An adage counsels "Go with the times, or with time you will go." In a larger sense, reinstituting the Middle Ages would be unwarranted, since they never disappeared. A surprise is how much that was felt to be (and sometimes was indeed) European and medieval took deep root across the Atlantic from Europe itself. The remains of these implantings—what I have christened the American Middle Ages—should prompt us at least now and again to reflect on the medieval period itself in all its exuberant and extravagant heterogeneity. The thousand years of this epoch remain so well bedded that its survivals are anything but deadwood. They live on. In doing so, they evolve. We should reflect also on how the last few centuries have pruned those original times to suit their needs, desires, and prejudices, and how the histories, presents, and futures of old and new worlds have been grafted together.

For a decade, I have luxuriated intermittently in immersing myself in the origins and reception of this story. The glee has made me perceive how I fell in love long ago not just, and not just directly, with the Middle Ages. Rather, I became enamored also through, and with, layers of medievalism that have laminated the medieval period. As when watching a statue mature through exposure to oxygen, we behold these coatings not as defacements but as enhancements. Our liking for the immutable radiance of gold, and our distaste for the darkening disfigurement of tarnish on silver, should not impede us from esteeming the process by which the natural red of copper patinates into verdigris.

In the last words of *Mont Saint Michel and Chartres*, Henry Adams left his readers with cold comfort. He maintained that the early twentieth century had forgone unity for multiplicity, faith in the Virgin for the technology of dynamos. The onetime historian arrived at his disaffection fair and square. For all his endless talents and achievements, he never latched onto a calling that would measure up to the presidential past of his storied family. A New England patrician, he forsook his native region and birthright for Washington. An intellectual of the first order, he turned his back on a professorship at the most highly rated American university of his day, biding his time for a form of recognition that would and could never come, a summons to become the sage laureate of the nation, éminence grise of chief executives in the US, or doyen of an as-yet uninvented profession—official public intellectual. He craved success by penning novels that he kept steadfastly anonymous, and he sought romance with an unattainable, or at least in his case unattained, younger married woman.

In 1919 Cram, the architect and Goth par excellence, had Adams's book reprinted for distribution to a much larger readership than it had reached in two infinitesimal private releases. He retailed collegiate Gothic architecture as a palliative for modernity, and he raised stout stone monasteries to house the future elite of America's military at West Point, and the crème de la crème of its leading families at other educational institutions throughout the country. None of this construction could hold off the Depression, ward off a Second World War, or keep tranquil any of the hornet's nests that lay ahead to be stirred. The Middle Ages could not repair all the drawbacks that Adams and Cram detected in their world and in themselves. More than one iteration of the Gothic revival took as its founding principle the urgency of contesting mind-numbing and heart-chilling technology. Out of the same necessity, we might consider administering ourselves a dram of Gothicism—but new and improved.

The Simplicity of Atonement

The fate of the story about the jongleur changes from year too year, from place to place, and from artist to artist. The tale acts as a litmus test that affords insight into the state of the cultures in which it has been received. The analytic holds valid less for the nature and degree of nostalgia in any given time and place than for cultural openness to a humble hero. An earlier chapter of this book contained a graph to present the drop in the relative frequency of the words *devout, faith, faithful, humble, humility, modesty,* and *simplicity* (see Fig. 5.13). All of these adjectives and nouns belong to the word cloud that cloaks the juggler, like a Greco-Roman god.

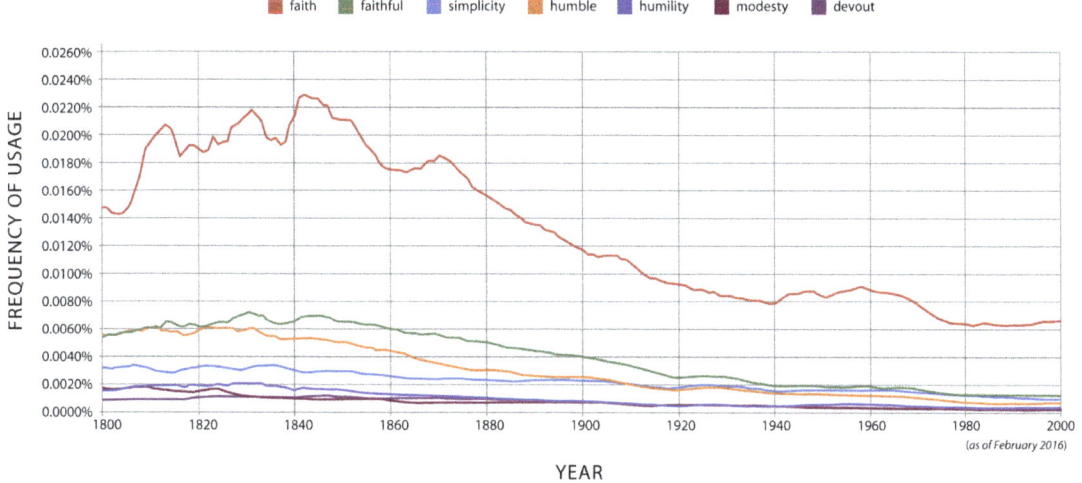

Fig. 5.13 Google Ngram data for qualities once thought to be characteristic of medieval people, showing a steady decline in frequency since 1850. Vector art by Melissa Tandysh, 2016. Image courtesy of Melissa Tandysh. All rights reserved.

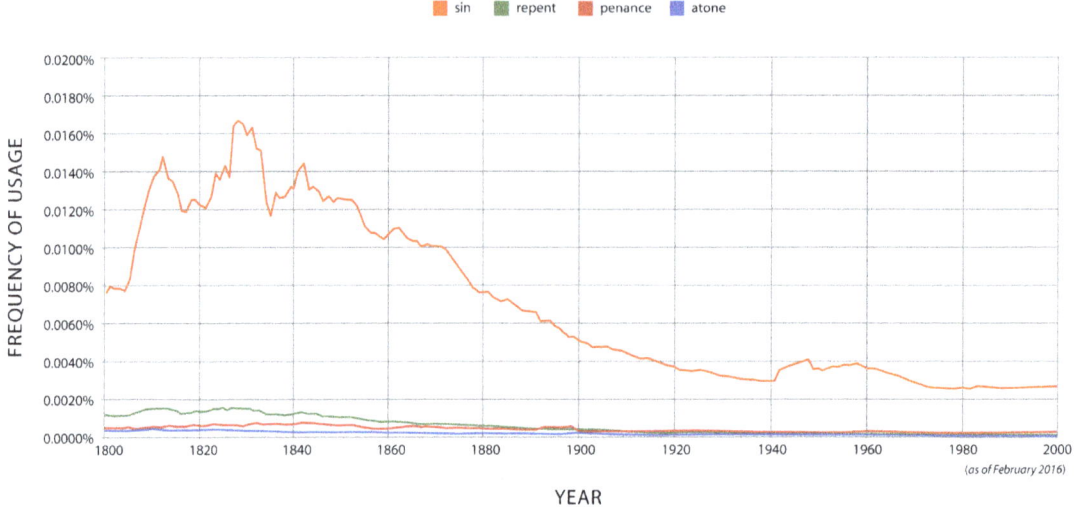

Fig. 5.14 Google Ngram data for "atone," "penance," "repent," and "sin." Vector art by Melissa Tandysh, 2016. Image courtesy of Melissa Tandysh. All rights reserved.

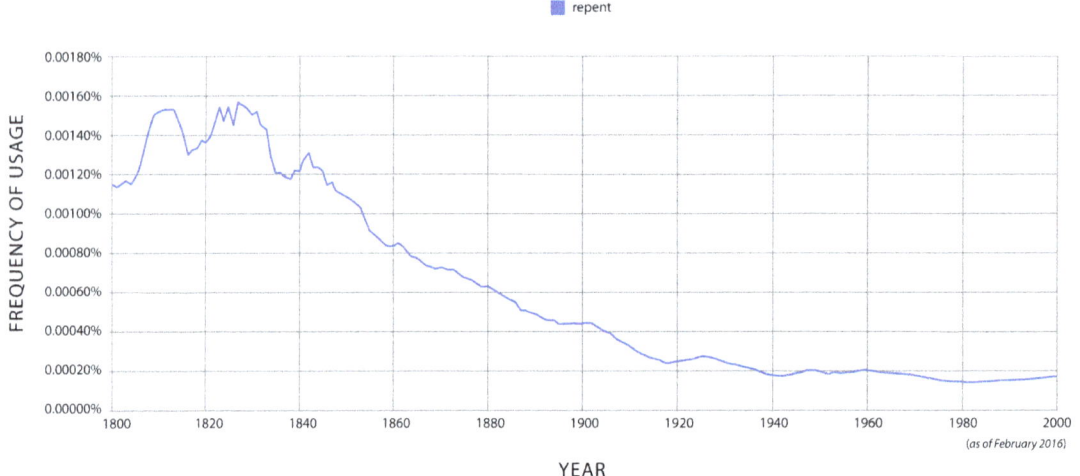

Fig. 5.15 Google Ngram data for "repent." Vector art by Melissa Tandysh, 2016. Image courtesy of Melissa Tandysh. All rights reserved.

The simplicity of the performer relates inextricably to the real or perceived *sins* for which he *repents*. This simple quality implies singleness, just as the etymology of monk gets at the idea of oneness. By the same token, *penance* is tied to *atonement*. Such reparation has encoded within it the notion of being at one with God. "At-one-ment" is a bona fide etymology, not a bon mot. All the key words and concepts italicized have seen relative declines in their usage (see Figs. 5.14–5.17).

For whatever reasons, we have ceased to operate within a substructure of sinfulness: we have become unrepentant or at least uninterested in repenting and atoning. The

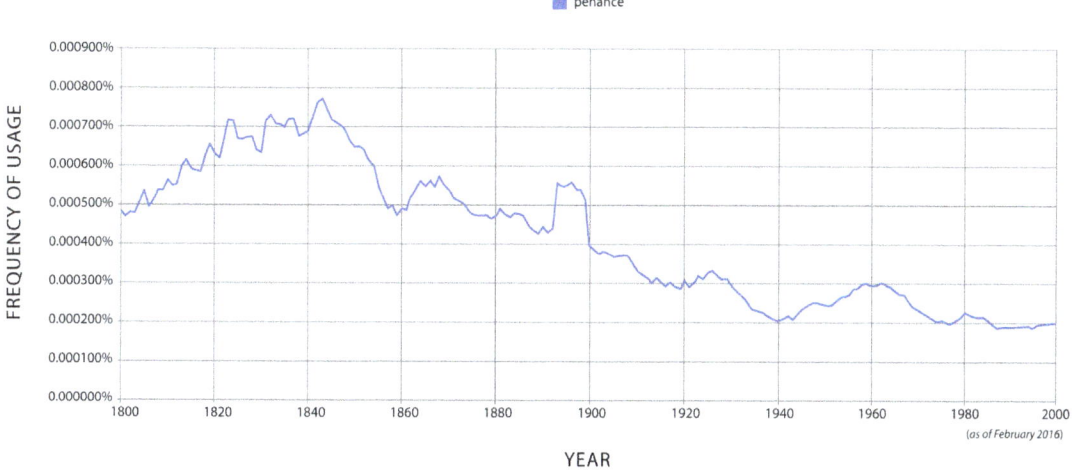

Fig. 5.16 Google Ngram data for "penance." Vector art by Melissa Tandysh, 2016. Image courtesy of Melissa Tandysh. All rights reserved.

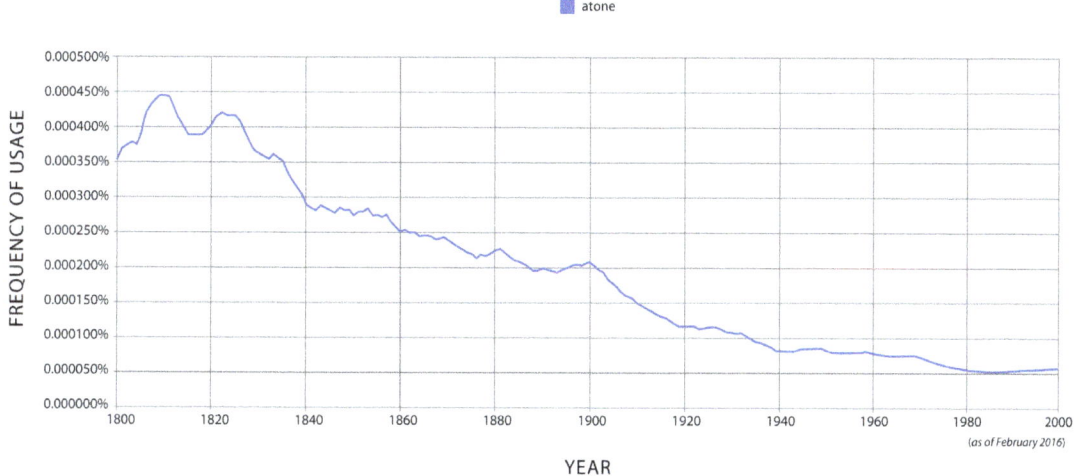

Fig. 5.17 Google Ngram data for "atone." Vector art by Melissa Tandysh, 2016. Image courtesy of Melissa Tandysh. All rights reserved.

outlier, unsurprisingly, is the unitalicized oneness (see Fig. 5.18), which brings us back appropriately to the square one of simplicity.

We have become more caught up in efforts to represent and analyze experience through algorithms in facts and figures—as confirmed by my readiness to regale you, dear reader, with graphs. But as the stock phrase runs, statistics can be made to prove anything. Figures, even human ones, can be manipulated, massaged, and twisted to all sorts of ends. We could frame overly simple or even simplistic arguments about the simplicity of yore in contrast to the complexity (or at least the supposed complexity) of today (see Fig. 5.19), or about the full-hearted faith of the past against the eye-rolling disbelief and hard-boiled cynicism of nowadays (see Fig. 5.20). O ye of little faith. The penitent could be argued to have lost ground to his opposite, the repeat offender or recidivist (see Fig. 5.21). Epiphanies emerge through sifting such numerical data, but future philologists (a band first envisaged by Ulrich von Wilamowitz-Moellendorff and Friedrich Nietzsche) must tread warily before allowing themselves to make fast-talking generalizations on the grounds of the computational hardware and software that have become widely available.

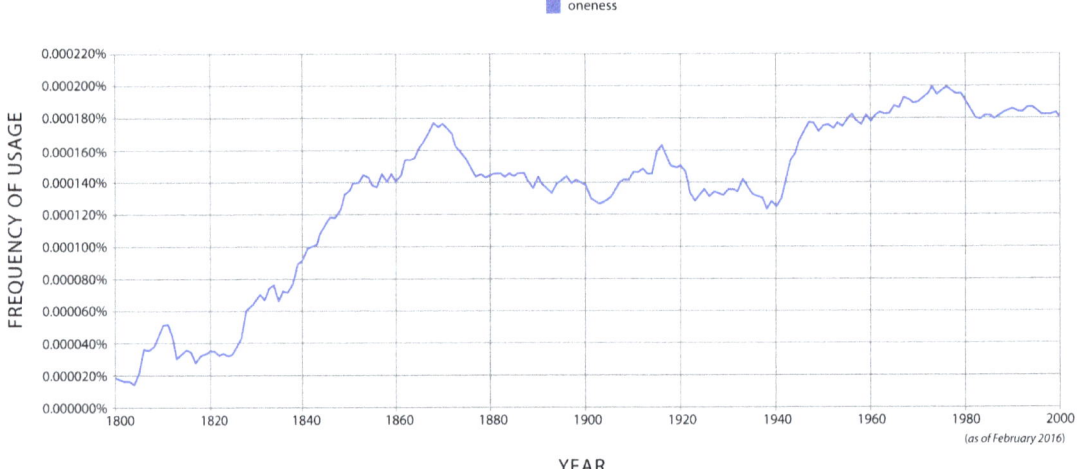

Fig. 5.18 Google Ngram data for "oneness." Vector art by Melissa Tandysh, 2016. Image courtesy of Melissa Tandysh. All rights reserved.

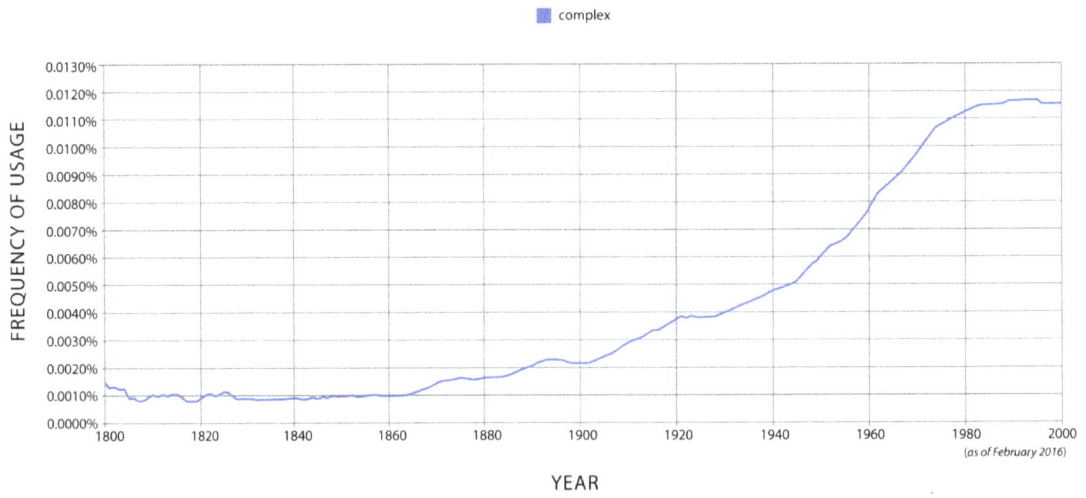

Fig. 5.19 Google Ngram data for "complex." Vector art by Melissa Tandysh, 2016. Image courtesy of Melissa Tandysh. All rights reserved.

A decade ago I began bandying emails back and forth with Barnaby Porter. His mother Barbara Cooney, illustrator and author of children's books, had decided even before his conception to name her firstborn male child after the protagonist in Anatole France's *Le jongleur de Notre Dame*, since she had fallen in love with the story. Her son, no longer a boy on the outside (but he sounded young on the inside), asked me at the end of our heart-to-heart what the narrative truly meant, and we swapped letters again on the topic much more recently too. All these pages are my rejoinder, at least for now. But let me explain my drift less coyly.

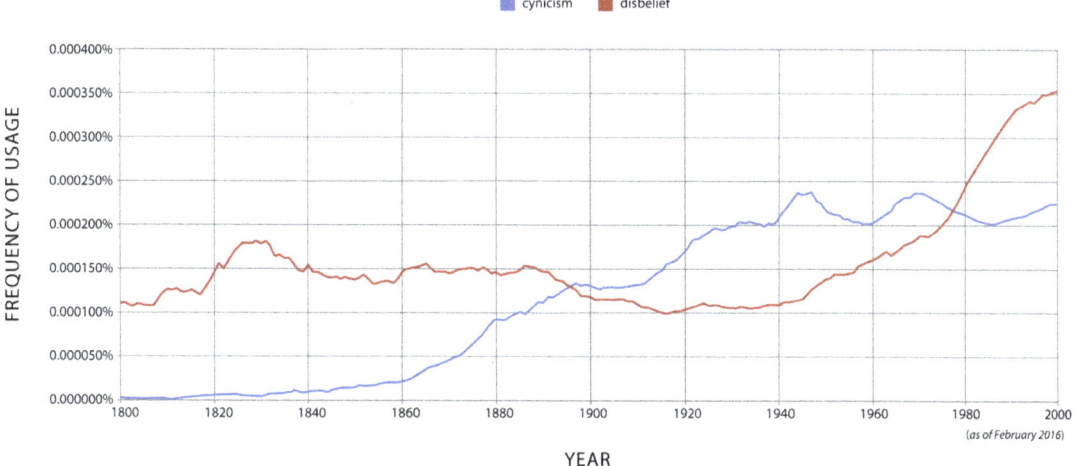

Fig. 5.20 Google Ngram data for "cynicism" and "disbelief." Vector art by Melissa Tandysh, 2016. Image courtesy of Melissa Tandysh. All rights reserved.

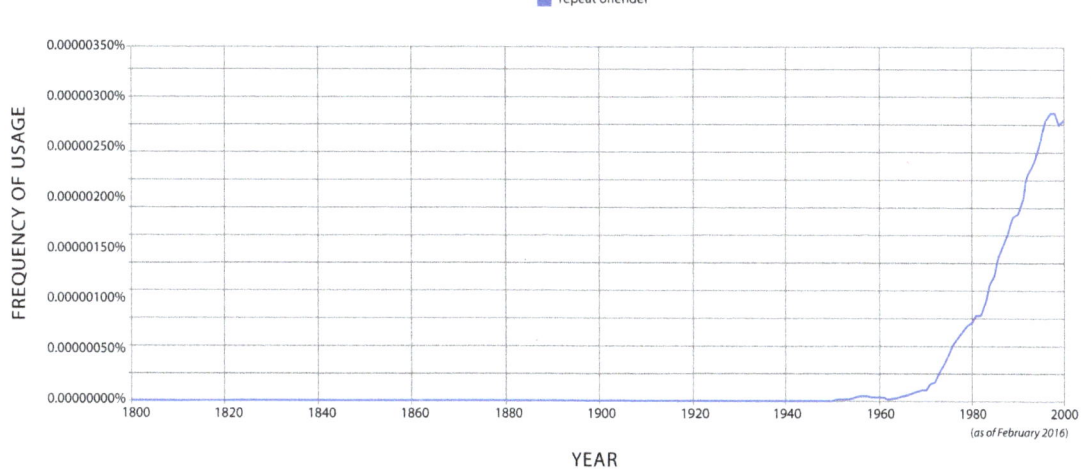

Fig. 5.21 Google Ngram data for "repeat offender." Vector art by Melissa Tandysh, 2016. Image courtesy of Melissa Tandysh. All rights reserved.

Through this book I aspire (a great verb for its serendipitous connection with Gothic steeples), as any person committed wholeheartedly to the humanities would do, to have contributed to the unending process of interpretation and recreation. My hope is that many more people will feel encouraged to come to grips with the significance of the tale and uncover verities that have eluded me, even if those truths have not escaped some of the more masterly minds than mine that have chosen to dance, juggle, sing, or play with the jongleur.

Individuals have made a stunning variety of this not-so-simply simple narrative. The multifariousness stands as a testament to the infinite inventiveness of the human mind. The medieval poem, Anatole France's story, Jules Massenet's opera, Mary Garden's co-option of the lead, R. O. Blechman's cartoon, and W. H. Auden's ballad, all in their supremely idiosyncratic manners, will energize readers to retell and recompose the tale afresh. Furthermore, each of these resourceful souls has demonstrated to the empirically minded that whenever the novelty of the tale palled, an individual talent could rescue it. They have done their job so well that the reception of *Our Lady's Tumbler* could be construed as an oddly underappreciated narrative feast or famine.

In odd and obstinate ways, the miracle resembles at its core the itinerant entertainer who plays its protagonist. It wanders through time and space, stopping in this or that culture until its performance becomes too routine and its audience jaded, passing on to the next, sometimes receding from view, only eventually to reemerge. The humble hero of this pious account has won the hearts of Catholics, Protestants, Jews, and agnostics, and nothing presupposes that his appeal must be restricted to those faiths. In an interview about her poetry and thought, the contemporary American poet Mary Rose O'Reilley adduced the juggler in a context that merits more than a fleeting look. Her spiritual background was eclectic, to say the least, since she was raised Catholic, became a practicing Quaker, developed a long passion for yoga, and grew curious ultimately about Buddhism and much more. In an interview in 2007, she first observed that "women of my generation were trained in indirection and self-effacement," then posited the expedience of differentiating between humility and the pose of being humble, and finally presented her view that by nature poetry constitutes "a device of indirection and self-erasure," which she set in a framework of Jungian psychology by [invoking his concept of the anima](). This is the Jung who knew our story well and used it self-defensively, to keep at bay the obligation to interpret unsought and unwanted amateur artworks. At this point O'Reilley's thoughts turned to our story. Her observations make of the juggler a patron saint, or a role model, who lends himself well to use by women and poets. In the reception of the poem and its adaptations, females have played no small part, but in recent decades they may not have gotten their fair share of attention among those who have reworked the story. Now may be a good time for them too to rethink and remake it.

The exemplum of the minstrel speaks to the potential for goodness in almost all human beings. Henry Adams waxed melancholic about the utility of the Middle Ages to modern man. First he demonstrated that the faith-based anthropocentrism of the medieval period had one uppermost meaning, embodied in Mary. Then he proved that the faith had lost its underpinning and had decayed. Yet the story of the tumbler outlasted Adams, surviving beyond the second half of the twentieth century. So too did his elegiac book. For the better part of a hundred years, it stood the test of time well, at least for an American readership. Its author was wrong to despair about the precariousness of everything medieval, at least where architecture enters the picture.

Gothic churches, college buildings, and skyscrapers manifest themselves across the North American continent with unostentatious omnipresence. Whatever our creeds may be, both the Old and New Worlds owe it to themselves not to be tone-deaf to their native-born cathedral cultures. Neither European countries nor the United States can afford the cost of forgetting their Middle Ages—original or revival. And when remembering, we should not allow antipathetic preconceptions about the period to crowd out memories of purer positives.

After the Second World War, the literary history of the Romance philologists Ernst Robert Curtius and (even more) Erich Auerbach absorbed the Middle Ages with redoubtable resignation and fathomless humanity. By projecting the period in all its incandescence and gloom, they handed on the torch to C. S. Lewis, J. R. R. Tolkien, Umberto Eco, and others. Today more than ever we need the cathedrals. Those great churches stretch from the tip-top of the finials of the pinnacles down by way of the gargoyles to the abyss of the subjacent crypts. To sum up the matter with an allusion to Victor Hugo's novel, we must think of Notre Dame as much as of the hunchback.

It is a woebegone culture that can engage with gusto in the gloating over another's misfortune that is known in German as *Schadenfreude*, meaning literally "harm-joy." Even sadder is if the same society has not even the most unexceptional niche for what we might call by the neologism *Freudenfreude*, translatable as "joy-joy." Ours is a time that defaults into disenchantment. A revealing tagline runs: "Happy endings are just stories that haven't finished yet." Other ways exist of facing life and literature than with such comedic negativism. With unique charm and beauty, the story of the juggler holds out the hope of redemption to those who may feel rough around the edges or unskilled in offering themselves. It tells of a life that its liver considers wasted, of an at first unfruitful foray and fray to make amends, and of a moment of grace that precipitates redemption at the very end. Even more than promising deliverance, the tale invites us to take joy in our talents, such as they may be. An ode to ordinariness, the narrative speaks to individuals who to others may not seem special, but who have the competence all by themselves to deliver and to attain spiritual satisfaction from the practice of whatever skills they have. Recollect that already in the thirteenth century the medieval exemplum was classified under the heading "Joy." If lessons can be extracted from the "example," they are universal. Unless sin disappears, self-questioning about talent vanishes, and the enrapturement of artistic self-expression loses its luster, the juggler will perdure in finding audiences and emulators.

At this moment, many guiding forces in our society emphasize nuts and bolts. In education, the hardnosed considerations take the form of a vocationalism that reposes upon science, technology, engineering, and mathematics, known as STEM for short. The added emphases contribute to a pattern that may limit our attractiveness and

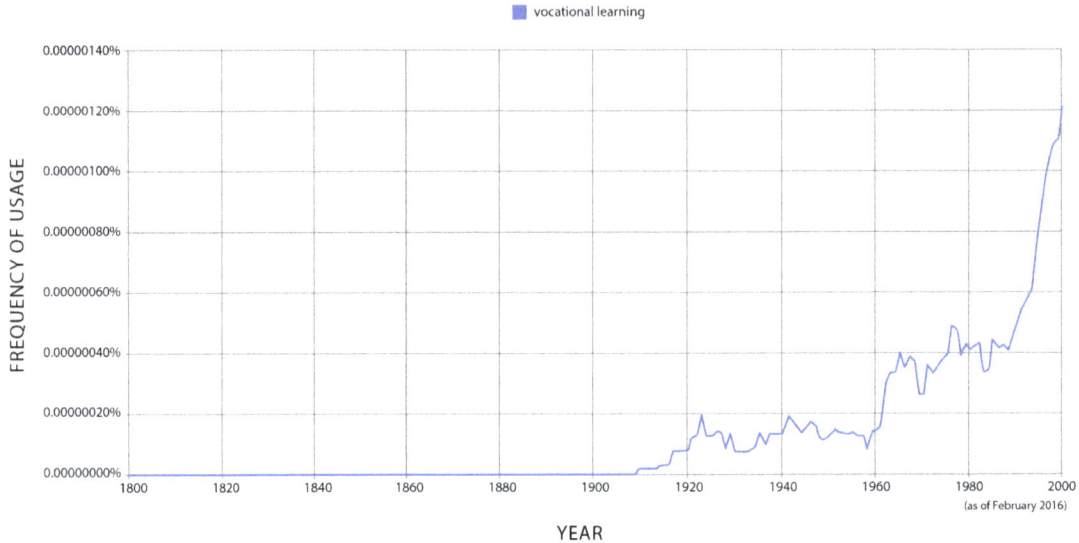

Fig. 5.22 Google Ngram data for "vocational learning." Vector art by Melissa Tandysh, 2016. Image courtesy of Melissa Tandysh. All rights reserved.

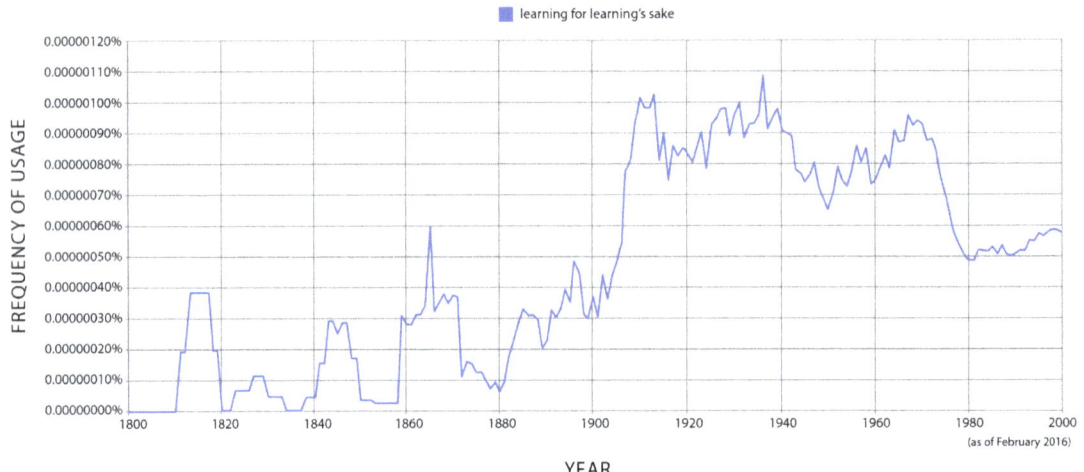

Fig. 5.23 Google Ngram data for "learning for learning's sake." Vector art by Melissa Tandysh, 2016. Image courtesy of Melissa Tandysh. All rights reserved.

competitiveness as a culture and civilization. The soaring stress on vocational learning need not entail automatically an abysmal abandonment of esteem for learning for learning's sake and art for art's sake … but the synchronicity of the two patterns is at the least suggestive (see Fig. 5.22–5.24). If we have only STEM, we will have lost STEAM: the arts must be part of our calculation. So too must be the humanities, so let us give the acronym a Yiddish twist: SHTEAM. The resources of these other creative and interpretative endeavors extend to the entire, boundless inventory of positive passions

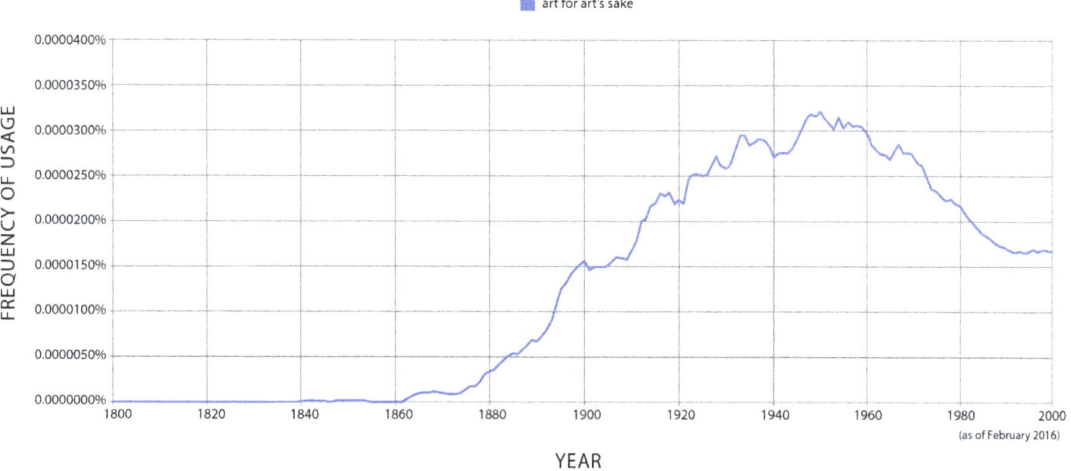

Fig. 5.24 Google Ngram data for "art for art's sake." Vector art by Melissa Tandysh, 2016. Image courtesy of Melissa Tandysh. All rights reserved.

and (yes) products that make cultures distinctive, balance work with pleasure, and on the whole suffuse life with significance. One proclamation in a sociology book that I have read and reread, perhaps still without comprehending it fully, seems to make a related suggestion, as a counterweight to an overemphasis on practicality: "There is the old legend of the 'jongleur de Notre Dame' who made acrobatics an instrument of Worship. All teachers of 'practical arts' ought to keep this in mind."

The last several decades, and especially the one of engagement with this narrative, have been for me positively medieval: end of story. A couple of decades ago it was posited that thanks to the advent of literary theory and a subsequent methodological eclecticism, medieval studies had undergone a renaissance. In my view, the rebirth will have taken place when we can say with a straight face that the field has undergone a Middle Ages, by which we will mean an affirmative transition rather than at best a neutral hiatus between two phases of cultural achievement that are held to be far greater. Above all, let us have faith: the juggler will not rest on his laurels for long. In the words of T. S. Eliot,

> We shall not cease from exploration
> And the end of all our exploring
> Will be to arrive where we started
> And know the place for the first time.

***

> Welcome to your destination, ladies and gentlemen.
> The safest part of your journey has come to an end.
>
> —Announcement to passengers reputedly made by
> pilots at the end of commercial air flights

Acknowledgments

> We do not need the tale of the *Jongleur de Notre-Dame* to teach us that a gift humbly offered to one's mother is not to be examined too critically.

It soothes the spirit to be immersed in a project in which gratitude stands in the forefront. The theme predisposes me to emulate the story's juggling paragon in demonstrating thankfulness. That said, profuse acknowledgments are considered in certain quarters an American affliction—a national overindulgence, the US academic equivalent of supersized meal portions. In this case the overserving is placed conveniently dead last. If you have no leaning toward overindulgence, stop right now. If you feel eager to verify nothing but the inclusion or omission of your own name, skip to the index: I will request that all proper nouns be immortalized there. Would that I could claim to have forgotten no one: nothing would bother me more than to be an ingrate or even to come across as ungrateful. But I must face the fact and own up to failure, since oversights will abound. If you belong to the distinguished company of the unjustly overlooked and undercredited, please forgive me. The one professorial qualification that I have ever had down pat is the legendary absentmindedness.

To confess that I have labored over these six volumes for most of this century sounds horrible, even though almost every minute of the toil has been lovely. Over what has become a *longue durée*, I have published passing little on the topic. In early 2004, I plunged into the thirteenth-century piece of poetry while preparing a talk for a workshop. More than a half decade later, those meager remarks wriggled into print as an essay in a volume propelled by Mary Carruthers. A dozen years ago, while basking in a gloriously gainful fellowship at the Netherlands Institute for Advanced Study, I submitted a thumbnail sketch of my research on *Le jongleur de Notre Dame*. Shortly thereafter, my investigation of the reception took shape in schematic form as an article. Just last year, I dashed off a couple of sides stimulated by the story as a tribute to a memorable colleague on his deathbed. While not putting words into print,

I have spewed forth plenty in formal oratory and absorbed even more in post-lecture discussion sessions.

Delving into the narrative of *Our Lady's Tumbler*, its modernization in both the short-story and operatic *Le jongleur de Notre Dame*, and the context of the modern reception within medieval revivalism has made my spirits soar for more than a decade. Stacks of printed materials have made the room where I hide away late at night into a Legoland-scale San Gimignano, spiked with paper-and-ink turrets. Although the paragraphs of my own prose are lined up page to page horizontally rather than vertically across space, they have grown into an ivory or at least a verbal tower where I can ascend for contemplation and solace. Perhaps I should go for broke and admit that the book itself gradually morphed into something even more ungainly—a do-it-yourself, cultural-historical cathedral. Think of the great church in Madrid that a lapsed Cistercian, Don Justo, cobbled together out of salvage materials.

Fig. 6.1 Cathedral of Justo Gallego Martínez. Mejorada del Campo, Madrid, 2005, CC BY-SA 3.0, https://commons.wikimedia.org/wiki/File:Cathedral_of_Justo_Gallego.JPG

In developing and completing this project, I have empathized with the juggler from the Middle Ages. Within Dumbarton Oaks Research Library and Collection, I have sometimes felt as extraneous as the minstrel regarded himself inside the abbey. Transplanted from my usual circus company in Cambridge, Massachusetts, I have occupied as my own home on the grange a residence just outside the walls of the facility in Washington, DC, where I work. By day I direct an institution with a refectory: what could be more monastic? In the wee hours I creep off to enact solitary devotions to the humanities and arts, as a means of reasserting equipoise after diurnal drudgery. Thus I turn out, despite lacking any and all skills in object manipulation, to resemble the jongleur after all.

Much of my industry has taken place mano a mano, or finger to plastic keyboard, in communing with digital devices. For all the foregone conclusions that search engines have coughed up, I owe far greater thanks to human beings than to computer servers. In particular, I have in mind the staffs of libraries, archives, and museums worldwide. In relatively few cases do the captions and credits particularize the individuals who have given their expertise and time to assist me, and the appreciation that I have expressed to these kindly people in e-mails, letters, and phone calls will have to suffice. Let me name just a small sampling: Patty Smith, the Adams National Historical Park; Carine Ruiz, Bibliothèque municipale Jacques-Lacarrière, Auxerre; Wanda Ray, Charles W. Capps, Jr. Archives and Museum; Wayne Kempton, the Episcopal Diocese of New York at The Cathedral Church of Saint John the Divine; Aura A. Fluet Sr., Library Services at the Episcopal Divinity School, Cambridge; Ken Grossi, Oberlin College Archives; first Peter Kiefer and then Tim Babcock, the Pennsylvania State University Archives; Ramses Peters, Katholiek Documentatie Centrum, Radboud Universiteit, Nijmegen, Netherlands; Christine Roussel, the Rockefeller Center Archives; Peter J. Johnson, the Rockefeller Corporate Office; Nancy Adgent, the Rockefeller Family Archive; Erika Gorder, Special Collections and University Archives, Rutgers University Libraries; Edward Probert, Canon Chancellor of the Salisbury Cathedral; Rebecca Cohn, San Jose State College; Deborah Kloiber, St. Catherine University Library, St. Paul, Minnesota; Peter Lysy and others, the University Archives at the University of Notre Dame; Jeffrey Gutkin, Horrmann Library, Wagner College; Irwin Lachof, Xavier University of Louisiana. The enumeration could and probably should balloon to fill a whole quire. These professionals contribute immeasurably to the preservation and transmission of knowledge that enriches the present through the past. Their generosity with their hours and expertise has moved me continually. For the many whom I have left unnamed, virtue is its own reward—and it may actually be enhanced by not being identified in a book as eccentrically contrarian as this one.

Often billeted four hundred miles or so from the library system upon which I rely most heavily, I gained from a succession of Harvard students there who did their bit in tracking down the printed materials that have been the lifeblood of my scholarship. At the risk of leapfrogging deserving names, let me point out in particular Kamila Lis, Emily Vasiliauskas, Alice Underwood, and Samuel Shapiro. Beyond undergraduate assistants, I put to use everything that the peerless library system of my university could furnish, including not only an extensive cross section from many of its constituent print collections, paper archives, and photo archives, but interlibrary loan, scan-and-deliver, and rare books. To say that I am grateful borders on bathos. Two further people whom I take extra special joy in mentioning are Teresa Wu and Alyson Lynch in Classics. They have unfailingly flanked me, not the least in the long steeplechase of receipts for purchases of used books, ephemera, and more as I built up slowly but surely an archive of both materials directly tied to the story and resources for images.

When I turned to the project full force, lengthened it, and illustrated it heavily, Raquel Begleiter entered the picture at Dumbarton Oaks. Her heartfelt encouragement and cool-headed reasoning made thinkable the development of a coherent archive, to keep in order and in good condition the original items that I scouted out for illustrations. I cannot overstate my esteem for her contributions and my admiration for her skills overall: she established a skeleton sturdy enough to survive to the end, despite unintentional efforts afterward to cause collapse. Eventually she handed the baton to Rebecca Frankel. As the book has looped through the editorial and production processes, Lane Baker became involved for a year to mop up permissions and produce proper captions and credits. Last but emphatically not least, Alona Bach, although occupied mainly with the related exhibit "Juggling the Middle Ages," has stepped up with both ability and alacrity to help out with last-minute repairs.

The Harvardian alumni of Dumbarton Oaks, by which I mean especially those who have logged a post-degree academic year or more working within the institution, have formed a supportive group. To name one name, Michael B. Sullivan, now the managing editor of the Loeb Classical Library, gave occasional assistance and also tendered ideas, which I much valued. Anna Bonnell-Freidin supplied me with an image of the Princeton campus and arranged for others through friends. Among short-termers, Shirin Fozi first mentioned to me Arthur Kingsley Porter's involvement in the discord over the war damage to the cathedral of Reims.

My closest colleague in Washington has been Yota Batsaki, executive director. As a comparatist and cultural historian through and through, she recognized with her customary perceptiveness how much this project meant to me and exhorted me to reserve slots in my calendar for completing it, even though my doing so has increased her own load. Her husband Jean-Christophe Maure and she, despite being drawn to the Enlightenment in values and midcentury modern in aesthetics, have smiled tolerantly upon my relentless gravitation to the Middle Ages and medievalism. Another person in the director's office who deserves to have her moniker flashing in bright lights on a big marquee is Marlee Clayton. Her title of senior executive assistant and project manager does not begin to map the horizons or convey the heaviness of the responsibilities she has shouldered to make this book and the related art installation click. Whenever anyone else has let me down or left me stranded, she has intervened with at least seeming equanimity to figure out how to maintain progress. It typifies her genial grit that when late in the game topic words needed to be tallied volume by volume, she simply (or not so simply) took on the task.

Dumbarton Oaks brings together, cheek by jowl, all the ingredients usually scattered around large educational institutions. I have imposed on all of our departments in this venture, especially the library, museum, publications, and finance, all with their own amazing passion, distinctive expertise, and characteristic values. Although it would become immediately invidious to list some and not all, leaving my thanks anonymous does not signify unawareness on my part that I have the best collaborators anywhere.

At the university that has been my home since 1981, I have the fortune of occupying a chair that honors Arthur Kingsley Porter, a historian of Romanesque art and architecture. My debt to the legacy of this great American medievalist goes beyond the mere funding of my professorship. In resolving to make this a massive manga monograph, I was inspired partly by the many photographs with which he illustrated some of his books. By the same token, I took to heart Henry Adams, who resigned tenure in Cambridge, Massachusetts, to take up being an independent scholar in Washington. While not emulating him by stepping down from my position, I have regarded him as a role model for the advantages he wrung from his situation in the nation's capital to acquire fresh perspectives on cultural changes.

To move from the dead to the quick, I will not give a checklist of the fellow classicists, medievalists, and comparatists from Harvard Square who have cheered me on and lavished their brilliance, but a full accounting would result in the slaughter of many cattle to enable a parchment scroll like what medieval heralds are sometimes depicted unfurling before proclaiming "Hear ye, hear ye!" Having had chances to talk shop with fellow professors like Dan Donoghue, Deborah Foster, Virginie Greene, Jeffrey Hamburger, Carla Heelan, Racha Kirakosian, Mike McCormick, Jószi Nagy, James Simpson, Diana Sorensen, Bill Stoneman, Richard Thomas, and Nicholas Watson, to offer only a representative sampling, has been a boon and a balm.

A few people within Byzantine studies or in its penumbra have been especially kindhearted and inspirational to me. Small talk and focused correspondence with Peter Brown, Réka Forrai, and Anthony Kaldellis leap to mind. Two long-standing Harvard colleagues from the field, John Duffy (now based mainly in Ireland) and Ioli Kalavrezou, have propped me both intellectually and personally more than they realize. Within Dumbarton Oaks, the sigillographer Jonathan Shea pointed me toward a couple of lead seals. More important, he pried open my eyes to the historical value of what might otherwise have remained nothing but toxic lead blobs about which to tease him. I have not tabulated how much heavy metal shows up across the six volumes, but the weight is respectable. All these good souls should not be held accountable for any mistakes, and even less culpable are the much-esteemed curators with whom I ought to have conferred about textile relics but did not: Gudrun Buehl and Betsy Williams, sorry! I regret also not having learned more from James Carder. To turn to a different program, colleagues in Garden and Landscape Studies will be surprised and (I hope) forgiving that I have blundered now and again into architectural history. They may wish that I had shared my ideas so that they could vet them and set them right before I perpetuated them between two covers. To the truehearted Pre-Columbianists who have cared to hear about this project and who have lent a helping hand, *un abrazo muy fuerte*.

Researchers from all over the globe have responded to my inquiries, and once again I will select two who will epitomize many others. A European with a faculty for armchair detective work was allured by a posting on academia.edu and solved a brain-twister for me: Otfried Lieberknecht pinpointed the correct Henri Marmier out of a few choices. Dr. Ingrid Biesheuvel in the Netherlands, Dr. Gradwohl-Schlacher in Austria, and Professor Emeritus Henry Phillips of the University of Manchester replied to specific queries. On this continent, Melissa Jordan Love provided in her master's thesis details on the acquisition by Worcester of a twelfth-century chapter house from a Benedictine priory.

One special gratification from this undertaking has been the creative agents with whom it has brought me into contact. The story has attracted exceptionally nice human beings. The authors and artists whom I have approached have been remarkably insightful and helpful. I have experienced nothing but marvelous humanity from the miniature bookmaker Maryline Poole Adams, the graphic designer R. O. Blechman, the musician Naji Hakim, the illustrator David and writer Mark Shannon, and the children's book author Tomie dePaola. The same magnanimity has held true of inheritors and literary executors of creators who no longer handle their own business affairs or who have passed away, such as the widow of the sculptor Arman, Edward Mendelson for the estate of the poet W. H. Auden, the son of the composer Juan Orrego-Salas, Barnaby Porter and other offspring of the children's book author Barbara Cooney, and Marina Tonzig for the artist Štěpán Zavřel.

Whom else should I single out? Over the years, I have been privileged to swap musings about the medieval minstrel with a friend who knows him inside out, Michel Zink. I acquired substantial insight about medievalism from reading Elizabeth Emery and talking with her. The other dedicatees, Piero Boitani, Mary Carruthers, Ilhi Synn, and Frits van Oostrom, all reminded me of the delights inherent in both rootedness within national traditions and transcendence of them through comparison, across literatures, media, and borders. At various instances, I was bedazzled by tête-à-têtes about *Le jongleur de Notre Dame* with David Ganz, Franco Mormando, and Richard Utz. Tom Hall of Notre Dame popped into the mail copies of *The Juggler* to remind me that at least at the University of Notre Dame, folks still care about the star of my story.

If I have two regrets about this book, the first is that I could not keep reappraising and amending it forever, and the second, that I have not carved out more than nanosecond-long entr'actes for discussing it with those who are dearest to me. My closest relatives refrained from staging an intervention to rein in what a clinical psychologist might diagnose as a monomania and to deprogram me. On the contrary, they egged me on or at a minimum tolerated with bemusement my idée fixe.

It would be hackneyed to profess that I owe everything to my parents, but sometimes such bromides hold true. My mother and father, in their wonderfully different fashions, instilled in my siblings and me love of story and history, art and architecture, religion and ethnicity, and far more. They passed on much of what I know about both America and Europe, as well as whetting in me curiosity about the other continents beyond those two continents. With their backing, I gravitated to the humanities and arts. With them as models, I learned to strive for empathy and to look for commonalities among human beings across divides that may be too easily overemphasized.

My sister has fielded queries from me about Slavic folklore and holy fools, my brother has stood at the ready as a font of knowledge where religion and literature loom large, and my Italianist, Germanist, and comparatist eldest daughter Saskia has entered the transgenerational chain of being by drawing my attention, with thanks to Mimmo Cangiano, to Giuseppe Prezzolini's diary. I have felt strength from the familial force field, encompassing my son-in-law Martin Eisner (a Dantist and medievalist, no less), brother-in-law Robert Thurston, and sister-in-law Lee Upton. In the next generation my nephew Alexander Thurston and his wife as well as my niece Theodora Ziolkowski and her groom have borne with me. Of course, academics have no monopoly on intelligence or culture. As a purported patriarch with the fairy-tale combination of three daughters, I would not want to infringe upon fatherly fairness by omitting Yetta Ziolkowski, Ada Horlander, or Ada's husband Dan Horlander. Last but not least, I must shout out a hearty *hola!* to Nola, Tullia, and Cayden, the next peer group of readers in the clan. All these relations give me strength, and I feel pride in these ties.

More than anyone else, my wife has had to endure hearing the bits and pieces of this obsession over and over again. As a forensic chemist, she has been accustomed to the scenes of homicides and other felonies for decades but hearing and reading what I do to the English language and to interpretation may be the goriest felony with which she has had to cope. To return from such concerns in the workplace as quality control and spatter patterns to my minstrel-maniacal maundering at home is more than should be asked of anyone. To take another metaphoric tack, she has kept me at once grounded and motivated to complete my spire. My fortieth anniversary present to Liz has been bringing the six volumes of this book into print and staging the exhibition, after which I will channel my impulses for mental hoarding in novel directions and allay her worries that I will devolve into an even stranger sort of Quasimodo, gamboling about among the gargoyles of my thoughts and prose.

Two top-notch copyeditors, each of whom brought preternatural patience and genuine genius to the project, wrangled over more than a year with my quip-filled English, jungle-like documentation, and ubiquitous images, to say nothing of my unyielding commitment to an idiosyncratic format. With my tinkering, I feared causing Peri Bearman to topple from anxiety and David Weeks to explode from apoplexy. All of us had to cope with the nightmare of captioning and credits as it dragged out. Finally, Melissa Tandysh, who long ago realized my requests for graphic art, replied instantly when I sought fixes, major or minor, in her handiwork.

Before allowing this sextet of volumes to close, I would like for the record to pull a Mary Garden by singing an aria in praise of Open Book Publishers. They dared to take on something gargantuan, with a presentation that pushed the nature of the book into terra incognita and with a timetable that would have been rejected out of hand by any other editorial house. They have delivered and then some. One of my main rewards to them is the promise that I will not return to them with anything else of this magnitude—but I would love to come back to their stable, with a mercifully smaller manuscript in tow.

Notes

who controls the present controls the past. George Orwell, *Nineteen Eighty-Four: A Novel* (London: Secker and Warburg, 1949), pt. 1, chapter 3.

Notes to Chapter 1

It would occur to only the most limited soul. Wilhelm Grimm, *Kleinere Schriften*, ed. Gustav Hinrichs, 4 vols. (Berlin: Ferdinand Dümmler, 1881–1887), 1:13–14: "Das Mittelalter zu erforschen, um es in der Gegenwart wieder geltend zu machen, wird nur der beschränktesten Seele einfallen; allein es beweist auf der andern Seite gleiche Stumpfheit, wenn man den Einfluss abwehren wollte, den es auf Verständnis und richtige Behandlung der Gegenwart haben muss."

he might reunite with his closest coevals. Henry Adams, *The Education of Henry Adams* (henceforth *EHA*), in Henry Adams, *Novels, Mont Saint Michel, The Education*, ed. Ernest Samuels and Jayne N. Samuels (New York: Library of America, 1983), 1181: "Perhaps some day—say 1938, their centenary—they might be allowed to return together for a holiday, to see the mistakes of their own lives made clear in the light of the mistakes of their successors; and perhaps then, for the first time since man began his education among the carnivores, they would find a world that sensitive and timid natures could regard without a shudder."

the fateful year. This phrase, translating the German *Schicksalsjahr*, has long been conventional in discussions of the Holocaust or Shoah. For example, see Avraham Barkai, "The Fateful Year 1938: The Continuation and Acceleration of Plunder," in *November 1938: From "Reichskristallnacht" to Genocide*, ed. Walter H. Pehle, trans. William Templer (New York: Berg, 1991), 95–122; Shaul Esh, "Between Discrimination and Extermination: 1938—The Fateful Year," *Yad Washem Studies on the European Jewish Catastrophe and Resistance* 2 (1958): 79–93.

loathsome anti-Semitism. Many articles and books have dealt in passing with Adams's anti-Semitism, but the topic awaits definitive treatment.

efforts to obliterate cultural centers. See Nicola Lambourne, *War Damage in Western Europe: The Destruction of Historic Monuments during the Second World War* (Edinburgh, UK: Edinburgh University Press, 2001).

The air strike on Coventry. The most recent and thorough coverage of the air attack has been offered by Frederick Taylor, *Coventry: Thursday, 14 November 1940* (London: Bloomsbury, 2015).

the Baedeker raids. The alternate name has been "Baedeker Blitz."

France

renowned tenor. Charles Friant.

Jérôme and Jean Tharaud. Their given names were Ernest and Charles. The writer Charles Péguy gave them the ones by which they are now known.

below the threshold. On the reception (or lack thereof) of the literature produced by the brothers, see Roger Mathe, "Pourquoi les Tharaud?," *Trames: Travaux et mémoires de l'Université de Limoges, Collection Français* 5 (1983): 89–98. This was a special issue, "Sur Jérôme et Jean Tharaud."

unwanted munitions. It should be conceded that in French, selected tales of the Virgin by the Tharaud brothers live on in recorded form on audio compact disc: "Les contes de la Vierge, d'après Jérome et Jean Tharaud," narrated by Pascal Nowak and Jean-Marie Frecon, with instrumental accompaniment by Gisela Melo (Versailles, France: Rejoyce, 2004).

on the wrong side. Mathe, "Pourquoi les Tharaud?," 91.

Wendelin Foerster. Jacques Monfrin, *Honoré Champion, 1874–1978* (Paris: Honoré Champion, 1978), 54, 57.

As habitués of this shop. Yvonne Foubert-Daudet, *La règle du je: Les frères Jérôme et Jean Tharaud, témoins et chroniqueurs d'un demi-siècle mouvementé* (Toulouse, France: Erès, 1982).

exhibition catalogue. Louis Gillet et al., *Les primitifs français: Contes de la Vierge*, Cahiers de la quinzaine, 6th series, vol. 7 (Paris: Cahiers de la quinzaine, 1904), 131–70. The heart of the volume comprises thirty black-and-white plates that reproduce artworks in the show.

reworking of Our Lady's Tumbler. Tharaud and Jean Tharaud, "Le Tombeor de Notre-Dame," in *Aux quatre coins de chez nous* (Paris: Journées du livre, 1931), 144–48.

Tales of the Virgin. Tharaud and Jean Tharaud, *Les contes de la Vierge* (Paris: Plon, 1940, repr. 1942, 1943, 1944, 1946, 1949, 1954, 1960). A selection with illustrations that does not include *Our Lady's Tumbler* was published in Spain (Barcelona: Ediciones Mediterráneas, 1942). Another illustrated version that does have it was brought out in Catalan forty years later: *Leyendas de la Virgen*, trans. Marià Manent, illus. Carles Planell, Panchatantra, vol. 2 (Barcelona, Spain: Casals, 1983), 57–61. A sampling from the tales was revised in textbooks for the use of students learning French as a foreign language: for Flemings, *Les contes de la vierge*, ed. L. Mees, Les bons auteurs, vol. 2 (Malines, Belgium: S. François, n.d.), and for Germans, *Contes de la Vierge: Devoirs pratiques*, ed. Arnold Leonhardi (Dortmund, Germany: Lensing, 1952).

Tales of Our Lady. Tharaud and Jean Tharaud, *Contes de Notre Dame* (Paris: Plon, 1943, repr. 1944, 1945, 1946, 1950, 1959).

Le jongleur de Notre-Dame. "Le Jongleur de Notre-Dame," in Tharaud and Tharaud, *Les contes de la Vierge* (Paris: Plon, 1944), 83–94 and iv–v.

Marianne. Marianne 7, no. 339, April 19, 1939, 1, 3.

their views on Judaism. On the Tharaud brothers, see Foubert-Daudet, *La règle du je*, 168–69. On early philo-Semitism, see Seth L. Wolitz, "Imagining the Jew in France: From 1945 to the Present," *Yale French Studies* 85 (1994): 119–34, at 121. On the range of their views, including anti-Semitism, in the 1920s, see Michel Leymarie, "Les frères Tharaud: De l'ambiguïté du 'filon juif' dans les années 1920," *Archives juives* 39.1 (2006): 89–109; Paul A. Moylan, "Jérôme and Jean Tharaud's Romantic Representation of Judaism," *French Review* 39.1 (1965): 69–77. On later anti-Semitism, see Herman Schnurer, "The Intellectual Sources of French Fascism," *Antioch Review* 1 (1941): 35–49, at 41.

admiration for Zionism. On the Tharauds' simultaneous anti-Semitism and Zionism, see Leymarie, "Les frères Tharaud"; Farouk Mardam Bey, "French Intellectuals and the Palestine Question," *Journal of Palestine Studies* 43.3 (2014): 26–39, at 27.

other undoctored forms of pious stories. Another was a version of "La Vénus d'Ille" (The Venus of Ille) by Mérimée; and a third was their retelling of the same story that lay behind Maeterlinck's "Sœur Béatrice."

anthologies of Marian miracles. See the French historian of medieval literature, Myrrha Lot-Borodine, trans., *Vingt miracles de Notre-Dame*, Poèmes et récits de la vieille France, vol. 14 (Paris: E. de Boccard, 1929); Gautier de Coinci, *Les plus beaux miracles de la Vierge*, trans. Gonzague Truc (Paris: Lanore, 1932). Truc was a French literary critic.

Acts of the Saints. In Latin, *Acta sanctorum* (Antwerp: apud Joannem Mevrsium, 1643–). The team effort has been overseen by the association of scholars, originally all Jesuits, known as the Bollandists.

a certain Guinehochet. In Latin, *Guinehocatus quidam*.

Go, peasant. John of Garland, *Parisiana Poetria*, ed. and trans. Traugott Lawler, Yale Studies in English, vol. 182 (New Haven, CT: Yale University Press, 1974), 78–79 (lines 422–31, Latin and English), 248 (note, with citation of one other version).

other medieval texts. For example, the name may have been lifted from a canon regular, active in the early thirteenth century, who left a plethora of Latin sermons and historical writings, as well as letters written during his years in the Mideast: see Jacques de Vitry, *The Exempla or Illustrative Stories from the Sermones vulgares of Jacques de Vitry*, ed. Thomas Frederick Crane, Publications of the Folk-Lore Society, vol. 26 (London: D. Nutt, 1890), 97, no. 123. Another possible source is Robert Bossuat, ed., *Bérinus, roman en prose du XIVe siècle*, 2 vols. (Paris: Société des anciens textes français, 1931–1933), 1:90, §103 (spelled in different manuscripts Guinehochés, Guinehochet, and Guignehochet).

Catholic theater of his day. Henry Phillips, *Le théâtre catholique en France au XXe siècle*, Littérature de notre siècle, vol. 37 (Paris: Champion, 2007).

Companions of Our Lady. In French, "Compagnons de Notre-Dame." See Jacques Cotnam, "Henri Brochet et le R. P. Émile Legault, c.s.c.: Rencontre et correspondance," *Tangence* 78 (2005): 45–89, at 48.

plays on Sister Beatrice. Henri Brochet, "Béatrice: Miracle de Notre-Dame, en trois actes," *Jeux, Tréteaux et Personnages* (May 1939): 143–78; (June 1939): 179–96; *Marie, reine de France et dame de Pontmain: Mystère en trois parties* (Paris: A. Blot, 1938).

Brochet's piece on the jongleur. The 33-page typescript, dated February 9–10, 1942, is entitled "Cadet Roussel, jongleur de Notre Dame: Un prologue et 3 actes par H. Brochet." The first character listed in the dramatis personae is "Notre Dame des Vertus, un statue." The scene involving the Madonna runs from the bottom of p. 28 to the bottom of p. 31.

Companions of Roger Good-Times. In French, "Compagnons de Roger Bontemps."

Guillaume Joseph Roussel. For information, see Louis-Marcel Raymond, "Un canadien à Paris," *Les cahiers des compagnons: Bulletin d'art dramatique* 3 (1947): 1–32, at 13; Cotnam, "Henri Brochet," 74, 83. From Henri Brochet, we also have a book that was published in 1952, apparently in Auxerre, under the title *Cadet Roussel danse sur les nuages: Un prologue et trois actes*.

Barber at the Fontaine des innocents. Cotnam, "Henri Brochet," 74n86: Joseph Aude, *Cadet Roussel, barbier à la Fontaine des Innocents: Folie en un acte* (Paris: Chez Barba, 1799). The mid-sixteenth-century Fontaine des Innocents is the oldest monumental fountain in Paris.

Brother Clown. Léon Chancerel, *Frère Clown, ou Le jongleur de Notre-Dame: Monologue par Léon Chancerel, d'après le miracle du ménestrel Pierre de Sygelar* (Lyon, France: La Hutte, 1943; 2nd ed., Paris: Librarie Théâtrale, 1956).

Léon Chancerel. For a broad backdrop to the productions of medieval theater by Chancerel and Ghéon, see Lynette Muir, "Résurrection des Mystères: Medieval Drama in Modern France," *Leeds Studies in English* 29 (1998): 235–48.

a version in French verse. "Mis en vers français par le Révérendissme Père Gautier de Coincy."

naïve, pious, and tender. Chancerel, *Frère Clown*, 4.

frequented the same theatrical circles. Chancerel, *Frère Clown*. From what Raymond indicates ("Un canadien à Paris," 12), Brochet and Chancerel belonged to the same social set. Many more details are forthcoming in Henry Phillips, "Jacques Copeau et le théâtre catholique: Une correspondance inédite avec Henri Brochet," *Revue d'histoire littéraire de la France* 104.2 (April–June 2004): 439–58. For an assessment of Chancerel, see Maryline Romain, *Léon Chancerel: Portrait d'un réformateur du théâtre français*, Collection Théâtre, vol. 20 (Lausanne, Switzerland: L'Âge d'Homme, 2005).

spiritual letters. Antoine-Marie Falaize, *Lettres spirituelles* (Paris: Cerf, 1945).

the Theophilians. Gustave Cohen, "Les Théophiliens," *The French Review* 12.6 (1939): 453–58; idem, "The 'Théophiliens': The Resurrection of the Medieval Theater," *Books Abroad* 25 (1951): 7–10.

Miracle of Theophilus. Rutebeuf, *Le miracle de Théophile*, transposed by Gustave Cohen (Paris: Delagrave, 1934).

restore its marvelous stained-glass colors. Cohen, "'Théophiliens': The Resurrection," 7.

came into print first in 1934. (Paris: Delagrave, 1934, 1935, 1938).

the professor's dulcet words of hope. Gustave Cohen, "Expériences théophiliennes," *Mercure de France* 48.927, vol. 273 (February 1, 1937): 453–77.

medieval literature had a share in both movements. The present chapter provides at least an amuse-bouche of information that gives an idea of how appetizing the results of an investigation could be into the roles of medieval literature in the French Underground. For other inquiries, see Roy Rosenstein, "A Medieval Troubadour Mobilized in the French Resistance," *Journal of the History of Ideas* 59.3 (1998): 499–520, and (on the Theophilians specifically) Helen Solterer, *Medieval Roles for Modern Times: Theater and the Battle for the French Republic* (University Park: Pennsylvania State University Press, 2010).

The legend of Theophilus. The oldest Greek renderings of the legend are preserved in two manuscripts of the tenth century. One of these texts takes the form of a supposed eyewitness account by a servant of Theophilus's. The most influential Latin translation of the legend is by a Neapolitan deacon of the ninth century, Paulus. In it, the priest is at the outset moved by piety and modesty to decline being elevated to bishop. The man chosen in his place then libels him and strips him of his priesthood. The pact with the devil is mediated by a Jew, and hinges on written repudiation of Christ and Mary.

the favorite Marian legend of the Middle Ages. Karl Plenzat, *Die Theophiluslegende in den Dichtungen des Mittelalters*, Germanische Studien, vol. 43 (Berlin: E. Ebering, 1926); Albert Gier, *Der Sünder als Beispiel: Zu Gestalt und Funktion hagiographischer Gebrauchstexte anhand der Theophiluslegende*, Bonner romanistische Arbeiten, vol. 1 (Frankfurt am Main, Germany: P. Lang, 1977); Jerry Root, *The Theophilus Legend in Medieval Text and Image* (Cambridge: D. S. Brewer, 2017).

Miracles of Our Lady. Gautier de Coinci, *Les miracles de Nostre Dame*, ed. V. Frédéric Koenig, 4 vols., Textes littéraires français, vols. 64, 95, 131, 176 (Geneva: Droz, 1955–1970), 1:50–176 (1.10, "Comment Theophilus vint a penitance").

the whole stage is shown. The full *mise en scène* is shown in an original drawing by Raoul-Roger Ballet, which serves as the frontispiece to the volume.

Golden Virgin. In French, *Vierge dorée*. The sculpture stands on a pillar, known technically as a trumeau, that divides the south transept portal of the cathedral. Rutebeuf, *Le miracle de Théophile*, 60.

Mystery of the Passion of the Theophilians. *Mystère de la Passion des théophiliens: Adaptation littéraire de Gustave Cohen, ... d'après Arnoul Greban et Jean Michel* (Paris: Richard-Masse, 1950), 9–10 (poem), 10 (*In memoriam*). The dedication opens with a verse *in memoriam* of "Louis Laurent [1918–1940], president of the Theophilians, senior officer cadet, killed as a volunteer, at the defense of the bridges of the Loire, June 20, 1940."

would serve again later as its director. On Chancerel as director of the Theophilians, see Solterer, *Medieval Roles*, 75, 96, 107n49. On the Comédiens-Routiers, see Jean Cusson, *Un réformateur du théâtre, Léon Chancerel: L'expérience Comédiens-Routiers, 1929–1939* (Paris: LaHutte, 1945).

Chancerel was drawn to God and religion. For instance, he jotted in his journal in 1927: "Longing to set up our life there at the foot of the cathedral, beneath its blessing, beneath its protection, and to work according to the discipline and the spirit that it enlarges." See Hubert Gignoux, *Histoire d'une famille théâtrale: Jacques Copeau, Léon Chancerel, les Comédiens-Routiers, la décentralisation dramatique* (Lausanne, Switzerland: Editions de l'Aire, 1984), 109.

only after 1940. Gignoux, *Histoire*, 167.

he wrote it in November of 1942. In Colomiers, a town near Toulouse where he had moved in October.

The dramatic group he oversaw unraveled. Romain, *Léon Chancerel*, 319–23.

entertainment programs. Chancerel, *Frère Clown*, 3.

Let's sing. Chancerel, *Frère Clown*, 5.

Nina Gourfinkel. Anne Grynberg, *Les camps de la honte: Les internés juifs des camps français, 1939–1944* (Paris: La Découverte, 1991), 183–86, at 185n; Lucien Lazare, *L'Abbé Glasberg* (Paris: Cerf, 1990), 41; Ruth Schatzman, "Nina Gourfinkel (1898–1984)," *Revue des études slaves* 63 (1991): 705–10, at 707–8, 708–9.

earned his sobriquet. Lazare, *L'Abbé Glasberg*, 41, 45.

allegedly also called him so. Countless references to this litter the Internet, but unfortunately none of them provides a source.

he was soon extolled. Lesley A. Wright, "La mort de Massenet: Réactions des contemporains," in *Massenet aujourd'hui: Héritage et postérité. Actes du colloque de la XIe biennale Massenet des 25 et 26 octobre 2012*, ed. Jean-Christophe Branger and Vincent Giroud, Centre interdisciplinaire d'études et de recherches sur l'expression contemporaine: Travaux, vol. 166 / Collection musique et musicology: Les cahiers de l'opéra théâtre, vol. 1 (Saint-Étienne, France: Publications de l'université de Saint-Étienne, 2014), 21–38, at 27.

curriculum of musical education. "Cours et conférences," *Revue de musicologie* 21 (1942): 10.

it played in the summer season. Giroud, "Le centenaire de la naissance: Massenet en 1942," in *Massenet aujourd'hui: Héritage et postérité. Actes du colloque de la XIe biennale Massenet des 25 et 26 octobre 2012*, ed. Jean-Christophe Branger and Vincent Giroud, Centre interdisciplinaire d'études et de recherches sur l'expression contemporaine: Travaux, vol. 166 / Collection musique et musicology: Les cahiers de l'opéra théâtre, vol. 1 (Saint-Étienne, France: Publications de l'université de Saint-Étienne, 2014), 65–94, at 87.

Saint-Étienne, France. See Blandine Devun, *La vie culturelle à Saint-Étienne pendant la deuxième guerre mondiale (1939–1944)* (Saint-Etienne, France: Publications de l'Université de Saint-Étienne, 2005); Giroud, "Le centenaire de la naissance."

commemorative stamp. The four-franc stamp in bluish green, measuring 18 × 22 mm, was designed by Paul-Pierre Lemagny and engraved by Antonin Delzers. It was issued on June 22, 1942, and ceased being sold on October 24.

Bastille Day. In French, *la fête nationale* and *le quatorze juillet*.

Holiday of the Federation. In French, *Fête de la fédération*.

Massenet was invoked. A postcard depicting Massenet highlights the caption (in French): "Families, take pride: thanks to you, France will live."

Henri Perrin. Henri Perrin, *Priest-Workman in Germany*, trans. Rosemary Sheed (London: Sheed and Ward, 1947).

a perfect sabotage. Henri Perrin, *Le capitaine Darreberg, héraut de Notre-Dame: Récit d'évasion, missions secrètes … à la R. A. F.* (Lyon, France: Emmanuel Vitte, 1956), 58–59.

His other pseudonyms. Jacques Baumel, *La liberté guidait nos pas* (Paris: Plon, 2004), 177.

Brotherhood of Our Lady. In French, *Confrérie Notre-Dame*.

Star of the Sea. Gilbert Renault, *On m'appelait Rémy*, 2 vols. (Paris: Librairie académique Perrin, 1966), 1:263–64, 278, 280, image between 288–89.

the cult of Fátima. Gilbert Renault, *Fatima: Espérance du monde* (Paris: Plon, 1957).

Cross of Lorraine. On the history of the cross of Lorraine, see François Le Tacon, *La croix de Lorraine: Du Golgotha à la France libre* (Woippy, France: Serpenoise, 2012), esp. 123–43 on the use of the cross during World War II.

organized in 1949. Les Jongleurs de Notre-Dame, Compagnie de Théâtre, Dole, founded by Monseigneur Boillon, curate of Notre-Dame.

staged in Paris. Forrest C. Pogue, *Pogue's War: Diaries of a WWII Combat Historian* (Lexington: University Press of Kentucky, 2001), 234.

a children's book. Anatole France, *Le jongleur de Notre-Dame* (Paris: Éditions de l'Amitié, 1944, repr. 1946).

in his mid-twenties. Eventually, Watrin would become a film animator.

The Revolt of the Angels. Anatole France, *La révolte des anges* (Paris: Calmann Lévy, 1946).

English translation. France, *The Revolt of the Angels*, trans. Wilfrid Jackson, illus. Pierre Watrin (New York: For the members of the Limited Editions Club, 1953).

luxury edition for connoisseurs. Jérôme Tharaud and Jean Tharaud, *Les contes de la Vierge*, illus. Pio Santini (Paris: Société d'éditions littéraires françaises, 1946).

his art for the book. Nineteen miniatures supplement the dropped initial capital letters that embellish each chapter.

1941 biography. *Images du Maréchal Pétain* (Paris: Sequana, 1941).

Charles Maurras. Samuel M. Osgood, *French Royalism under the Third and Fourth Republics* (The Hague: M. Nijhoff, 1960), 155–56.

forget what has preceded. In fact, *amnestia* in Greek means literally "forgetfulness."

A Pathway to Heaven. *A Pathway to Heaven*, trans. Antonia White (New York: Pellegrini & Cudahy, 1952); originally published as idem, *Le fil de la Vierge* (Paris: Plon, 1951).

gossamer. *Pathway to Heaven*, 37 (on Our Lady's threads).

recapitulation of the medieval tale. *Pathway to Heaven*, 7–21, at 7: "You probably know the story of *Our Lady's tumbler*. In case you do not know it or have forgotten it, it runs like this. A tumbler became a monk and observed with humble admiration how his brothers in religion consecrated their talents to the glory of the Mother of God. Finding himself too ignorant to produce such work as theirs, he shut himself in the chapel and, as an offering in Our Lady's honour, performed the acrobatics which had once ensorceled the crowds in the fair-ground in front of her statue. The prior, spying through a keyhole or a crack in the door, saw him turning his somersaults and thought his novice must suddenly have gone mad. He was about to intervene and put an end to this scandal when he saw the Virgin's statue come to life, descend the altar steps and wipe away the sweat from the tumbler's forehead with a fold of her blue cloak. This golden legend has inspired poets, novelists and musicians. It has even invaded the realms of Comic Opera. In the seminary at Bellerive it had provided the clerical students with a nickname for one of their colleagues, Calixte Merval."

Golden Legend. Besides the collection of hagiographies, Bordeaux evidences awareness of the little story of the monk and the bird: idem, *Pathway to Heaven*, 15, 16, 68.

tumbler of light. Bordeaux, *Pathway to Heaven*, 54, 81.

connoisseur of Madonnas. Bordeaux, *Pathway to Heaven*, 36, 117, 119.

God be praised! Bordeaux, *Pathway to Heaven*, 237, 239.

portrayed him as ugly. Compare Stith Thompson, *Motif Index of Folk-Literature: A Classification of Narrative Elements in Folktales, Ballads, Myths, Fables, Mediaeval Romances, Exempla, Fabliaux, Jest-Books, and Local Legends*, 6 vols., 2nd ed. (Bloomington: Indiana University Press, 1955–1958), D 1639.2.

the exact countercurrent. In 1924, an interpreter of it took to task his contemporaries who failed to appreciate literature and other arts as expressions of religion: "They need to apply that lovely old fable of Our Lady's Tumbler, and to remember that the artist normally honors God, not by preaching or teaching, but by practising his art!" See R. Ellis Roberts, "Arthur Machen," *Sewanee Review* 32 (1924): 353–56, at 354.

François Mauriac. For detailed insights into the similarities and differences between Bordeaux and Mauriac, see Gisèle Sapiro, "Salut littéraire et littérature du salut: Deux trajectoires de romanciers catholiques: François Mauriac et Henry Bordeaux," *Actes de la recherche en sciences sociales* 111.1 (1996): 36–58. She incorporated this material into her later book, *The French Writers' War, 1940–1953*, trans. Vanessa Doriott Anderson and Dorrit Cohn (Durham, NC: Duke University Press, 2014), 158–89. Sapiro's book is a tour de force of situating writers and their institutions within their broader social and political contexts.

defeated along with the Nazis. Sapiro, *French Writers' War*, 184.

Great Britain

the work of Irene Wellington. Wellington also handled minor features of the art. At that stage, she had not even reached the midpoint in her long and flourishing trajectory as a calligrapher and instructor of others in the craft. Her life and work are chronicled in Heather Child et al., *More than Fine Writing: The Life and Calligraphy of Irene Wellington* (Woodstock, NY: Overlook Press, 1987); this manuscript is listed, with the dates 1939–1942, on p. 136, with the alternative title *Del tumbeor Nostre Dame*.

William Morris. In due course, he established himself through his aptitude in stained glass and tapestry. See Lynne Curran, "Sax Shaw: His Contribution to the World of Tapestry," *Journal of Weavers, Spinners and Dyers* 200 (December 2001): 10–12.

new tradition of penmanship. In his handwriting, Johnston revived the use of the traditional broad-edged nib. His "foundational hand" influenced a generation of modern typographers.

a well-written codex. Peter Holliday, *Edward Johnston: Master Calligrapher* (London: British Library; New Castle, DE: Oak Knoll Press, 2007).

manuscripts from the Middle Ages and medieval-like texts. Already in 1925, Wellington lettered an illuminated manuscript of Morris's *The Defence of Guinevere*. In the second half of the same decade, she undertook, without concluding the effort, trial drafts for the medieval English Chester Pageant miracle play, *The Deluge*. In around 1943, she designed a manuscript form of Saint Francis's *Song of the Creatures* and another of poems from the major medieval songbook, the *Carmina Burana*, both in English translation. See Child et al., *More than Fine Writing*, 56–59, 68–69, 76–77, 86–87.

more convincing reality. She takes as her exemplar the earliest recension in *Romania* without naming its editor but instead only Gaston Paris, she singles out for praise the English translation by Eugene Mason, and she quotes with tacit approval the sentence "If it is stunning testimony to faith, it is also still a true poetic gem." See Wendelin (or Wilhelm) Foerster, "Del tumbeor Nostre-Dame," *Romania* 2 (1873): 315–25, at 316: "Si c'est un témoignage éclatant de foi, c'est plus encore un vrai joyau poétique."

United States

all the help they could get. From many examples, I pick one that is close to home for me. Robert Woods Bliss was a retired career diplomat and, in a studiously unflashy fashion, a remarkable philanthropist. In an address to the Harvard Club of Washington, DC in 1943 (seventy-five years ago), he envisioned that the center for Byzantine studies that his wife and he had endowed would shed the light of learning: "Now that dark nights have descended over Europe and eclipsed the great centres of mediaeval study in Prague, Budapest, Vienna, and other cities, it is our hope that Dumbarton Oaks will carry the lighted torch in the Western World." Dumbarton Oaks Archives, Administrative files, John S. Thacher correspondence, 1940–1949, April 8, 1943.

The Greatest Gift. MGM Miniatures, released September 5, 1942, directed by Harold Daniels, written by Karl Kamb, starring Edmund Gwenn as Bartholomew (the juggler), with Hans Conried as Father Fabian, Lumsden Hare as Father Cyprian, and Robert Emmett O'Connor as Brother Xavier. An English theater and film actor, Edmund Gwenn remains best known for having later delivered an Academy Award-winning performance as Kris Kringle in the 1947 *Miracle on 34th Street*. Kris Kringle has been a by-word for Santa Claus in the United States. The short was aired much later on television: in 1955, the American George Murphy, host of the variety show *MGM Parade*, included it in the December 14 episode (1.14).

married couple. Robert A. and Jarrett Wells Schmid, both originally from Montclair, New Jersey.

published our story. Unpaginated booklet, "Printed for the friends of Jarrett and Robert Schmid, Christmas 1944." Original French with English translation by Frederic Chapman. The pamphlet comprises a mere six bifolios, placed within a quarto that is folded over rather than cut to produce the cover.

Princeton University as an undergraduate. After taking his A.B. degree, he became an advertising executive in the media business.

Arnold Robert Verduin. Arnold R. Verduin, "Handsprings and Somersaults," *Journal of the National Education Association* 34.7 (November 1945): 151. The byline identifies him as resident at the time in Wichita, Kansas, and as former head of the history department at State Teaching College, New Paltz, New York. His most noteworthy accomplishment as an author may have been a piece about a beachcomber that appeared in *The New Yorker* in 1944; see idem, "High Wind at Coney," March 25, 1944: 61–62.

Notes to Chapter 2

The world becomes more amusing every year. Henry Adams, to Mabel Hooper La Farge, December 22, 1902, in Harold Dean Cater, *Henry Adams and His Friends: A Collection of His Unpublished Letters* (Boston: Houghton Mifflin, 1947), 532–33, at 533. Compare letter to John Hay, November 7, 1900, in Henry Adams, *The Letters of Henry Adams* (henceforth *LHA*), ed. J. C. Levenson et al., 6 vols. (Cambridge, MA: Harvard University Press, 1982–1988), 5:167–69, at 169.

the one-lira denomination. See Chester L. Krause and Clifford Mishler, *1994 Standard Catalog of World Coins*, ed. Colin R. Bruce II, 21st ed. (Iola, WI: Krause, 1993), 2038. The coins were first in nickel and later in stainless steel.

the area for signifying the date was enlarged. The usual format, in which the four digits of a year would be split with the first two on one side and the last two on the other, was expanded to allow for signaling both 1933 and 1934.

Ezquioga. William A. Christian Jr., "Tapping and Defining New Power: The First Month of Visions at Ezquioga, July 1931," *American Ethnologist* 14 (1987): 140–66.

referendum. Plebiscites are not always the best vehicles for successful democracy.

apparitions of Our Lady. Also called the Virgin of the Golden Heart, and Our Lady in the Hawthorn Tree. The five young visionaries were Fernande, Gilberte, and Albert Voisin, and Andrée and Gilberte Degeimbre. For the most reliable sources, see René Laurentin and Patrick Sbalchiero, *Dizionario delle "apparizioni" della vergine Maria* (Rome: ART, 2010), 111–12; Don Sharkey, "The Virgin with the Golden Heart: Beauraing, 1932–33," in *A Woman Clothed with the Sun: Eight Great Appearances of Our Lady in Modern Times*, ed. John J. Delaney (Garden City, NY: Hanover House, 1960), 213–38; John Beevers, *The Sun Her Mantle* (Westminster, MD: Newman, 1953), 182–89; Don Sharkey and Joseph Debergh, *Our Lady of Beauraing* (Garden City, NY: Hanover House, 1958), which is the only entire book devoted to "the complete story of Our Lady's appearances at Beauraing"; Fernand Toussaint and Camille Joset, *Notre-Dame de Beauraing: Histoire des apparitions* (Paris: Desclée De Brouwer, 1981); Herbert Thurston, *Beauraing and Other Apparitions: An Account of Some Borderland Cases in the Psychology of Mysticism* (London: Burns, Oates & Washbourne, 1934), 1–24.

convent school. The Sisters of Christian Doctrine Academy.

More than thirty times. Thurston, *Beauraing and Other Apparitions*, 4.

1,700,000. Thurston, *Beauraing and Other Apparitions*, 1.

Tilman Côme. The first name is sometimes written Tilmant. For information, see Thurston, *Beauraing and Other Apparitions*, 25–32.

Banneux. In the Belgian Ardennes, fifty miles northeast of Beauraing.

an eleven-year-old girl. She was named Mariette Beco. For a photograph, see Giuseppe Delabays, *La Madonna dei Poveri di Banneux-Notre-Dame*, trans. Ester Brinis (Balsamo, Italy: Paoline, 1949), between 32–33.

radiant with light. For the most reliable sources, see Laurentin and Sbalchiero, *Dizionario*, 104–6; Robert M. Maloy, "The Virgin of the Poor: Banneux, 1933," in *Woman Clothed with the Sun*, ed. Delaney, 239–67; Beevers, *The Sun Her Mantle*, 190–95; Léon Wuillaume, *Banneux, boodschap voor onze tijd: Verslag van de verschijningen, verklaring van de boodschap* (Banneux, Belgium: Voncken, 1983); Thurston, *Beauraing and Other Apparitions*, 33–40.

Onkerzele. In the diocese of Ghent.

many predictions. Thurston, *Beauraing and Other Apparitions*, 42: "She prophesies war and other calamities which threaten her country, and which can only be averted by prayer and the conversion of the people from infidelity. It was rumoured that she had foretold that there would be war within two years, but she denies this and declares that she has not been told when the blow will fall and what its exact nature may be."

the Church rejected. Laurentin and Sbalchiero, *Dizionario*, 556. Another instance would be the apparitions that Berthonia Holtkamp and Henri Kempenaers were supposed to have witnessed in 1933. The authenticity of these last-mentioned episodes was judged negatively by ecclesiastical authorities within the year. See ibid., 448.

throughout Belgium. At Chaineux, Etikhove, Lokeren, Melen, Rotselaer, and Tubise.

crisis in Flemish and Dutch literature. J. H. M. Anten, "De crisistijd van de jaren dertig: Gouden jaren voor de neerlandistiek," *Nederlandse letterkunde* 15.3 (2010): 262–72; Koen Rymenants et al., eds., *Literatuur en crisis: De Vlaamse en Nederlandse letteren in de jaren dertig*, AMVC-Publicaties, vol. 12 (Antwerp, Belgium: AMVC, 2010).

Our Lady's Dancer: A Little Miracle Play. F. J. Weinrich, *De danser van Onze Lieve Vrouw: Een klein mirakelspel*, trans. Wies Moens (Antwerp, Belgium: De Sikkel, 1930).

Wies Moens. All sources regarding his biography of Wies Moens, especially on the topic of Nazi activities, are to be parsed with close care. The fullest treatment of him to date is a case in point, since the family name of the first coauthor does not appear to be coincidental: Olaf Moens and Yves T'Sjoen, "Een historische en literaire inleiding," in Wies Moens, *Memoires* (Amsterdam: Meulenhoff, 1996), 9–77. See also Jan d'Haese, "Wies Moens," In *Oostvlaamse literaire monografieën*, vol. 4, Kultureel jaarboek voor de provincie Oost-Vlaanderen, Bijdragen, Nieuwe reeks, vol. 14 (Ghent, Belgium: 1981), 163–93.

College of the Holy Virgin. In Dutch, Heilige Maagdcollege, in Dendermonde.

Flemish Union. In Dutch, *Vlaamsche Bond*. Moens and T'Sjoen, "Een historische en literaire inleiding," 10.

Ghent remained the central locus. Bruno De Wever, "Vlaams-nationalisme in de Gentse regio, 1914–1945," *Handelingen der Maatschappij voor Geschiedenis en Oudheidkunde te Gent* 49.1 (1995): 265–81.

the so-called Flemish question. Camille Huysmanns, "The Flemish Question," *Journal of the Royal Institute of International Affairs* 9 (1930): 680–90, at 680.

Great Netherlands. In Dutch, *Groot-Nederland*. See Bruno De Wever, "Groot-Nederland als utopie en mythe," *Bijdragen tot de eigentijdse geschiedenis / Cahiers d'histoire du temps présent* 3 (1998): 91–108.

Afrikaans-speaking portion of South Africa. Yves T'Sjoen, "Achter de trommels: Het Afrikaner nationalisme als bouwsteen voor het ideologische discours van de Vlaamse Beweging (ca. 1875–1921)," *Werkwinkel* 2 (2007): 51–76.

avant-gardism. Artists of the period who pushed the boundaries of the status quo through innovation and experiment are labeled "avant-garde." See Geert Buelens, "Een avantgardist is (g)een groep: Over de wankele avantgardestatus van de flaminganten tijdens het interbellum," in *Avantgarde! Voorhoede? Vernieuwingsbewegingen in Noord en Zuid opnieuw beschouwd*, ed. Hubert F. van den Berg and Gillis J. Dorleijn (Nijmegen, Netherlands: Vantilt, 2002), 92–102, 223–24.

claim to literary-historical significance. Moens and T'Sjoen, "Een historische en literaire inleiding," 46.

expressionist poetry. Wies Moens, *De boodschap* (The message) (Antwerp, Belgium: De Sikkel, 1920).

school and amateur groups. In these observations, I am indebted to Staf Vos, *Dans in België 1890–1940* (Leuven, Belgium: Universitaire Pers Leuven, 2012), 279–80, who provides information on productions in 1930, 1931, and 1948.

other collaborative projects. Moens and T'Sjoen, "Een historische en literaire inleiding," 51.

Moens viewed his generation. Wies Moens, "Een katholiek-modern toneelrépertoire," *De Beiaard* 2 (1925): 27–48.

Play of Saint Bernard. In Dutch, *Sint Bernardus-spel*.

Companions of Our Lady. In French, *Compagnons de Notre Dame*.

German "legend play." Dietzenschmidt (pseudonym of a dramatist, born Anton Franz Schmid, who was also known as Anton Franz Schmidt and Peter Thomas Bundtschuch), *Compostella (Die St.-Jacobsfahrt): Legendespel in drie bedrijven*, trans. Wies

Moens, Wederlandsch Keurtooneel, vol. 1 (Ghent, Belgium: "'t Spyker," 1923). This play was later taken as the basis for the opera *Die Jakobsfahrt* (1936) by Fidelio Friedrich (Fritz) Finke.

The original-language edition from 1920. Dietzenschmidt, *Die Sanct Jacobsfahrt: Eyn Legendenspiel in drey Aufzügen* (Berlin: Oesterheld, 1920). The woodcut was by Johannes Othmar from Augsburg. At the corners of the illustrations are the signs of the four Gospel writers.

G. K. Chesterton's St. Francis. G. K. Chesterton, *S. Franciscus van Assisi*, trans. Wies Moens (Ghent, Belgium: Cultura, 1924).

an English volume on Saint Francis. This time Moens translated a drama by the English playwright and illustrator Laurence Housman: *Van Sint Franciscus: Negen taferelen uit het leven van de poverello*, trans. Wies Moens (Utrecht, Netherlands: De Gemeenschap, 1929–1930).

Flemish Popular Theater. In Dutch, Het Vlaamsche Volkstooneel, abbreviated as VVT. The group existed from 1924 to 1932. A comprehensive inventory of the archive for the group is available: see Jos Verhoogen and Geert Opsomer, *Inventaris van het archief van Het Vlaamsche Volkstooneel*, Reeks inventarissen en repertoria, vol. 24 (Leuven, Belgium: Kadoc, 1989).

Catholic theater producers. Frank Peeters, "Faam en waan van het modernistische theater in Vlaanderen: 1920–1929," in *Historische avant-garde en het theater in het Interbellum*, ed. Jaak Van Schoor and Peter Benoy (Brussels: ASP, 2011), 91–98, at 94.

intellectual elite. Evelin Vanfraussen, "'Ontbonden in dien stroom de puurste pracht!' Moens' veelvuldige volk en de Duitse bezetter," *Spiegel der letteren* 47.4 (2005): 355–76.

folk-connected. Vanfraussen, "'Ontbonden in dien stroom,'" 355, 356, 357, 360, 375, with additional references.

Dutch Literature Viewed from a Folk Perspective. In Dutch, *Nederlandsche letterkunde van volksch standpunt gezien* (Rotterdam, Netherlands: Dietsche Boekhandel, 1939, 2nd edition, Bruges, Belgium: Wiek op, 1941).

National Socialist party of Belgium. The organization was called Verdinaso, short for *Verbond van Dietse Nationaal Solidaristen* (Union of Diets National Solidarists).

unremarked and uncompensated later by the invaders. Vanfraussen, "'Ontbonden in dien stroom.'"

Flemish radio broadcasting. It was known in Dutch as *Zender Brussel*, in German as *Sender Brüssel*. The name can be translated with clunky literalism as "Transmitter Brussels" or less slavishly as "Brussels Station."

German translation. *Das flämische Kampfgedicht*, trans. Adolf von Hatzfeld (Jena, Germany: E. Diederich, 1942).

Carmelite college in Limburg. Els Van Damme, "'Met u of zònder u, altijd voor u': De 'volksverbonden' lyriek van Wies Moens," in *Verbrande schrijvers: 'Culturele' collaboratie in Vlaanderen (1933–1953)*, ed. Lukas De Vos et al. (Ghent, Belgium: Academia Press, 2009), 71–91 (with biographical and bibliographical details at pp. 86–91).

Germany above all. In German, *Deutschland über alles*.

Dutchland above all. In Dutch, "Dietsland over al."

The Pointed Arch. Wies Moens, *De spitsboog* (Bruges, Belgium: Wiek op, 1943).

Masson recalled. Marcel Lobet, *Arthur Masson, ou La richesse du cœur* (Gilly, France: Institut Jules Destrée pour la défense et l'illustration de la Wallonie, 1971), 53–56 (chapter 7, "Jongleur de la Wallonie"), at 52: "So it was that I became acquainted with fabliaux, tales to make us laugh, born apparently out of our Walloon region, and in which Gallic brio unleashes itself often into vast savagery, but sometimes grows tender too to the point of being no more than a fresh and stirring smile like an April posy. And so I learned the fabliau of *Our Lady's Tumbler*. You know how the poor jongleur, received in an abbey of monks, turns despondent at seeing that he is the only one unable to offer to the Madonna of the monastery a beautiful statue, a beautiful painting, the magnificent stained glass, or the elegant canticle that his fellow monks carve, paint, or compose with all their faith and their talents. He, the poor fellow, is not good for anything. All the same, he does what he can. Shutting himself off in the chapel, he performs before the Virgin the moves in his routine. He juggles, does acrobatics, sings, recites. He is discovered, and that is going to cause a scandal. But the good Virgin comes down from her pedestal and, before the stunned eyes of the brethren, comes to wipe the sweat that trickles from the face of the poor, exhausted trouvère.

"I cannot lay down at the feet of the Virgin of the 'Alma Mater' either learned works or noteworthy discoveries. I have only my tales, the naïve song of the clogs of Toine, the smile of his girls, and the stormy laugh of T. Déome. But I offer thus the best of what I have. An affectionate observer of our folk who, taken together, are good folk, simple, brave, colorful, and great lovers of droll and sly comedies, I have endeavored to make likable these worthy folk while writing stories in which, obviously, one would seek in vain a kindred spirit to that of the Prince of Ligne—stories that have not enriched the national patrimony but stories that have all the same cheered up decent folk."

T. Déome is the cousin of Toine, in Masson's fictitious world. The reference to the Prince of Ligne refers specifically to Charles-Joseph, the seventh Prince de Ligne, a field marshal known for his prowess, and a prolific writer renowned for his courtly elegance of style (in living as well as in writing).

jongleur of the Walloon region. In French, *Jongleur de Wallonie*.

Wintze, or Our Lady's Tumbler. E. H. Blondeel, *Wintze, of De Tuimelaar van O. L. Vrouw: Legendeverhaal* (Torhout, Belgium: Becelaere, 1933). The title page contains a reduced version of an illustration that is repeated as a full page later in the volume (p. 48); both display the main character with the Madonna and Child.

Wintze wins you over. Blondeel, *Wintze*, 59.

E. H. Blondeel. Born in the little town of Beveren (Roeselare), E. H. (Georges) Blondeel became a priest in 1942 and served later as a teacher at Sint-Lodewijkscollege in Bruges for nearly two decades. An article about Blondeel was published in the college's alumni magazine by J. Mûelenaere, "E. H. Georges Blondeel," *Haec olim* 12 (1961): 5–9.

Fig. n.1 E. H. Blondeel, seated third from right in front row, among his cohort of newly-ordained priests. Photograph, 1942. Photographer unknown. Image courtesy of Webwinkel Beeldbank Brugge. All rights reserved.

resided in Mont-Saint-Guibert. Subsequently, he was appointed as spiritual leader to communities of nuns, first in Ypres and later in Bruges. The book itself was published in Torhout, in West Flanders.

not far from both Beauraing and Banneux. To be precise, slightly less than forty miles (63 km) from Beauraing and a little less than seventy miles (117 km) from Banneux.

a practicing Catholic. His Catholicism is clear not only from the Church's nihil obstat and imprimatur, but also from the inscription in one surviving volume to "his former pupil, Brother Elias-Victor" ("zijn oud leerling Broeder Elias-Victor").

The Netherlands

the writer directed dramatic performances of Our Lady's Tumbler. "St-Vincent's College," *Het Ypersche*, January 26, 1929, 9; February 16, 1929, 16.

various other towns in Flanders. The newspaper accounts refer to Bruges, Roeselaere, and other unnamed towns and villages.

The Pious Minstrel. In Dutch, *De vrome speelman* (Amsterdam: "De Gulden Ster," 1933).

Reynard the Fox. August Defresne, *De psychologie van "Van den Vos Reynaerde"* (Amsterdam: Boonacker, 1920).

expressionism. August Defresne, "Het expressionisme in de huidige Duitse toneelschrijfkunst," *Groot Nederland* 22 (1925): 293–312, 406–29, 513–30, 625–42 (final page mispaginated).

any other Dutch-language author. In fact, the index of personal names in the biography includes no one mentioned in this study apart from Franz Werfel and Defresne's wife. For a study of Defresne's theatrical career, see Willy Philip Pos, *De toneelkunstenaar August Defresne: Toneelschrijver, regisseur, toneelleider* (Amsterdam: Moussault, 1971). His wife was Charlotte Köhler.

one or another theatrical company. His adaptation appeared during a spell from 1932 to 1938 when he was with the Amsterdam Stage Union (Amsterdamse Toneelvereniging).

Chamber of Culture. In Dutch, *Kultuurkamer*.

the photographic image. The photograph was taken by Godfried de Groot.

Charlotte Köhler. She is known to have performed the text in 1932, and to have resorted to it subsequently in school presentations. See Ferdinand Sterneberg, *Charlotte Köhler: "Klank en weerklank"* (Zutphen, Netherlands: Walburg Pers, 1977), 44, 129.

the mysticism of the thirteenth and fourteenth centuries. The preceding two quotations are plucked from *De vrome speelman*, 8, 9, respectively.

Broken Light. Anthonie Donker, *Gebroken licht* (Arnhem, Netherlands: Van Loghum Slaterus, 1934), 59. This and the citations of Donker in the following note expatiate upon information furnished in the postscript to Peter J. A. Nissen, "Jongleren voor de Moeder Gods: De voorgeschiedenis van een verhaal van Gerard Reve," *Maatstaf* 31 (1983): 45–50.

The fourteen-line poem. Anthonie Donker, *Grenzen* (Arnhem, Netherlands: Hijman, Stenfert Kroese & Van der Zande, 1928), 95, repr. in idem, *De einder: Verzamelde gedichten* (Arnhem, Netherlands: Van Loghum Slaterus, 1947), 152.

Dutch man of letters. Victor Emanuel van Vriesland, trans., *De potsenmaker van Onze Lieve Vrouwe*, illus. Bob Buys, De Uilenreeks, vol. 44 (Amsterdam: Bigot en Van Rossum, 1941), repr. in idem, *Gouden legenden: Verhalen van God en heiligen, vromen en zondaars*, ed. Antoon Coolen, illus. Karel Thole (Amsterdam: Meulenhoff, 1951; 2nd ed., 1953), 29–38. The text of the Dutch *Our Lady's Tumbler* is embellished with one full-page illustration (on p. 35), which depicts the tumbler in the middle of a backward handspring alongside an altar. A Madonna has descended and is approaching with a large towel.

Years ago, when seeking details about Vriesland's version through the Anglophone version of the search engine Google, I was amused to learn that keyboarding the Dutch word *potsenmaker* would induce the interrogative "Did you mean: potsmoker?" For general autobiographical information relating to this author, see Victor Emanuel van Vriesland, *Herinneringen verteld aan Alfred Kossmann* (Amsterdam: Em. Querido, 1969).

The Restaurant. August Defresne, *Het eethuis* (Maastricht, Netherlands: Leiter-Nypels, 1931), 9–17.

Vriesland's version. It appeared as a small clothbound book. If the title page is figured into the count, the volume contains six three-tone images by the artist and occasional book illustrator Bob Buys.

artists had played a role in the Resistance. "Hij beklemtoonde na de bevrijding steeds de belangrijke rol die kunstenaars in het verzet hadden gespeeld" ("After the liberation, he always emphasized the important role that artists had played in the Resistance"), http://www.historici.nl/Onderzoek/Projecten/BWN/lemmata/bwn3/vriesland

self-declared Zionist. Jaap Meijer, Victor Emanuel *van Vriesland als zionist: Een vergeten hoofdstuk uit de geschiedenis van het Joods nationalisme in Nederland*, Diasporade, vol. 2 (Heemstede, Netherlands: Jaap Meijer, 1976).

Vriesland sunk into despondency. One of his letters acknowledges that he "suffered from depression in the stark lazaretto of his isolation" ("In de barre leproserie van mijn isolement lijd ik aan depressies"), http://www.historici.nl/Onderzoek/Projecten/BWN/lemmata/bwn3/vriesland

to go under water. The Dutch *duiken* is cognate with the English verb *duck*. On awareness during the War of the word's metaphoric connotations, see Jeroen Dewulf, *Spirit of Resistance: Dutch Clandestine Literature during the Nazi Occupation* (Rochester, NY: Camden House, 2010), 86.

fled his homeland. Werfel did not return until thirty years posthumously, when his body was exhumed in Los Angeles for reburial in Vienna. He has been claimed ex post facto for honor by both Austria and Germany.

Fig. n.2 Franz Werfel. Photograph, ca. 1940, by Trude Geiringer.
Image courtesy of Leo Baeck Institute. All rights reserved.

Whether he would have wanted or even accepted kudos from either nation is disputable.

The Song of Bernadette. Franz Werfel, *Das Lied von Bernadette, Roman* (Stockholm: Bermann-Fischer, 1941). The book was translated into English for publication in 1942, and a movie was made of it already in 1943. The promotion for the film featured a painting made for the occasion by the archetypically American artist Norman Rockwell.

Fig. n.3 Advertisement for the film adaptation of Franz Werfel's *The Song of Bernadette*. Illustration by Norman Rockwell, 1943. Published in *Life*, December 13, 1943, 75.

ultimate values of our mortal lot. Franz Werfel, *The Song of Bernadette*, trans. Ludwig Lewisohn (New York: Viking, 1942), 7.

preeminence. Among other things, he held for two decades, from 1945 to 1965, the presidency of the Pen Club, the association of writers.

in 1902. On October 5.

Anatole France Society. In French, Société Anatole France. Held in The Hague, Nederlands Letterkundig Museum.

an undated publication. Gabriël Smit, trans., *De danser van Onze Lieve Vrouw* (Bussum, Netherlands: Ons Leekenspel, [1941?]).

seven miracles of the Virgin. The typography and printing of the miracles was the work of the publisher Charles Nypels. This presentation was reprinted in due course in Gabriël Smit, *Zeven Marialegenden*, illus. Cuno van den Steene (Utrecht, Netherlands: Het Spectrum, 1941, repr. 1944), 80–105.

a very Old French legend. Smit, *Zeven Marialegenden*, 108.

he also underscores. Smit, *Zeven Marialegenden*, 108: "Dat de hier geboden verzen de oorspronkelijke teksten niet op den voet volgen, spreekt welhaast vanzelf. Er werd—met behoud van den algemeenen opzet van het verhaal—voornamelijk naar gestreefd den geest dezer kostelijke vertelling voor den hedendaagschen lezer te doen herleven in een hem vertrouwde vorm."

Cuno van den Steene. He was associated with the progressive Catholic periodical *De Gemeenschap* (The community), published from 1925 to 1941.

a printer. For information, see Marianne van Laar and Karel van Laar, *Charles Nypels: Meester-drukker*, Goodwill, vol. 22 (Maastricht, Netherlands: Charles Nypels Stichting, 1986). The press was Het Spectrum; the printer, Charles Nypels.

In the Light. In Dutch, *In 't Licht*.

Smit's circumstances. See http://www.nederlandsepoezie.org/dichters/s/smit_gabriel.html

Netherlands Broadcasting. In Dutch, Nederlandsche Omroep.

Netherlands Chamber of Culture. In Dutch, Nederlandsche Kultuurkamer.

the opportunism of taking both sides. The evidence is presented fairly and concisely by Dewulf, *Spirit of Resistance*, 202–3.

addressed himself to religious topics. For instance, he wrote a "Requiem in Memory of His Mother," to honor a parent who had died when he was still a young man.

Psalms. In Dutch, *Psalmen* (1952).

In Wartime. The original title was the Latin *Tempore belli*, 1944 and 1946.

Praise of Mary and Other Poems. In Dutch, *Maria-lof en andere gedichten*.

A French Legend from the Twelfth Century. In Dutch, *De tuimelaar … een franse legende uit de twaalfde eeuw*. The book contains no indication of the printer.

far more for the size of the country. This point is made by Dewulf, *Spirit of Resistance*, 3.

Major Seminary. In Dutch, Grootseminarie.

Camp Haaren. Known in Dutch as Kamp Haaren, this "hostage camp" was located in the province of North Brabant.

prison and interrogation unit. In German, *Polizeigefängnis und Untersuchungsgefängnis*.

SS. In full, *Schutzstaffel*, "defense squadron."

Anton Mussert. On Mussert, see Dewulf, *Spirit of Resistance*, 41–42, 46–47.

Brabantia Nostra. On *Brabantia Nostra*, see J. (Jan) L. G. van Oudheusden, *Brabantia Nostra: Een gewestelijke beweging voor fierheid en "schoner" leven 1935–1951*, PhD diss., Katholieke Universiteit, Nijmegen, 1990 (Tilburg, Netherlands: Zuidelijk Historisch Contact, 1990), and, more accessibly, idem, "*Brabantia Nostra*: Rooms en romantisch regionalisme, 1935–1951," in *Constructie van het eigene: Culturele vormen van regionale identiteit in Nederland*, ed. Carlo van der Borgt et al., ANNO-historische reeks, vol. 8, Publicaties van het P. J. Meertens-Instituut voor Dialectologie, Volkskunde en Naamkunde van de Koninklijke Nederlandse Akademie van Wetenschappen, vol. 25 (Amsterdam: P. J. Meertens-Instituut, 1996), 123–39.

poet of the cultural and political reawakening. In Dutch, "Dichter van het Brabants Reveil."

the herald of Brabant. J. C. Bedaux, "Franciscus Josephus Henricus Maria van der Ven, Tilburg 2 september 1907–Tilburg 10 december 1999," *Jaarboek van de Maatschappij der Nederlandse Letterkunde* (2000): 129–31. After the war, Van der Ven set aside verse for his specialty of labor law and published prolifically in his new professional field. After retirement, he produced in rapid succession collections of poetry, once again under his pseudonym, with the publisher Brandon Pers in Tilburg: see http://www.cubra.nl/brandonpers/welcome.htm

Toward a Catholic Order. To give the full bibliography, Étienne Gilson, *Pour un ordre catholique* (Paris: Desclée de Brouwer, 1934). See Van Oudheusden, "*Brabantia Nostra*: Rooms en romantisch regionalisme," 128.

Étienne Gilson. For instance, in 1932, Étienne Gilson, *L'esprit de la philosophie médiévale* (The spirit of medieval philosophy) (Paris: J. Vrin, 1932) and, two years later, idem, *La*

théologie mystique de saint Bernard (The mystic theology of Saint Bernard) (Paris: J. Vrin, 1934).

student guild of Our Dear Lady. This point was made by Van Oudheusden, "*Brabantia Nostra*: Rooms en romantisch regionalisme," 125–26. On the guild, see B. J. M. van Raaij, "Het Brabants Studentengilde van Onze Lieve Vrouw: Een regionale katholieke studentenbeweging tussen antimodernisme en modernisme, 1926–1970," *Nordbrabants historisch jaarboek* 6 (1989): 155–206.

the core of the Netherlands. Cees van Raak, "En het strovuur brandt voort … Frank Valkenier en de verdere geschiedenis van de Brandon Pers," *Tilburg: Tijdschrift voor geschiedenis, monumenten en cultuur* 19.3 (2001): 97–105, at 98: "Brabant wordt zienderogen weer de kern der Nederlanden."

ready to invent them. Oudheusden, "*Brabantia Nostra*: Rooms en romantisch regionalisme," 130–33.

As a token of appreciation. This copy is in my possession.

Brabantia Mariana. Augustinus Wichmans, *Brabantia Mariana tripartita* (Antwerp, Belgium: apud Ioannem Cnobbaert, 1632).

the Duchess of Brabant. In Dutch, "De Hertogin van Brabant."

a little Marian chapel. Oudheusden, "*Brabantia Nostra*: Rooms en romantisch regionalisme," 133–34. The structure was sanctified in 1939.

the Lady of Moerdijk. In Dutch, "De Vrouwe van de Moerdijk."

boundary between the Netherlands and Belgium. With some distortion, it stands for what the Mason-Dixon line represents between the North and South in the United States. In this case, the line is a wide river and estuary called Hollands Diep. To the north of the water lies South Holland; to the south, North Brabant.

university teacher of medieval literature. Gryt Anne van der Toorn-Piebenga, *Middeleeuwse Marialegenden in modern Nederlands weergegeven, en van oorspronkelijke illustraties voorzien* (Baarn, Netherlands: Gooi, 1994), 61–64, with note on p. 92.

a prose version of the tale. Felix Rutten, *Novellen (Sittards dialekt)* (Sittard, Netherlands: Alberts, 1959), 7–15 ("Broeder Balderik"). The author had earlier published it as "Broeder Balderik," *Veldeke* 33.184 (December 1958): 49–52.

a short prose printed first in 1972. The short piece was published first in December of 1972 and again in the Christmas issue of 1974 in staff newsletters of a company where the housemate of the writer was employed. This "Guus van Bladel" was designated in Reve's works consistently as "the giver of the small picture of Notre Dame of Lourdes, 'shoe size 38.'" Full bibliographic details on the prose tale are available in Gerard Reve,

Archief Reve, ed. Pierre H. Dubois, annot. Sjaak Hubregtse, 2 vols. (Baarn, Netherlands: de Prom, 1981–1982), 2 ("1961–1980"): 21–23 (text), 219–20 (annotation). For analysis, see Peter J. A. Nissen, "Jongleren voor de Moeder Gods: De voorgeschiedenis van een verhaal van Gerard Reve," *Maatstaf* 31 (1983): 45–50.

discomfort with modernity. For context, see Otto Gerhard Oexle, "Das Mittelalter und das Unbehagen an der Moderne: Mittelalterbeschwörungen in der Weimarer Republik und danach," in *Spannungen und Widersprüche: Gedenkschrift für František Graus*, ed. Susanna Burghartz et al. (Sigmaringen, Germany: J. Thorbecke, 1992), 125–53.

pure Germanness. The term *Völkischkeit* (from the word *Volk*, "folk" or "people") means literally "folk-ishness."

This condemnation. Frank-Rutger Hausmann, "English and Romance Studies in Germany's Third Reich," in *Nazi Germany and the Humanities*, ed. Wolfgang Bialas and Anson Rabinbach (Oxford: Oneworld, 2007), 341–64, at 341, 345, 349.

German fairy tales. Christa Kamenetsky, *Children's Literature in Hitler's Germany* (Athens: Ohio University Press, 1984), 139–41.

His famous dictum. Anatole France, in *L'Humanité*, no. 6823, November 30, 1922, 1: "Il est beau qu'un soldat désobéisse à des ordres criminels."

Wilhelm Fraenger. Wilhelm Fraenger, *Die Masken von Rheims und der Legend "Der Tänzer unserer Lieben Frau" ins Deutsche übertragen von Curt Sigmar Gutkind* (Erlenbach, Switzerland: Eugen Rentsch, 1922).

he dismissed as failures. In Fraenger, *Die Masken von Rheims*, 40–42.

Religious Art in France. Émile Mâle, *Religious Art in France, the Thirteenth Century: A Study of Medieval Iconography and Its Sources*, Bollingen Series, vol. 90.2 (Princeton, NJ: Princeton University Press, 1984).

Romanesque Sculpture: Apostles and Jongleurs. Focillon, "Sculpture romane: Apôtres et jongleurs (études de mouvement)," *Revue de l'art ancien et moderne* 55 (1929): 13–28.

Previous research. Cahn, "Focillon's *Jongleur*," *Art History* 18.3 (1995): 345–62, at 355.

Curt Sigmar Gutkind

Curt Sigmar Gutkind. A thumbnail sketch of Gutkind can be found in Hans Reiss, "*Geisteswissenschaften* in the Third Reich: Some Reflections," *German History* 21 (2003): 86–103, at 98. For the fullest biographical background, see above all Frank-Rutger Hausmann, *"Vom Strudel der Ereignisse verschlungen": Deutsche Romanistik im "Dritten Reich,"* 2nd ed. (Frankfurt am Main, Germany: V. Klostermann, 2008), 244–51; Andreas F. Kelletat, "Auf der Suche nach einem Verschollenen: Dossier zu Leben und Werk des Romanisten und Übersetzers Curt Sigmar Gutkind (1896–1940)," in

Übersetzerforschung: Neue Beiträge zur Literatur- und Kulturgeschichte des Übersetzens, ed. idem et al., TRANSÜD: Arbeiten zur Theorie und Praxis des Übersetzens und Dolmetschens, vol. 85 (Berlin: Frank & Timme, 2016), 13–70. Other resources are Joseph Walk, ed., *Kurzbiographien zur Geschichte der Juden 1918–1945*, Leo Baeck Institute, Jerusalem (Munich, Germany: De Gruyter Saur, 1988), 132; *Lexikon deutsch-jüdischer Autoren*, 21 vols. (Munich, Germany: De Gruyter Saur, 1992–2013), 10:76–80.

Mussolini and His Fascism. The book was published in both Italian and German: Curt Sigmar Gutkind, *Mussolini und sein Fascismus*, with an introduction by Benito Mussolini (Heidelberg, Germany: Merlinverlag, 1928); *Mussolini e il suo fascismo* (Heidelberg, Germany: Merlinverlag, 1927).

labor and union issues. Wolfgang Schieder, *Mythos Mussolini: Deutsche in Audienz beim Duce* (Munich, Germany: Oldenbourg, 2013), 107–9.

personal audience. On March 1, 1927: see Schieder, *Mythos Mussolini*, 107.

dissertation director. In German, *Doktorvater* (literally, "doctor-father").

translation institute. In German, Dolmetscherinstitut, at the Städtische Handelshochschule Mannheim (later the Dolmetscherinstitut in Heidelberg).

Her husband directed the translation institute. On the internal politics within the translation institute and on the consequences of the national politics of the times, see Reinhard Bollmus, *Handelshochschule und Nationalsozialismus: Das Ende der Handelshochschule Mannheim und die Vorgeschichte der Errichtung einer Staats- und Wirtschaftswissenschaftlichen Fakultät an der Universität Heidelberg 1933–34*, Mannheimer sozialwissenschaftliche Studien, vol. 8 (Meisenheim am Glan, Germany: Hain, 1973), 121–23.

business school. In German, *Handelshochschule*.

Romance philologists. They included Erich Auerbach, Helmut Hatzfeld, Victor Klemperer, Ulrich Leo, Leonardo Olschki, and Leo Spitzer.

interned in Canada. The action was legal under the royal prerogative of Regulation 18B.

lost their lives. For an account of the vessel and its sinking, see Des Hickey and Gus Smith, *Star of Shame: The Secret Voyage of the Arandora Star* (Dublin, Ireland: Madison Pub., 1989); Maria Serena Balestracci, *Arandora Star: Dall'oblio alla memoria*, Belle Storie, Saggi, vol. 6 (Parma, Italy: MUP, 2008), 152 (on Limentani), 370n227 (on Gutkind). The tallies of deaths that have been published vary considerably. For clarification of the variations, see Peter and Leni Gillman, *"Collar the Lot!": How Britain Interned and Expelled Its Wartime Refugees* (London: Quartet Books, 1980), 209. For a more recent book on the interning, see Richard Dove, ed. *"Totally Un-English?": Britain's Internment of "Enemy Aliens" in Two World Wars* (Amsterdam: Rodopi, 2005).

Hans Hömberg

Cherries for Rome. In German, *Kirschen für Rom*.

contemporaneous book. *Jud Süß: Roman* (Berlin: Ufa-Buchverlag, 1941).

Jew Süss. The German title of the film is "Jud Süß," directed by Veit Harlan, who wrote the screenplay with Eberhard Wolfgang Möller and Ludwig Metzger. For context, see David Culbert, "The Impact of Anti-Semitic Film Propaganda on German Audiences: *Jew Süss* and *The Wandering Jew* (1940)," in *Art, Culture, and Media under the Third Reich*, ed. Richard A. Etlin (Chicago: University of Chicago Press, 2002), 139–57; Susan Tegel, *Jew Süss / Jud Süss (Germany, 1940)* (Trowbridge, UK: Flicks Books, 1996).

Popular Observer. In the full German, *Völkischer Beobachter: Kampfblatt der nationalsozialistischen Bewegung Großdeutschlands*. See Ernst Klee, *Das Kulturlexikon zum dritten Reich: Wer war was vor und nach 1945* (Frankfurt am Main, Germany: S. Fischer, 2007), 255–56.

The Juggler of Our Lady. In German, *Der Gaukler unserer lieben Frau*, illus. Ernst von Dombrowski (Vienna: Eduard Wancura, 1961).

three tales. "Der Gaukler unserer lieben Frau," 7–32, "Das eigentümliche Fräulein" (The peculiar young lady), 33–82, and "Die zwei Pasteten" (The two pies), 83–104.

additional remarks. Hömberg, *Der Gaukler unserer lieben Frau*, 108.

modern-day features. Despite the modern features, the story was taken as authentically medieval by Karl-Heinz Ziethen, *Virtuosos of Juggling: From the Ming Dynasty to Cirque de Soleil* (Santa Cruz, CA: Renegade Juggling, 2003), 6.

Here lies Mary's jongleur. Hömberg, *Der Gaukler unserer lieben Frau*, 32: "Hic iacet ioculator Mariae / artifex candidus / Vapor Ioannes."

collections of German art. Klee, *Kulturlexikon*, 118.

extreme rightist organizations. For example, consider the Deutsches Kulturwerk europäischen Geistes (German Cultural Society of the European Spirit) (1950–1996).

dissolved in 1998. In German, Verein Dichterstein Offenhausen (1963–1998).

After the War

writers and artists of any nation. See, for example, Anatole France, *Quatre nouvelles*, ed. Josef Longerich (Freiburg im Breisgau, Germany: L. Bielefeld, 1947), 13–20; idem, *Le petit soldat de plomb: Le jongleur de Notre-Dame*, ed. Georg Ahting and H. Richters-Franceschi, Neusprachliche Texte, vol. 124 (Dortmund, Germany: Lamberg Lensing, 1954).

a casualty of the Second World War. On the war and its effect on German medievalism, see Valentin Groebner, *Das Mittelalter hört nicht auf: Über historisches Erzählen* (Munich, Germany: C. H. Beck, 2008), 106–22, esp. at 117.

destroy the Gothic domes. Heinrich Heine, *On the History of Religion and Philosophy in Germany and Other Writings*, ed. Terry Pinkard, trans. Howard Pollack-Milgate (Cambridge: Cambridge University Press, 2007), 116. The original was first published as Henri Heine, "L'Allemagne depuis Luther," *Revue des deux mondes*, 3e ser., vols. 1, 4 (March, November, December 1834), repr. Heinrich Heine, "Zur Geschichte der Religion und Philosophie in Deutschland," *Der Salon* 2 (1835).

Church of the Augustinians. In German, Augustinerkirche.

Church of the Minorites. In German, Minoritenkirche. The Minorites are the Franciscans.

the renovating architect. Johann Ferdinand Hetzendorf von Hohenberg.

Votive Church. In German, Votivkirche, constructed between 1856 and 1878 by Heinrich Freiherr von Ferstel.

Mary of the Victory. In German, Maria vom Siege, built between 1868 and 1875 after a design by Friedrich von Schmidt.

Town Hall. Rathaus, built between 1872 and 1883 with Friedrich von Schmidt as architect.

The playwright. Joseph August Lux, *Das Gauklerspiel vor Unserer Lieben Frau*, or *Gauklerlegende*. For a listing of this unpublished play, see Wilhelm Kosch and Ingrid Bigler-Marschall, *Deutsches Theater-Lexikon: Biographisches und bibliographisches Handbuch*, 4 vols. (Klagenfurt, Germany: F. Kleimayr, 1953–1998), 2:1315. The typescript is Vienna, Austria, Österreichische Nationalbibliothek, Cod. Ser. N. 34081–34082 Han. The playwright's first name is frequently recorded with the alternate spelling Josef.

The Vision of the Blessed Lady. Joseph August Lux, *Die Vision der lieben Frau* (Berlin: Schuster & Loeffler, 1911).

The Play of Satan's World Judgment. In German, *Das Spiel von Satans Weltgericht oder Der Affe Gottes und der Gerechte: Ein zeitgemäßes Mysterium* (Vienna and Salzburg-Anif: Weiße Hefte, 1930).

God's Minstrel. In German, *Der Spielmann Gottes (Spiel)* (1930).

Play of a Holy Fool. In German, *Ein heilig Narrenspiel* (Vienna and Salzburg-Anif: Weiße Hefte, 1930).

From Death into Life. In German, *Vom Tod ins Leben: Ein Buch von Liebe, Tod und Jenseits* (Hammelburg, Germany: Drei Eichen, 1962).

earlier hymns. In German, *Vom Tod ins Leben: Ein Hymnus*, twelve pages published under the name of Rudolf Elmayer von Vestenbrugg (Zurich, Switzerland: Graphia, 1951), and six pages (ten sides of verse) under that of Elmar Brugg (Munich: Josef Gäßler, 1958).

The Jongleur of Our Beloved Lady. In German, "Der Spielmann Unserer Lieben Frau." In the novel, the key pages relating to our story are 254–71, 285–89, and 293.

construction engineer. The birth year of 1881 and death year of 1970 are attested in Werner Schuder, *Kürschners Deutscher Literatur-Kalender: Nekrolog 1936–1970* (Berlin: De Gruyter, 1973), 871. The alternative birth year of 1888 is also sometimes mentioned. He was born in 1881, in what is now the Croatian city of Pula, and died in 1970, in the Austrian metropolis of Graz, where he had lived much of the time until the spring of 1932. The fullest and most reliable information is available is Karin Gradwohl-Schlacher and Sabine Fuchs, "Rudolf von Elmayer-Vestenbrugg," in *Literatur in Österreich 1938–1945: Handbuch eines literarischen Systems*, vol. 1, *Steiermark*, ed. Uwe Baur and Karin Gradwohl-Schlacher, 3 vols. (Vienna: Böhlau, 2008–), 101–5; Karin Gradwohl-Schlacher, "Elmayer von Vestenbrugg (Elmayer-Vestenbrugg), Rudolf von; Ps. Elmar Vinibert von Rudolf, Elmar Brugg, Schriftsteller und Journalist," in *Österreichisches biographisches Lexikon (ÖBL) Online-Edition* 3 (Nov. 15, 2014).

his brother Willy. Willibald (Willy) Elmayer von Vestenbrugg, as had been his father Ludwig, was formerly a cavalry captain in the Austrian Imperial Army. The school is the Tanzschule Elmayer. On the brother and the school, see Thomas Schäfer-Elmayer, *Vom Sattel zum Tanzparkett: Die Lebensgeschichte meines Großvaters Willy Elmayer* (Vienna: Kremayr & Scheriau, 2014).

a host of different names. Such as von Elmayer-Vestenbrugg, Rudolf Elmar von Vinibert, Elmar Vinibert von Rudolph, Elmar Brugg, and Rudolph von Elmayer-Vestenbrugg: see Richard Bamberger and Franz Maier-Bruck, eds., *Österreich Lexikon*, 2 vols. (Vienna: Österreichischer Bundesverlag, 1966), 1:274.

lieutenant colonel. Obersturmführer (literally, "senior assault leader") in the Sturmabteilung-Wehrmannschaften ("Garrison of the Assault Division"). He is identified as having this rank in Rudolf von Elmayer-Vestenbrugg, ed., *SA.-Männer im feldgrauen Rock: Taten und Erlebnisse von SA.-Männern in den Kriegsjahren 1939–1940* (Leipzig, Germany: Hase & Koehler, 1941).

the brigade in Slovenia. Tone Ferenc, "The Austrians and Slovenia during the Second World War," in *Conquering the Past: Austrian Nazism Yesterday and Today*, ed. F. Parkinson (Detroit, MI: Wayne State University Press, 1989), 207–23, at 211–13.

Gravediggers of World Culture. Rudolf von Elmayer-Vestenbrugg, *Totengräber der Weltkultur: Der Weg des jüdischen Untermenschentums zur Weltherrschaft*, Kampfschriften der Obersten SA-Führung, vol. 2 (Munich, Germany: Zentralverlag der NSDAP, 1937).

Without Judah, without Rome. Rudolf von Elmayer-Vestenbrugg, *Georg Ritter von Schönerer, der Vater des politischen Antisemitismus, von einem, der ihn selbst erlebt hat* (Munich, Germany: F. Eher nachfolger, 1936, 2nd ed., 1942), 87: "Ohne Juda, ohne Rom / Wird gebaut Germaniens Dom!"

World Ice theory. In German, *Welteislehre*.

Hörbiger's system of deranged ideas. Brigitte Hamann, *Hitler's Vienna: A Portrait of the Tyrant as a Young Man*, 2nd ed. (London: Tauris Parke Paperbacks, 2010), 225–27, 431–32; Peter Levenda, *Unholy Alliance: A History of Nazi Involvement with the Occult*, 2nd ed. (New York: Continuum, 2002), 197–200. Such half-baked (or -frozen) thinking is a throwback, in an intellectually disordered and disheveled way, to the explanations for natural phenomena that Presocratic philosophers posited.

Heinrich Himmler. Others within the party opposed it strongly.

Storm Trooper training handbook. See Robert Bowen, *Universal Ice: Science and Ideology in the Nazi State* (London: Bellhaven, 1993); Edward P. Rich, *The Pazyryk Agenda: A Police Procedural* (self-published, Xlibris, 2004), 130–32. Not all this scholarship is readily verifiable, and the book by Bowen has been faulted: see the review by Mitchell G. Ash, in *German Studies Review* 18 (1995): 174–76. The German phrase translated here is "volksnah und volkswichtig."

his 1958 dissertation. "Studien zum Darstellungsbereich und Wortschatz des Beowulf-Epos."

Armanen Futhark. Futhark is a term to designate runic writing systems, while the modifier Armanen refers to a supposed class of priestly kings that held sway over the ancient Aryan-Germanic nation.

Guido von List. He wrote *Das Geheimnis der Runen* (The secret of the runes) to study the Armanen runes.

reviving Germanic paganism. Guido von List, *Deutsch-mythologische Landschaftsbilder*, 2 vols., 2nd ed. (Vienna: Guido-von-List-Gesellschaft, 1912), 2:592–93.

The Resurrection of the Dead. 367–471, with subsections "In the Catacombs" (410–62) and "Resurrection" (462–71).

another book of fiction. Elmar Brugg, *Sankt Stephan zwischen Staub und Sternen: Die Schicksalssymphonie eines Domes* (Hamburg, Germany: P. Zsolnay, 1956).

everything-in-one. In German, *das All-Eine*.

the unity of God and man. Angelika Pagel, "Jugendstil and Racism: An Unexpected Alliance," *RACAR: Revue d'art canadienne / Canadian Art Review* 19.1–2 (1992): 97–111, at 100–1, 103.

the infamous SS. From German *Schutzstaffel* (Defense Corps).

folkloristic journal. *Die Kunde*, "Tidings."

as an emblem. For example, the 6th SS-Gebirgs-Division "Nord" (Mountain Division North) used it.

SS Honor Ring. In German, *SS-Ehrenring*.

death's-head ring. Craig Gottlieb, *The SS Totenkopf Ring: An Illustrated History from Munich to Nuremberg* (Atglen, PA: Schiffer Military History, 2008), 19, 27, 31, 33, 47, 57.

Himmler. An avid Wagnerian, Himmler was predisposed to play at being a knight by his shallow and unsteady knowledge of supposed medieval heroic narratives and symbols. These accessories of knighthood included swords, daggers, and rings. See Gottlieb, *SS Totenkopf Ring*, 12.

The swastika and the Hagal-rune. The corresponding German reads: "Hakenkreuz und Hagall-Rune sollen uns den nicht zu erschütternden Glauben an den Sieg unserer Weltanschauung vor Augen halten." It appears in a letter signed by H. Himmler, dated June 6, 1939, to accompany bestowal of the SS death's-head ring upon SS-Gruppenführer Reinhard Heydrich.

in the SA and not the SS. That is, in the Storm Troopers and not in the *Schutzstaffel*.

Now it will also be evident. *Vom Tod ins Leben*, 474.

without recalling beliefs associated with them. At the same time, to a broader German and Austrian public at the time when he wrote, the Armanen futhark had become better known than any conventional medieval one, and nowadays many individual readers would not be aware of the Nazi associations from nearly seventy-five years ago.

Drei-Eichen-Verlag ("Three Oaks Press") published Vestenbrugg's novel. The firm had existed since before the war. It specialized in esoterica quite different from the occultism and pseudoscience promulgated by the Nazis, especially by Himmler's institute for archaeological and cultural history (*Ahnenerbe*, meaning "forefathers' inheritance"). Consequently, it has been reported that the publishers were persecuted. They may have deemed the esotericism of the novel appropriate to the general profile of the books they printed, without paying close attention to undercurrents of a very unpleasant past in *Von Tod ins Leben* (From death into life).

traveling folk. In German, the two main operative phrases are *fahrendes Volk* and *fahrende Leute*.

the same systematic persecution. Guenter Lewy, *The Nazi Persecution of the Gypsies* (Oxford: Oxford University Press, 2000).

common-law wife. No effort is made to preserve the emphasis in all other versions on the monasticism, or at least chastity, of the jongleur.

a character called Hanns. The name may be subsumed among the various German equivalents of the French Jean.

In the late twelfth century. The precise date was May 30, 1187.

a second miracle. See Johannes Agnellus, monk of Déols, *Liber miraculorum Beatae Mariae Dolensis*, in Jean Hubert, "Le miracle de Déols et la trêve conclue en 1187 entre les rois de France et d'Angleterre," *Bibliothèque de l'École des Chartes* 96 (1935): 285–300, at 296–300 (edition of Latin), and 292–93, 298–99 (analysis).

Saint George himself. *Vom Tod ins Leben*, 310.

Notes to Chapter 3

The cathedrals belong to France. Le Corbusier, *When the Cathedrals Were White* (New York: Reynal & Hitchcock, 1947), xxii.

right or proper reason. The phrase derives from what would be called in Latin *recta ratio*, which is modeled in turn upon the Greek expression *orthos logos*. On the origins of the heavily Aristotelian phrase, see J. M. Rist, "An Early Dispute about 'Right Reason,'" *The Monist* 66 (1983): 39–48. On the development of the concept over time, see Karl Bärthlein, "Zur Lehre von der *recta ratio* in der Geschichte der Ethik von der Stoa bis Christian Wolff," *Kant-Studien* 56.2 (1965): 125–55. On the Renaissance use of the idea, see Robert Hoopes, *Right Reason in the English Renaissance* (Cambridge, MA: Harvard University Press, 1962); Lotte Mulligan, "'Reason,' 'Right Reason,' and 'Revelation' in Mid-Seventeenth-Century England," in *Occult and Scientific Mentalities in the Renaissance*, ed. Brian Vickers (Cambridge: Cambridge University Press, 1984), 375–401.

art for art's sake. The French slogan from which the English derives is *l'art pour l'art*. The topic has been examined at length in Albert Cassagne, *La théorie de l'art pour l'art: En France chez les derniers romantiques et les premiers réalistes* (Paris: L. Dorbon, 1959); John Wilcox, "The Beginnings of l'art pour l'art," *The Journal of Aesthetics and Art Criticism* 11.4 (1953): 360–77. For earlier observations that trace the expression further back chronologically, see Joel E. Spingarn, "L'Art pour l'Art," *Modern Language Notes* 25 (1910): 95; F. Baldensperger, "L'Art pour l'Art," *Modern Language Notes* 27 (1912): 91.

a 1948 study by Wallace Fowlie. Wallace Fowlie, *The Clown's Grail: A Study of Love in Its Literary Expression* (Denver, CO: Alan Swallow, 1948), repr. as *Love in Literature* (Bloomington: Indiana University Press, 1965). I cite from the reprint.

voyou. A French word meaning something like "street urchin, hooligan."

This brother. Fowlie, *Love in Literature*, 80.

speechless. Fowlie, *Love in Literature*, 80: "The clown performs mute rites, as poetry always celebrates something silent, some wilfully silenced voice."

founder of a long race. Fowlie, *Love in Literature*, 81.

Richard Sullivan, Notre Dame Professor

practicing his art. Roberts, "Arthur Machen," 354.

The Juggler. The magazine was discussed in chapter 25, above.

cult of the Virgin. Thomas A. Kselman, *Miracles and Prophecies in Nineteenth-Century France* (New Brunswick, NJ: Rutgers University Press, 1983), 16–18, 198–200.

Sorin's own commitment. Marvin R. O'Connell, *Edward Sorin* (Notre Dame, IN: University of Notre Dame Press, 2001), 144 (on the sermon), 507–9 (on *Ave Maria*).

University of Our Lady of the Lake. In French, "L'Université de Notre Dame du Lac."

vowed to build a chapel. O'Connell, *Edward Sorin*, 143–44.

a copy of the Chapel of Loreto. It stands immediately behind the present Church of Loreto.

Our Lady of the Angels. In Italian, Santa Maria degli Angeli.

It imitated a church. In fact, its name is the Latin version of Italian *Porziuncola*, the small church protected inside the Basilica of Santa Maria degli Angeli about 2.5 miles (4 kilometers) from Assisi proper, and the place where the Franciscan movement started.

Portiuncula indulgence. The grant of remission was reputedly granted by Pope Honorius III in 1216, in response to reports of a private revelation to Saint Francis. Originally the indulgence, which became an entrenched practice before the end of the thirteenth century, was limited to the original Portiuncula chapel in Italy.

out of place and out of time. The technical terms would be *anatopical* and *anachronistic*, although only the second is commonly used.

Two of these hilltops. One was the Sacro Monte or "Sacred Mountain" of the Blessed Virgin in Oropa, province of Biella, constructed in 1617. The other was the Sacred Mountain of the Blessed Virgin of Succor in Ossuccio, province of Como (1635).

ready proximity of long-established pilgrimage sites. Michael P. Carroll, *Madonnas That Maim: Popular Catholicism in Italy since the Fifteenth Century* (Baltimore, MD: Johns Hopkins University Press, 1992), 3–4.

traveled several times. O'Connell, *Edward Sorin*, 618.

with a first stop in Lourdes. O'Connell, *Edward Sorin*, 641.

theme park for Marianism. The characterization of the Notre Dame campus in this way is meant neither irreverently nor disrespectfully.

Main Building. The edifice was constructed, starting in 1879, in a style that was designated at the time as "modern Gothic," although domes are not at all typical of architecture in that style.

the heart of the campus. Damaine Vonada, *Notre Dame: The Official Campus Guide* (Notre Dame, IN: University of Notre Dame Press, 1998), 75.

gilded image. The replica that tops off the Golden Dome was a gift from Saint Mary's College, Notre Dame's sister institution. It measures 16 feet tall and 2 long tons in weight. It brings the overall height of the building to 187 feet. Made of buffed bronze, it has been gilded and regilded a half dozen times with 23-karat gold. See Vonada, *Notre Dame*, 22; Richard Sullivan, *Notre Dame: Reminiscences of an Era* (Notre Dame, IN: University of Notre Dame Press, 1951), 141. Understood loosely, the gilding of Madonnas is a logical extension of the chrysography, the technique of golden highlighting, that was used on the Virgin and Child in medieval painting.

electric lighting. Thomas J. Schlereth, *A Dome of Learning: The University of Notre Dame's Main Building* (Notre Dame, IN: Notre Dame Alumni Association, 1991), 40.

crescent moon. The lunar shape echoes the base of the statue, which depicts the Virgin's feet trampling a serpent, with the horns of a crescent moon flanking them. The reptile alludes to her role in overcoming the consequences of Eve's part in the Fall, which involved a snaky seduction. See Genesis 3:13–15, Apocalypse (Revelation) 12:9. The moon and crown of twelve stars identify the Mother of God with the Woman of the Apocalypse described elsewhere in the Book of Revelation. See Apocalypse (Revelation) 12:1: "And there appeared a great wonder in heaven: a woman clothed with the sun, and the moon under her feet, and on her head a crown of twelve stars." *The Vulgate Bible: Douay-Rheims Translation*, vol. 6, *The New Testament*, ed. Angela M. Kinney, Dumbarton Oaks Medieval Library, vol. 21 (Cambridge, MA: Harvard University Press, 2013), 1360–61. All these elements were second nature in Christian iconography. Particularly pertinent is the type of statue known as the Marianum, which was beloved in northern German village churches from the mid-fifteenth century through the first half of the sixteenth: see Justin E. A. Kroesen and Regnerus Steensma, *The Interior of the Medieval Village Church*, 2nd ed. (Leuven, Belgium: Peeters, 2012), 347.

in Rome. In the Piazza di Spagna.

wended his way back to his former college. Sullivan, *Notre Dame*, 8. On Sullivan, see Harry Redcay Warfel, *American Novelists of Today* (New York: American Book Co., 1951), 417; see also Thomas Stritch, *My Notre Dame: Memories and Reflections of Sixty Years* (Notre Dame, IN: University of Notre Dame Press, 1991), 61, 161–62, on Sullivan and the relative paucity of writers from Notre Dame.

his early ambitions. Una M. Cadegan, "How Realistic Can a Catholic Writer Be? Richard Sullivan and American Catholic Literature," *Religion and American Catholic Literature: A Journal of Interpretation* 6 (1996): 35–61.

Virgin on the Dome. Sullivan, *Notre Dame*, 142–44: "Today the golden figure of Mary, tiny against the sky, with the great curve of the Dome rounding away golden beneath it, is a kind of symbol of all this University means. … The Dome and the statue on top of it in some kind of way which I do not clearly understand, and so cannot clearly explain, represent Notre Dame … I am inclined to feel that there is more than silly school spirit in this selection of the Main Building for general attention. … it is the fact that on the Dome there is a statue of Mary Immaculate—Notre Dame, Our Lady. … It merely seems necessary to indicate certain reasons why the statue on top of the

Dome—which is reverenced as a reminder of a woman who at one moment in time did something permanently important—stands in a way as the center, or core, of this masculine University."

under the title Inscripts. Samuel John Hazo, *Inscripts* (Athens: Ohio University Press, 1975), 49–98, quotation at p. 71.

Our Lady's Tumbler. Richard Sullivan, *Our Lady's Tumbler* (Chicago: Dramatic Publishing Co., 1940).

the grey drapes. *Our Lady's Tumbler*, 5.

dressed in the brown of Franciscans. Consequently, the actors in his play should properly be attired in robes of black and white, in lieu of the brown he proposes, which is associated today with Franciscan and, to a lesser extent, Carmelite friars.

Brother Wat. The name of Brother Wat is left unexplained. The form is attested, from the Middle Ages on, particularly as a shortening of Walter.

I do not earn my bread. *Our Lady's Tumbler*, 9.

offered his tumbling to Mary. *Our Lady's Tumbler*, 9: "Daily have I set before thee what trifling art I have." Brother Wat's insufficiency as a breadwinner is mentioned three more times, with the final instance occurring after he has fallen dead.

an exchange. *Our Lady's Tumbler*, 19: "Young Monk [*timidly*]. My lord—can tumbling please the Mother of God? Abbot. She is pleased with love, monsieur. [*He speaks softly.*] He has earned his bread."

A 1953 production. In this year, the script was duplicated for a production performed as part of a special Christmas program by a Catholic academy that had been founded in 1946 by the Brothers of Holy Cross. The duplication was accomplished using a mimeograph machine, which worked by forcing ink through stencils onto paper. The performance was reported in "Our Lady's Tumbler," *Cleveland Plain Dealer*, December 19, 1953, 28. Gilmour Academy was located in Gates Mills, an eastern suburb of Cleveland, Ohio. A connection to the playwright came through the fact that the Brothers were affiliated with the University of Notre Dame. If any other special explanations must be found for why the play would have been staged, at least two come to mind. One is that the theatrical work would have naturally been known to an order of brothers affiliated with a university dedicated to the name of Our Lady. Another is that local affection for the story could have lingered in the region of Ohio where the academy is situated, since it lies within the same diocese as Oberlin, where pageants on the theme had been performed.

No information is forthcoming. The Richard Sullivan papers (1873–1981, mostly 1930–1981) are in the University of Notre Dame Archives.

a modern musical version. Hannah Blue Heron, *That Strange Intimacy* (Victoria, BC: Trafford, 2005), 82–85. Following quotations are from pp. 85 and 83 respectively.

encyclical. "Fulgens Corona," September 8, 1953.

the decade of Mary. Una M. Cadegan, "Images of Mary in American Periodicals, 1900–1960," *Marian Studies* 46 (1995): 89–107, at 95.

R. O. Blechman, Cartoon Juggler

published in 1953. R. O. Blechman, *The Juggler of Our Lady: A Medieval Legend Adapted* (New York: Holt, 1953). The story of the conception and composition is recounted in R. O. Blechman, *Behind the Lines* (New York: Hudson Hills, 1980).

knew little about the holiday. Blechman, *Behind the Lines*, 23: "Preferably Christmas! If only he had said Halloween or New Year's Eve, I might have been happier, but Christmas! My mind was awash in Christmas notions all year round, and asking me to do something with this holiday was like asking me to dam a piece of the ocean."

would have been familiar with the tale. An enthusiastic reviewer took as a given that the story would be a known quantity: "Of course every one knows the legend of the juggler who entertained Our Lady with his art because he was a simple man who loved her and his art was all he knew." See Gouverneur Paulding, "An Old Legend in New, Charming Guise," *New York Herald Tribune*, December 6, 1953, A52.

the author reminisced. Blechman, *Behind the Lines*, 23.

any campus production before or since. This assertion is more or less verbatim what Conna Bell Shaw made in her reminiscences of the three stagings of the pageant: http://www.oberlin.edu/alummag/oampast/oam_winter/iwas.html

seemed to be instituting itself. The note concludes: "So the literary seed, after lying dormant 700 years, has flowered excitingly, until now 'The Juggler' has become one of the most pleasing tales of Christmastime." Thomas J. McCabe, *An Adaptation of the Story of Our Lady's Juggler*, illus. Raymond Lufkin (Tenafly, NJ: Private printing for the friends of Raymond Lufkin, 1951), endnote.

Rex Knight's Our Lady's Jester: A One-Act Play. London: Sir Isaac Pitman and Sons, 1952.

Master Punchinello. *Our Lady's Jester*, 5.

commedia dell'arte. In this form of theater actors wore the masks of specific character types. One is Pulcinella.

the beatitude of his playmate. *Our Lady's Jester*, 10.

a glory round his head. *Our Lady's Jester*, 10.

archaizing style. The stilted language bulges with words such as *nay* and *naught* and forms like *thou* and *thee*, *'tis*, *shalt*, and the like.

the parable of my own life. Blechman, *Behind the Lines*, 23.

The Age of Faith. New York: Simon and Schuster, 1950.

the author and his wife, Ariel Durant. The effort was not singlehanded, since after a long while Durant acknowledged the partnership of his wife Ariel.

spiritual bankruptcy of their own times. Norman F. Cantor, *The Civilization of the Middle Ages: A Completely Revised and Expanded Edition of* Medieval History: The Life and Death of a Civilization (New York: HarperCollins, 1993), xiv; John Van Engen, "The Christian Middle Ages as an Historiographical Problem," *American Historical Review* 91.3 (1986): 519–52, at 520–21.

publication of The Juggler of Our Lady. His first publication, it has been reprinted twice in English, both in his autobiographical dossier (introduced by Maurice Sendak) and by itself (New York: Stewart, Tabori & Chang, 1997). A few years ago, it was translated into French, in an edition that includes a small sampling of his other works: R. O. Blechman, *Le jongleur de Notre-Dame: Une légende médiévale réadaptée*, trans. Anne Krief ([Paris]: Gallimard Jeunesse, 2002).

eclipsed by the medievalism. "Religion: Cantalbert the Juggler," *Time*, Monday, October 5, 1953.

Franciscan who reviewed the volume. Eligius M. Buytaert, "Review of R. O. Blechman, *The Juggler of Our Lady*," *Franciscan Studies* 13.4 (1953): 138: "The drawings, partly in color, give quite an original, though modern, interpretation of the medieval version."

one-hit wonder. Blechman, *Behind the Lines*, 23: "When *The Juggler of Our Lady* was published and met with great acclaim, I associated success with the book but not with me, whom I considered undeserving. Convinced that success lay in producing other Jugglers, I set out to do more of them. *Son of the Juggler, Grandson of the Juggler, Grand Nieces and Nephews of the Juggler*—I turned them out with Catholic fervor, but to no effect. In the meantime the years went by, and, still desperately trying to produce offspring—*Cousin of the Juggler, Bastard of the Juggler*—I would not stop; I could not stop."

affinity for Christmas themes. His yuletide work has ranged from a lovely interstitial "Season's Greetings" on the CBS television network that aired in 1966, through an eleven-minute cartoon short on the Nativity in 1978 called *No Room at the Inn*, to *The Life of Saint Nicholas, as Transcribed in Pictures and Text* (New York: Stewart, Tabori & Chang, 1996).

seeking out foreign folktales. Most notably in a fifty-one-minute animated version of Igor Stravinsky's "The Soldier's Tale" in 1983. Beyond these bits of continuity, he innovated constantly afterward. In the fullness of time he became and has remained applauded for his creativity and wit as a cartoonist, animator, and illustrator. A culminating irony would be that nowadays many more would recognize his hand from major newspapers, magazines, and television than would have heard of the title that launched his career. He has had artwork in such venues as the op-ed page of *The New York Times*, the front cover of *The New Yorker*, and the pages of such magazines as *Esquire*, *Fortune*, *Harper's Bazaar*, *Rolling Stone*, and *Spin*; animations in television shows such as *Sesame Street*, series such as the PBS mystery show *Ghostwriter*, and commercials in many advertising campaigns. Eventually, he founded his own animation studio, The Ink Tank, in 1977.

animated short. By Terrytoons in Technicolor, produced by Gene Deitch, directed by Al Kouzel, based on the book by R. O. Blechman, with original music by Philip A. Scheib.

I am the Woolworth's. Leonard Maltin, *Of Mice and Magic: A History of American Animated Cartoons*, 2nd ed. (New York: New American Library, 1987), 125.

How the Grinch Stole Christmas. New York: Random House, 1957. The television special of 1966 was directed by Chuck Jones for Metro-Goldwyn-Mayer.

Named Cantalbert. Could his supposed incompetency, since he is preoccupied by all that he cannot do, account even subconsciously for the first syllable in his anomalous name?

rose without thorns. George Wells Ferguson, *Signs and Symbols in Christian Art* (New York: Oxford University Press, 1954), 37.

the rosary. For consideration of the origins of the rosary, see Anne Winston-Allen, *Stories of the Rose: The Making of the Rosary in the Middle Ages* (University Park: Pennsylvania State University Press, 1997), 13–30. For the Cistercian connection, see Andreas Heinz, *Louange des mystères du Christ: Histoire du rosaire, méditation de la vie de Jésus, compte tenu en particulier de ses racines cisterciennes* (Paris: Téqui, 1990).

I hope people won't be fooled. *Time*, October 5, 1953, 71–72, at 72.

Korean War. The war began on June 25, 1950, and it reached a close of sorts with a cease-fire on July 27, 1953.

Joseph R. McCarthy. McCarthyism has become synonymous with witch-hunt, thanks in no small part to *The Crucible*, a 1952 play written by the American playwright Arthur Miller in response to the sinister efforts of McCarthy's House Un-American Activities Committee to root out supposed communist sympathizers.

Janu-ary. As god of beginnings and transitions, he has dominion over gates and doorways: Janus is a divine janitor or "doorkeeper," from the noun *ianua* or "door."

sound recordings. Fred Waring and his Pennsylvanians, *'Twas the Night before Christmas*, 1953, Decca Records 45 rpm.

the relationship between the two. Bretel, "Le *jongleur de Notre-Dame*, un miracle pour enfants?," in *Grands textes du Moyen Âge à l'usage des petits*, ed. Caroline Cazanave and Yvon Houssais, Annales littéraires de l'Université de Franche-Comté, vol. 869 (Besançon, France: Presses universitaires de Franche-Comté, 2010), 277–97, at 285–86.

Blechman's development. For his subsequent development, see R. O. Blechman, *The Graphic Stories of R. O. Blechman: Talking Lines* (Montreal, Canada: Drawn and Quarterly, 2009).

Maurice Sendak observed. He offered the insight first in the introduction to Blechman's 1980 artistic biography, *Behind the Lines*, and adapted it in his preface to the 1997 reedition, fourth unnumbered side.

United Productions of America. Often designated UPA for short.

deliberate artistic experiment. Michael J. Barrier, *Hollywood Cartoons: American Animation in Its Golden Age* (New York: Oxford University Press, 1999), 548–51.

various short narratives. Through his art he brought to life fables by the Russian fabulist Ivan Andreevich Krylov and the fairy tale of the false prince by the German writer Wilhelm Hauff. He also illustrated a few books by the author of German children's books, Heinz Sponsel. See Ivan Andreevic Krylov, *Sämtliche Fabeln*, trans. Rudolf Bächtold (Zurich, Switzerland: Die Waage, 1960); Wilhelm Hauff, *Das Märchen von dem falschen Prinzen* (Dassel, Germany: Büttenpapierfabrik Hahnemühle, 1962); Heinz Sponsel, *Sango und die Inkagötter* (Stuttgart, Germany: Schwab, 1951); and other children's books with Sponsel on Christopher Columbus and Copernicus.

puppet plays. https://preetorius.lauteren.eu/lp.html

The Dancer of Our Lady. Wilhelm Preetorius, *Der Tänzer unserer lieben Frau* (Zurich, Switzerland: Die Waage, 1964).The unnumbered pages with art are printed in three colors, with handwritten text in black, and scissor cutouts in brown and gray. As in Blechmann's work, the graphic style is immediately recognizable as belonging to the second half of the twentieth century.

Life of the Fathers. For the reference to the *Vie des pères*, see Preetorius, *Der Tänzer*, first page of text (unnumbered): "the original of this legend derives from a collection of pious tales entitled *Vie des pères* written in thirteenth-century French."

scissor cuts. For an overview, see Ernst Biesalski, *Scherenschnitt und Schattenriß: Kleine Geschichte der Silhouettenkunst*, 2nd ed. (Munich, Germany: Callwey, 1978).

Emil Preetorius. Biesalski, *Scherenschnitt und Schattenriß*, 118–20, with illustrations.

At least one reviewer. For the first view, see the *Motion Picture Herald*, December 14, 1957, Product Digest Section 642: "With a deft, almost impressionistic use of line and color, and the deeply pleasant voice of Boris Karloff for narration, is told how eventually, in the monastery, the juggler's gift wields its influence. An unusual and novel effect is achieved by the use of small figures on the big CinemaScope screen." For the second, B. W. in *Kinematograph Weekly*, December 19, 1957, 14: "An unusual Terrytoon Cartoon in which is told a medieval folk tale. Although imaginatively handled, the treatment is too mannered and unusual to have as wide an appeal as its artistic qualities merit. Thus it must rate as Average."

Gene Deitch. For his recollections, see https://web.archive.org/web/20061102104316/http://genedeitch.awn.com/index.php3?ltype=chapter&chapter=14&page=4

wide-screen movies. The anamorphic lens series known as CinemaScope, created in 1953 and in use through 1967, permitted the creation of images up to a 2.66:1 aspect ratio, nearly twice as wide as the 1.37:1 ratio enabled previously by the Academy format.

highest achievement at Terrytoons. https://web.archive.org/web/20061102103731/http://genedeitch.awn.com/index.php3?ltype=chapter&chapter=15A&page=9

head of the studio. William M. Weiss.

the music. The composer was the American Philip A. Scheib.

the heading "Religion." In the category "Among the Other Books of the Week" (September 29, 1953).

ample justification. In speaking of miracles in 1888, Gaston Paris had already elevated *Our Lady's Tumbler* as "perhaps the masterpiece of the genre, thanks to its delightful and childlike simplicity." See Gaston Paris, *La Littérature française au Moyen Âge* (Paris: Hachette, 1888, 2nd rev. ed. 1890), 208: "l'histoire (chef-d'œuvre peut-être du genre par sa délicieuse et enfantine simplicité)."

graphic novels. R. O. Blechman, *The Juggler of Our Lady: The Classic Christmas Story*, foreword Jules Feiffer, introduction Maurice Sendak (Mineola, New York: Dover, 2015). In the "Foreword to the Dover Edition," Jules Feiffer points out that the term "graphic novel" was coined by Will Eisner for his experimental comic entitled *A Contract with God* (published in 1978). Other information suggests that the expression was first used in 1964.

Robert Lax, Poet among Acrobats

the being who leaves himself. Fowlie, *Love in Literature*, 83.

editors of The Jester. James Harford, *Merton & Friends: A Joint Biography of Thomas Merton, Robert Lax, and Edward Rice* (New York: Continuum, 2006), 9–12.

Cristiani Family Circus. Harford, *Merton & Friends*, 73–75; Michael N. McGregor, *Pure Act: The Uncommon Life of Robert Lax* (New York: Fordham University Press, 2015), 146–54; on the circus and conversion, see pp. 125–37 (chapter 8, "Aquinas and the Circus Beckon").

wandering minstrel. Robert Lax, *Circus Days & Nights*, ed. Paul J. Spaeth (Woodstock, NY: Overlook Press, 2000), 12: "Sometimes I layed [sic] down in the track … singling out a beautiful lady in the grandstands, or the fair flower she wore at her shoulder, looking at her wistfully, thinking, and not thinking, of all the dreams of romance. Lady, I am a beggar at the door of your castle. Your beauty has smitten me through the eyes and to the heart. You are Eleanor of Navarre and I am a troubadour."

Circus of the Sun. Journeyman Books, 1959.

circumstances in which he devised his book. Lax, *Circus Days & Nights*, 13.

want to make a movie ballet. Letter 49.2, in *When Prophecy Still Had a Voice: The Letters of Thomas Merton and Robert Lax*, ed. Arthur W. Biddle (Lexington: University Press of Kentucky, 2001), 108–9, at 108.

Acrobat's Song. Lax, *Circus Days & Nights*, 39 ("Acrobat's Song"): "Lady, / we are Thy acrobats; / jugglers; / tumblers / walking on wire, / dancing on air, / swinging on the high trapeze: / we are Thy children, / flying in the air / of that smile: / rejoicing in light."

the medieval lay brother. Lax, *Circus Days & Nights*, 90 ("Mogador's Book"): "It is not acrobatics on horseback. / It is ballet. / It is not comic ballet. / It is appropriately dignified praise. / An ancient / and very pure form / of religious devotion. / It is easy to compare it / to the childlike devotion / of the jongleur de Notre Dame; / But it is more mature, / more knowing."

videotape for children. Father Benedict Groeschel, C.F.R., *Children's Stories* (West Covina, CA: Saint Joseph Communications, 2008).

The Juggler of Notre Dame. The film was produced jointly by Walt Disney and the Paulist Brothers. The script and original score were the work of Lan O'Kun. The film was directed by Michael Ray Rhodes, and shot at San Juan Capistrano, a mission established by Franciscan friars in the late eighteenth century in southern California. The name of the location is not given within the film, since the claim is made that the church is named after Notre-Dame in Paris.

character of the juggler. In this case the performer is played by a career juggler, Carl Carlsson in real life.

a sculptor. Jonas is acted by a former professional football player, Merlin Olson.

Tony Curtis, Prime-Time Juggler

The Young Juggler. Tony Curtis and Barry Paris, *Tony Curtis: The Autobiography* (New York: Morrow, 1993), 178, 341. *The Young Juggler*, produced by William Frye, written by Joseph Stefano, directed by Ted Post, and coproduced by Curtleigh, had Tony Curtis playing the juggler (and serving as executive producer), with Nehemiah Persoff, Patricia Medina, Bert Freed, and Elisha Cook Jr. (Trick). It was originally to be entitled *The Juggler*, but a Kirk Douglas film by the same title (although on a different theme) already existed.

France and the United States. For the French, see Bernard Lesquilbet, "Christiane Lasquin," *Télé 60*, no. 795, January 17–23, 1960, 2. For the American, see J. P. Shanley, "Television," *America* 101.8, May 23, 1959, 378, on "Le Jongleur de Notre Dame." Aired on Sunday afternoon in May in *The Catholic Hour* by the National Broadcasting Company, this last one was an opera, directed by Richard J. Walsh, that had a cast drawn almost exclusively from Catholic University; the libretto was by Jean Anne Lustberg and the score by William Graves.

French press photo. Dated November 19, 1967. Conducting the Mass of "Le Jongleur de Notre Dame" is Father Mansot. The ceremony took place in Paris at the Cirque d'hiver ("Winter circus").

female juggler. Gipsy Bouglione.

fairground and traveling people. In French, *Aumônier des forains et des gens du voyage*.

during Lent. It was aired on March 29, 1960; Easter fell on April 17.

Feast of Fools. Max Harris, *Sacred Folly: A New History of the Feast of Fools* (Ithaca, NY: Cornell University Press, 2011). It was associated closely with Holy Innocents Day, the Feast of Asses, and other such celebrations.

January 6. The date is inaccurate, since the festival was customarily held on or about January 1.

W. H. Auden, *The Ballad of Barnaby*

We who must die. W. H. Auden, *For the Time Being: A Christmas Oratorio*, "Advent," III, in idem, *Collected Poems*, ed. Edward Mendelson (New York: Modern Library, 2007), 347–400, at 353.

Germanic literature. On his attraction to Old English and Old Norse literature, see Michael Alexander, *Medievalism: The Middle Ages in Modern England* (New Haven, CT: Yale University Press, 2007), 252–57; Chris Jones, *Strange Likeness: The Use of Old English in Twentieth-Century Poetry* (Oxford: Oxford University Press, 2006), 68–121 (chapter 2, "Anglo-Saxon Anxieties: Auden and 'the Barbaric Poetry of the North'").

Old English poems. These poems were included in W. H. Auden, *A Certain World: A Commonplace Book* (New York: Viking Press, 1970); *Deor* is on pp. 23–24.

translations from Old Norse poetry. The scholar was Paul Beekman Taylor. See Peter H. Salus and Paul B. Taylor, eds., *Völuspá, The Song of the Sybil: With the Icelandic Text*, trans. Paul B. Taylor and W. H. Auden (Iowa City: Windhover Press, University of Iowa, 1968); Paul B. Taylor and W. H. Auden, trans., *The Elder Edda: A Selection*, introduction Peter H. Salus and Paul B. Taylor, notes Peter H. Salus (London: Faber, 1969); W. H. Auden and Paul B. Taylor, trans., *Norse Poems* (London: Athlone, 1981). On the place of Iceland and its language in Auden's imaginative universe, see Paul Beekman Taylor, "Auden's Icelandic Myth of Exile," *Journal of Modern Literature* 24.2 (2000): 213–34.

Second Shepherds' Play. See Alexander, *Medievalism*, 255–56.

Ode to the Medieval Poets. W. H. Auden, *Collected Poems*, ed. Edward Mendelson (New York: Modern Library, 2007), 864.

girls' school in Connecticut. It was performed on May 23–24, 1969, at the now-defunct Wykeham Rise School for Girls in Washington, Connecticut. Harry Gilroy, "Auden Writes Opera Narrative for a Girls' School," *New York Times*, May 7, 1969, 36. The standard edition bears the dedication "for Chuck Turner": see Auden, *Collected Poems*, 824–27, where it is dated December 1968. For enlightenment about the text (which has only fourteen inconsequential differences among the various versions), see W. D. Quesenbery, *Auden's Revisions* (2008), http://audensociety.org/Audens_Revisions_by_WD_Quesenbery.pdf, 411.

longtime friend. Charles Turner is counted among the few students of the American composer Samuel Barber. See Peter Dickinson, "Charles Turner: Interview with Peter Dickinson, New York City, May 13, 1981," in *Samuel Barber Remembered: A Centenary Tribute*, ed. idem (Rochester, NY: University of Rochester Press, 2010), 73–79. The original score is held at the Gunn Memorial Library & Museum, in the Wykeham Rise Collection (cat. no. 1994.001.006).

sheet music. W. H. Auden, *The Ballad of Barnaby*, music by students of Wykeham Rise School in Washington, CT, realization Charles Turner (New York: G. Schirmer, 1969).

Epistle to a Godson. W. H. Auden, *Epistle to a Godson and Other Poems* (New York: Random House, 1972), 42–46.

a Christmas issue. *The New York Review of Books*, "Christmas Issue: 2," 13.11, December 18, 1969, cover.

cultivated a style. Steven Heller, *Edward Gorey: His Book Cover Art & Design* (Portland, OR: Pomegranate, 2015).

The Romance of Tristan and Iseult. Garden City, NY: Doubleday, 1955.

The Perfect Joy of St. Francis. Garden City, NY: Image Books, 1955.

Mont Saint Michel and Chartres. Garden City, NY: Doubleday, 1959. The latter was by Felix Timmermans. For reproductions of the covers, see Heller, *Edward Gorey*, 32, 40.

memorized the poet's whole canon. Alexander Theroux, *The Strange Case of Edward Gorey*, 2nd ed. (Seattle, WA: Fantagraphics Books, 2011), 104 (for this particular assertion), 108–16 (on broader connections between Auden and Gorey).

conventional definition. Auden holds to the usual verse form for ballads, iambic heptameters in sets of four. In this case, all twenty-four stanzas rhyme aabb.

rounded. In this usage the adjective means stanzaic.

relying heavily on dialogue. More than a quarter of the lines, twenty-six of the ninety-six, contain direct speech.

lack of Latin and illiteracy. "Now Barnaby had never learned to read, / Not *Paternoster* knew nor *Creed*." Auden, *Collected Poems*, 825.

faux-naïf. Lucy McDiarmid, *Auden's Apologies for Poetry* (Princeton, NJ: Princeton University Press, 1990), 4.

"Lady," cried Barnaby. Auden, *Collected Poems*, 827.

Glory to God in the highest. In Latin, "Gloria in excelsis Deo."

memorial service. See Iona and Peter Opie, eds., *The Oxford Book of Narrative Verse* (Oxford: Oxford University Press, 1983), 401. The broadside is mentioned in neither the printed program (Wednesday, October 3, 1973, 8:00 p.m.) nor by the report on the memorial service (a requiem Eucharist in the cathedral of Saint John the Divine) that was published in *The New York Times*, October 4, 1973, 48. But the broadside survives, with the text of the poem, together with the decorations by Gorey, on a single sheet of blue-gray paper, 30 × 26 cm. (10 ¼" × 11 ½") (New York: n.p., [1973], copyright 1972). It was listed in the Gotham Book Mart, Edward Gorey booklist (spring / summer 1975), no. 184.

universally loved or respected. For one of the more appreciative interpretations, see McDiarmid, *Auden's Apologies*, 4–7.

One critic. Mark Jarman, "Storytelling Verse from Oxford," *The Hudson Review* (1984): 491–95, at 495 (a review of *The Oxford Book of Narrative Verse*).

Another scholar. Damian Grant, "Verbal Events," *Critical Quarterly* 16.1 (1974): 81–86.

nothing more than fluff. For a brief defense of the "long and lovely" ballad against such denigration, see Alan Levy, *W. H. Auden: In the Autumn of the Age of Anxiety* (Sag Harbor, NY: Permanent Press, 1983), 80–81.

Alla Borzova. Alla Borzova, *The Ballad of Barnaby for Mixed Chorus a Cappella Poem by W. H. Auden* ([New York]: Euterpe Press, ASCAP, 2000).

Play of Robin and Marian. In French, *Jeu de Robin et de Marion*.

Lay of Our Lady. In French, *Lai de Notre Dame*.

Day of Wrath. In Latin, *Dies irae*.

The composer was won over to the poem. In the program notes to the premiere she stated: "Auden obviously liked his hero, and his poem has a strong appeal to the artistic profession. Barnaby was 'the finest tumbler of his day' and remained true to his talent, continuing to serve God with it until, literally, his last breath. 'Tumbling is all I have learnt to do,' he cries in front of the Virgin's statue, 'Mother of God, let me tumble for you.'"

blended the essences. Gilroy, "Auden Writes Opera Narrative," 36, quotes Auden as saying: "I consulted Anatole France, of course, but worked mostly from a medieval version of the story." On the signals of Auden's indebtedness to Wicksteed's translation, see Edward Mendelson, "*Our Lady's Tumbler* and 'The Ballad of Barnaby,'" *The W. H. Auden Society Newsletter* 27 (September 2006): 16–17.

posed as a historian. W. H. Auden, "The Art of Poetry No. 17," interviewed by Michael Newman, *Paris Review* 57 (1974), https://www.theparisreview.org/interviews/3970/w-h-auden-the-art-of-poetry-no-17-w-h-auden: "I've told people I'm a medieval historian when asked what I do. It freezes conversation. If one tells them one's a poet, one gets these odd looks which seem to say, 'Well, what's he living off?' In the old days a man was proud to have in his passport, Occupation: Gentleman. Lord Antrim's passport simply said, Occupation: Peer—which I felt was correct. I've had a lucky life. I had a happy home, and my parents provided me with a good education. And my father was both a physician and a scholar, so I never got the idea that art and science were opposing cultures—both were entertained equally in my home."

suggest an acquaintance. Nicholas Jenkins, "Auden in America," in *The Cambridge Companion to W. H. Auden*, ed. Stan Smith (Cambridge: Cambridge University Press, 2004), 39–54, at 45.

worshipped no / Virgin before the Dynamo. Auden, "New Year Letter (January 1, 1940)," in idem, *Collected Poems*, 195–241, at 235 (Part 3).

The Virgin & the Dynamo. W. H. Auden, "The Virgin & the Dynamo," in Auden, *The Dyer's Hand and Other Essays* (New York: Random House, 1962), 61–71.

The subject matter of a poem. "The Virgin & the Dynamo," 67.

Every beautiful poem. "The Virgin & the Dynamo," 71.

the Wicksteed translation. He received on loan from the Wykeham Rise School a copy of it which still survives. See Mendelson, *"Our Lady's Tumbler,"* 16, on the exemplar held in the Danowski Poetry Collection at Emory University.

Auden's influence on the Irish poet. See Douglas Houston, "Landscapes of the Heart: Parallels in the Poetry of Kavanagh and Auden," *Studies: An Irish Quarterly Review* 77.308 (Winter 1988): 445–59; John Redmond, "The Influence of Auden on Kavanagh's Poetic Development," *New Hibernia Review* 8 (2004): 21–34.

Vault of Champagne. The terminology in the second instance points clearly to the poet's reliance on the Wicksteed translation, where the movements are named in exactly these words, as opposed to the Butler, which refers to tricks rather than vaults, or the Kemp-Welch, which has somersaults rather than vaults.

deeply Christian. On the poet's religious views, see Arthur Kirsch, *Auden and Christianity* (New Haven, CT: Yale University Press, 2005), 141–66.

remains true to the last gasp. At the point of death, he professes before the statue of Mary that "Tumbling is all I have learnt to do."

the most famous poem by François Villon. In French, the poem is known variously as *Ballade des pendus* (Ballad of the hanged), *Epitaphe Villon* (Villon's epitaph), and, after its incipit, *Frères humains* (Human brothers), respectively.

The late-medieval poet's stock. Glen Omans, "The Villon Cult in England," *Comparative Literature* 18 (1966): 16–35; Robert E. Morsberger, "Villon and the Victorians: The Influence and the Legend," *Bulletin of the Rocky Mountain Modern Language Association* 23 (1969): 189–96.

an 1877 essay. First published in *The Cornhill Magazine* 36 (August 1877): 215–34. It was followed in rapid order by a short story, printed in *Temple Bar* 51 (October 1877): 197–212, under the title "A Lodging for the Night: A Story of Francis Villon," which purports to recount the events of a night in Villon's life.

Rabelais and His World. Mikhail Bakhtin, *Rabelais and His World*, trans. Helene Iswolsky (Cambridge, MA: MIT Press, 1968).

Work, Carnival and Prayer. The undated nineteen-page typescript draft of this lecture, with Auden's manuscript corrections, is held in the New York Public Library, Archives

& Manuscripts, Henry W. and Albert A. Berg Collection of English and American Literature, Berg Coll MSS Auden.

the primary task of the schoolteacher. The sentence is often quoted as an aphorism, always attributed to Auden, but not otherwise sourced.

much like a teacher. John Ciardi, "The Form is the Experience," *Art Education* 14.7 (October 1961): 16–22, at 21: "To show his heart was in the right place he took to sweeping out the chapel—that is a little like teaching school. It is not the essential process, but it is an act of devotion, but while he was at it he took to doing something I suspect teachers might do at times—when he was all alone he would sneak his rug and equipment in and juggle in front of the Virgin. He wanted to offer the one thing he knew how to do well."

poet's shaping of a poem. "The point I want to make is very simple. Any well-made thing is a praise. Anything joyously accomplished and roundly made is a praise. The offering was acceptable, you see, and any praise is acceptable, any supreme act of language, I don't care what it is, whether it is about a fish's eye, about the size of the universe—any superb language structure will endure because we need superb language structures. They are a kind of enzyme without which the human mind cannot function up to its best potential.

"As a matter of fact, they survive even the languages in which they are written. Many people walk today with high moments of Greek and Latin poetry and oratory in their heads simply because when a great language structure that really grows out of its medium and becomes the thing written and enters experience. Language is one of the profoundest things that human beings do, and anything that heightens that sense of language is meaningful and full and part of the total experience." Ciardi, "Form is the Experience," 22.

an introduction to poetry and to the criticism of it. John Ciardi, *How Does A Poem Mean?* (Boston: Houghton Mifflin, 1959).

an anxiety of influence. *The Anxiety of Influence: A Theory of Poetry* is a book (New York: Oxford University Press, 1973) by the American literary critic Harold Bloom. It makes many professors of literature nervous.

better lives ahead. *The Letters of Robert Lowell*, ed. Saskia Hamilton (New York: Farrar, Straus and Giroux, 2005), 400–1, at 40: (no. 407, "To John Berryman, March 18, [1962]").

Nina Nyhart. Nina Nyhart, "Our Lady's Tumbler," *Virginia Quarterly Review* 49.4 (1973): 555–57. Her attraction as a poet to the medieval performer would seem loosely related to the interest in clowning that she shows in "Captive Pierrot." This later poem is an ekphrasis on Paul Klee's painting by the same name that depicts this specific type of clown. But "Captive Pierrot" explores the inner life of a child costumed as a Pierrot, rather than the nature of the entertainer himself. See Nina Nyhart, "Two Poems after Paul Klee," *Poetry* 152.3 (1988): 141–42, analyzed by Carl R. V. Brown, "Contemporary Poetry about Painting," *English Journal* 81 (1992): 41–45, at 43–44.

contours. The six-line stanzas are rhymed with the mirror-image structure of abccba, in which the two c-rhymes carry the special weight of centrality, while those at the end are indispensable for sealing the metrical units.

Turner Cassity. Turner Cassity, "Our Lady's Juggler," *Poetry* 127 (1976): 343. The poem was reprinted in idem, *Hurricane Lamp* (Chicago: University of Chicago Press, 1986), 57.

Peter Porter. Peter Porter, *Max is Missing* (London: Picador, 2001), "Scrawled on Auden's Napkin," 48–49, at 49.

Music from Massenet to Peter Maxwell Davies

Young Folks' Picture History of Music. James Francis Cooke, *Young Folks' Picture History of Music* (Bryn Mawr, PA: Theodore Presser, 1925).

the picture to illustrate it. Cooke, *Young Folks' Picture History*, 11.

The Dancer of Our Dear Lady. *Der Tänzer unserer lieben Frau: Legendenspiel in 2 Akten für Soli, Chor und Orchester*.

two cases. The earlier of these is Friedrich Hedler, *Der Tänzer unserer lieben Frau: Ein Spiel nach altfranzösischen und altdeutschen Motiven* (Munich, Germany: Buchner, 1950). Hedler was a German dramatist and writer who had to his credit one play, *Floh im Ohr*, filmed in 1943. All of this is well and fine, but it must be stressed that the tale told by Hedler actually approximates that of the jongleur and the Holy Face of Christ in Lucca. For the later example, see below.

The Dancer of Our Blessed Lady. Konrad Karkosch and Ludwig Holzleitner, *Der Tänzer unserer lieben Frau: Ein Ballett-Libretto in 2 Akten nach der altfranzösischen Legende "Del Tumbeor Nostre-Dame" für Bühne, Film und Fernsehen* (Munich, Germany: Self-published, 1965). As the subtitle clarifies, the Karkosch and Holzleitner libretto deals with *Our Lady's Tumbler*.

true Volk education. See David B. Dennis, *Inhumanities: Nazi Interpretations of Western Culture* (Cambridge: Cambridge University Press, 2012), 172, 192–93.

music hall session. The French for the venue is *séance music hall*. The title is given alternately as *Jongleur* (without the definite article) and *Jongleurs* (in the plural). For letters connected with the composition, see Francis Poulenc, *Selected Correspondence 1915–1963*, trans. and ed. Sidney Buckland (London: Victor Gollancz, 1991), 26 (letter 9, Jean Cocteau to Francis Poulenc, September 2, 1918), 28 (letter 11). For catalogue information, see Carl B. Schmidt, *The Music of Francis Poulenc (1899–1963): A Catalogue* (Oxford: Clarendon Press, 1995), 25–27 (FP 10). For discussion, see Carl B. Schmidt, *Entrancing Muse: A Documented Biography of Francis Poulenc*, Lives in Music, vol. 3 (Hillsdale, NY: Pendragon, 2001), 58–66.

in 1921. To be precise, June 21, 1921.

costume. The costume can be seen in a photograph of Caryathis in the 1921 premiere of *La belle excentrique*: see Ornella Volta, *L'Ymagier d'Erik Satie* (Paris: Francis Van de Velde, 1979), 74. For the program of the show, see Paul Collaer, *Correspondance avec des amis musiciens*, ed. Robert Wangermée (Liège, Belgium: P. Mardaga, 1996), 82n1.

Litanies to the Black Virgin. In French, *Litanies à la Vierge Noire*: see Wilfrid Mellers, *Francis Poulenc* (Oxford: Oxford University Press, 1993), 75–79.

Dialogues of the Carmelites. In French, *Dialogues des Carmélites*, an opera with a libretto by the French author Georges Bernanos (1888–1948).

pray for his recovery. His hope was that if their prayers were answered, he might be able "to glorify God and the blessed martyrs of Compiègne with [his] music." Letter, dated July 10, 1954, quoted by John Howard Griffin, *Prison of Culture: Beyond Black Like Me*, ed. Robert Bonazzi (San Antonio, TX: Wings Press, 2011), 86.

a leitmotif in his writings. For instance, he asked: "Will God take into account my poor efforts—the Mass, the religious motets? Will He at least see them and me kindly, as another bungler, a jongleur de Notre Dame?" See John Griffin, "The Poulenc behind the Mask," in *The John Howard Griffin Reader*, ed. Bradford Daniel (Boston: Houghton Mifflin, 1968), 538–43, at 538. In a letter, he rambled, fusing two topics relating intimately to the Virgin Mary: "Perhaps Father Carré is right and I will always be the Jongleur de Notre-Dame. Did I tell you how overcome I was by Lourdes the other day? I had never seen a pilgrimage before. It was at once atrocious and sublime." See Francis Poulenc, *Correspondance, 1915–1963*, ed. Hélène de Wendel (Paris: Éditions du Seuil, 1967), 226; idem, *Selected Correspondence*, 220, letter 250. The composer's identification with the leading character of Massenet's opera inspired the title of a chapter partly about Poulenc in a musicological study: see Wilfrid Mellers, "*Un saint sensuel* and 'Le Jongleur de Notre Dame,'" in idem, *Celestial Music?: Some Masterpieces of European Religious Music* (Woodbridge, UK: Boydell, 2002), 230–43.

other scholastic contexts. A case in point would be a forty-page production of Vivian Merrill Young, *The Miracle of Jean the Juggler: A Musical Play in Three Scenes, Based on a French Folktale* (Chicago: H. T. FitzSimons, 1950), with music by Ruth Bampton. A version that shows clear debts to the libretto by Léna (although billed as being "based on a medieval legend") is by Sister Marcella M. Holloway, *The Little Juggler: A Miracle Play with Music* (New York: S. French, 1966), with music by Sister John Joseph Bezdek. Even so, the scope and nature of innovations and expansions made by Sister Marcella can be gauged by the list of characters: vegetable lady, fortune teller, balloon man, blue guitar man, Barnaby, children (Renee and five others), Brother Boniface the cook, Henri the donkey, the Virgin Mary, and four monks (Brother Piccolo, Brother Scribleus, Brother Da Vinci, and Father Abbot). The lead character is named Barnaby (an acknowledgment of Anatole France, of course), who early in the proceedings is befriended at a fair by the Man with the Blue Guitar. The events within the monastery culminate in Mary's bestowing upon the juggler a kiss. After this miracle, the performer returns to his itinerant life with the Man with the Blue Guitar and the donkey, but thanks to the miraculous token of affection from the Mother of God he is now accepted. For additional guidance, see Sister John Joseph Bezdek, *A Production Book for the Little Juggler* (performed in Macgowan Hall Playhouse, April 15, 16, 22, 23, 1967), in the library of the University of California, Los Angeles.

In 1967, Anatole France's story was refashioned in a musical play for language learning in both French as *Le petit jongleur* and Spanish as *El pequeño Bérnabe*: see Alan Garfinkel, "Notes and News," *Modern Language Journal* 62.3 (March 1978): 113–31, at 122–23.

one-act opera. Ulysses Kay, *The Juggler of Our Lady: A One-Act Opera*, libretto Alex King (New York: Pembroke Music, 1978) (Carl Fischer repr).

Alexander King. Born Alexander Koenig in Vienna. See Constance Tibbs Hobson and Deborra A. Richardson, *Ulysses Kay: A Bio-Bibliography*, Bio-Bibliographies in Music, vol. 53 (Westport, CT: Greenwood Press, 1994), 14, W60.

premiering in New Orleans. February 23, 1962, in the Xavier University Opera Workshop.

opera is not the medium for our time. Quoted in Hobson and Richardson, *Ulysses Kay*, 20.

a melodic triumph. "Kay's Opera a Melodic Triumph," *The Xavier Herald* 38 (February 1962): 1.

melodic affair. Frank Cagnard, "One-Act Opera Melodic Affair: Xavier Production Seems Popular Success," (New Orleans) *Times-Picayune*, February 25, 1962.

African-American press. *The Pittsburgh Courier*, February 17, 1962, 14.

modest national fanfare. The performance in Opera/South, in a double bill with William Grant Still's *Highway 1, U.S.A.*, was reported upon by Hamilton Bims, "An All-Black Opera Raises Its Voice," *Ebony* 28.4 (February 1973): 54–56. Both operas were broadcast internationally on the *Voice of America*.

Juan Orrego-Salas. Juan Orrego-Salas, *The Tumbler's Prayer = El saltimbanqui: A Ballet (Opus 48) Based on the Twelfth-Century Legend of "Our Lady's Tumbler,"* 1959, 35-page score.

sojourn in the United States. At the time he held his second Guggenheim Fellowship for Musical Composition.

an executive. William H. Johnstone was a vice president of the Bethlehem Steel Corporation.

a translation of Our Lady's Tumbler. The copy was of the version by Philip H. Wicksteed, as published by Thomas Bird Mosher.

the wife's younger son. The wife was Mildred ("Milly") C. Thomas Johnstone. Her first husband, whom she married in 1920, was Oliver Holton. Their son Tommy was killed in Middletown, NJ, in 1927. Juan Orrego-Salas reports that Milly Johnstone's immediate reaction to his idea was, "It's our commission, for Carmen's, your wife, coming to join us from Chile and in memory of Tommy, my son": personal communication, Juan Orrego-Salas, August 31, 2015. Other information is available in Juan Orrego-Salas, *Encuentros, visiones y repasos: Capítulos en el camino de mi música y mi vida* (Santiago, Chile: Ediciones Universidad Católica de Chile, 2005), 188–89, 202.

leapt upon the two-year-old. United Press, *The Independent* (St. Petersburg, FL) Saturday, July 23, 1927, 1, 18; *Time*, August 1, 1927.

commune in silence. The tumbler's style of worship resembles the collective monologue that the psychologist Jean Piaget sees as typifying preschoolers at play. In such togetherness, children speak, but to themselves. To what degree the shared silence is to be considered autistic or egocentric is for others to untangle.

In performance. The result was performed in 1960 as a concert and in 1961 as a ballet in Santiago, Chile.

tumbler or acrobat. The specific word is *saltimbanqui*. Shortly thereafter, the composer was invited to take up a position at Indiana University. Specifically, he was brought in to establish a Latin American Music Center and as a professor of composition. Not long after his installation in Bloomington, the local ballet performed the piece as *The Tumbler's Prayer*.

Another version is by the Swiss Rudolf Moser, "Der Gaukler unserer lieben Frau: Ein Legendenspiel für Bariton-Solo, Frauenchor, Männerchor, gemischten Chor, Orgel und Orchester: op. 68." Thus the title page. On the page on which the score begins, the heading reads "Der Gaukler unsrer lieben Frau nach der mittelalterlichen Legende zu einem Tanzspiel gestaltet von Senta Maria, Musik von Rudolf Moser, op. 68." The music is copyrighted 1991 by Gertrud Moser, but the index of his works indicates 1939 as the year of composition: see http://www.moser-stiftung.ch/index.php/werksverzeichnis.html. The composition, approximately ninety minutes in performance, contains a section (10–11) labeled *bourrée*, presumably a nod to Massenet. It has verbal notations and rubrication (37–39) to signal where acrobatic leaps may make sense.

Still farther afield, a major Australian composer of the twentieth century, Miriam Hyde, composed in 1956 for the combination of flute and piano "The Little Juggler," which may also be on our theme: National Library of Australia, Papers of Miriam Hyde, Box 2, MS 5260.

Le Jongleur de Notre Dame. Peter Maxwell Davies, *Le Jongleur de Notre Dame, a Masque for Mime, Baritone, Chamber Ensemble and Children's Band* (London: Chester Music, 1978).

chamber ensemble. The instrumentalists not only contribute to the drama by participating in the action, but also effectively speak in the performance. At points the sounds of the instruments imitate the voices of monks: the abbot, the baritone, is the only vocalist. For information on the masque, see Carolyn J. Smith, *Peter Maxwell Davies: A Bio-Bibliography* (Westport, CT: Greenwood Press, 1995), 39 (item W115).

plainsong. See *Peter Maxwell Davies Studies*, ed. Kenneth Gloag and Nicholas Jones (Cambridge: Cambridge University Press, 2009), 242. Plainsong, commonly known as Gregorian chant, is the body of traditional monophonic chants used in the liturgies of the Latin rite in the Western Church.

material relating to the Virgin. In 1966, he composed a work of musical theater in French, entitled *Our Lady of the Flowers* (*Notre Dame des fleurs*). In the masque, the statue of the Virgin is in general a far more active presence than in most other versions of the story. In 1967, the composer cofounded a new-music group called the Pierrot Players, after the stock character of *commedia dell'arte*. In 1972, he made a jester a salient character in his *Blind Man's Buff*, to which he had likewise attached the label "masque." This piece reaches a more optimistic, or at least less antimonastic, outcome than that of his *Jongleur de Notre Dame.*

made the Virgin Mary smile. Jane Birkhead, "Dramatic Music by P. Maxwell Davies," *Notes*, 2nd ser., 36.2 (December 1979): 484.

Mark. Since he was played by the English-born mime artist named Mark Furneaux.

enters a cloister. This setting harks back to an earlier work by the composer, since the 1965–1966 *Revelation and Fall* had as protagonist a woman vested in a blood-red habit as a nun.

a charming music theater piece. Birkhead, "Dramatic Music," 484.

chancel drama. Mark Schweizer, *The Clown of God: A Christmas Chancel Drama for Children's Choir* (Hopkinsville, KY: St. James Music Press, 1996). This version, set in twelfth-century England, is based loosely on Massenet's opera. The central character is an aging clown. Special emphasis is laid upon the legend of the sagebrush, a plant familiar from American cowboy westerns, which substitutes for the sage in Massenet.

The miracle takes place at a life-sized creche, which is associated with the nativity scene staged by Saint Francis.

An adaptation for performance in church by children, entitled *Le jongleur de Notre-Dame* (hyphenated thus), has been created and recorded by the composer Jean Humenry and the librettist Jean Louis Winkopp: see http://www.chantonseneglise.fr/chant.php?chant=13046

three poems. Naji Hakim, "Our Lady's Minstrel for Clarinet and Organ," http://www.najihakim.com/works/organ-and-other-instruments/our-lady-s-minstrel-for-clarinet-and-organ/. The composer uses verses from the 1898 translation into English by Isabel Butler. The text was suggested to him by his daughter, Katia-Sofia Hakim.

a one-hour musical. Entitled *The Juggler of Notre Dame: The Musical*, written and recorded by Stephen DeCesare: see http://www.musicaneo.com/sheetmusic/sm-159801_the_juggler_of_notre_dame_musical.html#159801

Notes to Chapter 4

What's past is prologue. The Tempest, Act 2, Scene 1.

Misremembering and Remembering

Prince. Prince Rogers Nelson (1958–2016) was a popular American musician. "Vicki Waiting" is the fifth track on his eleventh album, the soundtrack to the movie *Batman*.

imitations in other genres. The television series *Orange is the New Black*, which premiered in 2013, comes close to performing the story in one episode when it highlights a juggling act among the skits proposed by female prison convicts for a Christmas pageant: *Orange is the New Black*, season 1, episode 13 (season finale). But the notion of a juggler at Christmastide does not necessarily allude to the medieval tale and its afterlife. It could be mere coincidence.

It is possible to love the Middle Ages. Sheldon Christian, *Our Lady's Tumbler: A Modern Miracle Play* (Portland, ME: Anthoensen Press, 1948), v.

Maurice Vloberg. Maurice Vloberg, *La légende dorée de Notre Dame* (Paris: D. A. Longuet, 1921), 234.

more people should notice. John R. Dorsey, *Look Again in Baltimore*, photography James DuSel (Baltimore, MD: Johns Hopkins University Press, 2005), 86. The building is located at 43000 Roland Avenue.

physicists. For one example, see Philippe Nozières, "Some Comments on Bose-Einstein Condensation," in *Bose-Einstein Condensation*, ed. A. Griffin et al. (Cambridge: Cambridge University Press, 1995), 15–30, at 29 (in the acknowledgements): "This lecture was not given at the Trento workshop, but at a meeting held in Paris at the École Normale Supérieure on 9 June 1993 in honour of Claude Cohen-Tannoudji on his sixtieth birthday. I would like to take this occasion to renew my congratulations to Claude: Bose-Einstein condensation is far from his usual worries, but I am acting as 'le jongleur de Notre Dame.'" For another, see Anatole Abragam, "The Physicist Erwin Hahn," in *Pulsed Magnetic Resonance: A Recognition of E. L. Hahn*, ed. D. M. S. Bagguley (Oxford: Clarendon Press, 1992), 1–4, at 1, who likens the convention of offering a *Festschrift* to the gesture of Anatole France's *Le jongleur de Notre Dame* and concludes: "The message is clear: you may honour your fellow being by performing for him whatever you do best. It is the intent that counts."

a reviewer. W. W. Howells, review of *Evolution after Darwin*, vol. 2, *The Evolution of Man: Mind, Culture, and Society*, ed. Sol Tax, *Science*, n.s. 131.3413, May 27, 1960, 1601–2: "many authors make their offering by doing what they do best, like the juggler of Notre Dame, instead of feeling bound to stretch connections with Darwin himself."

comparability of the juggler and a judge. John Ladd, "The Place of Practical Reason in Judicial Decision," in *Rational Decision*, ed. Carl Joachim Friedrich, Nomos, vol. 7 (New York: Atherton Press, 1964), 126–44, at 138, quoting Karl N. Llewellyn, *Jurisprudence: Realism in Theory and Practice* (Chicago: University of Chicago Press, 1962), 90–91: "In a disparaging way, it has been said that all that lawyers and judges do is manipulate concepts. The judge, says Llewellyn, is a juggler, but, he adds, he should do it like Our Lady's Tumbler in the medieval tale: 'Let him tumble and juggle reverently; let him turn upon his juggling all that is best in him and all his skill.'"

If a physician would spell as follows. Paul P. Kies, *A Writer's Manual and Workbook*, 2nd ed. (New York: Appleton-Century-Crofts, 1964), 187.

modern languages studied in high school. Sam Dillon, "Foreign Languages Fade in Class—Except Chinese," *New York Times*, January 20, 2010; more specifically, Bertram M. Gordon, "The Decline of a Cultural Icon: France in American Perspective," *French Historical Studies* 22.4 (1999): 625–51.

poring over literature. Claire Kramsch and Olivier Kramsch, "The Avatars of Literature in Language Study," *Modern Language Journal* 84.4 (2000): 553–73.

Parisian circus-type entertainer. Chagall's oil on canvas from 1943 is in a private collection.

Czesław Miłosz. Czesław Miłosz, *The History of Polish Literature*, 2nd ed. (Berkeley and Los Angeles: University of California Press, 1983), 411. The first edition in English appeared in 1969.

an argument has been advanced. Prócoro Hernández Oropeza, "Inspiración o fusil el cuento de un anónimo árabe: Las fuentes de El alquimista, de Paulo Coelho," *Revista Inter-Forum*, 79, year 3 of publication (May 20, 2002).

original Portuguese edition. *O alquimista* (Rio de Janeiro, Brazil: Rocco, 1988), 7–11 ("Prefácio").

Getting a Rise from the Male Member

contains only male parts. *Musical Times and Singing Class Circular* 43.710 (April 1, 1902): 267.

Gothic crowns. See advertisement from *Esquire*, December 1941, for Dobbs Homburg "Gothic Crown."

girdled in similar architecture. A Canadian print advertisement from 1952 plugs a "Gothic girdle" for women.

one modern reader. David Adams Leeming, ed., *Storytelling Encyclopedia: Historical, Cultural, and Multiethnic Approaches to Oral Traditions around the World* (Phoenix, AZ: Oryx Press, 1997), 348–49, at 348 ("Deep in a crypt, he somersaults and dances naked for the Virgin every day").

The essence of religion. John P. Le Coq, *Vignettes littéraires: French Life and Ideals* (Boston: D. C. Heath, 1957), 58.

Treasures of the Kingdom. Ed. T. Everett Harré (New York: Rinehart, 1947), 351–56 (trans. Frederic Chapman), at 351: "In outstanding contrast to the cynical irony and skepticism of most of his writings, *Our Lady's Juggler*—also rendered into an opera—is unique for its tenderness and spiritual symbolism."

Love Never Ceases. In German, "Die Liebe höret nimmer auf" (pp. 125–28, Anatole France): Erika Horn, ed., *Es gibt noch Wunder …: Die schönsten Legenden* (Graz, Austria: Styria Steirische Verlagsanstalt, 1949).

A Century of Love Stories. Gilbert Frankau, ed. *A Century of Love Stories* (London: Hutchinson [1935?]), 993–97.

broad stereotypes. Take, for example, the string of generalizations about the typical traits of people from France that the author of a 1915 study of Anatole France adduced, without any temporization: "It is not enough to understand Anatole France; one also has to understand the French, the gay, sensual, garrulous French of the Middle Ages, the gay, sensual, courteous French of the seventeenth century, the gay, sensual, cynical French of Voltairian times, and the sensual, cynical French of to-day." See Walter Lionel George, *Anatole France* (New York: H. Holt, [1915]), 12–13.

The Yellow Book. From 1894 to 1896.

his many photographs. F. Holland Day, *Suffering the Ideal*, with an essay by James Crump (Santa Fe, NM: Twin Palms, 1995).

wine, women, and song. Day, *Suffering the Ideal*, 14–16.

Monk in Cell. Day, *Suffering the Ideal*, pl. 38 and 125; *F. Holland Day*, ed. Pam Roberts (Amsterdam: Van Gogh Museum, 2000), 127n44. *Vita Mystica* ca. 1900, platinum, 240 × 170 mm, The Royal Photographic Society, Bath, acquired from Mrs. Walter Benington, 1937 RPS 3585/2.

I'm not saying I am, either. Richard Corliss, "Radley Metzger: Aristocrat of the Erotic," *Film Comment* 9 (1973): 19–29, at 27. The film in question is *The Dirty Girls*, Audubon Films, 1964, screenplay by Peter Fernandez, directed by Radley Metzger.

Metzger's films. Elena Gorfinkel, "Radley Metzger's 'Elegant Arousal': Taste, Aesthetic Distinction, and Sexploitation," in *Underground USA: Filmmaking beyond the Hollywood*

Canon, ed. Xavier Mendik and Steven Jay Schneider (London: Wallflower, 2002), 26–39; Eric Schaefer, "Dirty Little Secrets: Scholars, Archivists, and Dirty Movies," *The Moving Image* 5.2 (2005): 79–105

erotic kitsch. Bart Testa, "Soft-Shaft Opportunism: Radley Metzger's Erotic Kitsch," *Spectator* 19.2 (1999): 41–55; http://cinema.usc.edu/assets/099/15905.pdf

glamorous European-accented romances. Richard Corliss, "That Old Feeling: When Porno Was Chic," *Time*, Tuesday, March 29, 2005, 5.

apologized. Alex Dobuzinskis, "Nude Virgin Mary Cover Prompts Playboy Apology," Reuters, US edition, December 12, 2008.

we adore you, Mary. "Te adoramos, María."

chockablock with Marianism. The Feast Day of the Immaculate Conception falls on December 8, the Feast Day of Our Lady of Guadalupe on December 12, and Christmas Day on December 25.

Playboy's Not So Virgin Mary. Kate Childs Graham, "Playboy's Not So Virgin Mary," *Religion Dispatches*, December 21, 2008, http://religiondispatches.org/playboys-not-so-virgin-mary

Until this juggling of proper nouns. René Étiemble, *Savoir et goût*, Hygiène des Lettres, vol. 3 (Paris: Gallimard, 1958), 28–29.

Barnes privileges the penis. Jane Marcus, "Laughing at Leviticus: *Nightwood* as Woman's Circus Epic," in *Silence and Power: A Reevaluation of Djuna Barnes*, ed. Mary Lynn Broe (Carbondale: Southern Illinois University Press, 1991), 221–50, at 228. She is discussing Djuna Barnes, *Nightwood* (New York: Harcourt, Brace, 1937), 26. Her interpretation is contested by Georgette Fleischer, "Djuna Barnes and T. S. Eliot: The Politics and Poetics of *Nightwood*," *Studies in the Novel* 30 (1998): 405–37, at 429n9.

Our Lady of the Limp. See Chapter 4.

Arman. His full name at birth was Armand Pierre Fernandez, while his full adult name was Armand P. Arman.

transculpture. In an interview recorded May 29, 1989, at the Mayor Gallery in London, in *Interviews-Artists*, vol. 4, *Patterns of Experience: Recordings 1988–2011*, ed. Nicholas Philip James (London: Cv Publications, 2011), 25.

this sculptural composition. The dimensions of the sculpture in inches are 90.9 height × 35.4 width × 32.3 deep (231 × 90 × 82 cm). It was produced at the Bonvicini foundry of Verona, Italy.

The Holy Virgin Mary. Paper collage, oil paint, glitter, polyester resin, map pins, and elephant dung on linen, 243.8 × 182.9 cm. The mixed-media piece attained notoriety in an exhibition called *Sensation* that traveled to London, Berlin, and New York.

raised in the Catholic Church. https://www.khanacademy.org/humanities/global-culture/identity-body/identity-body-europe/a/chris-ofili-the-holy-virgin-mary: "As an altar boy, I was confused by the idea of a holy Virgin Mary giving birth to a young boy. Now when I go to the National Gallery and see paintings of the Virgin Mary, I see how sexually charged they are. Mine is simply a hip hop version."

a scholarly article. Elizabeth Legge, "Reinventing Derivation: Roles, Stereotypes, and 'Young British Art,'" *Representations* 71 (Summer 2000): 1–23 (closing paragraph).

Jung's Jongleur

John Cowper Powys. John Cowper Powys, *Visions and Revisions: A Book of Literary Devotions* (Hamilton, NY: Colgate University Press, 1955), 117–27 ("Matthew Arnold"), at 127, where the quotation is preceded by the passage: "For it is the nature of poetry to heighten and to throw into relief those eternal things in our common destiny which too soon get overlaid. And some things only poetry can reach. Religion may have small comfort for us when in the secret depths of our hearts we endure a craving of which we may not speak, a sickening aching longing for 'the lips so sweetly forsworn.' But poetry is waiting for us, there also, with her rosemary and rue."

This collection of essays was first published in 1915. He draws the phrase "the lips… so sweetly forsworn" from a song in the section of Shakespeare's *Measure for Measure* about Mariana. Tennyson made this young woman the central figure of the poem he named after her, and we saw the same character captured in Millais's painting. Powys held that poetry offers two odorifous herbs, associated with remembrance and regret, respectively, to help cope with thwarted longing.

Powys mentioned the "jongleur of Paris" also in *A Glastonbury Romance* (New York: Simon and Schuster, 1932), 624; 2nd ed. (London: Macdonald, 1955; Picador, 1975), 600.

His conception of the unconscious mind. C. G. Jung, "Aion: Phenomenology of the Self," in *The Portable Jung*, ed. Joseph Campbell, trans. R. F. C. Hull, Viking Portable Library, vol. 70 (New York: Viking, 1971), 148–62.

since the Reformation. C. G. Jung, "Answer to Job," in idem, *Psychology and Religion: West and East*, trans. R. F. C. Hull, Bollingen Series, vol. 20, Collected Works, vol. 11 (New York: Pantheon, 1958), 461–62 (on the Assumption), 464 (for the specific quotation). Pope Pius XII proclaimed the doctrine of the Assumption in the encyclical *Munificentissumus Deus* on November 1, 1950.

Josef Elias. Josef Elias, *Der Tänzer unserer lieben Frau: Ein altes Legendenspiel für die Bühne* (Belp, Switzerland: Volksverlag Elgg, 1959). The Swiss pedagogue took as his point of departure the German translation that Wilhelm Hertz had published in 1886. Hertz's adaptation had been given a new lease on life by being reprinted, at the end of the Marian year of 1954, in the cultural journal *Atlantis*, which had been moved back to Germany from Switzerland only in 1950: Wilhelm Hertz, "Der Tänzer unsrer lieben Frau," *Atlantis* (December 1954): 565–66.

Rudolf Moser. Rudolf Moser, *Der Gaukler unserer lieben Frau: Ein Legendenspiel für Bariton-Solo, Frauenchor, Männerchor, gemischten Chor, Orgel und Orchester; Opus 68* (Arlesheim, Germany: Verlag der Werke Rudolf Moser, 1991). In English, the title means *Our Lady's Tumbler: A Legendary Play for Baritone Solo, Female Choir, Male Choir, Mixed Choir, Organ, and Orchestra; Opus 68*.

a letter. Letter to Mrs. Carol Jeffrey, July 3, 1954, in C. G. Jung, *Briefe*, ed. Aniela Jaffé, 3 vols. (Olten, Switzerland: Walter, 1972–1973), 2:405; trans. R. F. C. Hull, *Letters*, ed. Gerhard Adler and Aniela Jaffé, 2 vols., Bollingen Series, vol. 95.1–2 (Princeton, NJ: Princeton University Press, 1973–1975), 2 ("1951–1961"): 179.

create art for their own selves. "As the jongleur de Notre-Dame performs his tricks to honor the Madonna, so you paint for the self." Jung, *Briefe*, 2:405; *Letters*, 2:179.

Notes to Chapter 5

It is a sad old age. Etienne Gilson, *The Spirit of Medieval Philosophy* (London: Sheed & Ward, 1936), 425–26.

The Juggler's Prospects

many possible interpretations. Polysemy describes this branching out of meaning.

Roland Barthes. Roland Barthes, "The New Citroën," in idem, *Mythologies*, trans. Richard Howard and Annette Lavers (New York: Hill and Wang, 2012), 169–71. First published in French in 1957, in English in 1972.

the medieval cathedral as a consumer object. "I believe that the automobile is, today, the exact equivalent of the great Gothic cathedrals: I mean, a great creation of the period, passionately conceived by unknown artists, and consumed in its image, if not in its use, by an entire population which appropriates in it an entirely magical object." Barthes, "New Citroën," 169.

a major German newspaper. *Die Zeit*, May 27, 1988, reproduced in Magdalena Bushart, *Der Geist der Gotik und die expressionistische Kunst: Kunstgeschichte und Kunsttheorie 1911–1925* (Munich, Germany: S. Schreiber, 1990), 16, 248. The citation of the newspaper there has been unverifiable in editions available to me.

"transfer of empire" and "transfer of learning." From the Latin *translatio studii* and *translatio imperii*.

a phantasm. Alice Chandler, *A Dream of Order: The Medieval Ideal in Nineteenth-Century English Literature* (London: Routledge & Kegan Paul, 1971).

flight from modernity. Kenneth Clark, *The Gothic Revival: An Essay in the History of Taste* (London: Constable, 1928).

John Stuart Mill. John Stuart Mill, "The Spirit of the Age (1831)," in idem, *The Collected Works of John Stuart Mill*, ed. Ann P. Robson and John M. Robson (Toronto: University of Toronto Press, 1986), 22,1: 1.

order and innocence. Alice Chandler, "Order and Disorder in the Medieval Revival," *Browning Institute Studies* 8 (1980): 1–9.

Gropius vs. the Gothic Ivory Tower

Neither medievalism nor colonialism. Walter A. Gropius, "Not Gothic but Modern for Our Colleges: A Noted Architect Says We Cling Too Blindly to the Past, Though We Build for Tomorrow," *New York Times*, October 23, 1949, 16–18, at 16, final paragraph.

withdrawn into ivory towers. William H. Davenport, *The One Culture* (New York: Pergamon, 1970), 74.

an address in Chicago. He delivered his address in the Crystal Room at the Blackstone Hotel, an incongruously unmodernist landmark of Chicago, April 17, 1950.

Fig. n.4 Postcard of Blackstone Hotel, Chicago, IL (early twentieth century).

The ivory tower man is out. *Life*, June 7, 1968, 62.

best time of Gothic. Bushart, *Der Geist der Gotik*, 173–74.

manifesto for Bauhaus. The most ambitious attempt to set the movement within a European tradition from romanticism on is Staffan Källström, *Framtidens katedral: Medeltidsdröm och utopisk modernism* (Stockholm: Carlssons, 2000). For contextualization of Feininger's 1919 woodcut within the cultural milieu of the early Weimar Republic, see Alexander Nagel, *Medieval Modern: Art out of Time* (New York: Thames & Hudson, 2012), 241–47.

Must we take the word of our older alumni. Bainbridge Bunting, *Harvard: An Architectural History*, ed. Margaret Henderson Floyd (Cambridge, MA: Belknap Press, 1985), 228–29.

noun first cropped up. In 1770: see Thomas A. Gaines, *The Campus as a Work of Art* (New York: Praeger, 1991), 126.

stood up well to time. Arguably, they have endured better than the non-Gropius Allston Burr Lecture Hall, which lingers on in mostly ignored ugliness and functionlessness.

Gropius complex. Gropius, "Not Gothic but Modern."

Life magazine. The issue is dated April 7.

one of eight headings. The full run of captions is "Out of violence and chaos the Christian mind and spirit created a glowing era when men knew that all things were possible to faith—These saints and kings made the Church great—Daily Religion, it brought excitement and glory to men's lives—Monk, Abelard, a renowned teacher—Monk, Bacon a versatile scientist—Judgment, it sentenced people to heaven or to hell—The Cult of Mary, the virgin mother was a symbol of love, and heroine of legends like 'The Juggler'—A medieval map of the world."

the intense and simple faith of the Middle Ages. Le Coq, *Vignettes littéraires*, 58.

Norton Anthology of World Masterpieces. Maynard Mack, ed. *World Masterpieces*, 2 vols. (New York: W. W. Norton, 1956), 1:477–510 (introduction John C. McGalliard), 592–99 (trans. Kemp-Welch). Six years later this was reprinted as *The Continental Edition of World Masterpieces* (New York: Norton, 1962), 477–510, 584–91 respectively.

expelled from the compendium. The story was omitted from both the second and third editions: respectively, ed. Sarah Lawall, 6 vols. (New York: W. W. Norton, 2001–2002); ed. Martin Puchner (New York: W. W. Norton, 2012).

The Tumbler's Tumble

lost ground or altitude with dizzying rapidity. In 1974, Murray Sachs detected signs of a turnaround, but I remain unconvinced: see Murray Sachs, *Anatole France: The Short Stories* (London: Edward Arnold, 1974), 7.

lyrics that parody an aria. Pointed out by Linda Hutcheon, *A Theory of Parody: The Teachings of Twentieth-Century Art Forms* (New York: Methuen, 1985), xvi; Susan McClary, "This Is Not a Story My People Tell: Musical Time and Space According to Laurie Anderson," *Discourse* 12.1 (Fall–Winter 1989–1990): 104–28, at 113–15.

Problems in Prose. Paul Haines, *Problems in Prose*, 3rd ed. (New York: Harper & Brothers, 1950), 333. The first edition was in 1938, the second in 1944. At the end of the extract in the textbook, the compiler poses to student readers a half-dozen exacting questions about the selection. The interrogation commences by calling for collation of the taxonomies of Marian miracle legends that Gaston Paris and Henry Adams produced. The quiz concludes, "Comment on the poem about the Tumbler of Our Lady. First decide which lines make it charming, and then try to define the nature of its charm. What does Adams add to the story by his interpolated comments?"

less rewarding essays. Haines, *Problems in Prose*, 5th ed. (New York: Harper & Row, 1963), ix–x, at x.

The Joy of Reading. Charles Van Doren, *The Joy of Reading: A Passionate Guide to 189 of the World's Best Authors and Their Works* (Naperville, IL: Sourcebooks, 2008), 99–102.

which devotees have a right to recognition. Marjorie Glicksman Grene, *A Philosophical Testament* (Chicago: Open Court, 1995), 186.

Julie Harris. The account is provided in an undated first-person testimonial in *Guideposts*, accessed on line at http://www.guideposts.org/faith/stories-of-faith/holding-out-her-hand-in-faith

taken solace in the story. On the way to such responses, "A Note to the Reader" in one hand-sized book of the tale acknowledges: "The story itself has the basic theme, so comforting to us spiritual commoners, that Heaven does not disdain the humble gifts of humble people. Perhaps the same insight, or hope, may account for the popularity of the comparatively modern story of the little drummer boy who had no gift to bring to the Manger except his drumming and was glad to find that this was acceptable." See Walter Kahoe, *The Juggler of Our Lady: An Old Tale Retold*, illus. Gus Uhlmann (Moylan, PA: Rose Valley Press, 1977), on the first and second sides following the title page.

world literature. Joseph Remenyi, "The Meaning of World Literature," *Journal of Aesthetics and Art Criticism* 9 (1951): 244–51, at 249–50: "The religious sense of security which Dante's *Divine Comedy* offers, the spiritual delight that a medieval *conte dévot* [pious tale] such as *The Tumbler of Our Lady* gives, Don Quixote's wise madness, Hamlet's tragic hesitation, the fabliau-inspired earthiness of François Rabelais, Gulliver's sardonic relationship to his fellowmen, Tartuffe's hypocrisy, Faust's yearning for an affirmative philosophy, Rodion Raskolnikov's sense of guilt, Captain Ahab's tragic struggle with the White Whale, and many other examples taken from world literature, underpin the idea that the creative spirit makes life meaningful, and that world literature, while it does not sanction the formlessness of human existence, establishes a common link between the past and the present, the immediate and the future, the implicit and the intricate, the familiar and the unfamiliar." The article was reprinted in *World Literatures: Arabic, Chinese, Czechoslavak, French, German, Greek, Hungarian, Italian, Lithuanian, Norwegian, Polish, Romanian, Russia, Scottish, Swedish [and] Yugoslav*, ed. Joseph Remenyi et al. (Pittsburgh: University of Pittsburgh Press, 1956), 1–14.

searching for a deeper meaning. Remenyi, "Meaning of World Literature," 249.

English translations. Already in 1962, the text was "redacted into English prose": see Wilson Lysle Frescoln, *Old French Contes Dévots* (Wallingford, PA: Press of the Cheerful Snail, 1962). The title page bills the story in this way as the opening selection in a slim octavo with unnumbered pages. Yet the final line of the colophon reveals how far from the mass market this pint-sized collection of six medieval French pious tales was: "Twenty-six copies were printed, and the type has been distributed." The concluding past participle means definitively that after printing, the type used in producing the bookling was broken apart and replaced. The reason for the number of books in the printing is probably explained by the letter A that is penciled onto the verso of the title page to "The Tumbler of Our Lady": the translator and printer made one for each letter in the Roman alphabet as used in English. Whatever motivated this printing, and whoever received it, the little volume has been unknown and nearly impossible to find. In 1979, the tale received its first word-for-word translation into English with a reprint of the original text en face. The venue was a recherché journal: Everett C. Wilkie Jr., trans., "Our Lady's Tumbler," *Allegorica: A Journal of Medieval and Renaissance Literature* 4.1–2 (Summer–Winter 1979): 81–120.

Outside the Anglophone world, the story was printed in 1981 for the first time with a modern French translation facing the medieval French: Pierre Kunstmann, *Vierge et merveille: Les miracles de Notre-Dame narratifs au Moyen Âge* (Paris: Union générale d'éditions, 1981), 142–77. In 2003, a convenient paperback for researchers was published in France. This time it appeared with a fresh translation, a reprinting of the original poem, the text of Anatole France's version, and many supporting materials: Paul Bretel, *Le jongleur de Notre-Dame*, Traductions des classiques du Moyen Âge, vol. 64 (Paris: Honoré Champion, 2003).

reworking the tale. For instance, Mark Shannon wrapped up the prefatory remarks to his version by professing the hope that "this version keeps our acrobat's spirit as alive and engaging as ever."

The Juggler of the Mother of God. Galina Nikolaevna Gordeeva, "Zhongler bogomateri," in her poetry collection *Pocherk* (Moscow: Privately published, 2001). The poem is dedicated to the memory of Grigoriy Gorin ("pamiati Grigoriia Gorina").

put into Russian repeatedly. Natalia Nikitina and Natalia Tuliakova, "Translation of Anatole France's *L'Étui de nacre* in Russia: Reception and Perception," *Interlitteraria* 21.1 (2016): 79–94, at 80 (on the peaks of interest), 89 (on the number of translations), 92 (for the quotation).

at least sixteen times. Titles vary: *Akrobat*, *Zhongler svyatoi dery* (Jongleur of the Holy Virgin), *Zhongler Bogomateri* (Jongleur of the Mother of God), and *Prostoe serdtse* (Simple heart).

prestige of French in Japanese culture. Mitsuo Nakamura, "The French Influence in Modern Japanese Literature," *Japan Quarterly* 7.1 (1960): 57–65, at 61, 63.

no special notice. The reach of such transmission is limited: the Japanese of the tale is buried as only one selection within an extensive compendium. See Niikura Shun'ichi, trans. "Seibo no karuwazashi," in Niikura Shun'ichi, Kamizawa Eizō, and Amazawa Taijirō yaku, *Furansu chūsei bungakushū* (Poètes et romanciers du Moyen Âge), 4 vols. (Tokyo: Hakusuisha, 1990–1996), 4:407–26.

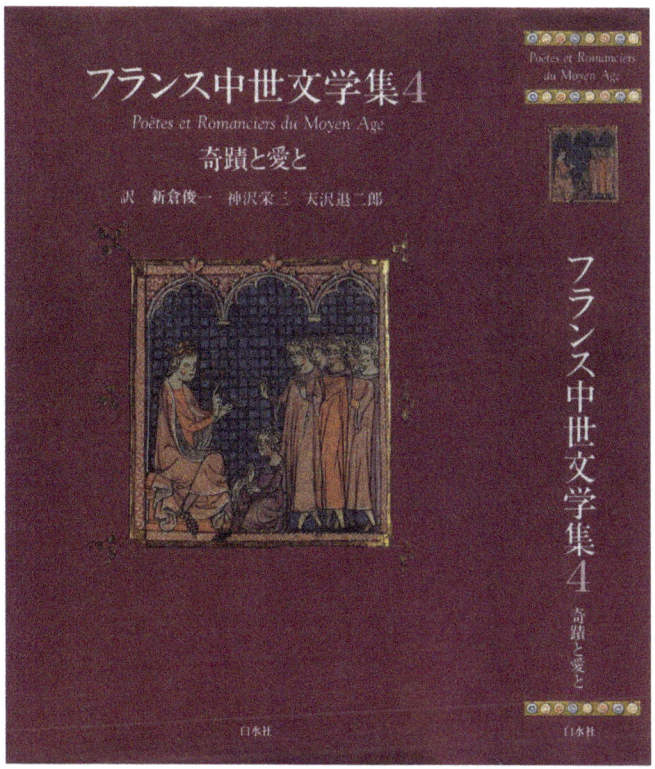

Fig. n.5 Front cover of Shin'ichi Nīkura, Eizō Kamizawa, and Taijirō Amazawa, eds. and trans., 奇蹟と愛と [Kiseki to ai to], vol. 4 of フランス中世文学集 [*Furansu chūsei bungakushū*] / *Poètes et romanciers du Moyen Âge* (Tokyo: Hakusuisha, 1996). Image courtesy of Harvard-Yenching Library. All rights reserved.

Michel Zink Reminds France

sequelae of the French Revolution. Beyond the historical layer to the famous lament, a literary one bears noting: Burke here deliberately echoes the final speech of the title hero in Johann Wolfgang von Goethe's 1773 melodrama, *Götz von Berlichingen*. Goethe's play exercised a deep international influence for a time. Walter Scott's first published work was his 1799 translation of it.

medieval pious tales. Michel Zink, *Le jongleur de Notre Dame: Contes chrétiens du Moyen Âge* (Paris: Le Seuil, 1999), 48–51, 199 (note).

Once upon a time. The original French reads "Il était une fois un jongleur."

simplifies the story. Michel Stanesco, "Le bruit de la source: Les contes chrétiens et la resonance d'éternité," in *Translatio litterarum ad penates = Das Mittelalter Übersetzen: Ergebnisse der Tagung von Mai 2004 an der Université de Lausanne = Traduire le Moyen Âge: Actes du colloque de l'Université de Lausanne (mai 2004)*, ed. Alain Corbellari and

Catherine Drittenbass (Lausanne, Switzerland: Centre de traduction littéraire, 2005), 331–44, at 337–38.

unaffected limpidity. Michel Zink, "Anatole France et moi," in *Medioevo e modernità nella letteratura francese: Moyen Âge et modernité dans la littérature française*, ed. Giovanna Angeli and Maria Emanuela Raffi (Florence: Alinea, 2013), 229–35, at 234.

not the best of my tales. Zink, "Anatole France et moi," 235.

quotation from Saint Bernard. Zink, *Le jongleur de Notre Dame*, 50–51.

Life of the Fathers. *Vie des Pères*, no. 10, ed. Félix Lecoy, *La Vie des Pères* (Paris: Société des anciens textes français, 1987), 1:141–75; Jacques Chaurand, ed., *Fou: Dixième conte de la Vie des Pères. Conte pieux du XIIIe siècle* (Geneva: Droz, 1971). For discussion, see Zink, *Poésie et conversion au Moyen Âge* (Paris: Presses universitaires de France, 2003), 162–63.

without making a secret of his dependence. Zink, "Anatole France et moi," 229–35.

the Tharauds. The preface to one wartime edition of *Les contes de la Vierge* (Paris: Société d'éditions littéraires françaises, 1944) refers explicitly to "our friend, Joseph Bédier" (p. v). In addition to the story of the tumbler, the collection includes "Le chevalier au Barizel" and "Le cierge de Rocamadour." The latter was already paired with *Of the Tumbler of Our Lady* by Alice Kemp-Welch.

Tales of the Middle Ages. In French, *Contes du moyen-âge*, illus. Pierre-Olivier Leclerc (Paris: Le Seuil, 2002).

the miracle of the jongleur was omitted. Bretel, "Le *jongleur de Notre-Dame*, un miracle," 281.

The book has been translated. Michel Zink, *El juglar de Nuestra Señora*, trans. Jorge Sans Vila (Salamanca, Spain: Sígueme, 2000); idem, *Príbehy a legendy stredoveke Evropy*, trans. Alena Lhotová and Hana Prousková (Prague: Portál, 2000); idem, *L'innamorato fedele*, trans. Costanza Ossola (Rome: Città Nuova, 2000).

We All Need the Middle Ages

R. O. Blechman's Juggler of Our Lady. Trans. Anne Krief.

I would not like to live in a world without cathedrals. Pascal Mercier, *Night Train to Lisbon*, trans. Barbara Harshav (New York: Grove, 2008), 171.

there is only medievalism. Stephanie Trigg, "Walking through Cathedrals: Scholars, Pilgrims, and Medieval Tourists," *New Medieval Literatures* 7 (2004): 9–33, at 33.

invoking his concept of the anima. Todd F. David, "Entering the House of the World: An Interview with Mary Rose O'Reilley," *Interdisciplinary Literary Studies: A Journal of Criticism and Theory* 9.2 (2007): 109–22, at 121: "Women of my generation were trained in indirection and self-effacement, which isn't *entirely* a bad thing. You have the ongoing job of learning the difference between humility and the pose of humility. ... Poetry is a device of indirection and self-erasure, as I see it, the territory of the anima, to put it in an old-fashioned way. And being a poet is not a very big deal in this business—I mean in the larger business of being human—I think of the Juggler of Notre Dame, or the family of acrobats in *The Seventh Seal*."

stories that haven't finished yet. The character Jane Smith (played by Angelina Jolie), over speakerphone to her husband John (Brad Pitt), in the 2005 action movie *Mr. & Mrs. Smith*.

whatever skills they have. See Grene, *Philosophical Testament*, 186: "The increasing place in school curricula of 'practical' subjects might not be a factor of cultural deterioration, if these subjects were not endowed with intrinsic cultural worth but actually treated as purely instrumental for objectively important achievements."

a sociology book. Florian Znaniecki, "Leadership and Followship in Creative Cooperation," in idem, *What are Sociological Problems?*, ed. Zygmunt Dulczewski et al. (Nakom, Poland: Wydawnictwo, 1994), 133.

renaissance. The expression "methodological renaissance" appears within quotation marks in Richard R. Glejzer, "The New Medievalism and the (Im)Possibility of the Middle Ages," *Studies in Medievalism* 10 (1998): 104–19, at 104. The earlier study cited is Peter Monaghan, "Medievalists, Romantics No Longer, Take Stock of Their Changing Field." *Chronicle of Higher Education*, October 30, 1998, A15–17.

We shall not cease from exploration. T. S. Eliot, "Little Gidding."

Notes to Acknowledgments

not to be examined too critically. Jean Misrahi, review of Sister Paul-Emile, *Le renouveau marial dans la littérature française depuis Chateaubriand jusqu' à nos jours* (Paris: Edition Spes, n.d.), in *The French Review* 15 (1942): 339–40, at 340.

a talk for a workshop. The workshop on "Rhetoric and the Non-Verbal Arts" took place in Villa La Pietra, Florence, from September 2–6, 2004.

an essay in a volume propelled by Mary Carruthers. "Do Actions Speak Louder Than Words? The Scope and Role of *Pronuntiatio* in the Latin Rhetorical Tradition, With Special Reference to the Cistercians," in Mary Carruthers, ed., *Rhetoric Beyond Words: Delight and Persuasion in the Arts of the Middle Ages*, Cambridge Studies in Medieval Literature, vol. 78 (Cambridge: Cambridge University Press, 2010), 124–50, at 137–42.

a thumbnail sketch of my research. "Juggling the Middle Ages," *Netherlands Institute for Advanced Study in the Humanities and Social Sciences NIAS Newsletter* 36 (2006): 18–22. These few pages alone were known to Antonie Hornung, "Durch Zeit und Raum: 'Del tumbeor Nostre Dame,'" in Antonie Hornung and C. Robustelli, eds., *Vivere l'intercultura-gelebte Interkulturalität: studi in onore di Hans Drumbl* (Tübingen: Stauffenburg-Verlag, 2008), 347–73.

a couple of sides stimulated by the story. "The Joy of Juggling, Words or Otherwise," in Kathleen Coleman, ed., *Albert's Anthology*, Loeb Classical Monographs (Cambridge, MA: Department of the Classics, 2017), 231–32.

in schematic form as an article. "Juggling the Middle Ages: The Reception of Our Lady's Tumbler and Le Jongleur de Notre–Dame," *Studies in Medievalism* 15 (2006 [printed 2007]): 157–197.

plenty in formal oratory. (1) "Our Lady's Tumbler: From Medieval Fantasy to Modern Fakelore," in "Folklore, Fantasy, and Film," a symposium sponsored by Folklore and Mythology, Harvard University, February 11–12, 2005. (2) "Juggling the Middle Ages: The Reception of Our Lady's Tumbler and Le Jongleur de Notre Dame," Yale Lectures in Medieval Studies, Yale University, November 9, 2006; Medieval Institute, University of Notre Dame; November 30, 2006; and Dumbarton Oaks, December 13, 2007. (3) "Tumbling into English: The Exemplary Medieval Past of the *Jongleur de Notre Dame*," Garnett Sedgewick Memorial Lecture, University of British Vancouver, March 2, 2007. (4) "Giving the Middle Ages a Tumble," in "Poets, Performers, and Other Mythical Creatures of the Middle Ages," a conference under the aegis of the UCLA Center for Medieval and Renaissance Studies, June 4, 2011. (5) "Henry Adams and the Melancholy of Medievalism," in "Madness, Melancholy, Myth," a conference under the aegis of the UCLA Center for Medieval and Renaissance Studies and the Freshman Cluster Course "Neverending Stories," May 31, 2014.

Bibliography

Abbreviations

EHA *The Education of Henry Adams*, in Henry Adams, *Novels, Mont Saint Michel, The Education*, ed. Ernest Samuels and Jayne N. Samuels, 715–1192. New York: Library of America, 1983.

LHA *The Letters of Henry Adams*, ed. J. C. Levenson et al. 6 vols. Cambridge, MA: Harvard University Press, 1982–1988.

Archives

Dumbarton Oaks Archives, Administrative files, John S. Thacher correspondence, 1940–1949.

Referenced Works

Abragam, Anatole. "The Physicist Erwin Hahn." In *Pulsed Magnetic Resonance: A Recognition of E. L. Hahn*, ed. D. M. S. Bagguley, 1–4. Oxford: Clarendon Press, 1992.

Acta Sanctorum. Antwerp: apud Joannem Mevrsium, 1643–. Largely online at www.patristique.org/Acta-sanctorum.html.

Alexander, Michael. *Medievalism: The Middle Ages in Modern England*. New Haven, CT: Yale University Press, 2007.

Anten, J. H. M. "De crisistijd van de jaren dertig: Gouden jaren voor de neerlandistiek." *Nederlandse letterkunde* 15.3 (2010): 262–72.

Ash, Mitchell G. Review of Edward P. Rich, *The Pazyryk Agenda: A Police Procedural*. *German Studies Review* 18 (1995): 174–76.

Auden, W. H. "The Art of Poetry No. 17," interviewed by Michael Newman. *Paris Review* 57 (1974), https://www.theparisreview.org/interviews/3970/w-h-auden-the-art-of-poetry-no-17-w-h-auden

—. *The Ballad of Barnaby*. Music by students of Wykeham Rise School in Washington, CT, realization Charles Turner. New York: G. Schirmer, 1969.

—. *A Certain World: A Commonplace Book*. New York: Viking Press, 1970.

—. *Collected Poems*, ed. Edward Mendelson. New York: Modern Library, 2007.

—. *Epistle to a Godson and Other Poems*. New York: Random House, 1972.

—. *For the Time Being: A Christmas Oratorio*, in idem, *Collected Poems*, ed. Edward Mendelson, 347–400. New York: Modern Library, 2007.

—. "New Year Letter (January 1, 1940)," in idem, *Collected Poems*, ed. Edward Mendelson, 195–241. New York: Modern Library, 2007.

—, and Paul B. Taylor, trans. *Norse Poems*. London: Athlone, 1981.

—. "The Virgin & the Dynamo," in idem, *The Dyer's Hand and Other Essays*, 61–71. New York: Random House, 1962.

Bakhtin, Mikhail. *Rabelais and His World*, trans. Helene Iswolsky. Cambridge, MA: MIT Press, 1968.

Baldensperger, F. "L'Art pour l'Art." *Modern Language Notes* 27 (1912): 91.

Balestracci, Maria Serena. *Arandora Star: Dall'oblio alla memoria*. Belle Storie, Saggi, vol. 6. Parma, Italy: MUP, 2008.

Bamberger, Richard, and Franz Maier-Bruck, eds. *Österreich Lexikon*. 2 vols. Vienna: Österreichischer Bundesverlag, 1966.

Barkai, Avraham. "The Fateful Year 1938: The Continuation and Acceleration of Plunder." In *November 1938: From "Reichskristallnacht" to Genocide*, ed. Walter H. Pehle, trans. William Templer. New York: Berg, 1991.

Barnes, Djuna. *Nightwood*. New York: Harcourt, Brace, 1937.

Barrier, Michael J. *Hollywood Cartoons: American Animation in Its Golden Age*. New York: Oxford University Press, 1999.

Barthes, Roland. "The New Citroën." In idem, *Mythologies*, trans. Richard Howard and Annette Lavers, 169–71. New York: Hill and Wang, 2012.

Bärthlein, Karl. "Zur Lehre von der *recta ratio* in der Geschichte der Ethik von der Stoa bis Christian Wolff." *Kant-Studien* 56.2 (1965): 125–55.

Baumel, Jacques. *La liberté guidait nos pas*. Paris: Plon, 2004.

Bedaux, J. C. "Franciscus Josephus Henricus Maria van der Ven, Tilburg 2 september 1907– Tilburg 10 december 1999." *Jaarboek van de Maatschappij der Nederlandse Letterkunde* (2000): 129–31.

Beevers, John. *The Sun Her Mantle*. Westminster, MD: Newman, 1953.

Benjamin, Walter. *Illuminations*, ed. Hannah Arendt, trans. Harry Zohn. New York: Schocken Books, 1969.

Biddle, Arthur W., ed. *When Prophecy Still Had a Voice: The Letters of Thomas Merton and Robert Lax*. Lexington, KY: University Press of Kentucky, 2001.

Biesalski, Ernst. *Scherenschnitt und Schattenriß: Kleine Geschichte der Silhouettenkunst*. 2nd ed. Munich, Germany: Callwey, 1978.

Bims, Hamilton. "An All-Black Opera Raises Its Voice." *Ebony* 28.4 (February 1973): 54–56.

Birkhead, Jane. "Dramatic Music by P. Maxwell Davies." *Notes*, 2nd ser., 36.2 (December 1979): 484.

Blechman, R. O. *Behind the Lines*. New York: Hudson Hills, 1980.

—. *The Graphic Stories of R. O. Blechman: Talking Lines*. Montreal, Canada: Drawn and Quarterly, 2009.

—. *The Juggler of Our Lady: A Medieval Legend Adapted*. New York: Holt, 1953; repr. New York: Stewart, Tabori & Chang, 1997. Repr. as *The Juggler of Our Lady: The Classic Christmas Story*, foreword Jules Feiffer, introduction Maurice Sendak. Mineola, New York: Dover, 2015. Trans. Anne Krief, *Le jongleur de Notre-Dame: Une légende médiévale réadaptée*. [Paris]: Gallimard Jeunesse, 2002.

—. *The Life of Saint Nicholas, as Transcribed in Pictures and Text*. New York: Stewart, Tabori & Chang, 1996.

Blondeel, E. H. *Wintze, of De Tuimelaar van O. L. Vrouw: Legendeverhaal*. Torhout, Belgium: Becelaere, 1933.

Bloom, Harold. *The Anxiety of Influence: A Theory of Poetry*. New York: Oxford University Press, 1973.

Blue Heron, Hannah. *That Strange Intimacy*. Victoria, BC: Trafford, 2005.

Bollmus, Reinhard. *Handelshochschule und Nationalsozialismus: Das Ende der Handelshochschule Mannheim und die Vorgeschichte der Errichtung einer Staats- und Wirtschaftswissenschaftlichen Fakultät an der Universität Heidelberg 1933–34*. Mannheimer sozialwissenschaftliche Studien, vol. 8. Meisenheim am Glan, Germany: Hain, 1973.

Bordeaux, Henry. *A Pathway to Heaven*, trans. Antonia White. New York: Pellegrini & Cudahy, 1952; orig. publ. idem, *Le fil de la Vierge*. Paris: Plon, 1951.

—. *Images du Maréchal Pétain*. Paris: Sequana, 1941.

Bossuat, Robert, ed. *Bérinus, roman en prose du XIVe siècle*. 2 vols. Paris: Société des anciens textes français, 1931–1933.

Bowen, Robert. *Universal Ice: Science and Ideology in the Nazi State*. London: Bellhaven, 1993.

Bretel, Paul. *Le jongleur de Notre-Dame*. Traductions des classiques du Moyen Âge, vol. 64. Paris: Honoré Champion, 2003.

—. "*Le jongleur de Notre-Dame*, un miracle pour enfants?" In *Grands textes du Moyen Âge à l'usage des petits*, ed. Caroline Cazanave and Yvon Houssais, 277–97. Annales littéraires de l'Université de Franche-Comté, vol. 869. Besançon, France: Presses universitaires de Franche-Comté, 2010.

Brochet, Henri. "Béatrice: Miracle de Notre-Dame, en trois actes." *Jeux, Tréteaux et Personnages* (May 1939): 143–78; (June 1939): 179–96.

—. *Marie, reine de France et dame de Pontmain: Mystère en trois parties*. Paris: A. Blot, 1938.

Brown, Carl R. V. "Contemporary Poetry about Painting." *English Journal* 81 (1992): 41–45.

Brugg, Elmar. [Rudolf Elmayer von Vestenbrugg]. *Sankt Stephan zwischen Staub und Sternen: Die Schicksalssymphonie eines Domes*. Hamburg, Germany: P. Zsolnay, 1956.

—. [Rudolf Elmayer von Vestenbrugg]. *Vom Tod ins Leben: Ein Hymnus*. Munich: Josef Gäßler, 1958.

Buelens, Geert. "Een avantgardist is (g)een groep: Over de wankele avantgardestatus van de flaminganten tijdens het interbellum." In *Avantgarde! Voorhoede? Vernieuwingsbewegingen in Noord en Zuid opnieuw beschouwd*, ed. Hubert F. van den Berg and Gillis J. Dorleijn, 92–102, 223–24. Nijmegen, Netherlands: Vantilt, 2002.

Bunting, Bainbridge. *Harvard: An Architectural History*, ed. Margaret Henderson Floyd. Cambridge, MA: Belknap Press, 1985.

Bushart, Magdalena. *Der Geist der Gotik und die expressionistische Kunst: Kunstgeschichte und Kunsttheorie 1911–1925*. Munich, Germany: S. Schreiber, 1990.

Buytaert, Eligius M. "Review of R. O. Blechman, *The Juggler of Our Lady*." Franciscan Studies 13. 4 (1953): 138.

Cadegan, Una M. "How Realistic Can a Catholic Writer Be? Richard Sullivan and American Catholic Literature." *Religion and American Catholic Literature: A Journal of Interpretation* 6 (1996): 35–61.

—. "Images of Mary in American Periodicals, 1900–1960." *Marian Studies* 46 (1995): 89–107.

Cahn, Walter. "Focillon's *Jongleur*." *Art History* 18.3 (1995): 345–62.

Cantor, Norman F. *The Civilization of the Middle Ages: A Completely Revised and Expanded Edition of* Medieval History: The Life and Death of a Civilization. New York: HarperCollins, 1993.

Carroll, Michael P. *Madonnas that Maim: Popular Catholicism in Italy since the Fifteenth Century*. Baltimore, MD: Johns Hopkins University Press, 1992.

Cassagne, Albert. *La théorie de l'art pour l'art: En France chez les derniers romantiques et les premiers réalistes*. Paris: L. Dorbon, 1959.

Cassity, Turner. "Our Lady's Juggler." *Poetry* 127 (1976): 343. Repr. in idem, *Hurricane Lamp*, 57. Chicago: University of Chicago Press, 1986.

Cater, Harold Dean. *Henry Adams and His Friends: A Collection of His Unpublished Letters*. Boston: Houghton Mifflin, 1947.

Chancerel, Léon. *Frère Clown, ou Le jongleur de Notre-Dame: Monologue par Léon Chancerel, d'après le miracle du ménestrel Pierre de Sygelar*. Lyon, France: La Hutte, 1943; 2nd ed., Paris: Librarie Théâtrale, 1956.

Chandler, Alice. *A Dream of Order: The Medieval Ideal in Nineteenth-Century English Literature*. London: Routledge & Kegan Paul, 1971.

—. "Order and Disorder in the Medieval Revival." *Browning Institute Studies* 8 (1980): 1–9.

Chaurand, Jacques, ed. *Fou: Dixième conte de la Vie des pères. Conte pieux du XIIIe siècle*. Publications romanes et françaises, vol. 117. Geneva: Droz, 1971.

Chesterton, G. K. *S. Franciscus van Assisi*, trans. Wies Moens. Ghent, Belgium: Cultura, 1924.

Child, Heather, H. Collins, A. Hechle, and D. Jackson. *More than Fine Writing: The Life and Calligraphy of Irene Wellington*. Woodstock, NY: Overlook Press, 1987.

Christian, Sheldon. *Our Lady's Tumbler: A Modern Miracle Play*. Portland, ME: Anthoensen Press, 1948.

Christian, William A., Jr. "Tapping and Defining New Power: The First Month of Visions at Ezquioga, July 1931." *American Ethnologist* 14 (1987): 140–66.

Ciardi, John. "The Form is the Experience." *Art Education* 14.7 (October 1961): 16–22.

—. *How Does A Poem Mean?* Boston: Houghton Mifflin, 1959.

Clark, Kenneth. *The Gothic Revival: An Essay in the History of Taste*. London: Constable, 1928).

Coelho, Paulo. *O alquimista*. Rio de Janeiro, Brazil: Rocco, 1988.

Cohen, Gustave. "Expériences théophiliennes." *Mercure de France* year 48.927, vol. 273 (February 1, 1937): 453–77.

—. "Les Théophiliens." *The French Review* 12.6 (1939): 453–58.

—. "The 'Théophiliens': The Resurrection of the Medieval Theater." *Books Abroad* 25 (1951): 7–10.

Collaer, Paul. *Correspondance avec des amis musiciens*, ed. Robert Wangermée. Liège, Belgium: P. Mardaga, 1996.

Cooke, James Francis. *Young Folks' Picture History of Music*. Bryn Mawr, PA: Theodore Presser, 1925.

Corliss, Richard. "Radley Metzger: Aristocrat of the Erotic." *Film Comment* 9 (1973): 19–29.

—. "That Old Feeling: When Porno Was Chic," *Time*, Tuesday, March 29, 2005, 5.

Cotnam, Jacques. "Henri Brochet et le R. P. Émile Legault, c.s.c.: Rencontre et correspondance." *Tangence* 78 (2005): 45–89.

"Cours et conférences." *Revue de musicologie* 21 (1942): 10.

Culbert, David. "The Impact of Anti-Semitic Film Propaganda on German Audiences: *Jew Süss* and *The Wandering Jew* (1940)." In *Art, Culture, and Media under the Third Reich*, ed. Richard A. Etlin, 139–57. Chicago: University of Chicago Press, 2002.

Curran, Lynne. "Sax Shaw: His Contribution to the World of Tapestry." *Journal of Weavers, Spinners and Dyers* 200 (December 2001): 10–12.

Curtis, Tony, and Barry Paris. *Tony Curtis: The Autobiography*. New York: Morrow, 1993.

Cusson, Jean. *Un réformateur du théâtre, Léon Chancerel: L'expérience Comédiens-Routiers, 1929–1939*. Paris: LaHutte, 1945.

Davenport, William H. *The One Culture*. New York: Pergamon, 1970.

Davies, Peter Maxwell. *Le Jongleur de Notre Dame, a Masque for Mime, Baritone, Chamber Ensemble and Children's Band*. London: Chester Music, 1978.

David, Todd F. "Entering the House of the World: An Interview with Mary Rose O'Reilley." *Interdisciplinary Literary Studies: A Journal of Criticism and Theory* 9.2 (2007): 109–22.

Day, F. Holland. *Suffering the Ideal*. With an essay by James Crump. Santa Fe, NM: Twin Palms, 1995.

De Wever, Bruno. "Groot-Nederland als utopie en mythe." *Bijdragen tot de eigentijdse geschiedenis/ Cahiers d'histoire du temps présent* 3 (1998): 91–108.

—. "Vlaams-nationalisme in de Gentse regio, 1914–1945." *Handelingen der Maatschappij voor Geschiedenis en Oudheidkunde te Gent* 49.1 (1995): 265–81.

DeCesare, Stephen. *The Juggler of Notre Dame: The Musical* (SDA Productions), http://www.musicaneo.com/sheetmusic/sm-159801_the_juggler_of_notre_dame_musical.html#159801

Defresne, August. *Het eethuis*. Maastricht, Netherlands: Leiter-Nypels, 1931.

—. "Het expressionisme in de huidige Duitse toneelschrijfkunst." *Groot Nederland* 22 (1925): 293–312, 406–29, 513–30, 625–42.

—. *De psychologie van "Van den Vos Reynaerde."* Amsterdam: Boonacker, 1920.

—. *De vrome speelman*. Amsterdam: "De Gulden Ster," 1933.

Delabays, Giuseppe. *La Madonna dei Poveri di Banneux-Notre-Dame*, trans. Ester Brinis. Balsamo, Italy: Paoline, 1949.

Delaney, John J., ed. *A Woman Clothed with the Sun: Eight Great Appearances of Our Lady in Modern Times*. Garden City, NY: Hanover House, 1960.

Dennis, David B. *Inhumanities: Nazi Interpretations of Western Culture*. Cambridge: Cambridge University Press, 2012.

Devun, Blandine. *La vie culturelle à Saint-Étienne pendant la deuxiéme guerre mondiale (1939–1944)*. Saint-Etienne, France: Publications de l'Université de Saint-Étienne, 2005.

Dewulf, Jeroen. *Spirit of Resistance: Dutch Clandestine Literature during the Nazi Occupation*. Rochester, NY: Camden House, 2010.

D'Haese, Jan. "Wies Moens." *Oostvlaamse literaire monografieën*, 4:163–93. Kultureel jaarboek voor de provincie Oost-Vlaanderen, Bijdragen, Nieuwe reeks, vol. 14. Ghent, Belgium: 1981.

Dickinson, Peter. "Charles Turner: Interview with Peter Dickinson, New York City, May 13, 1981." In *Samuel Barber Remembered: A Centenary Tribute*, ed. idem, 73–79. Rochester, NY: University of Rochester Press, 2010.

Dietzenschmidt [Anton Franz Schmid]. *Die Sanct Jacobsfahrt: Eyn Legendenspiel in drey Aufzüge*. Berlin: Oesterheld, 1920. Trans. Wies Moens, *Compostella (Die St.-Jacobsfahrt): Legendespel in drie bedrijven*. Wederlandsch Keurtooneel, vol. 1. Ghent, Belgium: "'t Spyker," 1923.

Dobuzinskis, Alex. "Nude Virgin Mary Cover Prompts Playboy Apology." Reuters, US edition, December 12, 2008, https://www.reuters.com/article/playboy/nude-virgin-mary-cover-prompts-playboy-apology-idUSN1250649220081213

Donker, Anthonie [N. A. Donkerslot]. *De einder: Verzamelde gedichten*. Arnhem, Netherlands: Van Loghum Slaterus, 1947.

—. *Gebroken licht*. Arnhem, Netherlands: Van Loghum Slaterus, 1934.

—. *Grenzen*. Arnhem, Netherlands: Hijman, Stenfert Kroese & Van der Zande, 1928.

Dorsey, John R. *Look Again in Baltimore*, photography James DuSel. Baltimore, MD: Johns Hopkins University Press, 2005.

Dove, Richard, ed. *"Totally Un-English?": Britain's Internment of "Enemy Aliens" in Two World Wars*. Amsterdam: Rodopi, 2005.

Durant, Will. *The Age of Faith: A History of Medieval Civilization—Christian, Islamic, and Judaic—from Constantine to Dante. A.D. 325–1300*. The Story of Civilization, vol. 4. New York: Simon and Schuster, 1950.

Elias, Josef. *Der Tänzer unserer lieben Frau: Ein altes Legendspiel für die Bühne*. Elgg, Switzerland: Volksverlag, 1959.

Elmayer-Vestenbrugg, Rudolf von. *Georg Ritter von Schönerer, der Vater des politischen Antisemitismus, von einem, der ihn selbst erlebt hat*. Munich, Germany: F. Eher nachfolger, 1936, 2nd ed. 1942.

—, ed. *SA-Männer im feldgrauen Rock: Taten und Erlebnisse von SA.-Männern in den Kriegsjahren 1939–1940*. Leipzig, Germany: Hase & Koehler, 1941.

—. *Vom Tod ins Leben: Ein Buch von Liebe, Tod und Jenseits*. Hammelburg, Germany: Drei Eichen, 1962.

—. *Vom Tod ins Leben: Ein Hymnus*. Zurich, Switzerland: Graphia, 1951.

—. *Totengräber der Weltkultur: Der Weg des jüdischen Untermenschentums zur Weltherrschaft*. Kampfschriften der Obersten SA-Führung, vol. 2. Munich, Germany: Zentralverlag der NSDAP, 1937.

Elmayer-Vestenbrugg, Rudolf von. See also Brugg, Elmar.

Esh, Shaul. "Between Discrimination and Extermination: 1938 –The Fateful Year." *Yad Washem Studies on the European Jewish Catastrophe and Resistance* 2 (1958): 79–93.

Étiemble, René. *Savoir et goût*. Hygiène des Lettres, vol. 3. Paris: Gallimard, 1958.

Falaize, Antoine-Marie. *Lettres spirituelles*. Paris: Cerf, 1945.

Ferenc, Tone. "The Austrians and Slovenia during the Second World War." In *Conquering the Past: Austrian Nazism Yesterday and Today*, ed. F. Parkinson, 207–23. Detroit, MI: Wayne State University Press, 1989.

Ferguson, George Wells. *Signs and Symbols in Christian Art*. New York: Oxford University Press, 1954.

Fleischer, Georgette. "Djuna Barnes and T. S. Eliot: The Politics and Poetics of *Nightwood*." *Studies in the Novel* 30 (1998): 405–37.

Focillon, Henri. "Sculpture romane: Apôtres et jongleurs (études de mouvement)." *Revue de l'art ancien et moderne* 55 (1929): 13–28.

Foubert-Daudet, Yvonne. *La règle du je: Les frères Jérôme et Jean Tharaud, témoins et chroniqueurs d'un demi-siècle mouvementé*. Toulouse, France: Erès, 1982.

Fowlie, Wallace. *The Clown's Grail: A Study of Love in Its Literary Expression*. Denver, CO: Alan Swallow, 1948. Repr. as *Love in Literature*. Bloomington: Indiana University Press, 1965.

Fraenger, Wilhelm. *Die Masken von Rheims und der Legend "Der Tänzer unserer Lieben Frau" ins Deutsche übertragen von Curt Sigmar Gutkind*. Erlenbach, Switzerland: Eugen Rentsch, 1922.

France, Anatole. *Le jongleur de Notre-Dame*. Paris: Éditions de l'Amitié, 1944, repr. 1946.

—. *Le jongleur de Notre-Dame*, trans. Frederic Chapman. [No place]: Printed for the friends of Jarrett and Robert Schmid, Christmas 1944.

—. *Le petit soldat de plomb: Le jongleur de Notre-Dame*, ed. Georg Ahting and H. Richters-Franceschi. Neusprachliche Texte, vol. 124. Dortmund, Germany: Lamberg Lensing, 1954.

—. *Quatre nouvelles*, ed. Josef Longerich. Freiburg im Breisgau, Germany: L. Bielefeld, 1947.

—. *La révolte des anges*. Paris: Calmann Lévy, 1946. Trans. Wilfrid Jackson, *The Revolt of the Angels*, illus. Pierre Watrin. New York: For the members of the Limited Editions Club, 1953.

Frankau, Gilbert, ed. *A Century of Love Stories*. London: Hutchinson, [1935?].

Frescoln, Wilson Lysle, trans. *Old French Contes Dévots*. Wallingford, PA: Press of the Cheerful Snail, 1962.

Gaines, Thomas A. *The Campus as a Work of Art*. New York: Praeger, 1991.

Garfinkel, Alan. "Notes and News." *Modern Language Journal* 62.3 (March 1978): 113–31.

Gautier de Coinci. *Les miracles de Nostre Dame*, ed. V. Frédéric Koenig. 4 vols. Textes littéraires français, vols. 64, 95, 131, 176. Geneva: Droz, 1955–1970.

—. *Les plus beaux miracles de la Vierge*, trans. Gonzague Truc. Paris: Lanore, 1932.

Geisel, Theodor Seuss [Doctor Seuss]. *How the Grinch Stole Christmas*. New York: Random House, 1957.

George, Walter Lionel. *Anatole France*. New York: H. Holt, [1915].

Gier, Albert. *Der Sünder als Beispiel: Zu Gestalt und Funktion hagiographischer Gebrauchstexte anhand der Theophiluslegende*. Bonner romanistische Arbeiten, vol. 1. Frankfurt am Main, Germany: P. Lang, 1977.

Gignoux, Hubert. *Histoire d'une famille théâtrale: Jacques Copeau, Léon Chancerel, les Comédiens-Routiers, la décentralisation dramatique*. Lausanne, Switzerland: Editions de l'Aire, 1984.

Gillet, Louis, Jérôme Tharaud, and Jean Tharaud. *Les primitifs français: Contes de la Vierge*. Cahiers de la quinzaine, 6th series, vol. 7. Paris: Cahiers de la quinzaine, 1904.

Gillman, Peter, and Leni Gillman. *"Collar the Lot!": How Britain Interned and Expelled Its Wartime Refugees*. London: Quartet Books, 1980.

Gilroy, Harry. "Auden Writes Opera Narrative for a Girls' School." *The New York Times*, May 7, 1969, 36.

Gilson, Étienne. *L'esprit de la philosophie médiévale*. Paris: J. Vrin, 1932. Trans. *The Spirit of Medieval Philosophy* (London: Sheed & Ward, 1936).

—. *Pour un ordre catholique*. Paris: Desclée de Brouwer, 1934.

—. *La théologie mystique de saint Bernard*. Paris: J. Vrin, 1934.

Giroud, Vincent. "Le centenaire de la naissance: Massenet en 1942." In *Massenet aujourd'hui: Héritage et postérité. Actes du colloque de la XIe biennale Massenet des 25 et 26 octobre 2012*, ed. Jean-Christophe Branger and Vincent Giroud, 65–94. Centre interdisciplinaire d'études et de recherches sur l'expression contemporaine: Travaux, vol. 166/Collection musique et musicology: Les cahiers de l'opéra théâtre, vol. 1. Saint-Étienne, France: Publications de l'université de Saint-Étienne, 2014.

Glejzer, Richard R. "The New Medievalism and the (Im)Possibility of the Middle Ages." *Studies in Medievalism* 10 (1998): 104–19.

Gloag, Kenneth, and Nicholas Jones, eds. *Peter Maxwell Davies Studies*. Cambridge: Cambridge University Press, 2009.

Gordon, Bertram M. "The Decline of a Cultural Icon: France in American Perspective." *French Historical Studies* 22.4 (1999): 625–51.

Gorfinkel, Elena. "Radley Metzger's 'Elegant Arousal': Taste, Aesthetic Distinction, and Sexploitation." In *Underground USA: Filmmaking beyond the Hollywood Canon*, ed. Xavier Mendik and Steven Jay Schneider, 26–39. London: Wallflower, 2002.

Gottlieb, Craig. *The SS Totenkopf Ring: An Illustrated History from Munich to Nuremberg*. Atglen, PA: Schiffer Military History, 2008.

Gradwohl-Schlacher, Karin. "Elmayer von Vestenbrugg (Elmayer-Vestenbrugg), Rudolf von; Ps. Elmar Vinibert von Rudolf, Elmar Brugg, Schriftsteller und Journalist." *Österreichisches biographisches Lexikon (ÖBL) Online-Edition* 3 (Nov. 15, 2014).

—, and Sabine Fuchs. "Rudolf von Elmayer-Vestenbrugg." In *Literatur in Österreich 1938–1945: Handbuch eines literarischen Systems*, ed. Uwe Baur and Karin Gradwohl-Schlacher, 1:101–5. 3 vols. Vienna: Böhlau, 2008–<2014>.

Graham, Kate Childs. "Playboy's Not So Virgin Mary." *Religion Dispatches*, December 21, 2008, http://religiondispatches.org/playboys-not-so-virgin-mary

Grant, Damian. "Verbal Events." *Critical Quarterly* 16.1 (1974): 81–86.

Grene, Marjorie Glicksman. *A Philosophical Testament*. Chicago: Open Court, 1995.

Griffin, John Howard. "The Poulenc behind the Mask." In *The John Howard Griffin Reader*, ed. Bradford Daniel. Boston: Houghton Mifflin, 1968.

—. *Prison of Culture: Beyond Black Like Me*, ed. Robert Bonazzi. San Antonio, TX: Wings Press, 2011.

Grimm, Wilhelm. *Kleinere Schriften*, ed. Gustav Hinrichs. 4 vols. Berlin: Ferdinand Dümmler, 1881–1887.

Groebner, Valentin. *Das Mittelalter hört nicht auf: Über historisches Erzählen*. Munich, Germany: C. H. Beck, 2008.

Groeschel, Benedict, C.F.R. *Children's Stories*. West Covina, CA: Saint Joseph Communications, 2008.

Gropius, Walter. "Not Gothic but Modern for Our Colleges: A Noted Architect Says We Cling Too Blindly to the Past, Though We Build for Tomorrow." *The New York Times Magazine*, October 23, 1949, 16–18.

Grynberg, Anne. *Les camps de la honte: Les internés juifs des camps français, 1939–1944*. Paris: La Découverte, 1991.

Gutkind, Curt Sigmar. *Mussolini e il suo fascismo*. Heidelberg, Germany: Merlinverlag, 1927, repr. 1928, with introduction by Benito Mussolini, *Mussolini und sein Fascismus*.

Haines, Paul. *Problems in Prose*. 3rd ed. New York: Harper & Brothers, 1950; 5th edition, New York: Harper & Row, 1963.

Hamann, Brigitte. *Hitler's Vienna: A Portrait of the Tyrant as a Young Man*. 2nd ed. London: Tauris Parke Paperbacks, 2010.

Hakim, Naji. "Our Lady's Minstrel for Clarinet and Organ." http://www.najihakim.com/works/organ-and-other-instruments/our-lady-s-minstrel-for-clarinet-and-organ

Harford, James. *Merton & Friends: A Joint Biography of Thomas Merton, Robert Lax, and Edward Rice*. New York: Continuum, 2006.

Harré, T. Everett, ed. *Treasures of the Kingdom: Stories of Faith, Hope, and Love*. New York: Rinehart, 1947.

Harris, Max. *Sacred Folly: A New History of the Feast of Fools*. Ithaca, NY: Cornell University Press, 2011.

Hauff, Wilhelm. *Das Märchen von dem falschen Prinzen*. Dassel, Germany: Büttenpapierfabrik Hahnemühle, 1962.

Hausmann, Frank-Rutger. "English and Romance Studies in Germany's Third Reich." In *Nazi Germany and the Humanities*, ed. Wolfgang Bialas and Anson Rabinbach, 341–64. Oxford: Oneworld, 2007.

—. *"Vom Strudel der Ereignisse verschlungen": Deutsche Romanistik im "Dritten Reich."* 2nd ed. Frankfurt am Main, Germany: V. Klostermann, 2008.

Hazo, Samuel John. *Inscripts*. Athens: Ohio University Press, 1975.

Hedler, Friedrich. *Der Tänzer unserer lieben Frau: Ein Spiel nach altfranzösischen und altdeutschen Motiven*. Munich, Germany: Buchner, 1950.

Heine, Heinrich. *On the History of Religion and Philosophy in Germany and Other Writings*, ed. Terry Pinkard, trans. Howard Pollack-Milgate. Cambridge: Cambridge University Press, 2007. First published as Henri Heine, "L'Allemagne depuis Luther," *Revue des deux mondes*, 3e ser., vols. 1, 4 (March, November, December 1834). Repr. Heinrich Heine, "Zur Geschichte der Religion und Philosophie in Deutschland." *Salon* 2 (1835).

Heinz, Andreas. *Louange des mystères du Christ: Histoire du rosaire, méditation de la vie de Jésus, compte tenu en particulier de ses racines cisterciennes*. Paris: Téqui, 1990.

Heller, Steven. *Edward Gorey: His Book Cover Art & Design*. Portland, OR: Pomegranate, 2015.

Hernández Oropeza, Prócoro. "Inspiración o fusil el cuento de un anónimo árabe: Las fuentes de El alquimista, de Paulo Coelho." *Revista Inter-Forum*, posted May 20, 2002, http://www.revistainterforum.com/espanol/articulos/052002artliter.html

Hertz, Wilhelm. "Der Tänzer unsrer lieben Frau." *Atlantis* (December 1954): 565–66.

Hickey, Des, and Gus Smith. *Star of Shame: The Secret Voyage of the Arandora Star*. Dublin: Madison Pub., 1989.

Hobson, Constance Tibbs, and Deborra A. Richardson. *Ulysses Kay: A Bio-Bibliography*. Bio-Bibliographies in Music, vol. 53. Westport, CT: Greenwood Press, 1994.

Holliday, Peter. *Edward Johnston: Master Calligrapher*. London: British Library; New Castle, DE: Oak Knoll Press, 2007.

Holloway, Marcella M. *The Little Juggler: A Miracle Play with Music*. New York: S. French, 1966.

Hömberg, Hans. *Der Gaukler unserer lieben Frau*, illus. Ernst von Dombrowski. Vienna: Eduard Wancura, 1961.

—. *Jud Süß: Roman*. Berlin: Ufa-Buchverlag, 1941.

Hoopes, Robert. *Right Reason in the English Renaissance*. Cambridge, MA: Harvard University Press, 1962.

Horn, Erika, ed. *Es gibt noch Wunder …: Die schönsten Legenden*. Graz, Austria: Styria Steirische Verlagsanstalt, 1949).

Housman, Laurence. *Van Sint Franciscus: Negen taferelen uit het leven van de poverello*, trans. Wies Moens. Utrecht, Netherlands: Nijmeegse Studentetoneel, 1929–1930.

Houston, Douglas. "Landscapes of the Heart: Parallels in the Poetry of Kavanagh and Auden." *Studies: An Irish Quarterly Review* 77.308 (Winter 1988): 445–59.

Howells, W. W. Review of *Evolution after Darwin*, vol. 2, *The Evolution of Man: Mind, Culture, and Society*, ed. Sol Tax. *Science*, n.s. 131.3413, May 27, 1960, 1601–2.

Hutcheon, Linda. *A Theory of Parody: The Teachings of Twentieth-Century Art Forms*. New York: Methuen, 1985.

Huysmanns, Camille. "The Flemish Question." *Journal of the Royal Institute of International Affairs* 9 (1930): 680–90.

James, Nicholas Philip, ed. *Interviews-Artists*, vol. 4, *Patterns of Experience: Recordings 1988–2011*. London: Cv Publications, 2011.

Jarman, Mark. "Storytelling Verse from Oxford." *The Hudson Review* (1984): 491–95.

Jenkins, Nicholas. "Auden in America," in *The Cambridge Companion to W. H. Auden*, ed. Stan Smith, 39–54. Cambridge: Cambridge University Press, 2004.

Johannes Agnellus. *Liber miraculorum Beatae Mariae Dolensis*. In Jean Hubert, "Le miracle de Déols et la trêve conclue en 1187 entre les rois de France et d'Angleterre." *Bibliothèque de l'École des Chartes* 96 (1935): 285–300.

John of Garland. *Parisiana Poetria*. ed. and trans. Traugott Lawler. Yale Studies in English 182. New Haven, CT: Yale University Press, 1974.

Jones, Chris. *Strange Likeness: The Use of Old English in Twentieth-Century Poetry*. Oxford: Oxford University Press, 2006.

Jung, C. G. "Aion: Phenomenology of the Self." In *The Portable Jung*, ed. Joseph Campbell, trans. R. F. C. Hull, 148–62. Viking Portable Library, vol. 70. New York: Viking, 1971.

—. "Answer to Job." In idem, *Psychology and Religion: West and East*, trans. R. F. C. Hull, 461–62. Bollingen Series, vol. 20, Collected Works, vol. 11. New York: Pantheon, 1958.

—. *Briefe*, ed. Aniela Jaffé. 3 vols. Olten, Switzerland: Walter, 1972–1973. Trans. R. F. C. Hull, *Letters*, ed. Gerhard Adler and Aniela Jaffé. 2 vols. Bollingen Series, vol. 95.1–2. Princeton, NJ: Princeton University Press, 1973–1975.

Kahoe, Walter. *The Juggler of Our Lady*, illus. Gus Uhlman. Moylan, PA: The Rose Valley Press, Christmas, 1977.

Källström, Staffan. *Framtidens katedral: Medeltidsdröm och utopisk modernism*. Stockholm: Carlssons, 2000.

Kamenetsky, Christa. *Children's Literature in Hitler's Germany*. Athens: Ohio University Press, 1984.

Karkosch, Konrad, and Ludwig Holzleitner. *Der Tänzer unserer lieben Frau: Ein Ballett-Libretto in 2 Akten nach der altfranzösischen Legende "Del Tumbeor Nostre-Dame" für Bühne, Film und Fernsehen*. Munich, Germany: Self-published, 1965.

Kay, Ulysses. *The Juggler of Our Lady: A One-Act Opera*, libretto Alex King. New York: Pembroke Music, 1978. Carl Fischer repr.

Kelletat, Andreas F. "Auf der Suche nach einem Verschollenen: Dossier zu Leben und Werk des Romanisten und Übersetzers Curt Sigmar Gutkind (1896–1940)." In *Übersetzerforschung: Neue Beiträge zur Literatur- und Kulturgeschichte des Übersetzens*, ed. idem, Aleksey Tashinskiy, and Julija Boguna, 13–70. TRANSÜD: Arbeiten zur Theorie und Praxis des Übersetzens und Dolmetschens, vol. 85. Berlin: Frank & Timme, 2016.

Kies, Paul P. *A Writer's Manual and Workbook*. 2nd ed. New York: Appleton-Century-Crofts, 1964.

Kinney, Angela M., ed. *The Vulgate Bible: Douay-Rheims Translation*, vol. 6, *The New Testament*. Dumbarton Oaks Medieval Library, vol. 21. Cambridge, MA: Harvard University Press, 2013.

Kirsch, Arthur. *Auden and Christianity*. New Haven, CT: Yale University Press, 2005.

Klee, Ernst. *Das Kulturlexikon zum dritten Reich: Wer war was vor und nach 1945*. Frankfurt am Main, Germany: S. Fischer, 2007.

Knight, Rex. *Our Lady's Jester: A One-Act Play*. London: Sir Isaac Pitman and Sons, 1952.

Kosch, Wilhelm, and Ingrid Bigler-Marschall. *Deutsches Theater-Lexikon: Biographisches und bibliographisches Handbuch*. 4 vols. Klagenfurt, Germany: F. Kleimayr, 1953–1998.

Kramsch, Claire, and Olivier Kramsch. "The Avatars of Literature in Language Study." *Modern Language Journal* 84.4 (2000): 553–73.

Krause, Chester L., and Clifford Mishler. *1994 Standard Catalog of World Coins*, ed. Colin R. Bruce II. 21st ed. Iola, WI: Krause, 1993.

Kroesen, Justin E. A., and Regnerus Steensma. *The Interior of the Medieval Village Church*. 2nd ed. Leuven, Belgium: Peeters, 2012.

Krylov, Ivan Andreevic. *Sämtliche Fabeln*, trans. Rudolf Bächtold. Zurich, Switzerland: Die Waage, 1960.

Kselman, Thomas A. *Miracles and Prophecies in Nineteenth-Century France*. New Brunswick, NJ: Rutgers University Press, 1983.

Kunstmann, Pierre, ed. and trans. *Vierge et merveille: Les miracles de Notre-Dame narratifs au Moyen Âge*. Paris: Union générale d'éditions, 1981.

Laar, Marianne van, and Karel van Laar. *Charles Nypels: Meester-drukker*. Goodwill, vol. 22. Maastricht, Netherlands: Charles Nypels Stichting, 1986.

Ladd, John. "The Place of Practical Reason in Judicial Decision." In *Rational Decision*, ed. Carl Joachim Friedrich, 126–44. Nomos, vol. 7. New York: Atherton Press, 1964.

Lambourne, Nicola. *War Damage in Western Europe: The Destruction of Historic Monuments during the Second World War*. Edinburgh, UK: Edinburgh University Press, 2001.

Laurentin, René, and Patrick Sbalchiero. *Dizionario delle "apparizioni" della vergine Maria*. Rome: ART, 2010.

Lawall, Sarah, ed. *The Norton Anthology of World Literature*. 6 vols. 2nd ed. New York: W. W. Norton, 2001–2002, 3rd ed. Martin Puchner. 6 vols. New York: W. W. Norton, 2012.

Lax, Robert. *Circus Days & Nights*, ed. Paul J. Spaeth. Woodstock, NY: Overlook Press, 2000.

—. *Circus of the Sun*. New York: Journeyman Books, 1959.

Lazare, Lucien. *L'Abbé Glasberg*. Paris: Cerf, 1990.

Le Coq, John P. *Vignettes littéraires: French Life and Ideals*. Boston: D. C. Heath.

Le Corbusier. *When the Cathedrals Were White*. New York: Reynal & Hitchcock, 1947.

Le Tacon, François. *La croix de Lorraine: Du Golgotha à la France libre*. Woippy, France: Serpenoise, 2012.

Lecoy, Félix, ed. *La Vie des Pères*. 3 vols. Paris: Société des anciens textes français, 1987–1999.

Leeming, David Adams, ed. *Storytelling Encyclopedia: Historical, Cultural, and Multiethnic Approaches to Oral Traditions Around the World*. Phoenix, AZ: Oryx Press, 1997.

Legge, Elizabeth. "Reinventing Derivation: Roles, Stereotypes, and 'Young British Art.'" *Representations* 71 (Summer 2000): 1–23.

Lesquilbet, Bernard. "Christiane Lasquin." *Télé 60*, no. 795, January 17–23, 1960: 2.

Levenda, Peter. *Unholy Alliance: A History of Nazi Involvement with the Occult*. 2nd ed. New York: Continuum, 2002.

Levy, Alan. *W. H. Auden: In the Autumn of the Age of Anxiety*. Sag Harbor, NY: Permanent Press, 1983.

Lewy, Guenter. *The Nazi Persecution of the Gypsies*. Oxford: Oxford University Press, 2000.

Lexikon deutsch-jüdischer Autoren. 21 vols. Munich, Germany: De Gruyter Saur, 1992–2013.

Leymarie, Michel. "Les frères Tharaud: De l'ambiguïté du 'filon juif' dans les années 1920." *Archives juives* 39.1 (2006): 89–109.

List, Guido von. *Deutsch-mythologische Landschaftsbilder*. 2 vols. 2nd ed. Vienna: Guido-von-List-Gesellschaft, 1912.

Llewellyn, Karl N. *Jurisprudence: Realism in Theory and Practice*. Chicago: University of Chicago Press, 1962.

Lobet, Marcel. *Arthur Masson, ou La richesse du cœur*. Gilly, France: Institut Jules Destrée pour la défense et l'illustration de la Wallonie, 1971.

Lot-Borodine, Myrrha, trans. *Vingt miracles de Notre-Dame*. Poèmes et récits de la vieille France, vol. 14. Paris: E. de Boccard, 1929.

Lowell, Robert. *The Letters of Robert Lowell*, ed. Saskia Hamilton. New York: Farrar, Straus and Giroux, 2005.

Lux, Joseph August. *Ein heilig Narrenspiel*. Vienna and Salzburg-Anif: Weiße Hefte, 1930.

—. *Das Spiel von Satans Weltgericht oder Der Affe Gottes und der Gerechte: Ein zeitgemäßes Mysterium*. Vienna and Salzburg-Anif: Weiße Hefte, 1930.

—. *Die Vision der lieben Frau*. Berlin: Schuster & Loeffler, 1911.

Mack, Maynard, ed. *World Masterpieces*. 2 vols. New York: W. W. Norton, 1956. Repr. as *The Continental Edition of World Masterpieces*. New York: Norton, 1962.

Mâle, Émile, *Religious Art in France, the Thirteenth Century: A Study of Medieval Iconography and Its Sources*, Bollingen Series, vol. 90, no. 2. Princeton, NJ: Princeton University Press, 1984. Originally published as *L'art religieux du XIIIᵉ siècle en France: Étude sur l'iconographie du Moyen Âge et sur ses sources d'inspiration*. Paris: Ernest Leroux, 1898.

Maloy, Robert M. "The Virgin of the Poor: Banneux, 1933." In *A Woman Clothed with the Sun: Eight Great Appearances of Our Lady in Modern Times*, ed. John J. Delaney, 239–67. Garden City, NY: Hanover House, 1960.

Maltin, Leonard. *Of Mice and Magic: A History of American Animated Cartoons*. 2nd ed. New York: New American Library, 1987.

Marcus, Jane. "Laughing at Leviticus: *Nightwood* as Woman's Circus Epic." In *Silence and Power: A Reevaluation of Djuna Barnes*, ed. Mary Lynn Broe, 221–50. Carbondale, IL: Southern Illinois University Press, 1991.

Mardam Bey, Farouk. "French Intellectuals and the Palestine Question." *Journal of Palestine Studies* 43.3 (2014): 26–39.

Mathe, Roger. "Pourquoi les Tharaud?" *Trames: Travaux et mémoires de l'Université de Limoges, Collection Français* 5 (1983): 89–98.

McCabe, Thomas J. *An Adaptation of the Story of Our Lady's Juggler.*, illus. Raymond Lufkin. Tenafly, NJ: Private printing for the friends of Raymond Lufkin, 1951.

McClary, Susan. "This Is Not a Story My People Tell: Musical Time and Space According to Laurie Anderson." *Discourse* 12.1 (Fall–Winter 1989–1990): 104–28.

McDiarmid, Lucy. *Auden's Apologies for Poetry*. Princeton, NJ: Princeton University Press, 1990.

McGregor, Michael N. *Pure Act: The Uncommon Life of Robert Lax*. New York: Fordham University Press, 2015.

Meijer, Jaap. *Victor Emanuel van Vriesland als zionist: Een vergeten hoofdstuk uit de geschiedenis van het Joods nationalisme in Nederland*. Diasporade, vol. 2. Heemstede, Netherlands: Jaap Meijer, 1976.

Mellers, Wilfrid. *Francis Poulenc*. Oxford: Oxford University Press, 1993.

—. "*Un saint sensuel* and 'Le Jongleur de Notre Dame.'" in idem, *Celestial Music?: Some Masterpieces of European Religious Music*, 230–43. Woodbridge, UK: Boydell, 2002.

Mendelson, Edward. "*Our Lady's Tumbler* and 'The Ballad of Barnaby.'" *The W. H. Auden Society Newsletter* 27 (September 2006): 16–17.

Mercier, Pascal. *Night Train to Lisbon*, trans. Barbara Harshav. New York: Grove, 2008.

Mill, John Stuart. "The Spirit of the Age (1831)." In idem, *The Collected Works of John Stuart Mill*, ed. Ann P. Robson and John M. Robson, vol. 22, part 1, p. 1. 33 vols. Toronto: University of Toronto Press, 1986.

Miłosz, Czesław. *The History of Polish Literature*. 2nd ed. Berkeley and Los Angeles: University of California Press, 1983.

Moens, Olaf, and Yves T'Sjoen. "Een historische en literaire inleiding." In Wies Moens, *Memoires*, 9–77. Amsterdam: Meulenhoff, 1996.

Moens, Wies. *De boodschap*. Antwerp, Belgium: De Sikkel, 1920.

—. *De danser van Onze Lieve Vrouw: Een klein mirakelspel*. Antwerp, Belgium: De Sikkel, 1930.

—. *Das flämische Kampfgedicht*, trans. Adolf von Hatzfeld. Jena, Germany: E. Diederich, 1942.

—. "Een katholiek-modern toneelrépertoire." *De Beiaard* 2 (1925): 27–48.

—. *Nederlandsche letterkunde van volksch standpunt gezien*. Rotterdam, Netherlands: Dietsche Boekhandel, 1939, 2nd ed. Bruges, Belgium: Wiek op, 1941.

—. *De spitsboog*, Bruges, Belgium: Wiek op, 1943.

Monaghan, Peter. "Medievalists, Romantics No Longer, Take Stock of Their Changing Field." *Chronicle of Higher Education*, October 30, 1998, A15–17.

Monfrin, Jacques. *Honoré Champion, 1874–1978*. Paris: Honoré Champion, 1978.

Morsberger, Robert E. "Villon and the Victorians: The Influence and the Legend." *Bulletin of the Rocky Mountain Modern Language Association* 23 (1969): 189–96.

Moser, Rudolf. *Der Gaukler unserer lieben Frau: Ein Legendenspiel für Bariton-Solo, Frauenchor, Männerchor, gemischten Chor, Orgel und Orchester; Opus 68*. Arlesheim, Germany: Verlag der Werke Rudolf Moser, 1991.

Moylan, Paul A. "Jérôme and Jean Tharaud's Romantic Representation of Judaism." *French Review* 39.1 (1965): 69–77.

Mûelenaere, J. "E. H. Georges Blondeel." *Haec olim* 12 (1961): 5–9.

Muir, Lynette. "Résurrection des Mystères: Medieval Drama in Modern France." *Leeds Studies in English* 29 (1998): 235–48.

Mulligan, Lotte. "'Reason,' 'Right Reason,' and 'Revelation' in Mid-Seventeenth-Century England." In *Occult and Scientific Mentalities in the Renaissance*, ed. Brian Vickers, 375–401. Cambridge: Cambridge University Press, 1984.

Nagel, Alexander. *Medieval Modern: Art Out of Time*. New York: Thames & Hudson, 2012.

Nakamura, Mitsuo. "The French Influence in Modern Japanese Literature." *Japan Quarterly* 7.1 (1960): 57–65.

Nikitina, Natalia, and Natalia Tuliakova. "Translation of Anatole France's *L'Étui de nacre* in Russia: Reception and Perception." *Interlitteraria* 21.1 (2016): 79–94.

Nissen, Peter J. A. "Jongleren voor de Moeder Gods: De voorgeschiedenis van een verhaal van Gerard Reve." *Maatstaf* 31 (1983): 45–50.

Nozières, P. "Some Comments on Bose-Einstein Condensation." In *Bose-Einstein Condensation*, ed. A. Griffin, S. Stringari, and David W. Snoke, 15–30. Cambridge: Cambridge University Press, 1995.

Nyhart, Nina. "Our Lady's Tumbler." *Virginia Quarterly Review* 49.4 (1973): 555–57.

—. "Two Poems after Paul Klee." *Poetry* 152.3 (1988): 141–42.

O'Connell, Marvin R. *Edward Sorin*. Notre Dame, IN: University of Notre Dame Press, 2001.

Oexle, Otto Gerhard. "Das Mittelalter und das Unbehagen an der Moderne: Mittelalterbeschwörungen in der Weimarer Republik und danach." In *Spannungen und Widersprüche: Gedenkschrift für František Graus*, ed. Susanna Burghartz et al., 125–53. Sigmaringen, Germany: J. Thorbecke, 1992.

Omans, Glen. "The Villon Cult in England." *Comparative Literature* 18 (1966): 16–35.

Opie, Iona and Peter, eds. *The Oxford Book of Narrative Verse*. Oxford: Oxford University Press, 1983.

Orrego-Salas, Juan. *Encuentros, visiones y repasos: Capítulos en el camino de mi música y mi vida*. Santiago, Chile: Ediciones Universidad Católica de Chile, 2005.

Oudheusden, J. (Jan) L. G. van. *Brabantia Nostra: Een gewestelijke beweging voor fierheid en "schoner" leven 1935–1951*. PhD diss., Katholieke Universiteit, Nijmegen, 1990. Tilburg, Netherlands: Zuidelijk Historisch Contact, 1990.

—. "*Brabantia Nostra*: Rooms en romantisch regionalisme, 1935–1951." In *Constructie van het eigene: Culturele vormen van regionale identiteit in Nederland*, ed. Carlo van der Borgt, Amanda Hermans, and Hugo Jacobs, 123–39. ANNO-historische reeks, vol. 8, Publicaties van het P. J. Meertens-Instituut voor Dialectologie, Volkskunde en Naamkunde van de Koninklijke Nederlandse Akademie van Wetenschappen, vol. 25. Amsterdam: P. J. Meertens-Instituut, 1996.

Pagel, Angelika. "Jugendstil and Racism: An Unexpected Alliance." *RACAR: Revue d'art canadienne/Canadian Art Review* 19.1–2 (1992): 97–111.

Paris, Gaston. *La littérature française au Moyen Âge*. Paris: Hachette, 1888, 2nd rev. ed. 1890.

Paulding, Gouverneur. "An Old Legend in New, Charming Guise." *New York Herald Tribune*, December 6, 1953, A52.

Peeters, Frank. "Faam en waan van het modernistische theater in Vlaanderen: 1920–1929." In *Historische avant-garde en het theater in het Interbellum*, ed. Jaak van Schoor and Peter Benoy, 91–98. Brussels: ASP, 2011.

Perrin, Henri. *Le capitaine Darreberg, héraut de Notre-Dame: Récit d'évasion, missions secrètes … à la R. A. F.* Lyon, France: Emmanuel Vitte, 1956.

—. *Priest-Workman in Germany*, trans. Rosemary Sheed. London: Sheed and Ward, 1947.

Phillips, Henry. "Jacques Copeau et le théâtre catholique: Une correspondance inédite avec Henri Brochet." *Revue d'histoire littéraire de la France* 104.2 (April–June 2004): 439–58.

—. *Le théâtre catholique en France au XXe siècle*. Littérature de notre siècle, vol. 37. Paris: Champion, 2007.

Plenzat, Karl. *Die Theophiluslegende in den Dichtungen des Mittelalters*. Germanische Studien, vol. 43. Berlin: E. Ebering, 1926.

Pogue, Forrest C. *Pogue's War: Diaries of a WWII Combat Historian*. Lexington, KY: University Press of Kentucky, 2001.

Porter, Peter. *Max is Missing*. London: Picador, 2001.

Pos, Willy Philip. *De toneelkunstenaar August Defresne: Toneelschrijver, regisseur, toneelleider*. Amsterdam: Moussault, 1971.

Poulenc, Francis. *Correspondance, 1915–1963*, ed. Hélène de Wendel. Paris: Éditions du Seuil, 1967.

—. *Selected Correspondence 1915–1963*, trans. and ed. Sidney Buckland. London: Victor Gollancz, 1991.

Powys, John Cowper. *A Glastonbury Romance*. New York: Simon and Schuster, 1932, 2nd ed. London: Macdonald, 1955/Picador, 1975.

—. *Visions and Revisions: A Book of Literary Devotions*. New York: G. A. Shaw, 1915, repr. Hamilton, NY: Colgate University Press, 1955.

Preetorius, Wilhelm. *Der Tänzer unserer lieben Frau*. Zurich, Switzerland: Die Waage, 1964.

Quesenbery, W. D. *Auden's Revisions* (2008), http://audensociety.org/Audens_Revisions_by_WD_Quesenbery.pdf

Raaij, B. J. M. van. "Het Brabants Studentengilde van Onze Lieve Vrouw: Een regionale katholieke studentenbeweging tussen antimodernisme en modernisme, 1926–1970." *Nordbrabants historisch jaarboek* 6 (1989): 155–206.

Raak, Cees van. "En het strovuur brandt voort … Frank Valkenier en de verdere geschiedenis van de Brandon Pers." *Tilburg: Tijdschrift voor geschiedenis, monumenten en cultuur* 19.3 (2001): 97–105.

Raymond, Louis-Marcel. "Un canadien à Paris." *Les cahiers des compagnons: Bulletin d'art dramatique* 3 (1947): 1–32.

Redmond, John. "The Influence of Auden on Kavanagh's Poetic Development." *New Hibernia Review* 8 (2004): 21–34.

Reiss, Hans. "*Geisteswissenschaften* in the Third Reich: Some Reflections." *German History* 21 (2003): 86–103.

Remenyi, Joseph. "The Meaning of World Literature." *Journal of Aesthetics and Art Criticism* 9 (1951): 244–51. Repr. in *World Literatures: Arabic, Chinese, Czechoslavak, French, German, Greek, Hungarian, Italian, Lithuanian, Norwegian, Polish, Romanian, Russia, Scottish, Swedish [and] Yugoslav*, ed. Joseph Remenyi et al., 1–14. Pittsburgh, PA: University of Pittsburgh Press, 1956.

Renault, Gilbert. *Fatima: Espérance du monde*. Paris: Plon, 1957.

Reve, Gerard. *Archief Reve*, ed. Pierre H. Dubois, annot. Sjaak Hubregtse. 2 vols. Baarn, Netherlands: de Prom, 1981–1982.

Rich, Edward P. *The Pazyryk Agenda: A Police Procedural*. Self-published, Xlibris, 2004.

Rist, J. M. "An Early Dispute about 'Right Reason.'" *The Monist* 66 (1983): 39–48.

Roberts, Pam, ed. *F. Holland Day*. Amsterdam: Van Gogh Museum, 2000.

Roberts, R. Ellis. "Arthur Machen." *Sewanee Review* 32 (1924): 353–56.

Romain, Maryline. *Léon Chancerel: Portrait d'un réformateur du théâtre français*. Collection Théâtre, vol. 20. Lausanne, Switzerland: L'Âge d'Homme, 2005.

Root, Jerry. *The Theophilus Legend in Medieval Text and Image*. Cambridge: D. S. Brewer, 2017.

Rosenstein, Roy. "A Medieval Troubadour Mobilized in the French Resistance." *Journal of the History of Ideas* 59, no. 3 (1998): 499–520.

Rutebeuf. *Le miracle de Théophile*, transposed Gustave Cohen. Paris: Delagrave, 1934.

Rutten, Felix. "Broeder Balderik." *Veldeke* 33.184 (December 1958): 49–52.

—. *Novellen (Sittards dialekt)*. Sittard, Netherlands: Alberts, 1959.

Rymenants, Koen, Kris Humbeeck, Jan Robert, and Jan Stuyck, eds. *Literatuur en crisis: De Vlaamse en Nederlandse letteren in de jaren dertig*. AMVC-Publicaties, vol. 12. Antwerp, Belgium: AMVC, 2010.

Sachs, Murray. *Anatole France: The Short Stories*. London: Edward Arnold, 1974.

Salus, Peter H., and Paul B. Taylor, eds. *Völuspá, The Song of the Sybil: With the Icelandic Text*, trans. Paul B. Taylor and W. H. Auden. Iowa City, IA: Windhover Press, University of Iowa, 1968.

Sapiro, Gisèle. *The French Writers' War, 1940–1953*, trans. Vanessa Doriott Anderson and Dorrit Cohn. Durham, NC: Duke University Press, 2014; orig. publ. idem, *La Guerre des écrivains, 1940–1953*. Paris: Fayard, 1999.

—. "Salut littéraire et littérature du salut: Deux trajectoires de romanciers catholiques: François Mauriac et Henry Bordeaux." *Actes de la recherche en sciences sociales* 111.1 (1996): 36–58.

Schaefer, Eric. "Dirty Little Secrets: Scholars, Archivists, and Dirty Movies." *The Moving Image* 5.2 (2005): 79–105.

Schäfer-Elmayer, Thomas. *Vom Sattel zum Tanzparkett: Die Lebensgeschichte meines Großvaters Willy Elmayer*. Vienna: Kremayr & Scheriau, 2014).

Schatzman, Ruth. "Nina Gourfinkel (1898–1984)." *Revue des études slaves* 63 (1991): 705–10.

Schieder, Wolfgang. *Mythos Mussolini: Deutsche in Audienz beim Duce*. Munich, Germany: Oldenbourg, 2013.

Schlereth, Thomas J. *A Dome of Learning: The University of Notre Dame's Main Building*. Notre Dame, IN: Notre Dame Alumni Association, 1991.

Schmidt, Carl B. *Entrancing Muse: A Documented Biography of Francis Poulenc*. Lives in Music, vol. 3. Hillsdale, NY: Pendragon, 2001.

—. *The Music of Francis Poulenc (1899–1963): A Catalogue*. Oxford: Clarendon Press, 1995.

Schnurer, Herman. "The Intellectual Sources of French Fascism." *Antioch Review* 1 (1941): 35–49.

Schuder, Werner. *Kürschners Deutscher Literatur-Kalender: Nekrolog 1936–1970*. Berlin: De Gruyter, 1973.

Schweizer, Mark. *The Clown of God: A Christmas Chancel Drama for Children's Choir*. Hopkinsville, KY: St. James Music Press, 1996.

Shanley, J. P. "Television," *America* 101.8, May 23, 1959: 378.

Sharkey, Don. "The Virgin with the Golden Heart: Beauraing, 1932–33." In *A Woman Clothed with the Sun: Eight Great Appearances of Our Lady in Modern Times*, ed. John J. Delaney, 213–38. Garden City, NY: Hanover House, 1960.

—, and Joseph Debergh. *Our Lady of Beauraing*. Garden City, NY: Hanover House, 1958.

Smit, Gabriël, trans. *De danser van Onze Lieve Vrouw*. Bussum, Netherlands: Ons Leekenspel, [1941?].

—. *Zeven Marialegenden,* illus. Cuno van den Steene. Utrecht, Netherlands: Het Spectrum, 1941, repr. 1944.

Solterer, Helen. *Medieval Roles for Modern Times: Theater and the Battle for the French Republic.* University Park: Pennsylvania State University Press, 2010.

Spingarn, Joel E. "L'Art pour l'Art." *Modern Language Notes* 25 (1910): 95.

Sponsel, Heinz. *Sango und die Inkagötter.* Stuttgart, Germany: Schwab, 1951.

Stanesco, Michel. "Le bruit de la source: Les contes chrétiens et la resonance d'éternité." In *Translatio litterarum ad penates = Das Mittelalter Übersetzen: Ergebnisse der Tagung von Mai 2004 an der Université de Lausanne = Traduire le Moyen Âge: Actes du colloque de l'Université de Lausanne (mai 2004),* ed. Alain Corbellari and Catherine Drittenbass, 331–44. Lausanne, Switzerland: Centre de traduction littéraire, 2005.

Sterneberg, Ferdinand. *Charlotte Köhler: "Klank en weerklank."* Zutphen, Netherlands: Walburg Pers, 1977.

Stevenson, Robert Louis. "François Villon: Student, Poet, and Housebreaker." *The Cornhill Magazine* (August 1877): 215–34.

—. "A Lodging for the Night: A Story of Francis Villon." *Temple Bar* (October 1877): 197–212.

Stritch, Thomas. *My Notre Dame: Memories and Reflections of Sixty Years.* Notre Dame, IN: University of Notre Dame Press, 1991.

Sullivan, Richard. *Notre Dame: Reminiscences of an Era.* Notre Dame, IN: University of Notre Dame Press, 1961.

—. *Our Lady's Tumbler.* Chicago: Dramatic Publishing Co., 1940.

Shun'ichi, Niikura, trans. "Seibo no karuwazashi." In Niikura Shun'ichi, Kamizawa Eizō, and Amazawa Taijirō yaku, *Furansu chūsei bungakushū* (Poètes et romanciers du Moyen Âge), 4 vols. Tokyo: Hakusuisha, 1990–1996. 4:407–26.

Taylor, Frederick. *Coventry: Thursday, 14 November 1940.* London: Bloomsbury, 2015.

Taylor, Paul Beekman. "Auden's Icelandic Myth of Exile." *Journal of Modern Literature* 24.2 (2000): 213–34.

—, and W. H. Auden, trans. *The Elder Edda: A Selection.* London: Faber, 1969.

Tegel, Susan. *Jew Süss/Jud Süss (Germany, 1940).* Trowbridge, UK: Flicks Books, 1996.

Testa, Bart. "Soft-Shaft Opportunism: Radley Metzger's Erotic Kitsch." *Spectator* 19.2 (1999): 40–57, http://cinema.usc.edu/assets/099/15905.pdf

Tharaud, Jérôme, and Jean Tharaud. *Les contes de la Vierge.* Paris: Plon, 1940. Repr. 1946, illus. Pio Santini. Paris: Société d'éditions littéraires françaises, 1946. Trans. Marià Manent, *Leyendas de la Virgen,* illus. Carles Planell. Panchatantra, vol. 2. Barcelona, Spain: Casals, 1983. Abbrev. editions: L. Mees, ed. *Les contes de la vierge.* Les bons auteurs, vol. 2. Malines, Belgium: S. François, n.d.; Arnold Leonhardi, ed. *Contes de la Vierge: Devoirs pratiques.* Dortmund, Germany: Lensing, 1952.

—. *Contes de Notre Dame.* Paris: Plon, 1943.

—. "Le Tombeor de Notre-Dame." In *Journées du livre: Aux quatre coins de chez nous* (Paris: J. Dumoulin, 1931), 144–48.

Theroux, Alexander. *The Strange Case of Edward Gorey.* 2nd ed. Seattle, WA: Fantagraphics Books, 2011.

Thompson, Stith. *Motif-Index of Folk-Literature: A Classification of Narrative Elements in Folktales, Ballads, Myths, Fables, Mediaeval Romances, Exempla, Fabliaux, Jest-Books, and Local Legends*. 2nd ed. 6 vols. Bloomington: Indiana University Press, 1955–1958.

Thurston, Herbert. *Beauraing and Other Apparitions: An Account of Some Borderland Cases in the Psychology of Mysticism*. London: Burns, Oates & Washbourne, 1934.

Toorn-Piebenga, Gryt Anne van der. *Middeleeuwse Marialegenden in modern Nederlands weergegeven, en van oorspronkelijke illustraties voorzien*. Baarn, Netherlands: Gooi, 1994.

Toussaint, Fernand, and Camille Joset. *Notre-Dame de Beauraing: Histoire des apparitions*. Paris: Desclée De Brouwer, 1981.

Trigg, Stephanie. "Walking through Cathedrals: Scholars, Pilgrims, and Medieval Tourists." *New Medieval Literatures* 7 (2004): 9–33.

T'Sjoen, Yves. "Achter de trommels: Het Afrikaner nationalisme als bouwsteen voor het ideologische discours van de Vlaamse Beweging (ca. 1875–1921)." *Werkwinkel* 2 (2007): 51–76.

Van Damme, Els. "'Met u of zònder u, altijd voor u': De 'volksverbonden' lyriek van Wies Moens." In *Verbrande schrijvers: 'Culturele' collaboratie in Vlaanderen (1933–1953)*, ed. Lukas De Vos, Yves T'Sjoen, and Ludo Stynen, 71–91. Ghent, Belgium: Academia Press, 2009.

Van Doren, Charles, ed. *The Joy of Reading: A Passionate Guide to 189 of the World's Best Authors and Their Works*. Naperville, IL: Sourcebooks, 2008.

Van Engen, John. "The Christian Middle Ages as an Historiographical Problem." *American Historical Review* 91.3 (1986): 519–52.

Vanfraussen, Evelin. "'Ontbonden in dien stroom de puurste pracht!' Moens' veelvuldige volk en de Duitse bezetter." *Spiegel der letteren* 47.4 (2005): 355–76.

Verduin, Arnold R. "Handsprings and Somersaults." *Journal of the National Education Association* 34.7 (November 1945): 151.

—. "High Wind at Coney." *The New Yorker*, March 25, 1944: 61–62.

Verhoogen, Jos, and Geert Opsomer. *Inventaris van het archief van Het Vlaamsche Volkstooneel*. Reeks inventarissen en repertoria, vol. 24. Leuven, Belgium: Kadoc, 1989.

Vitry, Jacques de. *The Exempla or Illustrative Stories from the Sermones vulgares of Jacques de Vitry*, ed. Thomas Frederick Crane. Publications of the Folk-Lore Society, vol. 26. London: D. Nutt, 1890.

Vloberg, Maurice. *La légende dorée de Notre Dame*. Paris: D. A. Longuet, 1921.

Volta, Ornella. *L'Ymagier d'Erik Satie*. Paris: Francis Van de Velde, 1979.

Vonada, Damaine. *Notre Dame: The Official Campus Guide*. Notre Dame, IN: University of Notre Dame Press, 1998.

Vriesland, Victor Emanuel van. *Herinneringen verteld aan Alfred Kossmann*. Amsterdam: Em. Querido, 1969.

—, trans. *De potsenmaker van Onze Lieve Vrouwe*, illus. Bob Buys, De Uilenreeks, vol. 44. Amsterdam: Bigot en Van Rossum, 1941. Repr. in idem, *Gouden legenden: Verhalen van God en heiligen, vromen en zondaars*, ed. Antoon Coolen, illus. Karel Thole. Amsterdam: Meulenhoff, 1951; 2nd ed. 1953.

Vos, Staf. *Dans in België 1890–1940*. Leuven, Belgium: Universitaire Pers Leuven, 2012.

Walk, Joseph, ed. *Kurzbiographien zur Geschichte der Juden 1918–1945*. Leo Baeck Institute, Jerusalem. Munich, Germany: De Gruyter Saur, 1988.

Warfel, Harry Redcay. *American Novelists of Today*. New York: American Book Co., 1951.

Werfel, Franz. *Das Lied von Bernadette: Roman*. Stockholm: Bermann-Fischer, 1941. Trans. Ludwig Lewisohn, *The Song of Bernadette*. New York: Viking, 1942.

Wichans, Augustinus. *Brabantia Mariana tripartita*. Antwerp, Belgium: apud Ioannem Cnobbaert, 1632.

Wilcox, John. "The Beginnings of l'art pour l'art." *The Journal of Aesthetics and Art Criticism* 11.4 (1953): 360–77.

Wilkie, Everett C., Jr., trans. "Our Lady's Tumbler." *Allegorica: A Journal of Medieval and Renaissance Literature* 4.1–2 (Summer–Winter 1979): 81–120.

Winston-Allen, Anne. *Stories of the Rose: The Making of the Rosary in the Middle Ages*. University Park: Pennsylvania State University Press, 1997.

Wolitz, Seth L. "Imagining the Jew in France: From 1945 to the Present." *Yale French Studies* 85 (1994): 119–34.

Wright, Lesley A. "La mort de Massenet: Réactions des contemporains." In *Massenet aujourd'hui: Héritage et postérité. Actes du colloque de la XIe biennale Massenet des 25 et 26 octobre 2012*, ed. Jean-Christophe Branger and Vincent Giroud, 21–38. Centre interdisciplinaire d'études et de recherches sur l'expression contemporaine: Travaux, vol. 166/Collection musique et musicology: Les cahiers de l'Opéra théâtre, vol. 1. Saint-Étienne, France: Publications de l'université de Saint-Étienne, 2014.

Wuillaume, Léon. *Banneux, boodschap voor onze tijd: Verslag van de verschijningen, verklaring van de boodschap*. Banneux, Belgium: Voncken, 1983.

Young, Vivian Merrill. *The Miracle of Jean the Juggler: A Musical Play in Three Scenes, Based on a French Folktale*. Chicago: H. T. FitzSimons, 1950.

Ziethen, Karl-Heinz. *Virtuosos of Juggling: From the Ming Dynasty to Cirque de Soleil*. Santa Cruz, CA: Renegade Juggling, 2003.

Zink, Michel. "Anatole France et moi." in *Medioevo e modernità nella letteratura francese: Moyen Âge et modernité dans la littérature française*, ed. Giovanna Angeli and Maria Emanuela Raffi, 229–35. Florence: Alinea, 2013.

—. *Contes du Moyen-Âge*, illus. Pierre-Olivier Leclerc. Paris: Le Seuil, 2002

—. *Le jongleur de Notre Dame: Contes chrétiens du Moyen Âge*. Paris: Le Seuil, 1999. Trans. Jorge Sans Vila, *El juglar de Nuestra Señora*. Salamanca, Spain: Sígueme, 2000; trans. Alena Lhotová and Hana Prousková, *Príbehy a legendy stredoveke Evropy*. Prague, Czech Republic: Portál, 2000; trans. Costanza Ossola, *L'innamorato fedele*. Rome: Città Nuova, 2000.

—. *Poésie et conversion au Moyen Âge*. Paris: Presses universitaires de France, 2003.

Znaniecki, Florian. "Leadership and Followship in Creative Cooperation." In idem, *What are Sociological Problems?*, ed. Zygmunt Dulczewski, Richard Grathoff, and Jan Włodarek (Nakom, Poland: Wydawnictwo, 1994).

List of Illustrations

Chapter 1

1.1 Winston Churchill walks through the ruins of Coventry Cathedral. Photograph by William G. Horton, 1941. Washington, DC, Library of Congress, Prints and Photographs Division. — 7

1.2 Charles Friant as Jean in Massenet's *Le jongleur de Notre Dame*. Photograph by Studio Harcourt, 1941 or earlier. Published in a program for the Théâtre national de l'Opéra Comique (January 19, 1941), 2. — 9

1.3 Cast list for Massenet's *Le jongleur de Notre Dame*, with German language instruction advertised at bottom (in German). Published in a program for the Théâtre national de l'Opéra Comique (January 19, 1941), 11. — 9

1.4 Cast list for Massenet's, with deluxe shoes advertised at bottom (in French). Published in a program for the Théâtre national de l'Opéra Comique (January 6, 1934), 15. — 9

1.5 From right to left, Jérôme and Jean Tharaud, in their garden. Photograph Agence de presse Meurisse, 1932, https://commons.wikimedia.org/wiki/File:Frères_Tharaud_a_Meurisse_1932.jpg — 10

1.6 Front page of *Marianne* 7, no. 339, April 19, 1939. — 13

1.7 Henri Brochet, with Virgin and Child on desk in left foreground. Photograph, date and photographer unknown. — 15

1.8 "Roger Bontemps." Illustration by Henri Gerbault, printed on lithograph promotional card, "Les chansons" (2nd series), by de Ricqlès & Cie, 1910. — 16

1.9 "Hippodrome au Pont de l'Alma: Cadet Roussel." Poster illustrated by Jules Chéret, printed by Chaix, 1882. — 16

1.10 Léon Chancerel. Photograph, 1942. Photographer unknown. — 17

1.11 Front cover of Léon Chancerel, *Frère Clown, ou Le jongleur de Notre-Dame* (Lyons, France: La Hutte, 1943). — 18

1.12 Front cover of Rutebeuf, *Le miracle de Théophile*, transposed by Gustave Cohen (Paris: Delagrave, 1934). — 18

1.13 The staging of *Le miracle de Théophile*. Photograph, 1933. Photographer unknown. Published in Rutebeuf, *Le miracle de Théophile*, transposed by Gustave Cohen (Paris: Delagrave, 1934), 3. — 19

1.14 Front cover of Gustave Cohen, *Mystère de la Passion des théophiliens* (Paris: Richard-Masse, 1950).   20

1.15 Alexandre Glasberg at Chansaye. Photographer unknown, ca. 1941–1944. Image courtesy of the Mémorial de la Shoah. All rights reserved.   22

1.16 Staging of Massenet's *Le jongleur de Notre Dame* outside the Cathédrale Saint-Charles Borromée, Saint-Étienne, France. Photograph, 1942. Photographer unknown. Saint-Étienne, Archives municipales, Bulletin municipal de 1942.   23

1.17 Four-franc Vichy French postage stamp with portrait of Jules Massenet to commemorate the centenary of his birth (1942).   23

1.18 First-day cover with portrait of Jules Massenet to commemorate the centenary of his birth (1942).   23

1.19 Holy card of children in supplication before the Virgin (Paris: A. Leclerc, 1944).   24

1.20 Postcard of the Virgin and Child, flanked by prominent French cathedrals and names of Marian miracle sites (1942).   24

1.21 Henri Perrin, *Le capitaine Darreberg*, 7th ed. (Corps: Association des pèlerins de La Salette, 1983), front cover. Courtesy of Association des pèlerins de La Salette.   25

1.22 Commemorative medallion (obverse) to honor Resistance, depicting Gilbert Renault (Colonel Rémy), ca. 1940–1944, by Jean-Paul Luthringer, struck in 1988 by Monnaie de Paris.   26

1.23 Commemorative medallion (reverse), depicting the Virgin with the Cross of Lorraine and the abbreviation CND (Confrérie Notre-Dame), by Jean-Paul Luthringer, struck in 1988 by Monnaie de Paris.   26

1.24 Front cover of Anatole France, *Le jongleur de Notre-Dame*, illus. Pierre Watrin (Paris: Éditions de l'Amitié—G. T. Rageot, 1944).   27

1.25 The monks are appalled by the juggler's improvised ritual. Illustration by Pio Santini. Published in Jérôme et Jean Tharaud, *Les contes de la Vierge* (Paris: Société d'éditions littéraires françaises, 1946), between pp. 172 and 173.   29

1.26 Henry Bordeaux. Photograph by Henri Manuel, date unknown. Reproduced on postcard stock (Paris, 1920).   29

1.27 The juggler performs. Illustration by Sax R. Shaw, calligraphy by Irene Wellington. Manuscript of *Del tumbeor Nostre Dame*, lines 223–25 (Edinburgh, 1942), fol. 10r. Courtesy of Newberry Library, Chicago, Illinois.   33

1.28 Preface to Anatole France, *Le jongleur de Notre-Dame*, trans. Frederic Chapman ([no place]: printed for the friends of Jarrett and Robert Schmid, Christmas 1944).   36

1.29 Cover illustration to the story "Handsprings and Somersaults" by Arnold Robert Verduin, published in 1945.   36

Chapter 2

2.1 Virgin Mary on crescent and globe, trampling serpent. One-lira Vatican commemorative coin (reverse), engraved by Aurelio Mistruzzi (1933).   39

2.2 "These four Ezquiogans saw the Virgin." Photograph by Charles Trampus, 1931. Published in *Le Miroir du monde* 2.78, August 29, 1931, 244.   40

List of Illustrations

2.3	"Ezquioga sera-t-il un nouveau Lourdes?" *Le Miroir du monde* 2.78, August 29, 1931, 243.	40
2.4	Postcard of the replica of the Lourdes grotto in Beauraing, Belgium (Brussels: Ernest Thill, 1930s).	42
2.5	Postcard recreating the apparition in Beauraing, Belgium (Brussels: Marco Marcovici, 1930s).	42
2.6	Postcard of crowd at the tree and bridge, locations of the apparition in Beauraing, Belgium (Brussels: Ernest Thill, 1930s).	43
2.7	"The crowd hearing the revelations of Côme Tilman, Beauraing." A bit left of the middle, bareheaded and facing the camera, the farmworker who experienced a miracle. Photograph, 1930s. Photographer unknown.	43
2.8	Postcard of the site of the apparition in Banneux, Belgium (Brussels: A. Dohmen, ca. 1934).	44
2.9	Postcard of Leonie Van den Dyck, the visionary of Onkerzele, Belgium, outside her home, ca. 1933.	44
2.10	Front cover of Franz Johannes Weinrich, *De danser van Onze Lieve Vrouw: Een klein mirakelspel*, trans. Wies Moens, woodcut by Prosper De Troyer (Antwerp, Belgium: De Sikkel, 1930).	46
2.11	Postcard of Het Heilige Maagdcollege, Dendermonde, Belgium (Brussels: Ernest Thill, 1930s).	46
2.12	Wies Moens. Photograph taken before 1926, photographer unknown.	47
2.13	Prosper De Troyer, self-portrait, 1929. From Frans Mertens, *Prosper De Troyer* (Antwerp, Belgium: Standaard, 1943), front cover.	48
2.14	Henri Ghéon. Drawing by Jean Veber, 1898, https://commons.wikimedia.org/wiki/File:Henri_Ghéon_by_Jean_Veber.jpg	48
2.15	Front cover of Dietzenschmidt [Anton Franz Schmid], *Die Sanct Jacobsfahrt: Eyn Legendenspiel in drey Aufzügen* (Berlin: Oesterheld, 1920). Woodcut by Johannes Othmar, 1920.	49
2.16	Front cover of Wies Moens, *De spitsboog* (Bruges, Belgium: Wiek op, 1943).	51
2.17	Arthur Masson in his student quarters in Louvain. Photograph, 1919. Photographer unknown.	52
2.18	Front cover of E. H. Blondeel, *Wintze, of De Tuimelaar van O. L. Vrouw: Legendeverhaal* (Torhout, Belgium: Becelaere, 1933).	53
2.19	August Defresne. Photograph by Hanna Elkan, 1940.	54
2.20	Charlotte Köhler as jongleur, in monastic habit. Photograph by Godfried de Groot, ca. 1933. Published on the front cover of August Defresne, *De vrome speelman* (Amsterdam: "De Gulden Ster," 1933).	54
2.21	Victor Emanuel van Vriesland, age 70. Photograph by Jacob de Nijs, 1962, CC BY-SA 3.0. The Hague, Nationaal Archief, https://commons.wikimedia.org/wiki/File:Victor_van_Vriesland_(1962).jpg	56
2.22	Victor Emanuel van Vriesland as a sad clown (top left), age 22. Photograph, 1914. Photographer unknown.	56
2.23	Title page of Victor Emanuel van Vriesland, trans., *De potsenmaker van Onze Lieve Vrouwe*, illus. Bob Buys, De Uilenreeks, vol. 44 (Amsterdam: Bigot en Van Rossum, 1941).	57

2.24 The juggler enters the monastery. Illustration by Bob Buys, 1941. Published in Victor Emanuel van Vriesland, trans., *De potsenmaker van Onze Lieve Vrouwe*, illus. Bob Buys, De Uilenreeks, vol. 44 (Amsterdam: Bigot en Van Rossum, 1941), 6. — 57

2.25 The juggler slips down into the crypt during prayer. Illustration by Bob Buys, 1941. Published in Victor Emanuel van Vriesland, trans., *De potsenmaker van Onze Lieve Vrouwe*, illus. Bob Buys, De Uilenreeks, vol. 44 (Amsterdam: Bigot en Van Rossum, 1941), 42. — 57

2.26 Gabriël Smit, age 42. Photograph, 1952. Photographer unknown. Image courtesy of Katholiek Documentatie Centrum, Radboud Universiteit, Nijmegen, Netherlands. All rights reserved. — 60

2.27 A monk discovers the juggler's performance. Illustration by Cuno van den Steene, 1945. Published in Gabriël Smit, *Zeven Marialegenden* (Utrecht, Netherlands: Spectrum, 1944), 80. — 61

2.28 Caricatures of Gabriël Smit, with note indicating that originally he belonged to the Old Catholic Church. Drawings by M. J. H. M. Wertenbroek, 1936. Image courtesy of Katholiek Documentatie Centrum, Radboud Universiteit, Nijmegen, Netherlands. All rights reserved. — 62

2.29 Front cover of Frank Valkenier [Frans van der Ven], *De tuimelaar van Onze Lieve Vrouw* (Tilburg, Netherlands: Private printing, 1944). — 63

2.30 Title page of Frank Valkenier [Frans van der Ven], *De tuimelaar van Onze Lieve Vrouw* (Tilburg, Netherlands: Private printing, 1944). — 63

2.31 Grootseminarie Haaren. Photograph, ca. 1942–1955. Photographer unknown. Image courtesy of Brabants Historisch Informatie Centrum. All rights reserved. — 64

2.32 Dedication of Frank Valkenier [Frans van der Ven], *De tuimelaar van Onze Lieve Vrouw* (Tilburg, Netherlands: Private printing, 1944). — 65

2.33 Title page of Augustinus Wichmans, *Brabantia Mariana* (Antwerp, Belgium: Joannes Cnobbaert, 1632). Munich, Bayerische Staatsbibliothek. — 66

2.34 Title page of Curt Sigmar Gutkind, *Mussolini e il suo fascismo* (Heidelberg, Germany: Merlinverlag, 1927), with introduction by Benito Mussolini. — 70

2.35 "Two Peoples and One Struggle." German postage stamp (12, with a supplement of 38). 1941. — 71

2.36 Postcard of the *Arandora Star* (before 1940). — 72

2.37 Süß shows off his wealth. Photograph, 1940. Photographer unknown. Published in J. R. George [Hans Hömberg], *Jud Süß: Roman* (Berlin: Ufa-Buchverlag, 1941), facing p. 32. — 74

2.38 Süß's elderly rabbi. Photograph, 1940. Photographer unknown. Published in J. R. George [Hans Hömberg], *Jud Süß: Roman* (Berlin: Ufa-Buchverlag, 1941), facing p. 97. — 74

2.39 The juggler arrives at the monastery. Illustration by Ernst von Dombrowski, 1961. Published in Hans Hömberg, *Der Gaukler unserer lieben Frau* (Vienna: Eduard Wancura, 1961), 13. — 76

2.40 The juggler performs before a smiling Madonna and Child. Illustration by Ernst von Dombrowski, 1961. Published in Hans Hömberg, *Der Gaukler unserer lieben Frau* (Vienna: Eduard Wancura, 1961), 25. — 76

2.41	Postcard of the Minoritenkirche, Vienna (Vienna: Kunstanstalt Kilophot, early twentieth century).	77
2.42	Postcard of the Votivkirche, Vienna (early twentieth century).	78
2.43	Postcard of the Kirche Maria vom Siege, Vienna (Vienna: K. Ledermann, early twentieth century).	79
2.44	Postcard of the Rathaus, Vienna (Vienna: K. Ledermann, early twentieth century).	79
2.45	Postcard of the Viennese Parliament, Rathaus, and Votivkirche (early twentieth century).	79
2.46	Georg Ritter von Schönerer. Engraving. F. F. Masaidek, *Georg Schönerer und die deutschnationale Bewegung* (Vienna: F. Schalk, 1898), frontispiece.	81
2.47	Hanns Hörbiger. Drawing, 1930. Artist unknown. Published in Rudolf von Elmayer-Vestenbrugg, *Rätsel des Weltgeschehens*, Kampfschriften der Obersten SA-Führung, vol. 4 (Munich: Eher, 1937), frontispiece.	81
2.48	The *hagal* rune. Vector art by Melissa Tandysh, 2016. Image courtesy of Melissa Tandysh. All rights reserved.	83
2.49	Guido von List. Photograph by Conrad H. Schiffer, 1909. Berlin, Deutsches Bundesarchiv, CC BY-SA 3.0.	83
2.50	*Hagal* runes flanking a swastika, on the title page of *Die Kunde* 4 (April 1936).	84
2.51	SS Totenkopf ring, with *hagal* rune visible. Image courtesy of Craig Gottlieb, 2015. All rights reserved.	85

Chapter 3

3.1	Wallace Fowlie, age 60. Photograph, 1968. Photographer unknown. Durham, NC, Duke University Archives Photograph Collection. Image courtesy of Duke University Libraries. All rights reserved.	91
3.2	Edward Sorin, with Madonna. Photograph, before 1890. Photographer unknown. Image courtesy of the University of Notre Dame Archives. All rights reserved.	93
3.3	*The Ave Maria* 10.9, August 30, 1919. Image courtesy of Ave Maria Press. All rights reserved.	93
3.4	Replica of the Chapel of Loreto, Saint Mary's, Notre Dame, IN. Photograph, before the Church of Loretto (sic) was built in front of it in 1886. Photographer unknown. Image courtesy of Sisters of the Holy Cross Archives and Records, Notre Dame, Indiana. All rights reserved.	94
3.5	Altar (with Madonna in center and *cap i pota*-style replica at left) in the replica of the Chapel of Loreto, Saint Mary's, Notre Dame, IN. Photograph, before 1886. Photographer unknown. Image courtesy of Sisters of the Holy Cross Archives and Records, Notre Dame, Indiana. All rights reserved.	94
3.6	Our Lady of the Angels, Notre Dame, IN, replica of the Porziuncola, Santa Maria degli Angeli, near Assisi, Italy. Photographer unknown. Image courtesy of the University of Notre Dame Archives. All rights reserved.	94

3.7	The Porziuncola, in the Basilica of Santa Maria degli Angeli, Assisi. Photograph by Ludmiła Pilecka, 2007, CC BY 3.0, https://commons.wikimedia.org/wiki/File:Santa_Maria_degli_Angeli_(Porcjunkula).JPG	94
3.8	Postcard of the Santuario di Oropa, Biella, Italy (Turin: S.A.C.R.O., 1943).	95
3.9	Postcard of the National Shrine Grotto of Lourdes, Mount St. Mary's University, Emmitsburg, MD (Gettysburg, PA: L. E. Smith Wholesale Distributors, date unknown).	96
3.10	The Grotto, University of Notre Dame, IN. Photograph, ca. 1896. Photographer unknown. Image courtesy of the University of Notre Dame Archives. All rights reserved.	97
3.11	Postcard of the Grotto, University of Notre Dame, IN (South Bend, IN: City News Agency, early twentieth century).	97
3.12	Postcard of the Basilica of the Sacred Heart and Main Building of the University of Notre Dame, IN (early twentieth century).	97
3.13	Workers maintaining the electric lights on the Main Building dome, University of Notre Dame, IN. Photograph, ca. 1922. Photographer unknown. Image courtesy of the University of Notre Dame Archives. All rights reserved.	98
3.14	La Colonna dell'Immacolata, Rome. Photograph by Wikimedia user Monopoli91, 2014, CC BY-SA 4.0, https://commons.wikimedia.org/wiki/File:Immacolatacolonnaroma.JPG	98
3.15	Postcard of the South Dining Hall, University of Notre Dame, IN (Notre Dame, IN: Notre Dame Bookstore, date unknown).	99
3.16	Richard Sullivan. Image courtesy of the University of Notre Dame Archives. All rights reserved.	99
3.17	Front cover of Richard Sullivan, *Notre Dame: Reminiscences of an Era* (Notre Dame, IN: University of Notre Dame Press, 1951).	99
3.18	Postcard of Sacred Heart Church and the Main Building by moonlight, University of Notre Dame, IN (Fort Wayne, IN: Fort Wayne Printing Co., early twentieth century).	100
3.19	To left, R. O. Blechman, *The Juggler of Our Lady: The Classic Christmas Story*, 3rd ed. (Mineola, NY: Dover Publications, 2015); to right, R. O. Blechman, *The Juggler of Our Lady: A Medieval Legend*, 1st ed. (New York: Henry Holt and Company, 1953). Photograph by Joe Mills, 2018.	104
3.20	R. O. Blechman at work. Photograph, November 2013. Photographer unknown. Image courtesy of R. O. Blechman. All rights reserved.	107
3.21	Boris Karloff, age 45. Photograph by MGM Studios, 1932, https://commons.wikimedia.org/wiki/File:Borris_Karloff_still.jpg	108
3.22	Boris Karloff as Frankenstein's monster in *The Bride of Frankenstein* (1935), CC BY-SA 4.0, https://commons.wikimedia.org/wiki/File:Boris_Karloff_as_Frankenstein's_monster.jpg	108
3.23	The Virgin's hand extends a rose to the juggler. Illustration by R. O. Blechman, 1953. Published in R. O. Blechman, *The Juggler of Our Lady: The Classic Christmas Story*, 3rd ed. (Mineola, NY: Dover Publications, 2015), 110 (unnumbered). Image courtesy of R. O. Blechman. All rights reserved.	110
3.24	Filming *The Fred Waring Show*. Photograph, ca. 1949–1954. Photographer unknown.	111

List of Illustrations 311

3.25 The tumbler dancing. Illustration by Wilhelm Preetorius, in Wilhelm Preetorius, *Der Tänzer unserer lieben Frau* (Zurich: Die Waage, 1964), 29. 113

3.26 The tumbler dancing. Illustration by Wilhelm Preetorius, in Wilhelm Preetorius, *Der Tänzer unserer lieben Frau* (Zürich: Die Waage, 1964), 31. 113

3.27 R. O. Blechman, cover art. To left, Hamlet with Yorick's skull; to right, Yorick the court jester with juggling ball. *Story*, Spring 1992. Image courtesy of R. O. Blechman. All rights reserved. 116

3.28 From left, Thomas Merton, Robert Lax, and Ralph de Toledano, editors of the *Jester*. Photograph, ca. 1937. Photographer unknown. New York, Columbia University Archives. Image courtesy of the Columbia University Archives. All rights reserved. 117

3.29 Tony Curtis as the juggler in *The Young Juggler*, dir. Ted Post (1960). Photograph, 1960. Photographer unknown. 120

3.30 Tony Curtis contemplates the Madonna in *The Young Juggler*, dir. Ted Post (1960). Photograph, 1960. Photographer unknown. 121

3.31 French prelates in a circus round watch a juggling performance. Photograph, 1967. Photographer unknown. 121

3.32 W. H. Auden, age 60. Photograph by Jill Krementz, 1967. 123

3.33 W. H. Auden, *The Ballad of Barnaby*, illus. Edward Gorey. Pre-existing poem and artwork, distributed to complement the Memorial Service in St. John the Divine, New York City, Wednesday, October 3, 1973. All rights reserved. 126

3.34 Hanged Criminals. Woodcut illustration to François Villon, *Le Grant Testament et le Petit, Son Codicille, Le Jargon et ses Balades*, 1st ed. (Paris: Pierre Levet, 1489), https://commons.wikimedia.org/wiki/File:PendusVillon.jpg 131

3.35 John Ciardi. Photograph from late 1950s, photographer unknown. Image courtesy of Rutgers University Libraries. All rights reserved. 133

3.36 Turner Cassity. Photograph, date and photographer unknown. Atlanta, GA, Emory University, Robert W. Woodruff Library. Image courtesy of Emory University Archives. All rights reserved. 134

3.37 Alfred Huth. Photograph by Ernst Huth, date unknown, CC BY-SA 3.0, https://commons.wikimedia.org/wiki/File:Alfred_Huth.jpg 137

3.38 Francis Poulenc. Photograph by Joseph Rosmand, before 1922. *Miniature Essays: Francis Poulenc* (London: J. & W Chester, 1922), 2. 138

3.39 Poster based on a watercolor by Léon Bakst, for a 1921 dance recital by Caryathis. 139

3.40 Caryathis, in a costume designed by Jean Cocteau, in a dance show that included a performance of *Le Jongleur*. Photograph, 1921. Photographer unknown. 139

3.41 Ulysses Kay, left foreground, at the reception after the premiere of his opera *The Juggler of Our Lady* at Xavier University, February 23, 1962. Xavier University of Louisiana Archives and Special Collections. Copyright by Xavier University of Louisiana. All rights reserved. 140

3.42 The juggler Colin and his musician are received by the monks. Ulysses Kay's opera *The Juggler of Our Lady* (1956), premiere at Xavier University, February 23, 1962. Xavier University of Louisiana Archives and Special Collections. Copyright by Xavier University of Louisiana. All rights reserved. 141

3.43	The drama unfolds within the monastery. Ulysses Kay's opera *The Juggler of Our Lady* (1956), premiere at Xavier University, February 23, 1962. Xavier University of Louisiana Archives and Special Collections. Copyright by Xavier University of Louisiana. All rights reserved.	141
3.44	Colin performs before the Madonna. Ulysses Kay's opera *The Juggler of Our Lady* (1956), premiere at Xavier University, February 23, 1962. Xavier University of Louisiana Archives and Special Collections. Copyright by Xavier University of Louisiana. All rights reserved.	141
3.45	The image of the Virgin with the jongleur after his collapse. Ballet Nacional Chileno, November 17, 1961, Viña del Mar, and Teatro Victoria, Santiago, April 19, 1962. Image courtesy of Juan Orrego.	144
3.46	The jongleur, holding his *vielle*, with one of the young women serving the Virgin. Ballet Nacional Chileno, November 17, 1961, Viña del Mar, and Teatro Victoria, Santiago, April 19, 1962. Image courtesy of Juan Orrego.	144
3.47	Sir Peter Maxwell Davies. Photograph by the University of Salford Press Office, 2012, CC BY 2.0, https://commons.wikimedia.org/wiki/File:Peter_Maxwell_Davies.jpg	145

Chapter 4

4.1	Google Ngram data for the phrase "Juggler of Notre Dame." Vector art by Melissa Tandysh, 2016. Image courtesy of Melissa Tandysh. All rights reserved.	151
4.2	Photograph of Czesław Miłosz, 1976, by G. Paul Bishop. Image courtesy of G. Paul Bishop. All rights reserved.	153
4.3	Konstanty Ildefons Gałczyński. Photograph by Henryk Hermanowicz, 1947, https://commons.wikimedia.org/wiki/File:KonstantyIldefonsGalczynski1947.jpg	153
4.4	Advertisement for J. B. Gothic bras. Showcard, 1940s.	154
4.5	"Notre-Dame, Quai de Montebello, Paris." Photograph by Bettina Rheims, 2009. Published in the series "Rose, c'est Paris." © Bettina Rheims. All rights reserved.	154
4.6	Front cover of Gilbert Frankau, ed., *A Century of Love Stories* (London: Hutchinson & Co., 1935?).	157
4.7	"Vita Mystica [Monk in Cell]." Photograph by F. Holland Day, 1900. Image courtesy of The Royal Photographic Society, Bath. All rights reserved.	158
4.8	A man looks at the front cover of the Mexican edition of *Playboy* (December 2008), featuring a suggestive Virgin Mary. Photograph, 2008. Photographer unknown. Image courtesy of Getty Images. All rights reserved.	161
4.9	Arman, *Jongleur de Notre Dame*, 1994. Cast bronze statue with brass and glass light fixtures, 231 × 90 × 82 cm. New York, Arman Studio. Photograph by Francois Fernandez. Image courtesy of Arman Studio, New York. All rights reserved.	164
4.10	Chris Ofili, *The Holy Virgin Mary*, 1996. Mixed media. Image courtesy of Chris Ofili. All rights reserved.	165

4.11	John Cowper Powys. Photograph, ca. 1930. Photographer unknown, https://commons.wikimedia.org/wiki/File:John_cowper_powys.jpg	167
4.12	Front row, left to right: Sigmund Freud, G. Stanley Hall, and Carl Gustav Jung; back row, left to right: Abraham A. Brill, Ernest Jones, and Sándor Ferenczi. Photograph, September 1909, at Clark University, Worcester, MA. Photographer unknown, https://commons.wikimedia.org/wiki/File:Hall_Freud_Jung_in_front_of_Clark_1909.jpg	168
4.13	Front cover of Josef Elias, *Der Tänzer unserer lieben Frau: Ein altes Legendenspiel für die Bühne* (Belp, Switzerland: Volksverlag Elgg, 1958).	169
4.14	The jongleur, in full motley with dunce cap, before the Madonna. Josef Elias, *Der Tänzer unserer lieben Frau: Ein altes Legendenspiel für die Bühne* (Belp, Switzerland: Volksverlag Elgg, 1958), 23.	170

Chapter 5

5.1	Advertisement from 1988 for the Citroën DS, featuring a quotation from Roland Barthes that compares automobiles and cathedrals.	176
5.2	Google Ngram data for "ivory tower." Vector art by Melissa Tandysh, 2016. Image courtesy of Melissa Tandysh. All rights reserved.	180
5.3	Lyonel Feininger, *Die Kathedrale*, cover design for the Bauhaus manifesto, 1919. Woodcut, 30.5 × 19 cm.	183
5.4	Google Ngram data for "corporate campus." Vector art by Melissa Tandysh, 2016. Image courtesy of Melissa Tandysh. All rights reserved.	184
5.5	Google Ngram data for "college campus." Vector art by Melissa Tandysh, 2016. Image courtesy of Melissa Tandysh. All rights reserved.	184
5.6	Google Ngram data for "university campus." Vector art by Melissa Tandysh, 2016. Image courtesy of Melissa Tandysh. All rights reserved.	185
5.7	Google Ngram data for "Anatole France" in five languages. Vector art by Melissa Tandysh, 2016. Image courtesy of Melissa Tandysh. All rights reserved.	188
5.8	Google Ngram data for "Jules Massenet" in English. Vector art by Melissa Tandysh, 2016. Image courtesy of Melissa Tandysh. All rights reserved.	189
5.9	Julie Harris. Photograph by ABC Television, 1973, https://commons.wikimedia.org/wiki/File:Julie_Harris_1973.JPG	190
5.10	Michel Zink, secrétaire perpétuel de l'Académie des inscriptions et belles-lettres, an *immortel* of the Académie française. Photographer: Brigitte Eymann. Copyright Académie des Inscriptions et Belles-Lettres, Paris. All rights reserved.	193
5.11	Front cover of Michel Zink, *Le jongleur de Notre Dame: Contes chrétiens du Moyen Âge* (Paris: Seuil, 1999). Image courtesy of Seuil. All rights reserved.	195
5.12	Joseph Bédier. Photographer unknown, 1920s, https://commons.wikimedia.org/wiki/File:Joseph_Bedier.jpg	196
5.13	Google Ngram data for qualities once thought to be characteristic of medieval people, showing a steady decline in frequency since 1850. Vector art by Melissa Tandysh, 2016. Image courtesy of Melissa Tandysh. All rights reserved.	199

5.14	Google Ngram data for "atone," "penance," "repent," and "sin." Vector art by Melissa Tandysh, 2016. Image courtesy of Melissa Tandysh. All rights reserved.	200
5.15	Google Ngram data for "repent." Vector art by Melissa Tandysh, 2016. Image courtesy of Melissa Tandysh. All rights reserved.	200
5.16	Google Ngram data for "penance." Vector art by Melissa Tandysh, 2016. Image courtesy of Melissa Tandysh. All rights reserved.	201
5.17	Google Ngram data for "atone." Vector art by Melissa Tandysh, 2016. Image courtesy of Melissa Tandysh. All rights reserved.	201
5.18	Google Ngram data for "oneness." Vector art by Melissa Tandysh, 2016. Image courtesy of Melissa Tandysh. All rights reserved.	202
5.19	Google Ngram data for "complex." Vector art by Melissa Tandysh, 2016. Image courtesy of Melissa Tandysh. All rights reserved.	202
5.20	Google Ngram data for "cynicism" and "disbelief." Vector art by Melissa Tandysh, 2016. Image courtesy of Melissa Tandysh. All rights reserved.	203
5.21	Google Ngram data for "repeat offender." Vector art by Melissa Tandysh, 2016. Image courtesy of Melissa Tandysh. All rights reserved.	203
5.22	Google Ngram data for "vocational learning." Vector art by Melissa Tandysh, 2016. Image courtesy of Melissa Tandysh. All rights reserved.	206
5.23	Google Ngram data for "learning for learning's sake." Vector art by Melissa Tandysh, 2016. Image courtesy of Melissa Tandysh. All rights reserved.	206
5.24	Google Ngram data for "art for art's sake." Vector art by Melissa Tandysh, 2016. Image courtesy of Melissa Tandysh. All rights reserved.	207

Acknowledgments

6.1	Cathedral of Justo Gallego Martínez. Mejorada del Campo, Madrid, 2005, CC BY-SA 3.0, https://commons.wikimedia.org/wiki/File:Cathedral_of_Justo_Gallego.JPG	210

Notes

n.1	E. H. Blondeel, seated third from right in front row, among his cohort of newly-ordained priests. Photograph, 1942. Photographer unknown. Image courtesy of Webwinkel Beeldbank Brugge. All rights reserved.	233
n.2	Franz Werfel. Photograph, ca. 1940, by Trude Geiringer. Image courtesy of Leo Baeck Institute. All rights reserved.	236
n.3	Advertisement for the film adaptation of Franz Werfel's *The Song of Bernadette*. Illustration by Norman Rockwell, 1943. Published in *Life*, December 13, 1943, 75.	236
n.4	Postcard of Blackstone Hotel, Chicago, IL (early twentieth century).	277
n.5	Front cover of Shin'ichi Nīkura, Eizō Kamizawa, and Taijirō Amazawa, eds. and trans., 奇蹟と愛と [Kiseki to ai to], vol. 4 of フランス中世文学集 [*Furansu chūsei bungakushū*] / *Poètes et romanciers du Moyen Âge* (Tokyo: Hakusuisha, 1996). Image courtesy of Harvard-Yenching Library. All rights reserved.	281

Index

Adam de la Halle (d. 1288) 128
Adams, Henry Brooks (1838–1918) 6, 35, 39, 125, 128–129, 160, 187, 198–199, 204–205, 213, 217–218, 228, 278, 284
  Adamsiana 128
  Education of Henry Adams 6, 128–129, 187, 217, 227
  Mont Saint Michel and Chartres 6, 125, 128, 187, 198, 260
Advent 104, 258
Africa, African 48, 166
African-American 140, 142, 266
Afrikaans 47, 230
Allied Powers 5, 27, 32, 35, 50, 64
America, American 12, 18, 34–35, 37–38, 54, 59, 75–76, 89–90, 92, 95–96, 102–106, 110–111, 113, 116–117, 120, 123–124, 127–128, 132–134, 136, 138–140, 142–143, 147, 150–151, 155, 158–160, 162–163, 173, 175–182, 185–187, 190–192, 197–199, 204–205, 209, 212, 214, 227, 236, 239, 250, 252, 254–256, 258–259, 261, 263, 266–268, 270–271
Americanism 38
Amsterdam 58, 234
Anderson, Laurie (b. 1947) 187
Anglican 34, 146
Anglophone 123, 235, 280
Anglo-Saxon 124, 259
Annunciation 17
anthropocentrism 204
anthropomorphism 107
anti-Semitism, anti-Semite 6, 11–12, 32, 73, 75, 80–82, 218–219
Antwerp 45, 66
Apollinaire, Guillaume (1880–1918) 75, 91
Arman (1928–2005) 163–164, 214, 273

Armanen 83–84, 245–246
Armanen Futhark 83, 245
Arreola, Juan José (1918–2001) 153
Arts and Crafts movement 34
Artz, Frederick Binkerd (1894–1983) 105
Asia, Asian 6, 37
Assisi 94–95, 231, 249
Atlantic 8, 72, 96, 105, 175, 179, 198
atonement 200, 199–207
Audenists 127
Auden, W. H. (1907–1973) 123–135, 159, 187, 204, 214, 258–264. *See also* "Ballad of Barnaby, The"
Auerbach, Erich (1892–1957) 205, 241
Australia, Australian 135, 192, 268
Austria, Austrian 6, 11, 32, 59, 73, 75, 77–78, 80–82, 86, 127, 137, 213, 235, 243–244, 246
Auxerre 15–16, 211, 220
Axis Powers 35, 50, 89

Baedeker raids 8
Bakhtin, Mikhail (1895–1975) 131–132, 262
"Ballad of Barnaby, The" 123–130, 132–133, 159, 258–259, 261
ballet, dance 5, 34, 45, 47, 49–50, 75, 80, 86, 88, 101–102, 112, 114, 118, 125, 136–139, 142, 148, 167, 169, 192, 194, 204, 229, 255, 257, 264, 267, 272
Banneux 43–44, 52, 56, 229, 233
Barnes, Djuna (1892–1982) 162, 273
Baroque 77
Barthes, Roland (1915–1980) 175–176, 276
Bastille Day 22
Bates, Katharine Lee (1859–1929) 103
Bauhaus 181–183, 277
Beauraing 41–43, 52, 56, 228–229, 233
Bédier, Joseph (1864–1938) 12, 125, 196, 282

Belgium, Belgian 9, 41–48, 50–52, 55–56, 65–67, 89, 229, 231–232, 239
Benedictine 35
Bénédictine 14, 149, 197
Beowulf 82, 245
Berlin 83, 85
Bernadette, Saint. *See* Soubirous, Bernadette
Bernanos, Georges (1888–1948) 265
Bernard of Clairvaux, Saint (1090–1153) 48, 195, 230, 239, 282
Berra, Lawrence Peter (Yogi) (1925–2015) 173
Berryman, John (1914–1972) 133, 263
Bethlehem Steel Corporation 142, 267
Bible 155, 250
Black Madonna 166
Blechman, R.O. (born Oscar Robert Blechman) (b. 1930) 103–116, 147, 187, 196, 204, 214, 252–256, 282
Blondeel, E.H. "Georges" (1916–1989) 52–53, 233
Bolshevik 192
Bonaventure, Saint (1221–1274) 118
Bordeaux, Henry (1870–1963) 11, 28–32, 225–226
Borrelli, Emmanuel-Raymond de, Vicomte (1837–1906) 75, 118
Borzova, Alla (b. 1961) 128, 261
Boston 158–159, 228
Boy Scouts 20
Brabant, Brabantine, Brabantism 52, 64–66, 238–239
Brazil, Brazilian 153, 192
Britain, British 8, 33–34, 71–72, 82, 127, 166, 171, 175, 178, 192, 226, 241, 274
British Commonwealth 175
Broadway 112
Brochet, Henri (1898–1952) 15–17, 220–221
Brother Clown, or The jongleur of Notre Dame, Monologue 17, 21, 221
Bruges 51–52, 232–234
Brun, Félix (1851–1926) 12
Buckley Jr., William F. (1925–2008) 160
Buddha, Buddhism 162, 204
Bühler, Fritz (1909–1963) 169
Burke, Edmund (1729–1797) 192, 281
Butler, Isabel (1869–1935) 134, 158, 262, 269
Byzantine 166, 213, 227

Cadet Roussel, jongleur de Notre Dame 16
Café Apollinaire 75
calligraphy 33–34, 226

Camp Haaren 63, 238
Canada, Canadian 72, 241, 245, 271
Carmelite 50, 138, 232, 251
Carruthers, Mary 209, 214, 284
cartoon animation 12, 107–108, 110–115, 118, 147, 204, 253–254
Caryathis [nom de théâtre of Elisabeth (Elise) née Toulemon Jouhandeau] 138–139, 265
Cassity, Turner (1929–2009) 134, 264
cathedrals 7–8, 22, 24, 77–78, 83, 89, 108, 147, 149, 155–156, 175–177, 179, 182, 186, 197, 205, 210–212, 222, 248, 260, 276, 282
Catholicism, Catholic 5–6, 10–12, 14–15, 18, 21, 24, 28, 30, 34, 45–46, 48, 50, 52, 59, 61–62, 64–67, 71, 80, 86, 92, 100, 102–104, 110, 117–118, 137–138, 145–146, 161–162, 166, 192, 204, 220, 231, 233, 237–238, 249–251, 253, 258, 274. *See also* Roman Catholic
Cervantes, Miguel de (1547–1616) 191
Chagall, Marc (1887–1985) 152, 271
Champion, Honoré (1846–1913) 11, 218, 280
Chancerel, Léon (1886–1965) 17–18, 20–21, 221–223
Chaplin, Charlie (1889–1977) 112, 160
Chesterton, Gilbert Keith (1874–1936) 49, 231
Chicago 112, 181, 251, 265, 277, 279
children's books 5, 27, 103, 112, 115, 142, 148, 153, 166, 186, 190, 192, 194, 203, 214, 224, 240, 255
Chile, Chilean 142–143, 192, 267
China, Chinese 6, 55, 271, 279
Chrétien de Troyes (1130–1191) 135
Christendom 124
Christianity, Christian 19, 39, 51, 59, 68, 77, 87, 90, 95, 102–104, 109–110, 115, 130, 148, 161, 166, 168, 192, 194, 228, 250, 253–254, 262, 278
Christmas, Christmastime 35–36, 67, 89, 92, 102–111, 115, 119, 122, 125, 146, 169, 190, 227, 239, 251–254, 256, 258–259, 268, 270, 273. *See also* yuletide
Christopher, Saint 176
Churchill, Winston (1874–1965) 7
Ciardi, John (1916–1986) 132–133, 263
Cistercian 101, 110, 117–118, 190, 210, 254, 284
Citroën DS 175–176
Civil Rights Act 1964 142
Clairvaux 101, 134, 137, 152
clandestine literature 62, 235

Claudel, Paul (1868–1955) 17
Cleveland 102, 251
Cocteau, Jean (1889–1963) 138–139, 264
Coelho, Paulo (b. 1947) 153, 271
Cohen, Gustave (1879–1968) 17–20, 221–222
Cold War 110, 113
Columbia University 116–117
Côme, Tilman 42–43, 228
Communism 51
Connecticut 124, 259
Cooney, Barbara (1917–2000) 203, 214
Copeland & Day 158–159
Copernicus, Nicolaus (1473–1543) 82, 255
Corliss, Richard (b. 1944) 159, 272–273
Coventry 7, 218
Coventry Cathedral 7
Cram, Ralph Adams (1863–1942) 35, 98, 158, 177, 199
Cristiani Family Circus 117, 257
Cristiani, Mogador 'Paul' Emerte (1931–1999) 117–118
Cross of Lorraine 26, 62, 224
Curtis, Tony (1925–2010) 104, 120–122, 258
Curtius, Ernst Robert (1886–1956) 205
Czech 59, 196
Czechoslovakia 6

Dachau 80
Dallas 138
dance. *See* ballet, dance
Dante Alighieri (1265–1321) 135, 162, 191, 279
Darreberg, Jacques (1916–1944) 25
Darwin, Charles (1809–1882) 270
Davies, Peter Maxwell (1934–2016) 135, 145–146, 264, 268
Day, Fred Holland (1864–1933) 95, 116, 128, 158–159, 223, 261, 272
Defresne, Marie August André Antoine (1893–1961) 53–56, 61, 234–235
Deitch, Gene (b. 1924) 114–115, 254, 256
Déols 86, 247
dePaola, Tomie (b. 1934 Thomas Anthony de Paola) 118, 214
De Troyer, Prosper (1880–1961) 46, 48
Dietzenschmidt, Anton Franz (1893–1955) 49, 230–231
Disney 108, 119, 257
Dombrowski, Ernst von (1896–1985) 75–76, 242
Dominican 17

Don Justo [Justo Gallego Martínez] (b. 1925) 210
Donkersloot, Nicolaas Anthonie (Nico) (1902–1965) 55, 234
Dostoevsky, Fyodor (1821–1881) 191
Douglas, Kirk (b. 1916) 120, 124, 258, 262
Dreyfus, Alfred (1859–1935) 11
Durant, Ariel (1898–1981) 106, 253
Durant, Will (1885–1981) 106, 253
Dutch 41, 45, 47, 49–53, 55, 58–60, 62–63, 66–67, 229–232, 234–235, 237–239

Eco, Umberto (1932–2016) 174, 205
Edinburgh 33–34
Eiffel Tower 155
Elias, Josef (1923–2000) 169–170, 275
Eliot, Thomas Stearns (1888–1965) 207, 273, 283
Elmayer von Vestenbrugg, Rudolf (1881–1970) 80–83, 85–88, 137, 244–245
England, English 7–8, 26, 28, 30, 33, 35, 49–50, 53, 58, 68, 70–71, 75, 82–83, 98, 102, 105–106, 108, 124–125, 131–132, 135–136, 142, 145, 151, 153, 157, 159, 165, 170, 175, 186–187, 189, 191, 194, 196, 215, 220, 224, 226–227, 231, 235–236, 240–241, 248, 253, 258–259, 262–263, 268–269, 271, 275–276, 279–280, 284
English Channel 7
Epiphany 122
Ernoul le Vieux de Gastinois (thirteenth century) 128
Esslingen am Neckar 114
Étiemble, René (1909–2002) 162, 273
Eucharist 260
Europe, European 6–7, 12, 19, 23, 35, 37, 41, 69, 71, 73, 90, 92, 125, 136–137, 146, 160, 175–177, 179, 181, 191–192, 197–198, 205, 213–214, 217–218, 227, 242, 265, 273, 277
Eve 119, 168, 250, 252
Ezquioga 40, 228

Fagan, Vincent F. (1898–1951) 98
Falaize, Antoine-Marie (1908–1942) 221
Farrand, Beatrix Cadwalader (1872–1959) 180
fascism, fascist 50–51, 70–72, 219, 241
Fátima 24, 26
Faustian 18
Feininger, Lyonel Charles (1871–1956) 182–183, 277
Ferstel, Heinrich Freiherr von (1828–1883) 243

Fidus (Hugo Höppener, 1868–1948) 84
Final Solution 73
Fitzgerald, F. Scott (1896–1940) 34, 173
Flanders, Flemish 41, 45–48, 50–53, 55–56, 67, 219, 229–231, 233–234
Focillon, Henri (1881–1943) 69, 240
Foerster, Wendelin (1844–1915) 11, 17, 218, 226
Fontaine des Innocents 220
Fowlie, Wallace (1908–1998) 91, 116, 248, 256
Fraenger, Wilhelm (1890–1964) 69, 240
France, Anatole (1844–1924) 150–151, 153, 156, 159, 170, 186–188, 191–193, 195, 203–204
France, Anatole (pen name of François-Anatole Thibault, 1844–1924) 5, 10–12, 16–17, 27–28, 30, 34–36, 55, 58, 60, 68–69, 75, 78, 100, 105, 112, 115, 118, 128–129, 132, 136–137, 224, 237, 240, 242, 261, 266, 270, 272, 278, 280, 282
France, French 6–12, 14–26, 28, 30, 33–35, 38, 41, 47–48, 50, 52–53, 55–56, 59–60, 62–63, 67–72, 75–76, 78, 86, 89, 92, 96, 98, 101, 105, 112, 114, 117, 120–124, 128–130, 133, 135–138, 140, 150–151, 156–157, 160, 162–163, 165, 175, 186–187, 192, 194–196, 218–221, 223–227, 230, 233, 237–238, 240, 247–249, 253, 255, 258, 261–262, 264–266, 268, 271–272, 276, 279–282
   Francophilia 7
   Francophone 41, 92
   French Academy 10, 28, 30, 196
   Frenchness 7, 68, 158
   French Revolution 92, 192, 281
Franciscan 101, 107, 117–118, 243, 249, 251, 253, 257
Francis of Assisi (1181–1226) 49, 95, 125, 226, 231, 249, 260, 269
Franco, Francisco (1892–1975) 11, 24, 28
Franco-Prussian War 24, 27, 73, 78
Frank, Annelies Marie (1929–1945) 58
Freudian 160, 165, 167
Freud, Sigmund (1856–1939) 157, 160, 167–168
Friant, Charles (1890–1947) 9, 218
Führer 41, 68, 82, 137
Futhark 83, 245

Gae, Nadine (1917–2012) 112
Gałczyński, Konstanty Ildefons (1905–1953) 153

Gallic 10, 157, 232
Garden, Mary (1874–1967) 54, 102–103, 112, 136, 147, 151, 156, 159, 187, 204, 215
Gauguin, Paul (1848–1903) 48
Gautier de Coinci (1177–1236) 17, 19, 187, 219, 221–222
Germanic 41, 47, 68, 76–77, 81–84, 124, 245, 258
Germanizing 81
Germanness 68, 72, 240
Germanosphere 69
Germany, German 5–6, 8–10, 12, 18, 20–21, 25, 27, 30, 34, 37, 41, 45, 47, 49–51, 53–56, 58–64, 66–77, 80–82, 85–86, 89, 105, 114, 136–137, 149, 169, 175, 182, 196, 205, 217, 219, 224, 230–232, 235, 238, 240–247, 250, 255, 264, 272, 275–276, 279
Ghent 47, 229–230
Ghéon, Henri (1875-1944, born Henri Vangeon) 15, 48, 221
Gilson, Étienne (1884–1978) 64, 173, 238, 276
Glasberg, Alexandre (1902–1981) 21–22
God 12, 19, 21, 31, 45–46, 61, 80, 84–85, 89–90, 92, 100, 116, 118–119, 122, 127, 130–132, 138, 152, 156, 160, 190–191, 195, 200, 222, 225, 235, 243, 245, 256, 260–261, 265, 268
Goebbels, Joseph (1897–1945) 73
Goethe, Johann Wolfgang von (1749–1832) 191, 281
Golden Legend 30–31
Golden Virgin 19
Gordeeva, Galina 191, 280
Gorey, Edward (1925–2000) 125–126, 260
Gospels 49, 158, 191, 231
Gothic 6–8, 18, 20, 24, 35, 51, 65, 77–78, 83, 88, 98, 108, 114, 123, 125, 130, 154–156, 175, 177–182, 185, 192, 199, 204–205, 243, 249, 271, 276–278
   architecture 7, 65, 123, 155, 178, 199
   de-Gothicization 8
   English Gothic 8
   Goth 155, 179, 199
   Gothicism 199
   Gothicist 35
   Gothophile 177
   neo-Gothic 77, 175, 179
   re-Gothicize 179
   revival architecture 175, 177, 179, 185, 199
Gourfinkel, Nina (1900–1984) 21, 223
Grant, Ulysses S. (1822–1885) 140

graphic novels 112, 115, 256
Graz 82, 244
Great Depression 41, 199
Greatest Gift, The 35, 227
Greece, Greek 118, 140, 159, 176, 199, 222, 225, 248, 263, 279
Gregorian 128, 268
Griffin, John Howard (1920–1980) 138, 265
Grimm, Jacob Ludwig Carl (1785–1863) 10–11
Grimm, Wilhelm Carl (1786–1859) 5, 10–11, 217
Groeschel, Benedict (b. 1933) 118, 257
Gropius, Walter Adolph Georg (1883–1969) 181–182, 184–185, 276–278
Guinehochet 14
Gutkind, Curt (also Kurt) Sigmar (1896–1940) 69–73, 240–241
Gutkind-Kutzer, Laura Maria (1896–1997) 71
Gwenn, Edmund (1877–1959) 227

Hagal rune 83–85, 246
Haines, Paul 187, 278
Haït, Ninon (née Weyl) (b. 1911) 21
Halloween 252
Hammerstein, Oscar, I (1847–1919) 136
Harlequin 91
Harris, Julie (1925–2013) 190, 279
Harvard University 181, 185
Hatzfeld, Helmut Anthony (1892–1979) 232, 241
Hazo, Samuel John (b. 1928) 100, 251
Heidelberg, University of 69
Heine, Heinrich (1797–1856) 77, 243
Hemingway, Ernest (1899–1961) 34
Hermans, Willem Frederik (1921–1995) 67
Heron, Hannah Blue (b. 1926) 102, 252
Hertz, Wilhelm (1835–1902) 69, 275
Higgins, Violet Moore (1886–1967) 194
Himmler, Heinrich (1900–1945) 82, 84, 245–246
Hitler, Adolf (1889–1945) 6, 12, 41, 50, 68, 70, 75–76, 80–82, 84–85, 240, 245
Hitlerism 80
Hohenberg, Johann Ferdinand Hetzendorf von (1733–1816) 243
Holland 65. *See also* Netherlands
Hollywood 120, 160, 255, 272
Holocaust 21, 217
Holtkamp, Berthonia 229

Holy Cross Brothers 92, 95
Holzleitner, Ludwig 137, 264
Hömberg, Hans (1903–1982) 73–76, 242
Hörbiger, Hanns (1860–1931) 81–82, 245
Housman, Laurence (1865–1959) 231
Houston 113, 262
Hugo, Victor Marie (1802–1885) 122, 149, 205
 The Hunchback of Notre Dame 122
Hungary, Hungarian 191, 279
Huth, Alfred (1892–1971) 136–137

Iceland, Icelandic 124, 259
Immaculate Conception 93, 96–97, 109, 273
Index of Prohibited Books 12
Indiana 92, 95, 225, 267
interwar period 67
Ireland, Irish 14, 72, 129, 158, 193, 213, 262
Irish Sea 72
Islam, Muslim 20
Italy, Italian 12, 28, 35, 39, 69–72, 93–95, 105, 160, 196, 229, 241, 249, 273, 279
Iverni, Petrus. *See* Siegelar [Sieglar, diocese of Cologne], Peter

Janus 111–112, 254
Japanese-American 37
Japan, Japanese 6, 37, 89, 162, 192, 280
Jesuits 219
Jesus Christ 12, 15, 24, 39, 86, 93, 122, 150, 155, 161–162, 166, 194, 222, 254, 264
Jewish, Jewishness 6, 12, 18, 50, 58–59, 68–69, 71, 73, 81–82, 104, 110, 217
Jewry 58, 71, 81
Jim Crow 142
John of Garland (ca. 1192–1275) 14, 220
Johnston, Edward (1872–1944) 34, 226
Johnstone, Mildred C. Thomas (1900–1988) 267
jongleur of Notre Dame 17, 22, 25–26
Judaism, Jew 6, 10, 12, 19–21, 32, 55, 58–59, 67–68, 70–73, 81, 86, 104, 117, 143, 204, 219, 222, 242
 Judeophilia 12
Judas 122
Julian of Norwich (ca. 1342-ca. 1416) 124
Jung, Carl Gustav (1875–1961) 167–168, 170–171, 204, 274–275

Karkosch, Konrad (1903–1987) 137, 264
Karl Alexander, Duke of Württemberg (1684–1737) 73

Karloff, Boris (1887–1969) 108, 255
Kavanagh, Patrick (1904–1967) 129, 262
Kay, Ulysses (1917–1995) 139–142, 266
Kempenaers, Henri 229
Kemp-Welch, Alice 134, 262, 278, 282
Kennedy, John F. (1917–1963) 104
King, Alexander (1899–1965) 140, 142, 266
King David 167
Klemperer, Victor (1881–1960) 241
Klimt, Gustav (1862–1918) 166
Knight of the Barrel, The 12
Knight, Reginald Frank Trinder "Rex" 105, 252
Köhler, Charlotte (1892–1977) 54, 234
Korea 192
Korean War 110, 254
Kristallnacht 6
Kutzer, Theodore (1864–1948) 71

La Salette 24–25
Latin 12, 14, 19, 64, 75, 98, 109, 112, 123, 125, 127–128, 130, 159, 219–220, 222, 247–249, 260–261, 263, 267–268, 276, 284
Latinity 14
Lawrence, D. H. (1885–1930) 167
Lax, Robert (1915–2000) 116–118, 256–257
Le Corbusier [Charles-Édouard Jeanneret-Gris] (1887–1965) 89, 186, 248
Leigh, Janet (1927–2004) 120
Le jongleur de Notre Dame 8–9, 11, 22–23, 27–28, 30, 35
Léna, Maurice (1859–1928) 17
Lent 122, 258
Leo, Ulrich (1890–1964) 241
Le tombeor de Notre-Dame 11
Lewis, Clive Staples (1898–1963) 174, 205
Liberation 27–28
Limburg 50, 67, 232
Limentani, Uberto (1913–1989) 72, 241
Lindbergh, Charles Augustus Jr. (1902–1974) 142
List, Guido von (1848–1919) 83–84, 245
Lommatzsch, Erhard (1886–1975) 75
London 26, 170
London, University of 71
Loreto 93–95, 249
Loretto 94
Louisiana 140–142, 211
Lourdes 24, 40–43, 59, 95–96, 103, 239, 249, 265

Lowell, James Russell (1819–1891) 133, 263
Lucullus (118-57/56 BCE) 73
Luftwaffe 8
Lux, Joseph (also Josef) August (1871–1947) 78, 80, 243

Madonna 16, 22, 31–32, 39, 49, 52, 66, 75–76, 78, 80, 86–88, 92–95, 97–98, 102, 105, 119, 121, 123, 129, 141, 143, 160–161, 163, 166, 170, 220, 225, 229, 232–233, 235, 249–250, 275
Madonna and Child 76, 78, 86, 93, 233
Maeterlinck, Maurice (1862–1949) 47, 219
Magi 122
Magnusson, Eiríkr (1833–1913) 124
Mâle, Émile (1862–1954) 69, 240
Malory, Thomas (1415–1471) 175
Malraux, André (1901–1976) 162
Manhattan 89, 108
Mannheim 69, 71–72
Marian, Marianism 11–12, 15, 17, 19, 24, 26, 31, 39–41, 45, 56, 66–67, 76, 80, 92–93, 95–96, 100, 103, 109, 128, 146, 161–162, 166, 196, 219, 222, 239, 249, 252, 261, 273, 275, 278. *See also* Mary
  Mariocentric 17
  Mariophanies 40, 45, 52
  visions 41
Marianne 12–13
Maribor 80–81
Marmier, Henri (1905–1982) 14
Mary 11–12, 15–16, 19–20, 24, 28, 30–31, 39–43, 45–47, 49, 55, 59, 62, 66–67, 75, 78, 86, 90, 92–98, 101, 103, 105, 109–110, 118–119, 130, 135, 137, 140, 146, 160–162, 166, 168, 186, 194, 204, 222, 238, 242–243, 249–252, 262, 266, 273, 278. *See also* Marian, Marianism
Mary, Lady of Pontmain 15
Maryland 96, 149
Mason, Eugene 226, 239
Massachusetts 133, 210
Massenet, Jules-Émile-Frédéric (1842–1912) 5–6, 8–10, 16–17, 22–23, 30, 35, 55, 68–69, 78, 100, 105, 135–137, 145, 151, 153, 156, 159, 170, 181, 186–187, 189, 197, 204, 223–224, 264–265, 267–268
Masson, Arthur (1896–1970) 52, 232
Mauriac, François (1885–1970) 30, 32, 226
Maurras, Charles (1868–1952) 30, 225
McCarthyism 254

McCarthy, Joseph R. (1908–1957) 110, 254
medieval 5–8, 11–12, 14–22, 28, 30–31, 33–35, 45, 48–50, 52, 54–56, 58–60, 62, 64–69, 75–78, 86, 90–92, 95, 100–103, 105–106, 109, 112–115, 118–120, 122–125, 128–136, 142–143, 145–146, 149–153, 156–159, 161, 163, 166, 170, 173–179, 186–187, 190–191, 194–195, 197–199, 204–205, 207, 210, 213–214, 219–221, 225–226, 238–239, 242, 246, 250, 253, 256–257, 261–263, 265, 270–271, 276, 278–281. *See also* Middle Ages
medievalism 34, 76, 107, 128, 177, 179, 181, 197–198, 212, 214, 243, 253, 258–259, 276, 282–284
Mediterranean Sea 93
Melville, Herman (1819–1891) 191
Memorial Hall 185
Mephistophelian 31
Mercier, Pascal [Peter Bieri] (b. 1944) 197, 282
Merton, J. Thomas (1915–1968) 116–118, 256–257
Metropolitan Museum of Art 125
Metzger, Radley (1929-2017 159–160, 162, 272–273
Mexico, Mexican 153, 160–162
Middle Ages 5, 7–8, 11, 14–15, 19, 27, 34–35, 39, 51, 53, 56, 58, 65, 67, 69, 75–77, 86, 89–91, 100–101, 105–107, 114, 117, 122, 124, 128–129, 134–135, 142, 149–150, 156–157, 159, 162, 173–179, 186–187, 192–199, 204–205, 207, 210, 212, 222, 226, 251, 253–254, 258, 270, 272, 278, 282–284. *See also* medieval
Middle English 124
Millais, John Everett (1829–1896) 274
Mill, John Stuart (1806–1873) 177, 276
Miłosz, Czesław (1911–2004) 153, 271
Mississippi 142
Moens, Aloisius or Aloïs Cesar Antoon "Wies" (1898–1982) 46–51, 53, 55, 61, 67, 229–232
Molière (1622–1673) 69, 191
Monaco 22, 112
monastic life 35, 47, 54, 109, 117, 125, 132, 149, 157, 210
Monroe, Marilyn [Norma Jeane Mortenson] (1926–1962) 120
Mont-Saint-Guibert 52, 233
Mont Saint Michel and Chartres. *See* Adams, Henry Brooks (1838–1918)

Morris, William (1834–1896) 33–34, 80, 124, 226
Moser, Rudolf (1892–1960) 169, 267, 275
Mosher, Thomas Bird (1853–1934) 105, 267
Mother and Child 155
Mother of God 12, 19, 24, 39, 41–43, 49, 55, 67, 86, 92–93, 102, 109, 146, 166, 191, 225, 250–251, 261, 280
Mount Carmel Seminary 138
Mount St. Mary's University 96
movies 25, 54, 73, 104, 108, 111–112, 114, 118–120, 122, 137, 147–148, 150, 159–160, 163, 167, 224, 227, 236, 242, 256–258, 270, 272, 283
Mulisch, Harry (1927–2010) 67
Munich 66, 80–81, 246
Murphy, George (1902–1992) 227
Mussert, Anton (1894–1946) 64, 238
Mussolini, Benito (1883–1945) 11–12, 28, 70–71, 241

National Socialism, National Socialist 50, 64, 68, 71, 73–76, 80–82, 84–85, 136–137, 231. *See also* Nazism, Nazi
Nativity 124, 146, 253
Nazareth 93
Nazification 137
Nazism, Nazi 5–8, 10, 21, 23, 26, 30, 32, 34, 39, 41, 50–51, 58–59, 61–64, 67–68, 70–71, 73–76, 80–85, 88, 137, 143, 226, 229, 235, 240, 244–246, 264. *See also* National Socialism, National Socialist
Nesbitt, John Booth (1910–1960) 75
Netherlands 41, 45, 47, 50–51, 53, 56, 58–62, 64–67, 89, 211, 213, 230, 234, 237–239, 284. *See also* Holland
New England 136, 198
New Orleans 142, 266
New World 12, 35, 90, 95, 177
New York 35, 38, 89, 104, 112–113, 115, 117, 125–127, 136, 164, 254, 259–260, 271, 276
Nietzsche, Friedrich (1844–1900) 202
Nigeria, Nigerian 166
Nobel Prize, Nobelist 12, 28, 32, 153
Norse, Nordic 68, 77, 81–84, 124, 258–259
Notre Dame 91–95, 98–100, 102, 117–119, 122, 132, 135–136, 138, 143, 145, 148–153, 155–156, 158–159, 162–164, 166–167, 170, 174, 187, 194–196, 203, 205, 207, 209–210, 214, 219–220, 230, 239, 248–250, 257–258, 261, 265, 268–270, 281–284

Notre Dame, University of 92–93, 96–100, 148, 211, 214, 250–251, 284
Nyhart, Nina Gibbon (b. 1934, Virginia) 133–134, 263–264

Oberlin College 103, 105, 211
Occupation 235, 261
Odyssey 140
Ofili, Chris (b. 1968) 165–166
Ohio 103, 251
Old French 68, 149, 196, 279
Old Norse 68, 81–83, 124, 258–259
Olivier, Laurence Kerr (1907–1989) 120, 271
Olschki, Leonardo (1885–1961) 71, 241
Onkerzele 44, 229
Onori, María Florencia (b. 1987) 161
Opéra Comique 9, 22
opera, French 265, 268
Oppenheimer, Joseph Süss (1698–1738) 73
O'Reilley, Mary Rose (b. 1944) 204, 283
Orrego-Salas, Juan (b. 1919) 142–143, 214, 266–267
Orwell, George [Eric Arthur Blair] (1903–1950) 217
Our Blessed Lady 78, 137, 155, 264
Our Lady's Dancer 45, 49–50, 229
Our Lady's Tumbler 5–8, 10–12, 14, 21, 28, 30, 33–34, 36–37, 45, 47, 50, 52–55, 59, 66, 68, 75–76, 78, 85–87, 89, 91–92, 100–103, 105–106, 109, 117–118, 124, 128–129, 134–138, 142–143, 146, 148–149, 151–152, 156, 158–160, 162, 168–169, 171, 173–174, 186–187, 190–191, 195, 204, 210, 218–219, 225, 232–235, 251, 256, 261–264, 266–267, 270–271, 275, 280, 284
Oxford 71, 124, 180, 260

Paris, Gaston (1839–1903) 11, 160, 186–187, 193–194, 226, 256, 278
Paris, Parisian 8, 22, 26–28, 69, 71, 75, 149, 152, 154–156, 193, 220–221, 224, 257–258, 270–271, 274
patriotism, jingoism 8, 12, 16, 20, 24, 32, 37, 39
Pearl Harbor 37, 89
Pennsylvania 100, 221
Perrin, Henri (1914–1954) 25, 224
Pétainist 30
Pétain, Philippe (1856–1951) 30, 35
pilgrimage 25, 40, 42, 49, 92, 95–96, 138, 249, 265

Pius IX [Giovanni Maria Mastai-Ferretti], Pope (1792-1878; r. 1846–1878) 93, 97
Pius XI [Ambrogio Damiano Achille Ratti], Pope (1857-1939; r. 1922–1939) 41
Pius XII [Eugenio Maria Giuseppe Giovanni Pacelli], Pope (1876-1958; r. 1939–1958) 103, 274
Poland, Polish 6, 73, 82, 153, 271, 279
Pontmain 15, 24
Porter, Barnaby 203, 214
Porter, Peter (1929–2010) 135, 264
Portiuncula 93, 95, 249. *See also* Porziuncola
Portugal, Portuguese 24, 153, 271
Porziuncola 94, 249. *See also* Portiuncula
Poulenc, Francis (1899–1963) 138, 264–265
Pound, Ezra (1885–1972) 135
Pourrat, Henri (1887–1959) 11
Powys, John Cowper (1872–1963) 167, 274
Preetorius, Emil (1883–1973) 114
Preetorius, Wilhelm (1915–1996) 113–114, 169, 255
Prince (1958-2016, stage name of Prince Rogers Nelson) 147, 270
Princeton University 35, 179, 183, 212, 227
Protestantism, Protestant 60, 204
psychoanalytic theories 160, 167
Puccini, Giacomo (1858–1924) 135
Pugin, Augustus Welby Northmore (1812–1852) 177
Pyrenees, Pyrenean 40–41, 59, 96

Quaker 204

Rabelais, François (1494–1553) 131, 191, 262, 279
Reformation 169, 274
Renaissance 11, 14
Renault, Gilbert (1904–1984) 25–26, 224
Resistance 6, 8, 18, 21, 25–28, 30, 56, 58, 62, 64, 217, 221, 235, 237–238
Reve, Gerard (1923–2006) 67, 234, 239–240
Reynard the Fox 53, 234
Rheims, Bettina (b. 1952) 154, 156, 240
Rhodes, Michael Ray (b. 1945) 257
Rimbaud, Arthur (1854–1891) 91
Rocamadour 12, 138, 282
Roman Catholic 41, 52, 60, 65, 80, 103. *See also* Catholic
Romance 11, 68, 71, 125, 194, 205, 240–241, 260
Romanesque 63, 69, 212, 240

Rome, Roman 14, 41, 52, 60, 65, 70, 73–74, 80–81, 96–98, 103, 111, 163, 176, 199, 236, 242, 245, 250, 280
Rothko Chapel 113
Roussel, Guillaume Joseph (1743–1807) 16, 211, 220
Ruskin, John (1819–1900) 80
Russia, Russian 132, 191–192, 255, 279–280
Rutebeuf (d. ca. 1285) 17–20
Rutten, Felix (1882–1971) 67, 239
Rüttgers, Severin (1876–1938) 69

Saint-Étienne 22–23
Saint John's, Newfoundland 72
Saint John the Divine 179, 211, 260
Saint Stephen's Cathedral 77
Ṣalāḥ ad-Dīn (Saladin) (1137-1193; r. 1174–1193) 20
Santa Claus 227
Santini, Pio (1908–1986) 28–29
SA (Sturmabteilung) 81, 85, 244, 246. *See also* Storm Troopers
Satan 19–20
Satie, Erik Alfred Leslie (1866–1925) 138, 265
Scheib, Philip A. (1894–1969) 254, 256
Schmidt, Friedrich von (1825–1891) 230, 243, 265
Schönerer, Georg Ritter von (1842–1921) 81, 245
Scott, Walter (1771–1832) 281
sculptures 69, 86, 93, 97, 119, 163, 167, 273
Segura y Sáenz, Pedro, Cardinal (1880-1957, r. 1927–1957) 41
Semitic 20
Sendak, Maurice (1928–2012) 103, 112, 253, 255–256
sexualization 155, 159, 162–163, 166
Shakespeare, William (1564–1616) 147, 191, 274
Shaw, Conna Bell 226, 252
Shaw, Sax R. (1916–2000) 33
Sherman, Alexander "Allie" (b. 1923) 104
Shoah 21–22, 58, 217
Sigelar [Sieglar, diocese of Cologne], Peter 17
Sister Beatrice 15, 55, 220
Slavic, Slavs 153, 191, 214
Slovenia, Slovenian 80–81, 244
Smit, Gabriël Wijnand (1910–1981) 60–62, 65–67, 237
Sorbonne 17, 71

Sorin, Edward (1814–1893) 92–93, 96, 249
Soubirous, Bernadette (1844–1879) 59, 96, 103
South Africa 47, 192, 230
Souvirón, José María (1904–1973) 142
Soviet 51, 89, 110–111, 131, 191–192
Spain, Spanish 40–41, 142–143, 150, 161–162, 192, 196, 219, 266
Spitzer, Leo (1887–1960) 241
SS (Schutzstaffel) 63, 82, 84–85, 238, 246
 Honor Ring 84, 246
Stalinists 68
Steene, Cunegondus "Cuno" Theodorus Emile van den (1909–1971) 60–61, 237
Stevenson, Robert Louis (1850–1894) 130
Stokes, Anne 155
Storm Troopers 80, 82, 86, 245–246. *See also* SA (Sturmabteilung)
Strauss, Richard (1864–1949) 135
Sullivan, Richard (1908–1981) 92, 98–101, 212, 248, 250–251
Swift, Jonathan (1667–1745) 191
Switzerland, Swiss 114, 169, 171, 267, 275
Symonds, John Addington (1840–1893) 159

Tales of the Middle Ages 196, 282
television, tv shows, made-for-tv movies 76, 89, 102, 104–105, 111–112, 114, 119–120, 136–137, 139, 147–148, 174, 227, 253–254, 270
Tennyson, Alfred (1809–1892) 274
Terry, Paul (1887–1971) 108, 114
Terrytoons 107, 109, 114–115, 254, 256
Tharaud, Jean (1877–1952) 10–12, 14, 28, 196, 218–219, 224, 282
Tharaud, Jérôme (1874–1953) 10–12, 14, 28, 196, 218–219, 224, 282
Theophilus, Theophilians 17–18, 20, 221–222
Third Reich 58, 80, 240, 242
Thirty Years' War 86
Tilburg 62, 238–239
Timmermanns, Leopold Maximiliaan Felix (1886–1947) 125, 260
Tolkien, J. R. R. (1892–1973) 124, 174, 205
Trappists 117
Turner, Charles (1928–2003) 134, 259

Ukraine, Ukrainian 21
Uncle Sam 12
Underground 10, 21–22, 25–26, 28
Union Army 140
United Productions of America 113

Universal Studios 122
Untermeyer, Louis (1885–1977) 104

Valéry, Paul (1871–1945) 60
Valkenier, Frank (1907–1999) 62–67, 238–239
Van den Dyck (Dijck), Leonie (1875–1949) 44
Van Gogh, Vincent Willem (1853–1890) 48
variety shows 111, 139, 227
Vatican 39
Ven, Frans van der. *See* Valkenier, Frank
Verduin, Arnold Robert (1905–1960) 36, 38, 227
Vichy, Vichyist 8, 11, 15, 21–23, 30, 32, 35
Vienna, Viennese 77–80, 83, 127, 140, 227, 235, 243, 245, 266
Villon, François (1431-ca. 1474) 91, 130–131, 262
Virgin and Child 15, 24
Virgin Mary 9–12, 15–16, 19, 24–26, 28, 30–31, 35, 37, 39–41, 43, 45–46, 48–49, 56, 59–60, 62, 66, 87, 90, 92–93, 95–96, 98, 101–103, 105, 109–110, 118–119, 123, 127–131, 135, 138, 140, 144–146, 150, 155, 160–163, 165–166, 168–169, 171, 186, 190, 192, 194, 196, 198, 218–219, 225, 228–229, 232, 237, 248–250, 261–263, 265–266, 268, 272–274, 280
Vloberg, Maurice (1885–1967) 17, 149, 270
Vriesland, Victor Emanuel van (1892–1974) 55–61, 66–67, 235

Wagner, Cosima (1837–1930) 135
Wagnerian 76, 246
Wagner, Richard (1813–1883) 68, 124
Walloon 41, 45, 47, 52, 232–233
Wall Street 183

Waring, Fred (1900–1984) 111, 139, 147, 254
Washington, D. C. 179, 198, 210, 212–213, 227, 259
Washington National Cathedral 179
Watrin, Pierre (1918–1990) 27–28, 224
Weimar Republic 68, 277
Weinrich, Franz Johannes (1897–1978) 45–47, 50, 53, 229
Wellington, Hubert (1879–1967) 33
Wellington, Irene (née Sutton, 1904–1984) 33–34, 226
Werfel, Franz (1890–1945) 59, 234–237
West Point 199
Wicksteed, Philip Henry (1844–1927) 105, 129, 134, 261–262, 267
Wilamowitz-Moellendorff, Ulrich von (1848–1931) 202
Wilde, Oscar (1854–1900) 158
World War I 7, 12, 35, 37, 41, 47, 51, 55, 68–69, 73, 136, 162
World War II 5–7, 21–23, 26–28, 30, 32, 34, 45, 47, 51, 59, 66–67, 73, 76, 80, 82–83, 86, 89, 114, 136–137, 143, 151, 186, 199, 205, 218, 224, 243–244

Yale University 179
Young Juggler, The 89, 120–122, 258
Ypres 53, 233
yuletide 146, 253. *See also* Christmas, Christmastime

Zink, Michel (b. 1945) 192–196, 214, 281–282
Zionism, Zionist 12, 58, 67, 219, 235
Zola, Émile (1840–1902) 60
Zurich 113, 169

The Juggler of Notre Dame and the Medievalizing of Modernity comprises six volumes available at https://www.openbookpublishers.com/section/101/1

www.ingramcontent.com/pod-product-compliance
Lightning Source LLC
Chambersburg PA
CBHW040741300426
44111CB00027B/2997